About the Author

George Odgers has made a significant contribution to Australians'
knowledge of the conflicts in which their country has been involved
and writes with authority and insight about the men and women who
have fought for Australia.

He has been a journalist with the *Argus* and the *Age* in Melbourne,
has worked with Channel 9, and is former head of historical studies in
the Department of Defence in Canberra. He served with the
Australian armed forces in the Second World War (New Guinea,
Bougainville and Borneo), the Korean War, the Malayan Emergency
and Vietnam.

His books include *Across the Parallel, Air War against Japan* and
Mission Vietnam.

100 YEARS
OF AUSTRALIANS AT WAR

George Odgers

LANSDOWNE

100 YEARS OF AUSTRALIANS AT WAR *is a revised and updated edition of* Diggers. *Lansdowne Publishing is proud to publish this paperback edition at the close of the 20th century to document the 100-year history of Australians involved in major conflicts worldwide.*

Published by Lansdowne Publishing Pty Ltd
Level 1, 18 Argyle Street, Sydney NSW 2000 Australia
First published in 1999

Copyright © 1994 and 1999 Department of Defence

Project Coordinator: Clare Wallis
Designer: Avril Makula

Set in Garamond on Quark Xpress
Printed in Australia by The Australian Print Group

National Library of Australia Cataloguing-in-Publication Data:
Odgers, George
100 Years of Australians at War

Includes index.
ISBN 1 86302 669 X.

1. Australia - Armed Forces - History 2. Australia - History, Military. I Title.

355.00994

In memory of all the Australians of the armed services who in the 20th century paid the supreme sacrifice in defence of their country.

CONTENTS

INTRODUCTION

Australians in Wars of the 20th Century

The 20th century was an historical era deeply scarred by war. The Commonwealth of Australia was proclaimed on this century's first day – the 1st of January, 1901, and, as though setting the mood for the coming years, the newly born nation was, on its birthday, already engaged not in one but two wars: the Boer War in South Africa and the Boxer conflict in China.

Neither of these wars caused great loss to Australia. But only a few years later two unimaginably devastating conflicts convulsed mankind. Australia was heavily involved in both and suffered grievous losses.

Because of their size and lethality these conflicts were named "world wars" – the First World War of 1914–1918 (10 million dead) and the Second World War of 1939–1945 (55 million dead).

Yet not even these horrendous slaughters put an end to the 20th century carnage.

It has been estimated that deaths caused by all the wars of the 20th century reached a total of at least 100 million.

Victory over the Axis powers in 1945 had been won at enormous cost in blood, tears and treasure. It was a bitter disappointment therefore that a great world victory had not been followed by a long period of peace and harmony. Instead dangerous rifts quickly opened between the victors – the Soviet communist block and the non-communist western powers. The era of the "cold war" had arrived.

The world was divided by what Winston Churchill called an "Iron

Curtain". The "Iron Curtain" never lifted for Churchill, who died in 1965, well before the Soviet Union, towards the end of the 20th century, abandoned its communist ideology.

On 25 June 1950 the Korean peninsula became the first major battleground in the struggle between the Communist nations and the western powers. The Australian Army, Navy and Air Force were at once involved in support of the United Nations in the fierce struggle to save South Korea from being crushed by communist North Korea and China. South Korea was saved.

All Australian defence forces were next involved in the Malayan Emergency in the years 1950–60, followed by another military emergency when the Indonesians "confronted" Malaysia and then by the long, drawn-out campaign in South Vietnam which ended for Australia when its combat forces were withdrawn in 1971.

In the Gulf War of 1990–91 Australian servicemen played a significant role with the United Nations which saw the overthrow of the forces of Iraq in its attempt to conquer Kuwait in the Persian Gulf.

During the century Australian servicemen also played an effective role in United Nations peacekeeping operations, mainly in Asia and Africa.

In 1995 members of an Australian medical support mission to the African state of Rwanda were witness to an horrendous episode of the Rwanda genocide of 1994–95. Their courage and steadfastness was responsible for saving hundreds of lives.

The Record

Australia's war record in the 20th century was both honourable and effective. In their many wars, courageous Australian soldiers, sailors and airmen encountered both triumph and disaster. The heroism and sacrifice of the Anzacs at Gallipoli and afterwards in France and Palestine were a triumph of the nation's spirit. Their bravery and sacrifice were continued at El Alamein, on the Kokoda Trail, at Kapyong in Korea and Long Tan in Vietnam. Their deeds have created, for Australia, a military heritage in which all Australians take pride.

1

DAY ONE OF THE COMMONWEALTH

Tuesday, the 1st of January 1901, is a day of great historical significance for Australians. It was a day celebrated in this country and throughout the world as the first day of the 20th century.

But, for Australia, the day had greater significance because it had been chosen as the day upon which the Commonwealth of Australia would enter world history.

With splendid timing the proclamation of Australia's emergence as a nation had been arranged to coincide with the birth of the 20th century.

On this momentous day Australia became a nation and at the same time joined the world in entering a new year and a new century.

In a blaze of colour, a brilliant cavalcade of soldiery from many parts of the British Empire, escorted a memorable parade which wound through Sydney streets on its eight-kilometre route to Centennial Park.

There before a huge and enthusiastic crowd, the first Australian Governor-General and Commander-in-Chief of all Australian naval and military forces (Lord Hopetoun) was sworn in. The oath was then administered to the Commonwealth Executive Council: Edmund Barton who was the first Australian Prime Minister and eight others who were members of the Cabinet.

Artillery then thundered in a 21-gun salute heralding the inauguration of the Commonwealth of Australia.

The shock of the artillery fire and the dazzling cavalcade of soldiery must have been a powerful reminder to many attending the celebration who had family members then experiencing combat service overseas.

At the time Australians were fighting in two wars. The States of New South Wales and Victoria had both contributed a naval brigade and the gunboat *Protector* had also been assigned by the South Australian Government to serve with the Royal Navy in China, where operations were in progress to suppress the Boxer uprising. At the same time volunteers in their thousands from all Australian States had been fighting in the South African War alongside contingents which rallied to the British cause from many parts of the Empire. Hundreds had lost their lives in combat or from deadly diseases.

Australian veterans of the military operations in the Sudan in 1885 took their places in the parade to Centennial Park as did young soldiers who had just returned from the war in South Africa.

They were joined by soldiers from all Australian States. Their new commander-in-chief was the Governor-General and they would now come under the direct control of the Commonwealth Minister for Defence, Sir James Dickson. Unfortunately Sir James died suddenly in his second week in office. The Western Australian statesman, Sir John (later Lord) Forrest, known as the "Emperor of the west" was appointed to replace him.

Sir John took over control of all Australian defence forces on 1 March 1901, a date accepted as the birthday of the Australian Army.

Captain Robert Muirhead Collins was appointed the first permanent head of the Defence Department. He had been, for 13 years, head of the Defence Department of the State of Victoria.

The NSW Lancers dressed in khaki and wearing slouch hats were also on parade, together with 305 school cadets and a Royal Australian Artillery band. The Life Guards in their glittering cuirasses and white plumed helmets were there; Dragoons in their scarlet tunics, Grenadier Guards in bearskins and Coldstream Guards in scarlet and blue. The Black Watch was represented as well as the Northumberland's Fusiliers and troops from Wales and Ireland. From India came the 9th Bengal Lancers and Sikhs and from Nepal the Fifth Ghurkhas in dark green and black.

To some Australians the strong military presence seemed to inject too great a military spirit into the nation's inaugural celebrations and there were some who warned against expectations that Australians should volunteer to contribute to wars that may not interest them directly.

The defence of Australia had been a vital consideration when the Australian people voted for Federation in a referendum in the late nineties. It was argued, justifiably, that the safety of the nation would be enhanced if the six Australian States federated and pooled their military resources into a single Federal army organisation.

This argument was put strongly in 1889 by Sir Henry Parkes, Premier of NSW, when he declared defence was the overarching justification for a Federated Australia.

On the eve of Federation Australian naval forces totalled 1898 while the military forces of the six States totalled 28,836. The task of welding all the soldiers into one army fell to an Imperial officer, Major General E. T. H. ("Curly") Hutton, who had commanded Australian troops in the South African war.

Hutton had a high opinion of Australian troops. "No man," he wrote, "be he Cromwell or Napoleon could drive Australian troops. But a strong and capable leader no matter how strict, could lead an Australian army to emulate – aye and surpass, if need be, the finest and most heroic deeds recorded in the annals of the British army."

While Hutton had great faith in the Australian soldiers his autocratic style led to clashes with his Australian political masters. His Australian service came to an end when the post of general officer commanding the Australian army was abolished.

After Australia's Federation, a British War Office paper proposed that Australia should be "encouraged" to establish a field force of 9,000 men in "the Imperial Australian Force". This force would be at the disposal of the Imperial Government in the event of war between Britain and one or more European powers.

Prime Minister Barton, aware of the opposition of members of the Commonwealth parliament towards any scheme which would remove Australian troops from Commonwealth control, explained that while the Commonwealth could be relied upon when the Empire was in peril, Australian opinion was unlikely to agree to any undertaking that required Australia to commit forces in advance of that situation.

But there was little cause for concern. The willing response of Australians to wars in New Zealand, the Sudan, South Africa and China had demonstrated with abundant clarity that they were ready and willing to volunteer for war service in defence of the Empire. They were strongly pro-British and for any political leaders to oppose assistance to Britain in a defence emergency was to court political suicide. Moreover a strong united Empire would mean greater security for its component parts and Australians, concerned with the recurrent turbulence in Asia and the sudden rise of Japan, felt the need for a great and powerful friend.

2

AUSTRALIANS IN THE BOER WAR

The South African republics of the Transvaal and Orange Free State declared war on Britain on 11 October 1899.

In a bid for a quick victory the Boer armies seized the initiative and thrust swiftly into the British territories of Natal and Cape Colony.

In this crisis, Australians at once answered the call of Empire as thousands volunteered to fight the Boers.

When hostilities began in South Africa, Australia had not achieved Federation (which came on 1 January 1901, when the Commonwealth of Australia was proclaimed). So the six separate Australian States raised, trained and despatched their own armed contingents to the veldt. Other parts of the British Empire did likewise.

Tension and antagonism between Briton and Boer had for decades disturbed the political calm of southern Africa. Cape Colony on the southernmost tip of Africa had long been a key strategic station on the sea route between Europe, Asia and Australasia. The First Fleet bound for Botany Bay with its convict passengers had called there in October 1787 to replenish supplies for the first white settlement in New South Wales.

The Dutch were the first Europeans to settle permanently at the

Cape. They were joined there by French and German migrants. During the Napoleonic wars the Cape was seized and retained by Britain as part of the peace settlement of 1814.

The Dutch (or Boer) settlers resented the British takeover, especially when the British abolished slavery in the colony. They were unable to accept the concept of equality for black people and were angered by British failure to compensate them adequately for the loss of their slaves.

The Boer farmers were so alienated that large numbers packed their belongings into covered wagons and took part in the "Great Trek" to the north where they could be free from British control. There they established the Afrikaner republics of Orange Free State and Transvaal which the British Government recognised in 1852.

More friction developed when the discovery of gold and diamonds in the Boer republics attracted a flood of newcomers from all parts of the world including Britain and Australia. The Boers feared their future was threatened by the newcomers. Their leader, President Paul Kruger, a stern Calvinist whose way of life resembled that of a character from the Old Testament, treated the newcomers (the Boers called them "Uitlanders") harshly. He denied them political rights while at the same time taxing them heavily and forcing them into military service.

Blood was spilled in 1881 when Boers attacked and defeated a small British force at Majuba Hill. In 1896, tension was at flash point when Dr Starr Jameson, leading a party of British adventurers, invaded Boer territory. The raid deteriorated into a fiasco. The raiders were captured and handed over to the British for punishment.

Finally the Boers, aware that a British army corps 46,000 strong was to be sent to South Africa and concluding that a war was inevitable, decided to strike first. On 9 October 1899 they despatched an ultimatum demanding that the British military build-up in South Africa should cease and when, as expected, no reply was received, declared war two days later.

The Boers feared the British intended to destroy their independence and incorporate them in British South Africa. They would have none of that and were making intense preparations for war. They armed their troops with modern artillery and the effective German Mauser rifle which could kill at 2500 yards. Their men were self-reliant, hardy, highly mobile and familiar with the countryside. Fighting for their own homeland they would be a formidable enemy.

When war came the Boers were ready and fired the first shots. Some 14,000 Transvaalers invaded Natal while another 6000 soldiers from the Orange Free State moved from the west to join up with the Transvaalers in a campaign to seize Ladysmith, a vital rail junction and garrison town. At the same time other elements of the Free State army advanced into Cape Colony were the northern districts rebelled against Britain and joined the Boers.

While the Boers were grimly determined and well-armed, they had no credible strategic plan to win the war. They aimed to lay siege to the towns of Mafeking, Kimberley and Ladysmith. This was ill advised because it would tie up most of their available forces in static warfare.

Thousands of Uitlanders including many Australians who feared being trapped within the Boer republics, made a hurried exit to British territory. In Natal they joined British war units and within 10 days of the outbreak of war the Imperial Light Horse, which had many Australians in its ranks, fought a battle at Elandslaagte, defeating a Boer invading force which lost 67 men killed.

Most Australians at home were convinced that war could not be avoided. They followed developments in South Africa with intense interest, condemning the oppressive treatment of the Uitlanders. Many protest meetings were held.

Immediately war came, Australia, Canada, New Zealand, Ceylon and India rallied loyally to "the mother country". Amid demonstrations of patriotic fervour, volunteers marched through Australian city streets to the tunes of "Rule Brittania" and "Soldiers of the Queen". A balladist wrote verses warning the Boers that Australians were on the way:

> *I'm coming, Oom Paul Kruger,*
> *To have a talk with you;*
> *A word into your ear, old man –*
> *I am the kangaroo,*
> *The emu and the 'possum,*

And the eucalyptus tree –
In other words Australia;
And this I say to thee –
Now Mister Oom Paul Kruger,
Just let my father be.

The loyalty so enthusiastically displayed was a source of comfort to Britain because of underlying concern that a Boer military victory might trigger revolts elsewhere and lead to the disintegration of the Empire. It provided moral support in the face of the great hostility displayed in Europe, especially in France and Germany, as well as the dissent of anti-imperialists in Britain and Australia. The press of the major European powers was rabidly anti-British. The Kaiser had praised the Boers for their response to the Jameson raid and France was still smarting over the Fashoda affair of 1898 when France and Britain were on the brink of war over the Sudan.

Even before hostilities began, the Government of Queensland had offered (in July 1899) that if war came Queensland could send 250 mounted infantry with a machine-gun section. On 28 September a conference of Australian military commandants was held in Melbourne and a scheme was agreed for the sending of a joint Australian contingent numbering 2,500 of all arms, more than half to be mounted. This plan was set aside, however, when the British War Office cabled that it would accept Australian forces on the basis of two squadrons each of 125 men from NSW and Victoria and one each from the other colonies. Thus the Australian aim to achieve national impact by bringing all Australian contingents together in one large force was not achieved.

Altogether some 50 Australian units from all States saw active service in the South African war. They included mounted infantry, Imperial bushmen, Citizens' bushmen, mounted rifles, artillery and an army medical unit. In addition, after the Federal Government took responsibility for Australian defence on 1 January 1901, eight battalions of Commonwealth Horse were formed and sent.

By chance, members of the NSW Lancers were in England in 1899 for training with British cavalry at Aldershot. Two days before war was declared they were at Waterloo Station, about to leave for Australia. But their destination was changed to Cape Town and they received a flattering reception from Londoners as they departed for the war in the troopship *Nineveh*. They landed in South Africa less than three weeks after hostilities began. They were the first colonial troops to arrive.

A detachment of the Lancers were horsed and equipped and sent forward to De Aar in Cape Colony where they joined Lieutenant General Lord Methuen's force which had been tasked to relieve the besieged diamond town of Kimberley. On 22 November the Lancers came under fire for the first time near Belmont where a Boer force was compelled to retreat after losing heavily. The Lancers were in action again two days later in a sharp engagement at Graspan.

After the minor victories in Cape Colony British spirits had risen, only to fall again during "Black Week" (10–15 December 1899) when the enemy inflicted defeats at Stormberg, Magersfontein and Colenso. The action at Stormberg resulted in the loss of 600 British soldiers taken prisoner. Magersfontein near Kimberley was an even greater disaster when an attack on 11 December by the Highland and Guards Brigades was defeated with heavy losses including the deaths of most of the officers in the forward battalions. The veldt where they died was a shambles. "There'll be many a sore heart in Scotland today," a saddened Highlander said after the holocaust. The NSW Lancers were again in action at Magersfontein as escorts for the Royal Horse Artillery, and were subjected to heavy enemy fire.

Into Action

After a passage of 28 days from Melbourne, the troopship *Medic* arrived at Cape Town on 26 November with the first contingents from Victoria, South Australia, Western Australia and Tasmania. A total of 588 officers and men with 189 horses and nine mules disembarked. The soldiers went into camp close to the western slopes of Table Mountain. Queensland and NSW units including the NSW Army Medical Corps arrived in early December. They were hurried to the front and committed to the campaign to lift the siege of Kimberley.

The medical unit opened a hospital at Orange River Station while the Queensland Mounted Infantry went to Belmont, the NSW Mounted Rifles to De Aar and the Victorian Mounted Rifles and all infantry units to Enslin, a railway siding on the line to Kimberley.

The five companies of Australian infantry were drawn together to form the first Australia-wide military force, designated the 1st Australian Regiment and commanded by Colonel J. C. Hoad. However, the British command had by now decided that much greater mobility for their forces was needed than at first envisaged. So the 1st Australian Regiment was converted to mounted infantry and absorbed into the 1st Mounted Infantry Brigade under Major General E. ("Curley") Hutton, who in 1892 had been commandant of the military forces of NSW.

The first Australian soldiers to die in the South African War were killed at Sunnyside on New Year's Day 1900. They were troopers D. C. McLeod and V. S. Jones of the Queensland Mounted Infantry who had arrived in South Africa during "Black Week".

The Queenslanders were part of a column consisting of 250 Queenslanders, 100 Canadians, 40 British regulars and an artillery unit sent to attack a Boer laager (camp) known as Sunnyside's kopje (small hill) north west of Belmont.

Jones was shot dead when his advanced patrol clashed with Boer pickets. Four out of the five members of his patrol were hit by enemy fire.

The Boers were caught by surprise in their laager and after two hours of fighting ran up a white flag. Some 50 were killed and 40 taken prisoner. The rest fled leaving behind all their tents, wagons, equipment and forage.

"The Queensland Mounted Infantry," wrote war historian Alec Hill,[1] "were fortunate in their first action to enjoy success at the cost of only two killed and two wounded, the first Australian casualties of the war ... small as it was Sunnyside was the first success after a series of reverses and indeed was the imperceptible moment when the tide of Boer success began to ebb. Moreover the Queenslanders' skill in attack helped to modify the unfavourable opinion of colonials then current among British regulars."

Leading "A" Company of the Queenslanders in this attack was Captain Harry Chauvel who was later to become a world famous leader of mounted troops when in the First World War he commanded the Desert Mounted Corps in Palestine.

In an ambush near Colesberg on 16 January 1900, two soldiers from New South Wales were killed when 100 Boers suddenly emerged from kopjes to attack a small mixed patrol.

On 9 February 1900 a troop of some 20 Western Australians led by Captain Hatherly Moor and a squadron of Enniskillen Dragoons were patrolling east of Slingersfontein when they encountered a Boer commando of 400 men. The Western Australians, ordered to a flank, were attacked by the Boers from three sides. Throughout the day the 20 Western Australians fought off the encroaching Boers with great skill and courage. Although their strength was reduced by death and wounds they answered an enemy surrender demand with a defiant display of bayonets. The Western Australian journalist and novelist Alfred ("Smiler") Hales learned later from a Boer in hospital of the epic fighting qualities of these WA men in this action. He wrote:

> We sprang up eagerly and dashed down some hills meaning to cross the gully and charge up the kopje where the men were waiting for us. They did not fire on us as regular soldiers always do – volley after volley straight in front of them – but everyone picked his man and shot to kill. They fired like lightning never dwelling on the trigger, yet never wasting lead. All around us our boldest and best dropped until we dare not face them. We dropped to cover and tried to pick them off, but they were cool and watchful.
>
> We tried to crawl from rock to rock to hem them in but they, holding their fire until our burghers moved, plugged us with lead. To move upright to cross a dozen yards meant certain death. They did not play wild music. They only clung close as climbing weeds to rocks and shot as we never saw men shoot before and never hope to see men shoot again.
>
> They got ready to sweep the hill with artillery, but our

> *Commandant, admiring those brave few who would not budge*
> *before us, in spite of our numbers, sent an officer to them to ask*
> *them to surrender, promising them all the honours of war. But*
> *they sent word to come and take them if we could. "Go back*
> *and tell your commandant, Australia is here to stay," they said.*
> *We tried to rush them under the cover of the artillery fire but*
> *they only held the posts with stouter hearts and shot the*
> *straighter when the fire was hottest. We could do nothing but lie*
> *there and swear at them though we admired their stubborn*
> *pluck. They held the hill till all their men were safe, and then*
> *dashed down the other side. They made off carrying their*
> *wounded with them. They were but twenty and we were 200.*[2]

In this action the Western Australians lost Lieutenant G. Hensman
and Corporal Michael Conway. Conway was killed while attempting to
comfort the wounded Hensman as he lay dying.

Next day the Western Australians were paraded before the brigade
commander, Major General R. Clements, and praised for their gallantry.
A brigade order of the day declared:

> *The General Officer commanding wishes to place on record his*
> *high appreciation of the courage and determination shown by a*
> *party of 20 men of the Western Australians, under Captain*
> *Moor. By their determined stand against 300 to 400 men they*
> *entirely frustrated the enemy's attempt to turn the flank of the*
> *position.*

After the bloody fiascos of Colenso, Stormberg and Magersfontein,
Lord Roberts was sent from England to take over from Sir Redvers
Buller as commander-in-chief in South Africa. Roberts, 67, who arrived
in January 1900 had Major General Lord Kitchener as his chief of staff.

Buller remained as field commander in Natal and suffered another
severe reverse at Spion Cop near besieged Ladysmith. When Buller's
forces attacked on 23–24 January 1900 the Boers were in positions
overlooking the British objective and were able to pour heavy fire down

on the confined space on Spion Cop, turning it into an acre of massacre. The British lost 322 killed or died of wounds, 533 wounded and 300 taken prisoner. Boer losses were also heavy.

No purely Australian formations were fighting on the Natal front in the campaign to relieve Ladysmith. But many individual Australians, mostly Uitlanders, served in the British units engaged. The bravery and skill of many of these soldiers has been recorded in detail by R. L. Wallace.[3]

By February 1900 the popular Lord Roberts was ready to mount a counter-invasion of Boer territory. His command had been heavily reinforced and he now had available five divisions including a whole division of cavalry commanded by Lieutenant General John French. Attached to French's division were the NSW Lancers, the Queensland Mounted Infantry and the NSW Medical Corps. Transport was provided by 4,000 drivers, 11,000 mules and 9,600 oxen.

The Invasion of Orange Free State

The massive drive into the Orange Free State was under way by early on 12 February. Relying on speed and surprise French's cavalry division thrust rapidly into Boer territory with the intention of relieving Kimberley. The NSW Lancers on the right flank came under artillery fire. But with 40 kilometres of the veldt to cover, they ignored it and swept on. Near the Modder River the cavalry came under fire from Boers on kopjes but at the end of the day French held two forts and was camped on the north bank.

So severe was the effect of hard riding and the blazing heat that hundreds of exhausted horses were lost. The route of the advance was littered with the corpses of 500 animals which had been either killed by the hard riding or shot after becoming lame or exhausted.

The task of the cavalry was to ride "like the wind" to the relief of Kimberley. They had to save it from the Boers and also from Cecil Rhodes who had warned Roberts he was to make the relief his first priority or he (Rhodes) would surrender it to the Boers.

On 15 February the cavalry headed for Kimberley. They bypassed the Boer-held trenches of Magersfontein which had proved such an obstacle to the Guards and Highland Brigades in December. When Boers attempted to block the cavalry sweep, a massed charge scattered them. The Boers broke everywhere, jumped on their horses and rode for their lives.

The arduous ride was taking a heavy toll of the division with the men on half rations and horses dropping dead with hunger, heat and exhaustion. Conditions were made worse by veldt fires. But the cavalry swept on in wave after wave through a long nek and across the plain to enter Kimberley that night. The four months' siege had ended.

Describing his exhilarating experience. Captain Chauvel of the Queensland Mounted Infantry wrote: "We had a glorious ride from Belmont, fighting more or less all the way after the second day. The day after we arrived (at Kimberley) we had a hard day's work fighting to drive the Boers out from around Dronfield."

The bearer company of the NSW Medical Corps had the distinction of being the only medical unit to keep up with the cavalry on the ride to Kimberley.

General Piet Cronje, the Boer commander at Magersfontein, had been outmanoeuvred by swift cavalry thrust and he was forced to abandon his strong fixed defences and retreat with 6,000 men as quickly as he could towards Bloemfontein, his capital and supply base. He did not make it. Australians of the NSW Mounted Rifles located Cronje's force at Paardeberg. There on the sandy banks of the river his men went to earth digging trenches for horses, bullocks and women. The Boer leader de Wet rushed up from the south to their relief but was too late. He found the British all around Cronje's laager, blasting him with artillery which sent great clouds of red dust into the air. After a 10-day siege Cronje surrendered. Some 117 Boers had been killed and they lost another 4,250 who went into captivity. Cronje was exiled to the island of St Helena.

Kimberley had been relieved and now Paardeberg had fallen, giving the British their first great victory of the war.

Boer morale had been shattered but some 7,000 made another stand at Dreifontein. After brushing aside this opposition, Roberts entered Bloemfontein, the capital of Orange Free State on 13 March, just 30 days after he had set his massive drive in motion. No attempt was made to hold the capital. The Boers had reached the end of their tether.

Meanwhile, to add to the Boer catalogue of disasters the British in Natal had relieved Ladysmith after a siege lasting 118 days. Gripped by a wave of pessimism and despair the Boers fled in chaos across the sodden veldt. On 28 February, as Buller's cavalry rode into Ladysmith, the tail end of a great Boer trek could be seen: a long, winding stream of wagons and riders moving with undisciplined speed in Zululand.

In the wake of these defeats the Boers made overtures for peace, but these were summarily rejected. Some Boers had believed that other nations would come to their aid with military forces and were bitterly disappointed when this did not happen. Even worse was the knowledge that the British colonies had volunteered freely to come to the aid of Britain.

The aftermath of victory was not kind to Australians: disease caused more Australian deaths in South Africa than did Boer weapons. At Bloemfontein enteric fever struck hard. Unclean water polluted with dead horses and human waste from Cronje's laager at Paardeberg turned the capital into a pest hole, infecting the army. More than 80 members of the Queensland Mounted Infantry were in hospital at the end of March 1900. At one stage at Bloemfontein 2,000 soldiers were in hospital.

The NSW Army Medical Corps set up a hospital in the Orange Free State military barracks. Reinforcements from Australia saw the unit's strength grow to 240 including 14 nursing sisters who arrived with the second contingent. They cared for fever victims both Boer and Briton and their dedication and efficiency established them as pre-eminent among Australian units in South Africa.

So deadly was the outbreak of disease that fatigue parties had to work long hours to meet the demand for graves. One of the Australian nurses counted 20 funerals in one day.

After the fall of Bloemfontein and the relief of Ladysmith the war appeared to be over. All that was necessary, it seemed, was for the remaining Boer commandos to lay down their arms. This did not happen.

Lord Roberts, after pausing to replace the heavy loss of horses and to build up supplies and stocks of arms and ammunition, launched what was believed would be the final British offensive. On 3 May the drive to Pretoria, the capital of the Transvaal Republic, began. He had a large army of 44,000 soldiers, 11,000 horses and 22,000 mules drawing 5500 carts. With this force went 3,000 mounted soldiers from the Australian contingents. The Boers could muster only 15,000 armed men and could offer little more than token opposition.

Johannesburg fell to Roberts on 30 May. The Boers also withdrew from Pretoria and the city capitulated to Roberts on 3 June. President Kruger had left Pretoria three days earlier and in 1904 died in exile in Switzerland.

But the struggle continued. Battle was joined again on 12 June at Diamond Hill. Australians were represented in this action by four squadrons of the NSW Mounted Rifles with Western Australians in support. They came under heavy fire when they galloped across the plain near a Boer farm. They then dismounted and charged the Boers with fixed bayonets. The Boers retreated taking their dead and wounded with them. "Banjo" Paterson, the Australian war correspondent, praised the actions of two Australian officers (Lieutenants W. Harriott and P. Drage) who were killed in this battle. He wrote: "Harriott and Drage stood up urging the men on and calling them by name. They actually got their pipes and filled them while the Boer bullets whizzed past and splattered in little grey patches on the rocks."

By May 1900 the end of Mafeking's ordeal was in sight. Two British relief columns had joined together and were poised to raise the siege. With these columns were the Imperial Light Horse, whose second-in-command was Major W. "Karri" Davies, an Australian, the Queensland Mounted Infantry and Australian Citizens' Bushmen.

The defenders of Mafeking were amazed on 17 May when, in semi-darkness, a light horse major and eight troopers with ostrich plumes in their hats clattered into the market square at 7 pm. They were led by "Karri" Davies and included Corporal Ernest Warby of Sydney who had volunteered to join Davies in his daring bid to be first into Mafeking. The Imperial Light Horse had lost 22 killed and wounded in an encounter with the besiegers the day before. But after two hours' fighting the Boers had decamped.

Mafeking had been besieged for 217 days. The end of this siege was the signal for an extraordinary and prolonged outburst of celebration and rejoicing throughout the Empire.

After the fall of Pretoria and Kruger's flight, most Boers had had enough of the war. Convinced their cause was lost, they were on the point of surrendering. But younger, more ruthless and energetic leaders such as de Wet and de la Rey who had proved outstanding in battle were totally opposed to surrender. They were determined to carry on a guerilla war to rekindle the spirit of resistance. To overcome the numerical superiority of the British they would organise elite striking forces which would rely on mobility and elusiveness. To contain the guerillas the British would need greater numbers at a time when the War Office was pressing for troop reductions. Kitchener, who succeeded Roberts as commander-in-chief, demanded 30,000 more men to cope with the new style Boer campaign.

With the guerilla phase of the war soon under way, "Koos" de la Rey had to capture supplies from his enemies so that he could carry on the fight. In August 1900 he led 3000 Boers against a post at Brakfontein on the Elands River in western Transvaal which was rich in stores of all kinds. Defending the post were 105 NSW Citizens' Bushmen, 141 Queensland Mounted Infantry, 42 Victorian Bushmen, 9 Western Australians, 2 Tasmanians and 201 Rhodesian Volunteers.

The Boers attacked on 4 August and their shells, falling within the defences, killed hundreds of animals and caused 32 casualties. Overnight the defenders dug in and held out against shell and rifle fire. A relief force was stopped by the Boers and a second relief column turned back in the mistaken belief that the post had already been relieved.

During the 11 days' siege the Boer artillery fired 1800 shells into the two-hectare camp area. Lieutenant J. Annat led a patrol of Queenslanders in an attempt to silence a troublesome pom-pom. They forced the burghers manning the gun to retire. On 6 August Annat was killed when a shell exploded near him.

On 9 August de la Rey called on the defenders to surrender, offering them honourable terms and a safe conduct to a British camp. He was told that if he wanted the supplies in the camp he would have to come and get them. Colonel C. Hore, the British commander, emphasised the firm resolve of the defenders when he said to the Boers: "I cannot surrender, I am in command of Australians who would cut my throat if I did."

For 10 days the Boers poured artillery fire and Mauser bullets into the defences. An Australian burial party, caught in the open, had to shelter in a partly dug grave until the fire subsided.

But the Boers, although heavily outnumbering the defenders, were not prepared to risk a frontal attack and after ten days packed up and faded away empty-handed. On 16 August the post was relieved by a column commanded by Lord Kitchener.

The weary defenders at Elands River were the victors of one of the finest exploits of the Boer War. The famous British author, Arthur Conan Doyle paid them this tribute:

> *The stand at Brakfontein on the Elands River appears to have been one of the finest deeds of arms of the war. Australians have been so split up during the campaign that though their valour and efficiency were universally recognised, they had no single large exploit which they could call their own. But now they can point to Elands River as proudly as the Canadians at Paardeberg ... they were sworn to die before the white flag would wave above them. And so fortune yielded as fortune will when brave men set their teeth ... when the ballad makers of Australia seek for a subject, let them turn to the Elands River, for there was no finer fighting in the war.*[4]

The Boer guerilla campaign began to hurt and the British reacted with harsh measures. A "scorched earth" policy was started, involving the burning of Boer houses and crops. With their menfolk absent on guerilla war missions Boer women and children were rounded up and placed in concentration camps. Blockhouses were built and garrisoned. Barbed-wire barriers were set up to protect railway communications. These counter-measures incensed the Boers and their women were especially bitter, and more irreconcilable. Outside the large towns the ubiquitous activities of the guerillas kept large areas of the Boer republics beyond British control.

One Boer general, Jan Smuts, led a commando unit to within 50 miles of Cape Town endeavouring to incite the Cape Dutch to rise in revolt against British rule.

Coping with the Boers was difficult and dangerous and required the commitment of large forces to prevent Boer attacks on isolated areas and weakly garrisoned towns, convoys and sections of railways. An ever-present danger existed of sudden ambushes and forays costing lives and the loss of supplies.

The Australians were not always successful in battle. On 12 June 1901 the 5th Victorian Mounted Rifles were camped for the night at Wilmansrust near Middleberg. Because of a faulty picket line they were completely surprised and overwhelmed by 150 Boer fighters. Within minutes the attack was over and 19 Victorians lay dead including the medical officer. Many Australians, separated from their weapons, surrendered but were released after the Boers left with their loot.

This defeat had an unfortunate sequel. The British regular officer who commanded the Australians, Major General Stuart Beatson, openly described the 5th Victorians as a "fat-arsed, pot-bellied, lazy lot of wasters". The insults were strongly resented and later when the Victorian Private James Steel was heard to say "We'll be a lot of fools to go with him again," he and two other Victorians were arrested, charged with inciting to mutiny, found guilty and sentenced to death. Kitchener, however, commuted the sentences to prison terms.

Later when the Australian Prime Minister Edmund Barton sought information on the cases, the War Office informed him that legal flaws had been found in the court martial proceedings and that the Judge Advocate General had ordered the immediate release of the three and the quashing of the convictions.

In a sharp action on 30 October 1901, Victorians of the Scottish Horse suffered heavy casualties at Gun Hill when the Boers attacked a poorly sited gun position. The Boers stripped the dead and wounded Australians of clothes and valuables, leaving them naked on the ground. The Boers themselves lost an estimated 60 killed. In another battle at Onverwacht on 4 January 1902, the 5th Queensland Imperial Bushmen lost 13 killed and 17 wounded.

Breaker Morant

Another serious disciplinary matter involving Australian soldiers arose shortly before the war ended. Two Australians officers, convicted at a court martial for the murder of Boer prisoners, were executed at Pretoria by a firing squad on 27 February 1902. They were Lieutenants Harry Morant and P. J. Handock. A third officer, Lieutenant G. R. Witton, was convicted on the same charge and also sentenced to death. Field Marshal Kitchener confirmed the death sentences on Morant and Handcock but commuted Witton's sentence to life imprisonment. The three officers were all members of the Bushveldt Carbineers, a special force operating against guerillas in the northern Transvaal. All three were found guilty of shooting prisoners but acquitted of a further charge of shooting a German missionary. Morant admitted shooting prisoners but justified this action because of orders from a superior office that prisoners were not to be taken and also by the stress of guerilla warfare.

Morant, a colourful character and a great horseman, was well known in Australia as a contributor of ballads to the Sydney Bulletin under the pen-name "Breaker". Game to the last he refused a blindfold and spoke to the firing squad of Cameron Highlanders urging them, "Shoot straight, don't make a mess of it."

The fate of the two officers and the Wilmansrust affair caused resentment and controversy in Australia and confirmed the view that in future disciplinary action involving Australian servicemen should always be in the hands of Australian military authorities.

The Last Phase

In December of 1901 Australia agreed to send 1,000 mounted troops to be designated the Australian Commonwealth Horse. Large Numbers volunteered and the commitment was increased to 4,000. Only four of the eight battalions formed actually reached South Africa before the war ended. The first battalion sailed for South Africa on 19 February 1902.

The drastic measures taken against the enemy slowly bore fruit. They unsuccessfully sued for peace in March 1901 and finally accepted the loss of their independence when they signed the peace of Vereeniging on 31 May 1902, bringing the war to its inevitable end.

Australian Forces sent to South Africa 1899–1902

A total of 16,175 Australian soldiers and 16,134 horses were sent to South Africa. British and Empire troops taking the field totalled 450,000 of whom colonial volunteers from outside South Africa totalled 31,000. Another 53,000 came from South Africa itself.

The contributions of individual Australians States were:

	OFFICERS	OTHER RANKS
New South Wales	314	5,796
Victoria	193	3,372
Queensland	149	2,739
South Australia	89	1,437
Western Australia	67	1,162
Tasmania	36	821
	848	15,327

Australian casualties in South Africa were 1,400 in all categories and of these 251 were killed in action or died of wounds and 267 died of diseases.

The Australian fighting man by his initiative, dash and courage made a great contribution to the success of the British Empire operations in South Africa. However, it was clear that Australia's impact would have been far greater had the many individual contingents not been scattered throughout South Africa in small units attached to larger non-Australian forces.

Australian courage was rewarded by a substantial number of decorations including the highest award for gallantry, the Victoria Cross, which was awarded to six Australians. All were decorated for rescuing wounded men under fire. They were:

> **Captain Neville Howse**, a medical officer of the NSW Medical Corps for gallantry in action at Vredefort on 24 July 1900. Howse, the first Australian to be awarded a Victoria Cross, faced heavy crossfire to pick up a wounded man and carry him to safety.
>
> **Lieutenant G. Wylly** of the Tasmanian Imperial Bushmen received his award for rescuing a wounded man at Warm Bad, Transvaal, on 1 September 1900.
>
> **Trooper J. H. Bisdee** also of the Tasmanian Imperial Bushmen earned the award on the same day in similar circumstances.
>
> **Lieutenant Frederick Bell** of the Western Australian Mounted Infantry received the decoration for gallantry at Brakpan on 16 May 1901.
>
> **Trooper J. Rogers** of the South African Constabulary earned his award for repeated acts of bravery in the Orange Free State on 15 June 1901.
>
> **Lieutenant L. C. Maygar** of the 5th Victorian Mounted Rifles won the award at Geelhoutboom in Natal on 23 November 1901. Maygar survived the South African war only to be killed in action near Beersheba in Palestine in 1917.

3

WAR AGAINST
THE BOXERS

All Australian colonies were deeply involved in the bloody fighting in South Africa when another call to arms came from China, via Britain, for help in containing and defeating a dangerous threat to all foreigners in China by the fanatical Chinese secret society known as the "Boxers".

The colonies of New South Wales, Victoria and South Australia responded at once by offering some 460 members of the Victorian and NSW naval brigades and the gunboat *Protector*, flagship of the South Australian naval forces, and its crew of 96.

When in June 1900 the call for military help came, the Australian naval brigade units were being prepared for the South African War and their diversion to China resulted in the first Australian involvement in a war on the mainland of Asia.

The Australian soldiers were to join an international force composed of sailors, marines and soldiers from Britain, France, Italy, Russia, America and Japan tasked to protect the lives of Christian missionaries and other foreign nationals and to defend their economic interests.

China's immense size, huge population and enormous resources and potential, coupled with the weakness of the ruling Manchu dynasty, made her vulnerable to external pressures.

In the second half of the 19th century Western industrial nations and emergent Japan vied with each other to extract concessions, privileges and leaseholds from the Chinese. Japan, eager to detach Korea from China, succeeded in its aim when the Chinese were crushed in the Sino-Japanese war of 1894–95. Sensing a likely disintegration of the Chinese state, other nations increased the pressure on China for concessions and spheres of interest.

These unfortunate circumstances were the cause of growing unrest in the Chinese community. With patience finally exhausted many Chinese joined the "Righteous Harmonious Fists" or "Boxer" movement. Secretly encouraged by the Empress Dowager, the angry Boxers vowed to "exterminate the foreigners".

But however much China suffered from the foreign "devils", there was no way such a drastic solution could be tolerated by the Europeans who lived and traded there. The Boxers murdered Christian missionaries, both male and female, and Chinese converts to Christianity. Rape and pillage were widespread and Western property was put to the torch. A crisis point was reached in May 1900 when the Empress permitted Boxers to demonstrate openly against foreigners in the walled city of Peking (now Beijing) and an Imperial Chinese Army 18,000 strong joined thousands of undisciplined Boxers in the streets. Chaos reigned in the capital and the Diplomatic Corps sent urgent appeals for more guards to be provided from a multinational fleet standing off the coast. Some 1,500 Europeans were slaughtered by the Boxers. At Tientsin the Boxers waved the heads of murdered missionaries as they occupied the city.

The Empress ordered all foreign diplomats to leave Peking, but before they could do so Baron Von Kettler, the German Minister, was killed by Boxers. This aroused a furious response from the German Kaiser who urged German marines to "take no prisoners ... kill him when he falls into your hands".

The siege of Peking now began with the insurgents and Chinese troops firing on the embassies. In June an additional Allied force of

2,000 sailors and marines from the multinational fleet set off from the coast to relieve the legations but were forced back by the Boxers and the Chinese army.

Alarmed for the safety of their nationals, eight nations joined together in forming an international relief force.

On 28 June 1900 the British Government cabled Australia asking that warships of the Royal Navy then serving on the Australian Station be released for service in China. They were released at once and in addition the State of Victoria offered 200 men of the naval brigade (commanded by Commander Frederick Tickell) for service in China. As well, NSW offered another 260, to be commanded by Commander Francis Hixson. The commitment of the South Australian gunboat HMCS *Protector* together with 96 officers and men brought the total to 556. *Protector* was to be commanded by Captain William Creswell, a former Royal Navy officer who had served on the China Station. Included in the NSW force was a detachment of "disguised" soldiers designated the "NSW Marine Light Infantry".

In the Victorian Legislative Assembly the Hon. C. C. Salmon declared that no better means could be adopted of ensuring peace than by assisting in China at once. "The terrible occurrences in China," he said, "had sent a thrill of horror right through the civilised world." Mr H. B. Higgins doubted the wisdom of the decision. "The people will be wanting to know whether we in these colonies are to be expected to volunteer each time to contribute valuable lives and money in aid of wars which may not interest us directly," he said.

The Victorian and NSW contingents left Sydney on the liner *Salamis* on 9 August and the *Protector* three days later.

On the 9 September the contingents, after inspections at Woosung, arrived at Taku on the Gulf of Chihli where they became part of the British Contingent Field Force in China.

However, most of the fighting had already taken place. The Taku forts had been captured on June 17, opening the way for contingents of the international force to land.

By 14 July the international force had taken the city of Tientsin. A 20,000-strong Allied force had then pushed on to Peking which was relieved on 14 August after the defenders had endured a desperate 55-day siege. The relief took place before the substantial German expeditionary force, despatched to avenge the murder of the German Minister in Peking, could take part in the rescue. Deprived of the glory of lifting the siege the Germans now cast about to find some way of justifying their high-speed sea dash from Europe.

On 24 September the Australians were ordered to take part in a foray against the Peitang forts in a force of 8000 men which included British, Russians and Australians. The Australian contribution was 300 (150 from Victoria and 150 from NSW including 25 marines of the Light Infantry). The Australians were angered to learn when they arrived at Peitang that the Russians had already stormed the forts where after the action only four dead Chinese were found. The Australians, hungry and tired after a march of 18 miles, had arrived too late.

On 6 October the first Australian to die in China was buried. He was Private T. J. Rogers of the NSW Marine Light Infantry, who fell victim to influenza. At the time 25 per cent of the contingent were on the sick list. Four days later the New South Welshmen were ordered to Peking where they carried out guard duties at the British Legation and the Llama temple.

HMCS *Protector* became HMS *Protector* when she arrived in China and came under Royal Navy control. *Protector* spent her time shuttling men and stores between ports and carrying despatches. By the beginning of November the Admiralty decided it could dispense with her services and she was released on 2 November to return to Adelaide.

On 12 October, 250 Australians joined a force of 8,500 men (including British, German, French and Italian soldiers) in a foray to Pao Ting-fu where they were to deal with the murderers of missionaries. The force, under French Brigadier General Bailloud, reached Pao Ting-fu, the provincial capital of Chihli, after a 10-day march. But the city offered no resistance. Some Australians were directed to guard a number of Boxers who were to be held and then handed over for execution. The force returned to Tientsin after being in the field for 25 days during which they experienced no fighting.

Towards the end of 1900 after the Boxers had been dispersed, the fighting in North China quickly subsided. With few active military duties to be performed, the Australians were tasked to support the civil administration. In Peking, Lieutenant Staunton Spain of the NSW contingent was put in charge of fire fighting. Victorians in Tientsin formed the nucleus of the police force. Others were employed in the railway service as guards and ticket collectors. Some understandably resented being used in non-military duties.

Lieutenant General Sir Alfred Gaselee, the British Commander, wrote to Prime Minister Edmund Barton praising the Australian naval brigades. "It only remains for me to say how excellent an effect has been produced by the appearance in so remote a stage as North China by these fine Contingents from the Australian Commonwealth." The Mayor and Council of Tientsin presented each member of the contingent with an illuminated souvenir.

After serving through the bitterly cold winter months, members of the contingent were withdrawn to Australia. They arrived at Sydney on the transport *Chingtu* on 25 April 1901.

Of the total of 556 Australians who had served in the war of the Boxers, six had died, including Staff Surgeon J. Steel.

4

THE FIRST WORLD WAR

The Last Man and The Last Shilling

A bullet fired by a teenage assassin in Sarajevo, capital city of Bosnia-Herzegovina in the Balkans, ignited the spark which exploded into the First World War, one of the most lethal and destructive conflicts in history.

It was a conflict in which 60,000 Australians were to lose their lives in battle and another 150,000 would be wounded.

The fatal shot was fired on 28 June 1914 by an 18-year-old Bosnian student, Gavrilo Princip. It killed the Archduke Franz Ferdinand, heir to the Austro-Hungarian throne. The outraged Austrians saw this murder as a slavonic challenge to the teutonic world.

Relations between Austria and neighbouring Serbia had long been turbulent and Austria, believing that Serbia was implicated in the Sarajevo crime, and confident of the backing of Germany (as an insurance against Russia intervening to defend Serbia), declared war on Serbia on 28 July 1914.

A fatal chain reaction now set in. Tsarist Russia mobilised in support of Serbia. The German war machine, then the world's most powerful, advanced to meet both the Russian armies in the east and Russia's ally, France, in the west.

The Germany army mounted a lightning campaign (based on the Schlieffen Plan) to crush all French resistance. To gain a military advantage over France, the Germans overran Belgian territory. For this violation, Britain, a guarantor of Belgian neutrality, declared war on Germany on 4 August and despatched the British Expeditionary Force across the Channel to France. "The lamps are going out all over Europe. We shall not see them lit again in our lifetime," declared a saddened Sir Edward Grey, the British Foreign Secretary.

Only the Italians, then allied to the Germans and Austro-Hungarians, stood aloof and ultimately turned their backs on the central powers and joined the "Allies" (Britain, France and Russia), as did Japan.

Japan was allied to Britain through the Anglo-Japanese Treaty of 1902. The existence of this treaty was not altogether favourably accepted by Australians, although Japan's naval strength added to Australia's maritime security.

The Sarajevo assassination was the immediate cause of the war, but the fundamental causes lay deep in 19th-century history. The war had been preceded by decades of international tensions arising from nationalism, fuelled by rivalry over colonial expansion in Africa, Asia and the Pacific. In the Balkans a lethal mix of race, religion and culture had set the stage for a bloodbath.

Fear of aggression led to an unprecedented arms race. The major European nations had been organising and training great conscript armies. Navies expanded, especially that of Germany which aimed to rival the Royal Navy. Guns and ammunition poured from the factories of the industrialised nations.

On 29 July, Britain sent a warning signal to Australia indicating that war was imminent. When it came on 4 August, the Australian people rallied solidly behind "the mother country". They were aware that although the war was chiefly between European countries the outcome would affect the entire world. Australians believed that if Britain was threatened, so was Australia.

Andrew Fisher, Leader of the Labor Party and soon to become Prime Minister, was greeted with thunderous applause at Colac, Victoria, when on 31 July he pledged Australia's "last man and last shilling" to the British cause.

Even before the declaration of war, Prime Minister Cook had sent a cable to the British Government offering the services of the RAN and "to prepare and despatch an expeditionary force of 20,000 men of any suggested composition to any destination desired by the Home Government ... the force ... to be at complete disposal of Home Government. Cost of despatch and maintenance will be borne by the Government. Australian press notified accordingly". Britain accepted gratefully and asked that the force be sent as soon as possible.

Spurred on by the fear of aggressors, Australians had responded powerfully to the dangers they saw and had laid solid foundations upon which the nation's defences could be built.

In 1911 the Government had established the Royal Military College, Duntroon, in Canberra, to alleviate the serious shortage of professionally trained army officers. An RAN College, modelled on Osborne and Dartmouth in England, was opened at Geelong in 1913 with a first intake of 26 cadets.

Following the "astounding" victory of the Japanese Navy over the Russian Navy in Tsushima Straits in 1905, and the strong German challenge to Britain's world naval supremacy, Australians had begun to entertain seriously the possibility of invasion and in 1911 compulsory military training was introduced. All schools were required to join the scheme and by December 1913 a total of 55,850 junior cadets were under training.

Defence factories were built and an armament industry began to take shape. Although aviation was in its infancy, Australians were quick to grasp the strategic significance of air power. By 1913 land had been acquired at Point Cook, Victoria, where in the following year the Central Flying School was established. On 17 August four army officers began the first military flying training course. One of the four, Lieutenant (later Air Marshal Sir) Richard Williams was first to qualify as a pilot and later became the first Chief of the Air Staff (RAAF).

In 1914 the Australian Army had a strength of 45,645. However, the promised Australian expeditionary force would have to be a volunteer force because the Defence Act did not permit compulsory service beyond Australian shores.

As soon as volunteers were invited to enlist, eager recruits besieged recruiting stations to sign up for war. Only the fittest were accepted, leading to the bitter disappointment of those rejected. Soon columns of young men were marching into training camps near the capital cities.

Brigadier General (later Major General Sir) William Throsby Bridges was appointed to command the force which he named the Australian Imperial Force (AIF). It was composed of infantry, artillery and light horse. It was to be a compact Australian force not split up as in South Africa to form elements of British Army formations.

A division, the 1st Australian Division (AIF) was organised. Volunteers from NSW formed the Division's 1st Brigade, comprising the 1st, 2nd, 3rd and 4th Battalions, each of 1,023 men; the 2nd Brigade (Victoria) comprising the 5th, 6th, 7th and 8th Battalions and the 3rd Brigade: 9th Battalion, Queensland, 10th South Australia; 11th Western Australia and 12th half Tasmania and half Western and South Australia.

The 1st Light Horse Brigade (2,226 strong) was composed of the 1st Regiment, NSW, 2nd Regiment, Queensland, and 3rd Regiment, South Australia and Tasmania. It was commanded by Colonel (later Lieutenant General Sir) Harry Chauvel.

The Navy Goes to War

Warships of the RAN were already on their way to war stations when news was received that a state of war existed with Germany. At 12.30 pm on 10 August, five days later, the Australian Navy was placed under the control of the British Admiralty.

The nation was proud of its Navy, a modern ocean-going force ready for immediate action. It comprised the powerful battle cruiser HMAS *Australia* of 19,200 tons, four cruisers, three destroyers and two submarines. *Australia* with its superior speed and 12-inch (30.48 cm) guns was capable of destroying the whole of the German Pacific squadron singlehanded. The RAN fleet had been created largely in the image of the Royal Navy. Of its 3,800 permanent personnel, some 850 were on loan from the Royal Navy.

When war came, the Australian Navy commander, Rear Admiral Sir George Patey, considered it was his supreme duty to seek out and destroy the German Pacific squadron which operated from a strong base at Tsingtao in China. The German squadron included two armoured cruisers, the *Scharnhorst* and *Gneisenau*. However, HMAS *Australia* alone was more than a match for them.

The Germans proved elusive. Fearing the crushing supremacy of Allied naval power if Japan joined the Allies, they had melted into the vast expanses of the Pacific.

The RAN suspected the German squadron might be at Rabaul, capital of Germany's New Guinea colonies. Admiral Patey sped north with the intention of torpedoing any naval units found at Rabaul but when his squadron searched the harbour on 11 August they found it empty of warships. The quarry was at Pagan in the Caroline Islands some 2,500 kilometres away and was planning to make for the west coast of South America and thence back to Germany.

Meanwhile on 6 August the British Government had asked Australia to take part in the "great and urgent Imperial service" of seizing German wireless stations in the south-west Pacific, thus delivering a fatal blow to German naval activities. Australia was to destroy stations on Yap, Nauru and New Guinea.

Australia at once organised a joint army-navy force known as the Australian Naval and Military Expeditionary Force (AN and MEF). Patey was required to escort this force to Rabaul since the whereabouts of the German squadron was still not known. Command of all troops was given to Colonel Williams Holmes, an Australian veteran of the South African War.

The AN and MEF was off New Britain in the transport *Berrima* by 11 September and two armed parties were sent ashore, one at Herbertshoe and the other at Kabakaul near Rabaul. The Australians quickly subdued the German forces, losing two officers and four men killed and a number wounded in action. On 13 September the British flag was hoisted at Rabaul and within a few weeks most of German New

Guinea, Bougainville and the Admiralty Islands had been occupied. On 21 September 40 German soldiers and 110 local recruits marched into Rabaul and laid down their arms.

The RAN suffered the loss of one of its two submarines, *AE1*, on 14 September when it failed to return from a patrol near Rabaul. Its loss was a mystery. Searches by navy ships saw no sign of the submarine or any of its three officers and 32 men.

The *Sydney-Emden* Fight

By mid-September many newly formed units of the 1st Division AIF marched through the streets where relatives proudly crowded to see them. By the end of the month orders were given for the battalions to embark on troopships. But these orders were cancelled when the *Gneisenau* and *Scharnhorst* suddenly appeared off Samoa. However, shortly afterwards these German cruisers raided Tahiti a further 1000 miles from Australia and the Government ordered the embarkation to proceed. New Zealand and Australian troopships gathered in King George's Sound, the harbour of Albany in Western Australia. On 1 November 36 transports, escorted by four warships (the British cruiser *Minotaur*, the Japanese cruiser *Ibuki* and the Australian cruisers *Melbourne* and *Sydney*), sailed out of the harbour. They were joined at sea by another two troopships from Western Australia.

As the great convoy transporting the Australian Imperial Force cleared the harbour at King George's Sound, the German Pacific squadron was about to engage a British squadron off Coronel, South America. In the battle which followed the British were decisively beaten. It was the view of Admiral Patey that had the Australian squadron been allowed immediately to seek out and destroy the German squadron, the Coronel disaster would have been averted. However, the German squadron was annihilated a month later (on 8 December 1915) in the Battle of the Falkland Islands.

The German Pacific Squadron had earlier forced the AIF convoy to be delayed and now the *Minotaur* which was in command of the convoy's escorting warships was ordered to South Africa, as part of a rapid redeployment of British naval units resulting from the German

Squadron's victory at Coronel. HMAS *Melbourne* took *Minotaur's* place and the great troop convoy ploughed on through the Indian Ocean.

Meanwhile, the 3,592-ton German cruiser *Emden* which had earlier been detached from the German Pacific squadron to undertake "a special mission" had embarked on one of the most daring careers of maritime destruction in naval history, creating havoc mainly in the Indian Ocean. In a few weeks *Emden* sank or captured 25 Allied steamers and two warships as well as setting oil tanks ablaze at Madras. In a sudden foray into the Malacca Straits, *Emden* sank the Russian cruiser *Zemtchug* and the French destroyer *Mousquet* near Penang. Clearly *Emden's* presence endangered the Australian convoy.

Emden now entered Indian Ocean waters through which the AIF convoy was moving. The raider, unaware of the convoy's presence, appeared off Cocos Island on 9 November and sent an armed party ashore which destroyed the cable and wireless station. The AIF convoy was close by to the east and picked up distress signals sent by the Cocos staff. They sent the message: "Strange ship approaching," then "SOS" followed by silence. At 7.15 am HMAS *Sydney* was sent at full speed to investigate and two hours later sighted *Emden*.

Sydney outgunned *Emden*. The raider opened fire first at extreme range and hit *Sydney* 15 times. *Sydney* replied with her 100 lb shells (compared with *Emden's* 38-pounders) and inflicted much greater damage. *Emden* caught fire and her funnels went over the side. Her steering gear was destroyed. By 11 am *Emden* gave up the fight and steering by her engines deliberately ran aground on North Keeling Island. At 11.10 am Captain J. T. C. Glossop of *Sydney* informed the convoy it was safe with the message: "*Emden* beached to avoid sinking". Troops on the decks of the transports were drilling as they listened to the distant thumping of naval gunfire and cheered lustily when they heard the news. To celebrate the victory they were given a half holiday.

Sydney had lost four killed and 12 wounded. *Emden* suffered 134 killed and 65 wounded. The battle had been fierce but when Captain Glossop met the vanquished Captain Karl von Muller on the quarterdeck he permitted the German captain to retain his surrendered sword. Von Muller was widely acclaimed for the chivalry and humanity with which he discharged his duties.

Except for the cruiser *Konigsberg* which was bottled up by the British Navy in the Rufigi River in East Africa, the Indian and Pacific oceans were now free of significant German naval units and as a result *Melbourne* and *Sydney* were ordered to the Atlantic and *Australia*, after sinking a German liner off South America, became the flagship of the Second Battle Cruiser Squadron of the British "Grand Fleet". *Konigsberg* stayed in the Rufigi River until she was destroyed in July 1915 with the help of HMAS *Pioneer*.

The great troop convoy steamed steadily on to Colombo and on 15 November, HMAS *Sydney* which had followed with many wounded German sailors on her decks, sailed quietly up the harbour between the crowded Australian transports. The air was still. Captain Glossop had asked that there be no cheering to celebrate the Australian naval victory. Young Australian soldiers were witnessing for the first time the ugly side of war. Human emotions broke through the barriers of allegiance in this silent gesture of compassion for the maimed and dying enemy sailors.

The convoy sailed on, reaching Aden at the end of November. Shortly after passing Aden word came that the Australian and New Zealand troops would disembark not in England but in Egypt, for Turkey had entered the war on Germany's side on 30 October. Together the Australians and New Zealanders were to form a corps under General W. R. (later Field Marshal Lord) Birdwood, a British cavalry officer. After training for combat in a camp near Cairo they would go to the front from Egypt. British command had changed the plan to accommodate the colonial troops in England because difficulties had been encountered in England in the provision of winter camps not only for the Canadian contingent but for British troops as well. Once Turkey entered the war it was agreed that the Australians should be accommodated in Egypt.

The Australians began disembarkation at Alexandria on 3 December and settled into a huge tented camp at Mena where the 1st Australian Division was together on land for the first time near the pyramids and close to the Libyan desert. By mid-December the task of training the division for war was in full swing. Birdwood's corps of two divisions was organised as follows:

Corps Headquarters (a British unit with a staff of British officers).

1st Australian Division.

New Zealand and Australian Division comprising:

New Zealand Infantry Brigade

4th Australian Infantry Brigade (Commander, Colonel John Monash)

1st Australian Light Horse Brigade

New Zealand Mounted Rifles Brigade.

A second Australian AIF contingent began arriving on 1st February and camped next to the New Zealanders on the other side of Cairo at Zeitoun.

Gallipoli

The German war plan in Europe was a simple one. First, a concentrated massive blow to knock France out of the war and then, with one enemy eliminated, an about-face to the east to deal with Russia. It came close to success.

On the other hand the Allies, while striving to hold the Germans in France, had high hopes that the Russian armies advancing into East Prussia would force the Germans to switch substantial forces from France to the east, thus easing the pressure on the Western Front.

But the Russians were bundled out of East Prussia, losing some 1,500,000 men. They were almost annihilated on 31 August 1914 at the Battle of Tannenberg.

In their advance on Paris the Germans swept over most of Belgium and clashed with the small British Expeditionary Force of five divisions at Mons. The British and French armies west of Verdun then retired. It seemed that nothing could hold the German onslaught and their advance guard was soon within 32 kilometres of Paris.

But by September the German advance had faltered and the decisive battle of the Marne (6–10 September) put an end to Germany's hopes of a "knockout" result on the Western Front. By 14 September the

German Army was back on the Aisne River and the immediate threat to Paris was removed. As the Allies had hoped, the Germans were weakened at a critical moment by the withdrawal of the Germany Army Corps to reinforce the Eastern Front against the Russian "steamroller". At the height of the battle, the French Army commandeered 600 Paris taxis to rush 6,000 reinforcements to the front in relays.

By early 1915 the Russians were in a pitiable state and to add to their woes Turkey had entered the war on Germany's side, cutting communications between Russia and her Western allies through the Straits of the Dardanelles. Much-needed munitions for Russia were "bottled up". In addition, Turkey mounted an aggressive campaign through Armenia into the Russian Caucasus and launched another army across the Sinai desert to "liberate" Egypt from the British and seize control of the international choke point of the Suez Canal. However, this Turkish campaign turned into a fiasco. The Australian Army was not involved, although for a time two Victorian battalions manned trenches along the Suez Canal.

However, the Turkish campaign in the Caucasus alarmed the Russians and the Grand Duke Nicholas appealed to the British Government to organise a demonstration or an Allied diversionary operation against Turkey to force them to withdraw.

The British responded at once by developing a plan to seize Constantinople. It was considered feasible to knock Turkey out of the war and that a number of Balkan states would then join the Allies.

Winston Churchill, First Lord of the Admiralty, was an ardent advocate of the project but the great killing match on the Western Front was draining Allied manpower and no troops could be spared from that vital theatre. The British Government decided therefore to see what could be done by naval action alone.

During February and early March 1915 a British fleet attacked the guns in the outer forts of the Dardanelles. But the results were disappointing. A major attack was then made on 18 March by a combined British-French naval force and for a time the Turkish gunners opposing the Allies were demoralised and their guns almost silenced.

However, later that day three Allied naval units struck Turkish mines and were lost. The operation was called off.

So far naval action alone had failed and it was decided that a joint army-navy expedition could succeed in seizing the Gallipoli peninsula and opening the way to Constantinople. A total of 75,000 troops could, after all, be found. A British Regular Army division, the 29th, was available and the Anzac corps of two divisions could provide 30,000 Australians and New Zealanders. Also available were one French division which included Zouaves and Foreign Legionnaires, and the Royal Naval Division. All were to be commanded by General Sir Ian Hamilton.

All over the Mediterranean the dogs were barking loudly that an assault on Gallipoli by an Allied army was in the making. Mail began arriving in Alexandria marked "Constantinople Force, Egypt". The Middle East was thick with Turkish agents who provided Liman von Sanders, the German general commanding the Turkish Army at the Dardanelles, with accurate estimates of Hamilton's forces.

Thoroughly alerted to what was going on, the Turks quickly increased their army in the area fivefold and steeled themselves for the coming battle. Panic gripped the Turkish capital, Constantinople, where an exodus was under way.

Hamilton's staff prepared operational plans in Alexandria. The Anzacs were still an unknown quantity but they would be the first to attempt the hazardous assault on the precipitous Gallipoli peninsula where rugged ridges covered with entangling scrub would impede their advance.

The veteran 29th Division was to make the main landings around Cape Helles on the "toe" of the peninsula. In addition, to create diversions and confuse the enemy, the French would land at Kum Kale on the Asiatic side of the Dardanelles and the Royal Naval Division would demonstrate at Bulair.

With the dramatic announcement on 1 April 1915 that all leave was cancelled came the Australians' full realisation that the ultimate test of combat was near at hand. At Mena camp the news jolted the Anzacs into hectic activity as last-minute preparations were made and they embarked on maritime transports for a secret destination which turned out to be the Greek island of Lemnos. Thence on the night of 24 April the convoy carrying the flower of Australian youth, and with them the hopes and fears of a young nation, glided quietly through the Aegean Sea towards their appointment with destiny – Gallipoli.

The Australians were given the formidable task of landing on the peninsula at Gaba Tepe, 21 kilometres north of Cape Helles. They were to advance inland at once and seize points of the Bay of Kilia which would put them in place to block attempts by the Turks to threaten the 29th Division, which was to land soon afterwards at Cape Helles under cover of a naval bombardment.

The Australian 3rd Brigade was to land first as a covering force at Gaba Tepe. Birdwood, hoping for the advantage of surprise, declined the support of a preliminary bombardment which would have alerted the Turkish defences. The 3rd Brigade (comprising men of the "outer" States – Tasmania, Queensland, South and Western Australia) arrived off Gaba Tepe at about 2 am on 25 April. They were transferred to pinnaces and at the point of dawn the keels of their boats grounded in the shallows of a beach later named "Anzac Cove".

Unfortunately they had been carried a mile north of the intended landing place. But the Australians did not hesitate. They paused briefly to fix bayonets and then scrambled up the steep slope to scatter Turkish defenders who fled from ridge to ridge.

Albert Facey, a 20-year-old private in a Western Australian battalion (the 11th) described the landing thus:

> *This was it. We were scared stiff – I know I was – but keyed up and eager to be on our way. We thought we would tear right through the Turks and keep going to Constantinople. Troops were taken off both sides of the ship on to destroyers … all went well until we were making the change to rowing boats …*
> *Suddenly all hell broke loose; heavy shelling and shrapnel fire commenced. The ships that were protecting our troops returned the fire. Bullets were thumping into us in the rowing boats. Men were being hit and killed all around me. When we were cut*

> *loose to make our way to the shore was the worst period. I was*
> *terribly frightened. The boat touched bottom some thirty yards*
> *from shore so we had to jump out and wade to the beach. The*
> *Turks had machine guns sweeping the strip of beach where we*
> *landed ... there were many dead already when we got there.*
> *Bodies of men who reached the beach ahead of us were lying all*
> *along the beach and wounded men were screaming for help ...*
> *we used our trenching tools to dig mounds of earth and*
> *sheltered from the firing until daylight ... the Turks never let*
> *up ... the slaughter was terrible.*[1]

By 8 am, 8,000 Australian troops were ashore and fighting a confused series of skirmishes in impossible terrain where there was no front line. Although weighted down by their 40 kilogram (80 lb) packs, Australians heeding their instructions to "keep going at all costs" managed to clamber through the tangled mess of ridges and ravines and a few were rewarded with a dazzling glimpse of the narrows from the highest point.

But the Turks were not long in responding strongly to the danger and were fighting desperately to throw the invaders back into the sea before they could consolidate.

A resolute Turkish military leader, Mustapha Kemal, commanded the *Turkish 19th Division*, a reserve force based only a short distance from where the Australians were scaling the main ridge. He observed their movements at 9.30 am and immediately sent his best regiment to counter their advance. By the afternoon, pressure by Kemal's men was forcing the Australians back.

By nightfall the position at the beachhead had become critical. The Anzacs were virtually besieged in a small enclave. The British fleet was offshore in strength but there was little naval guns could do to help. Desperate calls were coming in for reinforcements and ammunition. The beach was jammed with stragglers who had lost touch. Casualties exceeded 2,000 and the wounded lay over the entire end of the beach.

Meanwhile at Cape Helles the British 29th Division had encountered a serious setback. Troops landing from the transport *River Clyde* were decimated when fired on by entrenched Turks.

At the end of the day General Birdwood feared a fiasco and was persuaded to urge Hamilton to order the evacuation of the beachhead. Hamilton did not agree. He told Birdwood that his corps must dig themselves right in and stick it out. The Australians set to work at once, alternately digging in the rough unyielding ground and then firing their weapons. Soon the hillsides were honeycombed with excavations. The terrain soon looked like a vast mining camp and the Australian term "Digger" began to be heard. By the following year Australian soldiers used the term generally to mean one of their kind.

Hamilton, in his message to Birdwood, had added that the RAN submarine *AE2* had penetrated the narrows and torpedoed a Turkish gunboat at Chanak. The *AE2* had been assigned the hazardous task of attempting to get through the Dardanelles and "to run amok generally". The submarine set out on its perilous mission early on 25 April and after spine-chilling adventures was sunk five days later in the Sea of Marmara by a Turkish torpedo boat. The entire crew became prisoners of the Turks.

To add strength to the advance of the 29th Division from Cape Helles, Hamilton sent two brigades (2nd Australian and the New Zealand) from the Anzac area to the Cape and on 10 May they were ordered to attack towards Krithia. But in advancing 1,000 yards the Australians encountered a wall of small arms fire and in one hour lost 1,056 men killed, wounded and missing.

On 15 May General Bridges, the Australian 1st Division commander, was mortally wounded by a sniper and died three days later on the hospital ship *Gascon*. The General's body was later taken to Australia and buried on Russell Hill overlooking the Royal Military College, Canberra.

On the day after Bridges died, another soldier, Private John Simpson, was also killed by a sniper. Simpson, who enlisted under the name of Kirkpatrick, was a stretcher bearer who became famous as "the man with the donkey". He used the donkey to carry wounded to safety through the perils of sniper fire and shrapnel in Monash valley. There were in fact several brave men who used donkeys to transport their wounded comrades at Gallipoli, and they are all honoured in

Australian's proud memory of the man named Simpson. On May 19 Simpson's luck gave out and he was killed bringing out two wounded men. He is commemorated by a statue at the Australian War Memorial, Canberra.

By mid-May the Turks were far from defeated and suddenly before dawn on 18 May, General Birdwood was awakened in his dugout at Anzac Cove with the news that Turkish troops were streaming en masse towards the Anzac trenches.

Some 42,000 enemy troops from four divisions had been assembled at night before the Anzac lines with orders to demolish the Anzac bridgehead in a single blow.

Fortunately the Anzacs had received reinforcements including the 1st Light Horse Brigade (without horses). But with only 12,500 men available for front line fighting they were outnumbered three to one and were compressed into 162 blood-soaked hectares of a shallow triangle resting on the sea behind them.

A Turkish onslaught was expected. On the previous day a Royal Navy reconnaissance aircraft had reported the massing of the Turkish troops and the Anzacs were ordered to stand to arms at 3 am next morning. Within minutes of that time shadowy forms and a long line of bayonets were seen in the half darkness.

Gunfire soon erupted and all along the Anzac front the Turks now jumped from their cover and charged towards the Anzac lines, while the excited Australians and New Zealanders poured a lethal small arms fire into them as they yelled Egyptian slang words such as "Baksheesh" and "Saida".

An awful slaughter ensued as Turkish officers drove their men towards the Anzac wall of fire. As soon as one line of Turks was annihilated another line formed up and was promptly cut down. When some Turks managed to get into the Anzac lines, quick bayonet work despatched them. Some Anzacs, wild with excitement, risked death by sitting astride the parapets to get a better view and from there pumped lead into the yelling Turks.

This ill-conceived offensive was the enemy's greatest disaster of the Gallipoli campaign. Some 10,000 Turks fell compared with Anzac losses of 160 killed and 468 wounded. On 24 May a truce had to be arranged so that the dead lying in front of the Anzac trenches could be buried.

In the heat of summer the sufferings of the Anzacs were increased. Swarms of disease-carrying flies invaded the peninsula. Lice and fleas made life miserable. The Anzacs stood at their posts under the threat of shellfire that never ended. They dug, tunnelled and carried heavy burdens along dusty precipitous tracks. Weakened by monotonous rations they fell easy victims to debilitating diseases such as dysentery, paratyphoid and diarrhoea which attacked thousands. Only serious cases of illness could be evacuated. A chronic shortage of fresh water persisted. A supreme luxury was to bath in the Aegean, but this was attended by the risk of death or wounding from Turkish shells, a risk the diggers were more than willing to face.

The bitter struggle continued in the southern end of the peninsula where Hamilton's troops tried repeatedly to destroy the Turkish defences in the olive groves around Krithia. But the result was a costly stalemate.

Lone Pine and the NEK Disaster

The Turks reinforced their army and so did the British. By August Hamilton would have five additional divisions at his disposal while the Turks built up to 16 divisions overall.

The Gallipoli campaign was now approaching its climax. Hamilton had 110,000 troops and developed a new battle plan which involved the landing of the British IX Corps at Suvla Bay north of the Anzac bridgehead. This force and the Anzacs would converge and dominate the Narrows.

The landing at Suvla Bay on the night of 6 August was accomplished successfully but a wretched display of poor military leadership saw the initial advantage of surprise dissipated. The Turks were given ample time to react and pushed the British force back across the Suvla Plain. An RAN Bridging Train provided facilities in support of the Suvla landing.

Further south tremendous struggles developed when the British attacked yet again at Cape Helles and shortly afterwards the Australian 1st Brigade with two added battalions struck the Turks at Lone Pine.

Both actions were intended to draw Turkish attention away from the main assault.

The attack at Lone Pine which began at 5.30 pm on 6 August was a desperate adventure. Whistle blasts sounded the attack and the Australians dashed 100 yards through scrub on a narrow front to reach the strongly held Turkish trenches. They then discovered that the Turks had roofed over their trenches with pine logs. But the Australians forced their way into the trenches and desperate struggles followed in the dark passages with rifle and bayonet and sometimes with bare hands.

By 6 pm the Australians had taken Lone Pine. They then repulsed Turkish counterattacks and held their gains. But the cost was heavy. By 10 August the six Australian battalions engaged had lost 80 officers and 2,197 men in action while the Turkish 16th Division lost 6,930.

The battle of Lone Pine is a highlight of Australian legend. The gallantry of the Australians was recognised by the award of no less than seven Victoria Crosses – four of them to one battalion, the 7th.

The main thrust in the attempt to seize control of the Dardanelles began on 6 August. A force of 20,000 (including Australians of the 4th Brigade, New Zealanders, British and Indians) was given the task of breaking out north from the Anzac bridgehead and capturing the key Turkish positions atop Chunuk Bair.

By next morning, New Zealand infantry were only 1,000 yards from Chunuk Bair. But other elements of the Anzac force were far from their objectives.

If, as expected, the New Zealanders had taken Chunuk Bair by dawn on the 7th August, they would be in a position to attack towards the enemy trenches on a position called "the Nek". The Australian 3rd Light Horse Brigade would, at the same time, attack the Nek from their positions at Russell's Top.

The Light Horsemen had orders to attack at 4.30 am on 7 August, by which time it was expected that the New Zealanders would have been in possession of Chunuk Bair for an hour. But this was not to be. The advance everywhere had been held up and the imminent Light Horse attack was now seen as a feint which would give vital assistance to the New Zealand attack on Chunuk Bair.

The hazardous frontal assault by the Australian Light Horse Brigade was to be in four waves each of 150 men. The first two waves would come from the 8th Light Horse (Victorians) and the second two from the 10th Light Horse (Western Australians).

The assault was preceded by an intense half-hour bombardment by artillery and naval gunfire. Unaccountably this barrage which in any case missed most of the Turkish front line trench stopped at 4.23 am which was seven minutes too early.

In the hush that followed the Turks only 18 metres away took advantage of the situation to emerge from their shelters and get ready to meet the assault.

Eager and confident, the Australians of the 8th Light Horse Regiment leapt from their trench precisely at 4.30 am to be met by a lethal small arms barrage. They had taken barely five or six steps before all lay dead, dying or wounded on the ground in front of their trench.

The second line of lighthorsemen waited two minutes and in spite of the terrible carnage, sprang forward only to be cut down. The 10th Light Horse now filed into the vacant places in the trench knowing that they were facing certain death. One commander, believing that the attack could not succeed, appealed unsuccessfully for it to be stopped. Another officer told his men as they waited to face the Turkish guns, "You have ten minutes to live."

So the killing went on. Within minutes several hundred Australians lay dead or wounded on the blood-soaked ground at the Nek and other nearby positions. For this incredible sacrifice they gained no ground. But their heroic example helped greatly to ennoble the name of Anzac in history.

Evacuation

The grim struggle at Gallipoli continued but after the reverses of August the expedition was doomed. As winter approached the Australians awaited their future. A decision to evacuate was in the air, a decision which Hamilton believed was "unthinkable" and would, if undertaken, result in heavy casualties.

After months of exhausting combat and harsh conditions the surviving members of the 1st Australian Division were withdrawn to Mudros and replaced in the line by the Australian 2nd Division, commanded by Lieutenant General J. G. Legge.

Hamilton had come under increasing criticism for his conduct of the failed campaign and a strongly adverse report on conditions at Gallipoli, written by Keith Murdock, Australian journalist, came into the hands of Asquith, the British Prime Minister. On 7 December the British Command ordered Hamilton to "shorten the front by evacuating Anzac and Suvla". A week later the Anzacs began moving from their front line trenches to the beaches and there embarked for Egypt.

Warnings that the withdrawal would lead to a bloodbath were not realised. By the night of 20 December 1915 the entire Anzac force had been withdrawn with only two casualties.

Gallipoli had failed to achieve its objective, but it was not without valuable results for the Allies. It forced the Turks to concentrate the greater part of their army to defend threatened Constantinople, thus lessening the pressure on Egypt and assisting Russia in defence. The Turks had suffered severe losses, with 66,000 killed.

Britain and her Allies had sent half a million men to Gallipoli and of these 33,532 were killed, 78,518 wounded and 7,689 missing. Australian losses were 7,600 killed or died of wounds and 19,000 wounded.

The Anzacs were amazed and unbelieving when told they must leave the peninsula. Some were angry; some turned to poetry. A sergeant wrote these lines of verse to capture the poignant hurt to those who were leaving behind their dead comrades:

> Not only muffled in our tread
> To cheat the foe.
> We fear to rouse our honoured dead
> To hear us go.
> Sleep sound old friends, the keenest smart
> Which more than failure wounds the heart
> Is thus to leave you, thus to part.

But worse was to befall the Australians when they joined battle again in France.

The Half Flight

In May 1915, while the Anzacs were locked in battle on the Gallipoli peninsula, Australia's fledgling military aviation force was in action against the same enemy in Mesopotamia (Iraq). A "half flight" recruited and trained at Point Cook, Victoria, was sent to provide military aviation support for a British army commanded by Major General C. V. Townshend, which was advancing up the River Tigris towards Amara. Flying in primitive flying machines, which included Longhorn, Shorthorn, Caudron and Martinsyde aircraft, they carried out reconnaissance and bombing missions.

On 30 July 1915 one of the Australian pilots, Lieutenant G. Merz of Ballarat, became the first pilot of an Australian aviation unit to die in air operations when, after a forced landing in a Caudron, he was killed in a running fight with hostile Arabs. Another Australian of the Half Flight, Captain T. W. ("Tommy") White (who in 1949 was appointed Minister for Air), was taken prisoner near Baghdad during a daring raid to cut enemy communications.

On 29 April 1916 nine Australians of the Half Flight together with 13,000 troops were taken prisoner when Townshend surrendered at Kut, after the Turkish forces had been boosted by troops sent from the Dardanelles. It was not until February 1917 that Kut was retaken by the British who then pressed on to take the major prize of Baghdad on 11 March 1917.

The Somme, France 1916

Gallipoli was a watershed in Australian history. The young nation grieved for the loss of the flower of a generation who had been left behind on the harsh slopes of an ancient alien shore. But at the same time they felt intensely proud that their country had been part of a great adventure and had established a noble tradition.

The veterans themselves were changed men. They had survived an horrendous baptism of fire. They found it very hard to believe that after the sacrifices the Australians had endured the battle had been lost. But win or lose the Australian fighting man had shown he had the courage, the determination and the skill to fight for his country. With pride they continued to wear the faded tunics and battered hats which identified them as Gallipoli veterans. "Men clung to their Australian uniforms till they were tattered to the limit of decency," wrote historian Charles Bean.

News of the dramatic events at Gallipoli had greatly stirred Australians back home and resulted in an unprecedented expansion of the Australian army as recruits responded to the urgent call to arms and joined the ranks. The surge of enlistments resulted in the AIF growing by 100,000 between May and September of 1915. In one month, July 1915, enlistments totalled 36,000.

Three more Australian divisions (the 3rd, 4th and 5th) were created. One of the new divisions (the 3rd, to be commanded by the famous Major General John Monash) was formed in Australia and would go direct to England. The distinguished Australian Light Horse commander, Major General Chauvel, was appointed to command the Anzac Mounted Division comprising the Australian 1st, 2nd and 3rd Light Horse Brigades and the New Zealand Mounted Rifles Brigade whose men were now reunited with their horses back in Egypt. Many other Australians were recruited into the Camel Corps.

In order to give a veteran character to the reorganised Australian divisions, new battalions and brigades were formed by splitting half the oldest ones and then using reinforcements to expand each half into a whole. Thus, although the reinforcements were raw they became members of experienced battle units within which the knowledge and discipline of the veterans quickly rubbed off. Expansion created unexampled opportunities for promotion. Young company commanders suddenly found themselves leading battalions. Veteran privates quickly became non-commissioned officers.

The Anzac force was now organised into two Army corps. Lieutenant General Birdwood was given command of I Anzac Corps (1st, 2nd Australian and the New Zealand Divisions) and General A. J. Godley was appointed to command II Anzac Corps (then the 4th and 5th Australian Divisions).

By early 1916 the Turks were no longer committed to the active defence of the Dardanelles and the Allied leaders in the Middle East believed they would decide to move against the vital British-controlled Suez Canal and "set the East in a blaze". But the Turks would face formidable British forces including the Anzacs now withdrawn from Gallipoli and the newly arrived Australian 8th Brigade. Mounted troops were in demand in Egypt and Australian Light Horsemen just back from Gallipoli joined in operations to defend the Nile Valley against the Senussi.

Reports of the advance of Turkish forces across the Sinai desert caused the British command to send Australian troops to establish defence posts along a 30-mile front of the canal.

However, the Turkish threat did not develop and the substantial forces in Egypt were soon regarded as being a major source of reinforcements for the Western Front where a massive campaign was in the making.

At Chantilly, France, in December 1915, high-level decisions on military strategy were agreed by representatives of the French, Russian, British and Italian Governments. The Chantilly conference defined the "principal fronts" of the war to be where the enemy maintained his greatest strength. These were the Eastern Front (Russia), the Western Front (France) and the Southern Front (Italy). To avoid too great a dispersion of available Allied military strength, these fronts would receive the maximum reinforcement in fighting men and materials and would mount coordinated offensives against the enemy. The French were eager to attack on the Western Front and wanted the Germans tied down as much as possible in the other fronts so that reinforcements would not be brought to the West. A major French-British offensive was in preparation, with the opening blow to fall on 1 July 1916.

Minor theatres such as Salonika would be maintained only at their existing strength. Egypt, where large Allied forces were now available following the termination of the Gallipoli campaign, was to be adequately defended.

The Germans saw an Allied offensive in the making in France and were determined to get in first. They decided to attack Verdun which they knew would be rigorously defended because of its symbolic importance to the French. They hoped, with their superiority in heavy artillery, to bleed the French armies white. They believed that once France was defeated, Russia must follow and England would then be alone.

The mammoth struggle for Verdun began on 21 February 1916 heralded by a tremendous artillery barrage which rained high explosives, gas, shrapnel and tear gas shells at the rate of 100,000 rounds an hour. It seemed nothing could survive the bombardment, yet when the German soldiers advanced after the barrage lifted they were opposed by French soldiers firing machine guns. 25 February was a day of disaster when the French surrendered Fort Douaumont. But the French rallied to the cry. "They shall not pass." General Henri Pétain was sent to command their forces and Verdun was saved. Horrific losses on both sides were close to 350,000. Yet the frontline at Verdun had moved but little.

Verdun underlined the Allied need for greater military strength in France and it was no surprise when eight days after the battle began the 1st Australian Corps (1st and 2nd Australian and the New Zealand Division) was ordered from Egypt to the Western Front. Embarkation began on 13 March. In May the 4th and 5th Divisions were ordered to follow but the Anzac Mounted Division would remain in Egypt. From that point on the AIF was divided and would fight in two theatres of war – the Western Front and the Middle East.

Although hostile submarines were active, the Anzacs voyaged safely through the Mediterranean and began disembarking from their troopships at the crowded port of Marseilles. The French people at once warmed to the breezy friendliness of the Australians and soon were referring to them as "les bons soldats". Australian regimental bands performed the Marseillaise with the "Diggers" whistling the anthem and cheering. They revelled in the welcoming atmosphere and the delights of the early French spring. "Their journey up the Rhone Valley," wrote Charles Bean, "with the orchards in blossom and, beyond, the winding blue river and distant Alps – was like a plunge into fairyland."

The troops were a little disappointed when their troop trains bypassed Paris. The weather became wet and cold as they neared the operational zone in northern France and soon they began to hear, in the distance, the crump of exploding shells and saw at night the gash of gun flashes in the pale white flares above the battlefield. Ominously they were issued with steel helmets and gas masks. They would soon encounter the horrors of gas war, flamethrowers, batteries of machine guns and incredibly heavy artillery bombardments.

So in April 1916 the vanguard of the Australian Army from Egypt arrived at the Western Front where the carnage of war had been far greater than at Gallipoli. Hundreds of thousands of war-weary soldiers continued to besiege each other along a line of trenches, forts and defence posts arrayed for hundreds of kilometres between the English channel near Calais to the mountains of Switzerland. The Allied armies had no less than 160 divisions and the Germans 120 facing them. The manpower strength of the British Army (including by early July 100,000 Australians and New Zealanders) far exceeded the million mark. Reinforcements from England, predominantly members of Kitchener's New Army of volunteers eager to do their bit, were pouring into France in preparation for the major offensive on the Somme. High hopes were entertained for a war-winning breakthrough opening a wide breach in the German defences through which British and French cavalry would rush to divide and defeat the enemy.

It was the practice of the high command to assign new divisions in the British area to a relatively quiet sector (known as the "Nursery") southeast of the industrial centre of Armentières. There on 7 April 1916, I Anzac Corps took over responsibility from the British 2nd Corps.

The Australians faced a more formidable foe than at Gallipoli. The Germans were bold, better trained and better equipped than their Turkish allies.

Fighting was at first confined to sniping and active patrolling. Sudden gas alarms were experienced. British troops to the north of the Australians suffered 400 casualties from clouds of chlorine and phosgene gas which also floated across the Australian rear area but caused only one Australian casualty.

Suddenly on 5 May 1916 a deluge of shells and bombs struck the Australian 20th Battalion, causing 100 casualties. The Germans entered the battalion's trenches, capturing a number of prisoners and two of the "secret" Stokes mortars. On 30 May a similar bombardment struck the Australian 11th Battalion, inflicting heavy casualties.

As the time for the great Anglo-French offensive on the Somme drew near, "trench raids", mostly for the purpose of gaining intelligence information from enemy prisoners, were increased by both sides. The first such Australian raid, carried out on the night of 5 June by a party of carefully briefed Australians of the 7th Brigade, was a success; it raised the confidence of Australian Troops.

Raids were stepped up further: the Allied command ordered as many raids as possible for the period between 20 and 30 June (the 10 days prior to the start of the Somme offensive). In this period the Anzac Corps mounted ten raids with great vigour, turning the Nursery from a quiet area into one of marked tension. The corps suffered heavily – 773 casualties were reported.

Meanwhile the preliminary artillery preparation designed to destroy as much of the German defences as possible had got under way by 24 June. On 25 June two siege batteries of the Australian garrison artillery joined in the bombardment. The bump of the shells exploding could be heard in southeastern England. By the time the infantry attacked, some 1,738,000 shells had been despatched.

At 7.30 am on 1 July, with a blazing summer sun climbing high in the sky, the bombardment suddenly stopped. Then all along the front, wave after wave of British soldiers climbed out of the trenches into no man's land and made for the German lines. In spite of the heavy bombardment many Germans quickly emerged from their dugouts and exacted horrific losses on the advancing British troops, who were impeded by the shattered landscape and their heavy burdens of arms and equipment. In less than two weeks on the Somme no less than 100,000 British troops were killed, wounded or were missing. Nevertheless the British and French had struck a heavy blow. A wedge had been driven into the German line, but it did not lead to the hoped-for major breakthrough.

Although they had not taken part in the massive opening offensives by the Anglo-French armies which began on 1 July, all four Australian infantry divisions then in France were to have roles in the Somme campaign. By early in July the 1st and 2nd Australian Divisions were withdrawn from the Armentières area and were under orders to concentrate near Amiens by 13 July for the continuation of the Somme offensive.

In the meantime, to support the offensive the high command had decided to mount a strong feint attack to the north near the village of Fromelles. The aim of this diversion was to deter the Germans from sending reinforcements from the northern area to bolster their forces under attack on the Somme. Two divisions, the 5th Australian and 61st British, were to be employed in the Fromelles operation. The 5th Australian had just entered the line to relieve the 4th Australian which was to join the 1st and 2nd Divisions on the Somme.

The Fromelles attack was to begin at 6 pm on 19 July, after a final seven-hour bombardment beginning at 11 am on the same day. All three brigades of the Division (the 8th, 14th and 15th) were to be in the front line trenches for the attack, although using only two each of their battalions for the actual fighting.

The majority of the troops in the 5th Division had never been in the front line before and were far from ready for the operation. Nevertheless, as Charles Bean wrote, "The Australians were in great fettle and were cheered to see the German parapets leaping into the air in shreds."

Abundant signs of the coming attack warned the Germans and they poured heavy artillery barrages into the Australian front lines, causing heavy casualties to the 8th Brigade which suffered further casualties from the fire of "friendly" artillery as they advanced towards the German breastworks. The German defenders fled before them. The 8th and 14th Brigades quickly seized 1,000 yards of the enemy front system and formed a line of posts. The 15th Brigade had to attack where no man's land was widest and within a few minutes of the cessation of supporting Allied artillery fire was met with fierce German machine gunfire and shot to earth with many of its leaders killed. The survivors were forced to seek shelter in ditches and furrows. Those who followed found only dead and wounded comrades with the Bavarians firing freely at everything that moved.

The 61st Division fared little better. It was caught in heavy German fire during its assembly and advance into no man's land. The men were pinned down and then forced back. The 61st was later ordered to return to its own lines to prepare for a renewed attack which would be attempted next day. But the position was deteriorating rapidly. All reserves of the Australian division were quickly drawn into the battle and a fierce and lethal struggle continued throughout the night. The captured German lines were held most bravely until next morning the 8th Brigade were driven back, casting a shadow over the morale of the remaining troops. Their retreat rendered the position of the 14th Brigade ever more perilous and it too was ordered to retire to the Australian lines now packed with wounded and dying.

After the fighting ended, Australian soldiers, risking death repeatedly, re-entered no man's land under fire to rescue wounded comrades. It was an inspiring display of selfless heroism and humanity.

Thus Australia's first major battle on the Western Front had quickly ended in disaster, due in part to the inadequacy of the artillery support. The 5th Division had lost 5,533 men in little more than one night, 400 of whom had been marched off the battlefield to German prisoner-of-war camps. The 61st Division with a loss of 1,547 soldiers and the Germans with a 1,500 loss fared better. The battle had shattered the 5th Division which would not for a long time be ready again for offensive action.

Fromelles was a severe reverse. The primary aim of persuading the Germans to "milk" their Somme front of troops had failed. The enemy was not deceived, concluding at once that the thrust at Fromelles was a mere feint. As Charles Bean commented, "The value of the result was tragically disproportionate to the cost."[2]

Pozières

Shortly after the 5th Australian Division's action at Fromelles, the 1st Australian Division was ordered into battle at Pozières, the key to the area just north of the Somme. Four attacks on Pozières from 13-17 July had failed to dislodge the German defenders who were retarding the British advance in this salient. Now the commander of the Reserve Army (General Hubert Gough) had been ordered to take over. Summoning General H. B. Walker, the commander of the 1st Australian Division, to his headquarters, Gough greeted him with the words: "I want you to go into the line and attack Pozières tomorrow night!"

Just after midnight on 23 July, the confident Australians of the 1st Brigade (from NSW) and the 3rd Brigade (from Queensland, South Australia, Western Australia and Tasmania) attacked on a front 1.6 kilometres wide towards the centre of Pozières village. They advanced swiftly, shooting and bayoneting Germans they encountered and quickly achieved a striking success. They captured three key objectives, although impeded on the way by the churned-up terrain and surface rubble created by the great mincing machine of the artillery of both sides, which was dominating the land battle on the Somme. A German counterattack at dawn was shot to pieces.

After the fighting the triumphant Australians smoked German cigars and donned shiny German spiked helmets as they dug trenches for the next phase of operations.

Except for the striking success of the Australians at Pozières, the big British push on that day had not been successful.

The only part of the Australian objectives not achieved was 4,277 metres of the OG ("Old German") lines. But the whole area had been so cratered and pulverised by the artillery bombardments that the OG lines could not be found. Elsewhere stubborn Germans held out and bitter close-fought battles ensued in which two Australians won Victoria Crosses (Private John Leak and Lieutenant A. S. Blackburn).

The Germans did not take the loss of Pozières lightly and set about retaking it. They methodically bombarded the Australian positions, switching the greater part of the artillery resources of the *IV German Corps* on to them. The whole area was deluged with shells. Australians buried by trench cave-ins were being constantly dug out, some alive, some dead or wounded. The main approach to Pozières was so lined with dead that it was named "Dead Man's Road".

The 1st Division had lost 5,285 men. It had held grimly to its gains but many of its dazed and exhausted men were no longer capable of working or fighting. No human beings could be expected to endure more, and the 2nd Division was now moved into the swirling horror of Pozières to relieve it.

Systematically and endlessly the enemy artillery continued to flay the tortured terrain into a sea of shell craters.

Major-General Legge, the division's commander who was criticised for his conduct of the operation, sought and was given permission to attack again. However, furious German shellfire disrupted the task of digging communications and "jumping off" trenches. Nevertheless the Division attacked on the night of 4 August after an intense artillery barrage, and seized the Pozières crest and the OG second line. At dawn next day a German counterattack was shattered by Australian machine gunfire.

The 2nd Division was now more exhausted even than the 1st. In a twelve-day tour of duty at the front, it lost 6,848 men. It was relieved by the 4th Division which was ordered to take over and carry out an attack to the north.

One of the most graphic descriptions of the monstrous horrors of Pozières was penned by a Melbourne journalist, Lieutenant J. A. Raws of the 23rd Battalion, who with his brother was later killed in the battle. He wrote:

> … we lay down terror-stricken along a bank. The shelling was awful … we eventually found our way to the right spot out in no man's land. Our leader was shot before we arrived and the strain had sent two other officers mad. I and another new officer took charge and dug the trench. We were shot at all the time … the wounded and killed had to be thrown to one side. I refused to let any sound man help a wounded man; the sound man had to dig … we dug on and finished amid a tornado of bursting shells. I was buried with dead and dying. The ground was covered with bodies in all stages of decay and mutilation and I would, after struggling from the earth, pick up a body by me to

*try and lift him out with me and find him a decayed corpse ...
I went up again the next night and stayed there. We were
shelled to hell ceaselessly. X went mad and disappeared ... there
remained nothing but a charred mass of debris with bricks,
stones, girders and bodies pounded to nothing ... we are lousy,
stinking, unshaven, sleepless ... I have one puttee, a dead man's
helmet, another dead man's protector, a dead man's bayonet. My
tunic is rotten with other men's blood and partly spattered with
a comrade's brains ...*[3]

All three divisions of I Anzac Corps were now committed to a plan
for driving a wedge behind the German bastion of Thiepval by
occupying Mouquet farm, north of Pozières. The 4th Division began an
advance on this objective on 10 August. Twice in August and again on
3 September the Australians fought their way into the farm only to be
forced out again.

Embittered Australian soldiers regarded the Monquet farm mission
as a grave military miscalculation. The route to the farm was constantly
subjected to artillery barrages and was clearly in the view of German
observers. Enemy shells came in from the front, the flank and the rear
so that the whole area became a sea of shell craters. Australian casualties
totalled 6300.

The Australian troops were given a break during September-October
when the Corps was transferred to the comparatively tranquil Ypres
salient for "a rest". But by November the corps was back on the Somme.
The Australian 5th Division, recovered from the Fromelles action, was
also moved to the Somme area.

The onset of a particularly severe winter now made the task of
holding the line very grim. Trenches and shell-torn fields dissolved into
vast quagmires as soon as the winter rains came. The strain of just trying
to walk through the morass of mud in trenches and fields left men
exhausted.

A blizzard on 18 November put an end to major operations on the
Western Front and the epic Somme campaign wound down. It had
lasted four and a half months. Three million men had fought in a

dreadful struggle which had cost the British 475,000 casualties. The French lost 195,000 and the Germans 500,000.

Three Australian divisions had lost 23,000 men in less than seven weeks. Those Australians who endured the Somme could never forget the horrors of Pozières. Nor could the grieving relatives of the casualties. As Charles Bean wrote, "The ridge [Pozières] was more densely sown with Australian sacrifice than any other place on earth."

The results in the Somme campaign in terms of ground won from the enemy were ludicrously small. Nowhere had the allies advanced more than seven miles. But clearly the Allied cause was making progress. The bloodletting on the Somme and at Verdun had weakened German morale and in a very real sense this was bringing ultimate victory closer. The surrender of German soldiers had increased. General Ludendorff, the German chief of staff, informed his superiors at the end of 1916 that the German Army was "absolutely exhausted".

France, 1917

After the harsh winter on the Somme the spirits of the Australians rose in the spring of 1917. They bounded even higher when to their astonishment it was apparent that the German troops were withdrawing. On 17 March patrols of the 2nd Division advanced to the northern outskirts of Bapaume. The town was burning as patrols of the 5th Division made a small attack and found German trenches were empty. The 30th Battalion passed through the smoke-filled streets and were just in time to see Germans disappearing in the distance.

It soon became clear, however, that this was not a disorderly retreat, but a well-planned manoeuvre: the Germans were simply shortening their front and moving into the immensely strong Siegfried Line (known to the Allies as the Hindenburg Line). This move would exchange their bulging front line for a well-sited line which could be garrisoned by 13 fewer divisions and which bristled with every device of the defence art. It had several lines of bold earthworks, deep dugouts and great belts of wire. Russian prisoners and local French civilians had been conscripted for the task of building it.

The Anzac Corps advanced rapidly as the Germans pulled back and on 2 April took part with the British V Corps in the capture of a whole string of villages fringing the Hindenburg Line, including Noreuil, seized at dawn by the 13th Australian Brigade. On 9 April the 1st Australian Brigade captured Hermies taking more than 200 German prisoners. On the same day, the British began the battle of Arras. Buoyed by the German retreat and the American's declaration of war, the troops were keyed up and the outcome was one of Britain's most effective battles of the war. A real breakthrough seemed possible and the enemy was badly rattled.

On 11 April the Australian 4th Division entered the battle with the urgent task of seizing part of the Hindenburg Line near Bullecourt, south-east of Arras. The 4th Cavalry Division would then pass through any breach created in the line. A new weapon, the tank, was to attack ahead of the Australians (the 4th and 12th Brigades) and flatten the German wire defences. But the tanks failed to reach the wire ahead of the infantry and were soon stalled and on fire all over the battlefield. Allied artillery was not permitted to operate and as a result terrible small arms fire swept the battleground. Germans emerged in large numbers from their underground galleries and fired on the Australians from the flank and rear. The 4th Division had swept deep into the German line but the thrust was too narrow.

Australian casualties were extremely heavy. The 4th Brigade with 3,000 men in action suffered 2,339 casualties and the 12th, 950. Some 1,100 were taken prisoner.

Charles Bean was caustic about the Army commander. He wrote:

> ... everyone was aware that the 4th Division had been
> employed in an experiment of extreme rashness, persisted in by
> the Army commander after repeated warnings and that the
> experiment had failed with shocking losses.[4]

On the 3rd of May the Australians were committed to another attack at Bullecourt. Two brigades of the 2nd Division (5th and 6th) attacked first and succeeded in seizing and holding sections of the Hindenburg Line. The 6th Brigade which had thrust through the line on a narrow front was attacked on both flanks, but held its position. The 7th Brigade joined the battle against the stubborn 27th (Wurttemberg) Division. After fierce fighting the 2nd Division held most of its original first objective.

Troops of the 1st Division were now committed and by the 7th May the 5th Division was also committed to the second battle of Bullecourt which ended in mid May when the Germans withdrew after the failure of their final attempt to recapture Bullecourt.

The Australians had withstood no less than seven major counterattacks. Their achievement was described by General Haig as "among the great deeds of the war". It had cost the Australians 7,000 casualties.

The major French offensive in April had quickly turned into a fiasco and disillusioned French *poilus* mutinied in 16 of the French Army corps, creating fears of the disintegration of the French war effort.

The United States had entered the war on 6 April but as against this the French mutinies and the dissolution of the Russian armies threatened by the Russian revolution of March 1917 had created the gravest Allied crisis of the war. Britain and the dominions were almost alone against the Germans on the Western Front.

Messines

After Bullecourt, General Haig made preparations for an offensive which had the major objective of freeing the Belgian North Sea ports from the German grip, thus helping to disrupt the German submarine campaign which threatened England with starvation.

As a preliminary, the British forces planned to eliminate a German salient south of Ypres which enclosed the Messines ridge. Enemy possession of the Messines ridge was a potential obstacle to the British plan. Three Army corps were committed, including II Anzac Corps (the New Zealand, 3rd Australian and the 25th British Division). The 4th Australian Division was also committed. The 3rd Australian under

Major General John Monash had arrived in France in December 1916 and had gained operational experience in a series of raids on the German trenches.

On 7 June a million pounds (454,545 kilograms) of explosives were detonated in tunnels under the Messines ridge. German trenches above were obliterated. The vibration was felt in London. Members of the 1st Australian Tunnelling Company had taken part in the tunnelling operations.

Immediately after the 19 explosions had torn immense craters in the German lines, Allied troops rose from their trenches and rushed the enemy, capturing nearly 7,000 dazed Germans. The advance was swift. The New Zealanders quickly captured the Messines ridge with the 3rd Australian and 25th British Divisions on the flanks.

On the Anzac front in the afternoon two brigades of the 4th Australian Division moved through the terrain occupied by the British and New Zealanders. They encountered a German bombardment preceding an enemy counter thrust and suffered casualties. But a British barrage broke up the German attack.

Messines was an immense success, eliminating the German salient south of Ypres.

Ypres

On 31 July 1917, the Allies continued the offensive aimed at liberating the Belgian ports. The start of the campaign had been delayed at the political level because of fears of the consequences of further heavy casualties.

The Allies struck with 20 divisions across the flat Flemish plain where the heavy preliminary bombardments had destroyed the surface drainage and the autumn rains, falling a month early, had created an unbelievable ocean of mud.

The Australian 3rd Division was in action on the first day, but carried out little more than a demonstration. North of Ypres the Allied divisions made some progress. But at 4 pm the skies opened and the battlefield was deluged with rain for days. The troops found it almost impossible to follow their artillery barrages across a mass of water-filled shell craters.

Six weeks into the battle the I Anzac Corps was committed. On 16 September after a night march through Ypres the 1st and 2nd Australian Divisions took over a section of the battlefront at Glencorse Wood. On 20 September a new attack was launched. The two Australian divisions were part of the centre of the attack and for the first time they advanced side by side, winning famous landmarks of previous battles. The Australians were elated at the successful outcome of the Battle of Menin Road as the action was named, but they had suffered 5,000 casualties in achieving it.

On 26 September the 4th and 5th Australian Divisions attacked and quickly captured both Polygon Wood and the outskirts of Zonnebeke. This success was followed by another successful attack on the main Broodseinde ridge on 4 October in which both Anzac corps were engaged. The four Australian divisions involved advanced on the objective side by side.

As the Australians rose to advance they clashed head on with a German force which was attacking them at the same time. Australian Lewis gunners at once opened fire. The German line broke and the Australians rolled over them. After sharp fighting around German pillboxes the ridge was won.

It appeared to the Allied military leaders that a breakthrough was possible and in spite of the implacable mud an attack on the Passchendaele ridge was mounted on 12 October.

The New Zealanders were stopped by fire from pillboxes and most of the 3rd Australian Division was bogged down in the mud. Ultimately the Canadian Corps captured the Passchendaele heights.

By 14 November all five Australian divisions had been withdrawn from the Ypres battlefield. The Australians had won three decisive battles – Menin road, Polygon Wood and Broodseinde. In eight weeks' fighting they had suffered 38,000 casualties.

As with the Somme battle of 1916, little territory had been won by the campaign in Belgium, but attrition had again taken its toll on the German Army.

Conscription

In 1916 the conscription of Australian men for service in the war theatre became an intense issue on the home front. It came to a head in 1916 because Australian casualties in the great battles of the Western Front in that year thinned army ranks and the demand grew for reinforcements to maintain the strength of Australian military formations. At the same time the flow of recruits was dwindling.

In mid-1916 Australia had only 7,000 reinforcements available in Britain. Some 80,000 more men were needed in four months, but the reservoir of willing volunteers was drying up. In Australia, public opinion was passionately divided on the issue of conscription for war service overseas. One major faction feared that without compulsion the war would be lost for lack of sufficient military strength and that Australia had not fully accepted responsibility to commit soldiers to the battle. The opposing faction contended that because the Australian continent was not in danger of invasion conscription was not needed. The issue hung on whether the existence of the nation and the liberty of its people was at stake.

The Labor Government of W. M. Hughes decided that a referendum was needed on the issue. This was held on 28 October 1916 and the plan to conscript young men for war services overseas was rejected by a margin of 72,476 votes. Soldiers serving overseas voted for conscription.

The conscription issue split the Labor Party and Hughes joined with Liberal members of the House of Representatives to form a "Nationalist" Party.

In 1917 enlistments for overseas war service flagged again and the Hughes government decided on a second referendum. The poll took place on 20 December 1917 and the "no" vote had increased its margin to 94,152. Soldiers serving overseas again favoured conscription but by a smaller majority.

It was abundantly clear that conscription would not be adopted short of a dangerous direct threat to Australia.

From Egypt to Damascus

The strategic Suez Canal was vital to British Empire communications and the conduct of the war. Britain was bound to defend it strongly and in early 1916 had ample means to do so when Egypt and the canal zone were flooded with a host of evacuated troops from the Dardanelles. However, the bulk of these forces, including the Australian infantry divisions, were quickly transported to France to take part in the battles of the Western Front. Left behind in Egypt to defend the area were the superb Australian Light Horsemen, who were now part of the Anzac Mounted Division under General Chauvel.

But the British General, Sir Archibald Murray, had more than the defence of Egypt in mind. He planned to reconquer the Sinai Peninsula. He built up a great fortified system which reached out to the British base of Romani, now the head of the rail line. Work on a pipeline to bring water from the Nile was in progress. On the Turkish side, the railway through Palestine now extended southwards to Beersheba. A strong body of Turkish soldiers struck at Oghratina and Katia in April, 1916. The Anzac Mounted Division was sent to the scene but the enemy had withdrawn.

The Australian Light Horsemen were delighted on returning from Gallipoli to be reunited with their horses and committed to a form of warfare suited to their talents and temperament. Murray regarded his three Australian Light Horse brigades and the New Zealand brigade, as "the only really reliable mounted troops that I have … any work entrusted to these excellent troops is invariably well executed."

In July of 1916 the Turks made an imprudent bid to invade Egypt and despatched a column of some 16,000 troops across the desert against Romani, the strongly held British base in the Sinai forward of the canal zone. General Chauvel was to play a key role in the coming battle and he disposed his Light Horsemen so that they could envelop any Turkish force which attempted to envelop Romani. Romani itself was defended by the British 52nd Division.

At 1 am on 4 August with wild yells of "Allah! Allah!" the Turks attacked two Australian Light Horse regiments comprising 500 rifles which were thinly spread in a three-mile screen to the south of Romani. As the Turks closed on them, the Australians pulled back as planned, to entice the Turks to continue their advance. But they soon turned to fight again. Late in the day the British reserves were committed, including the New Zealanders and Yeomanry, and the exhausted Turks began to surrender in large numbers. At 4 am on 5 August the Light Horse attacked with the bayonet and hundreds more Turks were showing the white flag.

Although the Turkish force was not completely destroyed, the threat of an invasion of Egypt had been dispelled. Mounted troops pursued the Turkish remnant. When the battle ended the Turks had lost 5,250 killed or wounded and almost 4000 captured. British losses were 1,130, the majority being Australians and New Zealanders.

Romani was a significant victory. The British after first checking the enemy assault had routed the attackers, destroying half their force and driving the remnant out of the oasis area into the waterless desert. The Anzac mounted troops could now operate freely throughout the area. As a result of the victory the outlook in the Middle East changed for the better and the British held hopes of driving the Turks from Palestine.

Murray's army advanced to El Arish which it entered on 21 December to find it abandoned. Two days later the Anzac Mounted Division and the Camel Corps fought all day against an enemy force at Magdhaba where they stormed and overcame the defences. On 9 January 1917 they captured Rafa.

By March 1917, the Sinai peninsula was virtually clear of the enemy. General Murray's army was comfortably disposed before Gaza in southern Palestine. Elsewhere, particularly in eastern Europe, the war outlook was grim.

British strategists hoped that Turkey at least could be knocked out of the war and urged Murray to plan a maximum effort against the Turks with the glittering symbolic prize of the Holy City to draw him on. But Murray was rebuffed when he asked for reinforcements. He already had, however, a superb military asset in his mounted forces, mainly the Anzacs.

Murray wasted no time. He launched an attack on Gaza in thick fog on 26 March and by noon his mounted troops had swept past Gaza township to the east and north and had reached the sea 3.2 kilometres beyond. A Turkish general had been captured and the mounted Anzacs had broken into the northern suburbs. However, Murray's attacking force had been directed that unless Gaza fell by sunset the mounted troops must be withdrawn, otherwise they would be in danger of being denied water. To the Australian Light Horsemen, victory had appeared certain when, to their great disappointment the word came to pull out. They brought back with them their wounded and some of their dead.

Murray in reporting to his superiors in London showed a lack of candour in claiming the outcome was successful when clearly it was not. He was given permission to try again. But when he attacked Gaza again on 18 April the Turks had had time to strengthen their defences. The attack failed at a cost of 6,000 British casualties.

This second failure led to Murray's recall and his replacement in June by General Sir Edmund Allenby, who was transferred from the 3rd Army in France. Command of all three divisions of mounted troops, soon to become known as the "Desert Mounted Corps" was given to Chauvel, who thus became the first Australian corps commander. He was promoted to Lieutenant General. The New Zealander General E. W. C. Chaytor, succeeded him as commander of the Anzac Mounted Division.

The Turks continued to strengthen their defences which extended from Gaza on the coast to Beersheba some 20 miles inland. Allenby's plan was to seize Beersheba first using Chauvel's Desert Mounted corps to attack them from the east and north.

Success at Beersheba with its precious wells was crucial. On 31 October three British infantry divisions stormed their objectives west of the town while the Australian 2nd Light Horse Brigade took control of the Hebron road to the north to block the approach of any Turkish reinforcements. To the east 2000 men of the Anzac Mounted Division attacked dismounted, but progress there was slow.

Chauvel's orders were to storm Beersheba, which had to be won before nightfall. The situation was becoming grave because the British forces would soon be in urgent need of 400,000 gallons of water.

Chauvel had two Light Horse brigades south of the town and he decided to commit the nearest one, Brigadier General William Grant's 4th Brigade. His two leading regiments (the 4th and 12th) with the 11th following were assembled five miles from Beersheba. Only a few hours of daylight remained. Chauvel decided. "Put Grant straight at it," was his terse order. Grant at once mounted his horse and galloped off to his brigade. For the first time the Light Horse was to act as cavalry. They had no swords, only their rifles and bayonets for a hazardous cavalry charge against entrenched infantry.

At 4.30 pm now four miles from Beersheba, the Light Horsemen, eager for action and for victory, moved off at the trot. Soon the pace speeded up to a canter and then to a gallop as direction and formation were established. The outcome of the battle was at stake depending on an audacious rush of resolute cavalrymen. "All rode for victory and Australia."[5]

Turkish artillerymen opened fire followed by machine guns which were silenced by a British artillery battery. As they neared the Turkish trenches rifle fire, wild and high, opened up and then the Light Horsemen were on the enemy jumping the main Turkish trench, dismounting and turning to engage the Turks in ugly hand-to hand fighting. Beersheba and its vital wells were thus taken in one of Australia's finest military actions.

Australian casualties, mostly at the trenches, were light: the 4th and 11th Regiments lost 31 killed and 35 wounded. Victory meant water for the parched horses. Novelist Frank Dalby Davison wrote movingly of how "the smell of water, cold and sweet, was released in the dusty air. Standing weary and patient out among the ridges, the horses smelled it and a whinny ran from line to line. Throughout the night … the horses were let in … to drink with slackened girths and bitless mouths at the wells of Beersheba".[6]

A distinguished Australian soldier was mortally wounded on the battlefield. He was Lieutenant Colonel L. C. Maygar, winner of the Victoria Cross in South Africa. While leading the 8th Light Horse Regiment he had been hit by fire from a German aircraft. He died the next day.

After the brilliant victory at Beersheba, Allenby continued his onslaught on Gaza, which fell on 6 November. The Turks, although badly mauled, managed for a time to establish a line 32 kilometres further north. But Allenby's thrusts brushed them aside and his men drove rapidly northwards through modern Jewish settlements to Ramleh, Ludd and Jaffa which fell on 16 November. At Ludd, 40 Australian Light Horsemen galloped down and captured a Turkish column of 300 men.

Allenby was nearing Jerusalem which for centuries had been under Muslim rule. The British Government strongly desired its liberation which would be a great psychological boost to the Allied cause. Allenby continued his coastal thrust to mislead the Turks and then advanced with his right into the Judaean hills which were the natural defence of Jerusalem. The Turks, well-equipped and well-entrenched, resisted strongly, but on 8 December in pouring rain British infantry accompanied by the Australian 10th Light Horse Regiment drove the Turks from their lines and next day the 60th (London) Division entered Jerusalem to an hysterical welcome by Jews and Christians.

The surrender ceremony which took place on 11 December was a low-key affair. Allenby, who could be irritated by too much pomp, dismounted and walked briskly through detachments of troops (including Australian Light Horsemen) and proceeded through the Jaffa Gate to an ancient terrace near the Tower of David. The year had ended in triumph for the Allies in the Middle East.

After the fall of Jerusalem, the British repulsed a Turkish bid to retake the city and then advanced into the Jordan valley. The Anzac Mounted Division helped to outflank Jericho, prompting the Turks to withdraw so that the Australians occupied the ancient village on 21 February 1918.

A month later, on 22 March, in a move to encourage T. E. Lawrence's Arabs who were conducting effective guerilla operations against Turkish garrisons in Arabia, Allenby launched a strong raid across the Jordan. The raiding force, which included the 2nd Australian Light Horse Brigade, seized Amman. To hamper the Turks the raiders destroyed sections of the Hejaz railway. During the raid, the Australians and New Zealand Mounted Rifles captured Es Salt. But after stiff fighting they were forced to pull back.

On 30 April a repeat raid across the Jordan was mounted and again Australian Light Horsemen occupied Es Salt. Severe fighting developed. The 4th Australian Light Horse Brigade, which had the task of guarding the Jordan crossing, was forced back by the Turks, while the 60th (London) Division and two brigades of the Australian Mounted Division could not dislodge the Turks from their positions. As a result on 4 May the raiders withdrew across the Jordan.

The British Government was eager to exploit the fall of Jerusalem and Prime Minister Lloyd George proposed that Allenby follow up his success by knocking Turkey out of the war completely. To strengthen Allenby's hand, reinforcements were to be sent to Palestine from Mesopotamia and France. But the massive German offensive which began in France in March 1918 put a sudden end to this line of thinking. Instead, Allenby had to part with two divisions and other units of his command to reinforce the Western Front. In place of a major war-winning offensive in Palestine and Syria, he was now reduced to conducting an active defensive. Nevertheless, looking ahead, he continued to develop ambitious plans for the day when he could give full scope to the four divisions of horsemen soon to be at his disposal, including two Indian cavalry divisions.

In June 1918 it was proposed that half the Australian Light Horse in Palestine be sent to France as infantry reinforcements. But fortunately, after protests both from Allenby and Australian sources, this proposal was rejected.

The burning heat of summer in the pestilential Jordan valley had to be endured by the Australian Light Horse who were committed to the defence of the Jordan river bridgeheads in an area, which at the southern end, was 397 metres below sea level. While Allenby's plans were on hold, they suffered the searing heat of the valley, oppressed by the heavy moisture-laden atmosphere and the dense palls of dust. Many suffered from malaria, sandfly fever and severe stomach disorders.

The Turkish soldiers suffered even more and enemy strength was rapidly melting away in wholesale desertions. Food was scarce. Troops dressed in rags were scourged by disease. Their baggage animals could barely hobble because of lack of food.

On 14 July a German battalion of the Asia Corps attacked and captured the important hill of Abu Tellul. But a swift counterattack by the Australian 1st Light Horse Brigade recovered the position and the enemy abandoned plans for an offensive in the Jordan valley.

By September 1918 Turkish strength in the Middle East was declining fast, while Allenby with a much stronger and better equipped army was poised to strike a terminal blow.

British military activity in the Jordan valley and beyond, together with some masterly ruses of deception, led the Turks to believe Allenby's coming offensive would strike mainly on the Jordan flank. Instead, the great bulk of his army was concentrated on a 24-kilometre front on the extreme west near Jaffa on the Mediterranean coast.

On 19 September 1918, Allenby's army struck the opening blows of the battle of Megiddo. Four divisions of infantry broke through the enemy lines north of Jaffa. Racing through the gaps thus created, two of General Chauvel's cavalry divisions (the 4th and 5th Indian) began a famous ride. Moving first at the trot they streamed north along the coastal plain, crossed the Carmel range and poured down into the plain of Esdraelon behind the Turkish armies. El Afule, a key defence centre, was galloped down and soon the cavalry had clattered into Nazareth from which the German commander, Limon von Sanders, was forced to make a hurried exit. By the 23rd September the cavalry had seized the ports of Haifa and Acre.

Meanwhile the Australian Mounted Division had passed through the Carmel range and the 3rd Light Horse Brigade captured 8,000 Turkish soldiers at Jenin. The 5th Brigade destroyed the rail lines north of Samaria.

On 22 September Allenby informed Chauvel that his intention was to employ the cavalry to push on to Damascus, one of the oldest cities in the world. The Australian Mounted Division was to advance on Damascus along the western shores of Lake Tiberias followed by the 5th Indian Division.

On 25th September Chauvel sent the 4th Light Horse Brigade to take Semakh, a key point on the southern side of Lake Tiberias.

1. *Sydney, 1 January 1901 – the birthday of the Commonwealth of Australia. The inauguration of the new nation was the occasion of a brilliant military parade of British Empire and Australian troops.*

2. The 15th Battalion AIF marches through Melbourne before going off to war.

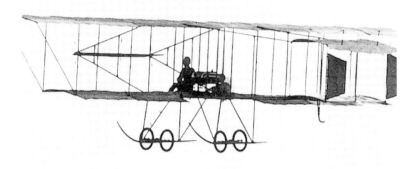

3. *Australia's first trainee military pilots learned to fly in this type of flimsy fabric-and-wire aircraft – the Bristol Box Kite.*

4. *A friendly boxing match on HMAS* Melbourne *at Bermuda in 1915.*

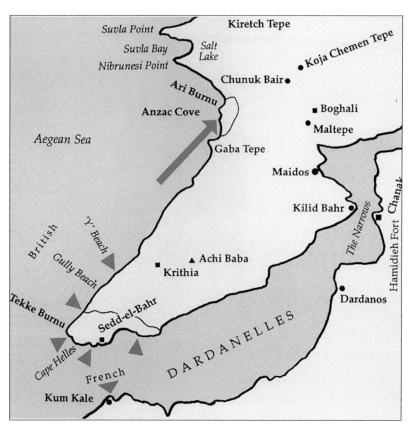

5. Allied landings in the Dardanelles and on the Gallipoli Peninsula.

6. Private John Simpson, who enlisted as John Simpson Kilpatrick, alongside his donkey carrying a wounded soldier.

7. Soldiers of the 8th Battalion in an abandoned Turkish position at Bolton's Ridge, the day after the Gallipoli landing.

8. The AE2 *which managed to penetrate the Dardanelles, before she was lost in action.*

9. Australian dead in the trenches in Gallipoli.

10. Australian troopers of the Light Horse went to Gallipoli without their mounts. The trooper on the right, W. H. R. Woods, was one of the first to be killed in Gallipoli.

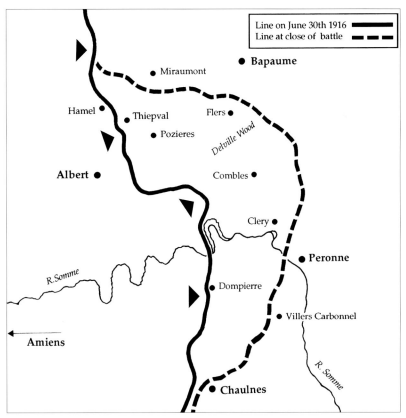

11. Battlefields of the Somme.

12. Soldiers of the 3rd Australian Division at Armentiéres.

13. A desolate scene at Pozières as stretcher bearers carry out the wounded under a flag of truce. In less than seven weeks, three Australian divisions lost 23,000 men. Those Australians who endured the Somme never forgot its horrors.

14. Australians wounded at the dressing station beside the Menin Road in September 1917.

15. Portrait of three First World War diggers. These were men of the 5th Battalion in the Suez defences, outside a shelter made from waterproof sheets. They had just arrived from Gallipoli and were about to face service in the desert.

16. Light Horsemen in a sector of the bridgehead at Ghoraniye in May 1918.

17. Australians, gassed near Villers Bretonneux, await the result of the battle of Amiens in 1918.

18. Motor transports of No 3 Squadron Australian Flying Corps at Tarciennes in Belgium.

19. Robert Menzies, the Prime Minister of Australia, announces Australia's declaration of war on Germany on 3 September 1939.

20. The Courier Mail *Brisbane* announces Britain's declaration of war.

21. Victorian recruits
for the 6th Division
at Puckapuntal in
November 1939.

22. Australian troops
advance into Bardia
in their first battle in
the Western Desert,
3 January 1941.

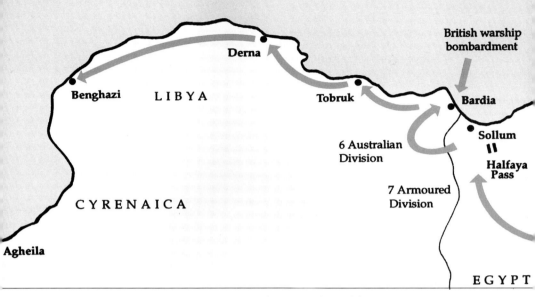

Mediterranean Sea

British warship bombardment

Derna

Benghazi

LIBYA

Tobruk

Bardia

6 Australian Division

Sollum

Halfaya Pass

CYRENAICA

7 Armoured Division

Agheila

EGYPT

23. *Australia's first land victories in the Second World War.*

24. *Australians of the 6th Division outside Tobruk after its capture.*

25. *Tomahawk aircraft pilots race to their aircraft to intercept enemy raiders in the Western Desert, November 1941.*

26. *Women of AWAS (Australian Women's Army Service) attending to a jeep.*

27. Wounded from Tobruk are ferried to a hospital ship in the harbour.

28. *Air crew of an RAAF squadron off-duty in the Western Desert.*

29. *Sharing a match with a native carrier before setting out along the Kokoda Trail.*

Meanwhile on 21 September British and Australian airmen had turned the Wadi Fara into a valley of death as vanquished Turkish troops made a desperate bid to escape. Turkish transport, artillery and foot soldiers were devastated. By nightfall two Turkish armies west of the Jordan had been destroyed.

The rout of the Turkish armies spread eastwards of the Jordan where the Anzac Mounted Division, having crossed the river, advanced on Amman which fell on 25 September. There was little resistance, for the German and Turkish forces were intent solely on fleeing north towards Deraa, which was no haven because it was about to be entered by the Arabs.

On 29 September the Turkish remnants surrendered to the Australian Light Horse at Ziza. In a strange turn of events the Australian brigade commander allowed the Turks to keep their arms: then together the Australians and Turkish prisoners defended the trenches overnight to ward off threatened attacks by Arab tribesmen who appeared ready and anxious to kill and loot the defeated Turks.

Further north on 29 September Chauvel sent the 4th Australian Light Horse Brigade to take Semakh, a key point at the southern end of Lake Tiberias. Semakh was rushed and seized although half the horses of an Australian machine gun squadron were hit. The 11th Regiment captured 364 enemy at Semakh but lost 14 killed and 71 wounded.

Tens of thousands of demoralised Turkish and German refugees were attempting to reach Damascus, pressed from behind by the victorious British Army and the Arabs. Chauvel's cavalrymen were moving rapidly north to take the ancient city of 300,000 people, hindered only by the resistance of Turkish rearguards and German machine gunners, who were easily dealt with.

On reaching the outskirts of Damascus, the Australian Mounted Division was ordered to isolate the city. Two of its Light Horse Brigades (the 3rd and 5th) were to cross the Barada gorge which enters the city from the east and then ride on to straddle the road to Homs. But Wilson of the 3rd Brigade reasoned that if he took that route he would not arrive in time to block the enemy escape route. He boldly decided he would risk a short cut through the centre of the crowded city.

At 5 am on 1 October, Wilson, believing the Turks were still in control, began his extraordinary ride. With scouts probing ahead, the Western Australian 10th Light Horse entered the city, whose streets were heaped with dead and wounded humans and dead and maimed animals. Scattered small-arms fire greeted them but mostly it was into the air as a greeting from welcoming Arabs.

The 3rd Brigade galloped past a Turkish barracks with thousands of armed Turks assembled. But apparently they were so demoralised by their wretched condition and the hardships they had endured that they made no attempt to use their weapons. The Australians boldly demanded to see the city governor and informed him his situation was hopeless; the city was surrounded by Chauvel's cavalry. They then asked for an Arab guide and continued their ride towards the Homs road. By 7 am they were clear of the deliriously happy inhabitants who had crowded around them wanting to shower gifts and hospitality upon them. They clattered on, capturing 500 enemy troops and 37 machine guns.

Soon after Wilson's brigade had risked all by entering Damascus and then left the city, Lawrence of Arabia arrived on the heels of the advance guard of an Indian cavalry brigade. The Arabs believed they had shared the honour of first entry. But they were mistaken: the Western Australian Light Horsemen had already entered and passed right through the centre of the city.

Damascus was in chaos, but Chauvel quickly restored order and then, with the 5th Cavalry Division leading, pushed on to Homs and Aleppo, which was abandoned by the Turkish army on 26 October. On 30 October Turkey surrendered unconditionally to the Allies.

Victory was complete. The Australian Light Horse contribution to that victory was fully acknowledged. In a tribute, Allenby wrote:

> ... they have shared in the campaign which achieved the destruction of the Turkish Army and the conquest of Palestine and Syria and throughout they have been in the thick of the fighting ... I have found them eager in advance and staunch in defence ... they have earned the gratitude of the empire and the admiration of the world.

Australian Airmen in the Middle East

Australia was quick to recognise the great potential of aviation in war, and in December 1915 had decided to organise an Australian Flying Corps. At Point Cook, No. 1 Squadron of that corps was created. It was to have 12 aircraft in three flights and its composite role in operations was to be fighter/bomber/reconnaissance. The squadron was committed to operations against Turkey and on arrival in Egypt on 14 April 1916 was placed under the control of the 5th Wing, Royal Flying Corps.

The squadron was equipped in Egypt with the somewhat ancient BE (British Experimental) 2c aircraft. These warplanes were inferior in speed, climb, manoeuvrability and fighting power to the German aircraft they would have to meet in air combat. The Middle Eastern theatre of war was regarded in London as a "side show" and the improved machines which were coming out of the aircraft factories were reserved for the vital "tumult in the clouds" then taking place over the battlefields of France. In consequence the Allied pilots in the Middle East, with inferior machines, would have little chance of surviving in air combat against the German airmen. Nevertheless, the Australians flew them in desperate encounters and did excellent work. Later the tables would be turned on the Germans after the British and Australian pilots were provided with fighting machines which completely outclassed those of the Germans.

During the battle of Romani in July-August 1916 the German air force raided Egypt aggressively. The Australians took to the air to intercept but their inadequate aircraft were generally unable to even climb up to the enemy aircraft. However, they hit back with bombing raids on ground forces, although well aware that should the Germans take off to meet them, they had small hope of beating them off. On 22 December ten of the Australian machines bombed the Turks in support of the Anzac Mounted Division when it captured Magdhaba.

In a bombing raid on 20 March 1917, Lieutenant Frank McNamara of Rushworth, Victoria, won the first Victoria Cross awarded to an Australian airman. Although he was wounded and weak from loss of blood, McNamara landed behind the enemy lines near a Turkish mounted force and rescued a member of his squadron who had been forced down.

Beersheba, Gaza, Jerusalem and Jaffa had, by the end of 1917, fallen to the advancing British Army and by March 1918 the days of shortage and inferior equipment ended for No 1 Squadron when it was completely equipped with Bristol fighters, one of the finest combat aircraft produced in the First World War. During this period Major Richard (later Air Marshal Sir Richard) Williams of Moonta, South Australia, was emerging as an outstanding air leader. He was the first Australian military pilot to graduate as a pilot in Australia and after long service in the theatre of war was appointed commanding officer of No 1 Squadron in May 1917. By June 1918 Allenby was preparing for his great "knockout" blow against Turkey and at this vital stage, Williams was promoted to lieutenant colonel and put in charge of the 40th (Army) Wing of the Royal Flying Corps which would be the air striking force in the coming battle. To increase its strength, the Wing was allotted two additional squadrons, one of DH9as (bombers) and one of SE5as (fighter scouts).

In the lead-up to Allenby's big offensive, Williams' squadrons kept the skies clear of enemy aircraft. Australia's No 1 squadron with its new fighters and expert technical backing completely dominated the aerial battle in this period, destroying 15 enemy planes in combat. Two Bristols of No 1 took on a formation of six Pfalz scouts, the new German fighter, and forced them all down.

Access to Allied air space was denied to enemy aircraft, which not only protected Allied forces on the ground but "blinded" the enemy commanders about British activities and intentions. Allenby was able to concentrate his powerful forces in secret. As soon as any German reconnaissance aircraft appeared near Allied-held territory it was shot down or driven off.

When Allenby's divisions were about to attack in the battle of Megiddo (known also as "Armageddon") No 1 Squadron had the honour of delivering the first blow. The squadron had been allotted a giant Handley Page twin-engined bomber aircraft, the only one sent to the theatre. Piloted by Captain Ross Smith and carrying sixteen 112 lb (51 kg) bombs, it took off at 1.15 am on 19 September to begin the battle by bombing the important central telephone exchange and temporarily wrecking the railway junction at El Afule. Other aircraft attacked nerve centres and communications so that the Turks remained in ignorance of Allenby's operations further south.

Widespread bombing and strafing attacks were made on retreating enemy cavalry and infantry and on air installations and aircraft. Not a single enemy aircraft was able to take off from Jenin and El Afule during the course of the battle because of the constant surveillance of Corps squadrons.

The disaster which befell the Turkish army in the Wadi Fara on 21 September at the hands of Williams' air corps has been mentioned above. It was a massacre. Williams wrote later, "The Turkish Seventh Army ceased to exist and it must be noted that this was entirely the result of attack from the air."

At this time the Arab force led by Lawrence of Arabia was in trouble north of Amman and Lawrence called for help. He informed Allenby that his followers "were being wrecked by air impotence", following attacks by the German air force based on Deraa.

On 22 September Captain Ross Smith was called on to help out. Williams sent Ross Smith two Bristol fighters and they quickly restored the situation by shooting down German intruders. In order to keep his aircraft operating, Ross Smith also used his Handley-Page to carry petrol, food and spares. Lawrence later declared that the appearance of the "biggest aeroplane in the world" and the shooting down of the German planes brought thousands of Arab recruits to his Army.

Allenby's triumph was swift. The Turks were utterly crushed and within a few weeks the war ended and No 1 Squadron returned to Egypt. On 19 February 1919 when its members were about to embark for home, Allenby attended a farewell parade at Kantara, Egypt, and paid a high tribute to the squadron.

Major Addison (Addison succeeded Williams as commanding officer), officers and men:

> *It gives me considerable pleasure to have this opportunity of*
> *addressing you prior to your return to Australia. We have just*
> *reached the end of the greatest war known to history. The*

operations in this theatre of the war have been an important factor in bringing about the victorious result. The victory gained in Palestine and Syria has been one of the greatest in the war, and undoubtedly hastened the collapse that followed in other theatres. This squadron played an important part in making this achievement possible. You gained for us absolute supremacy of the air, thereby enabling my cavalry, artillery and infantry to carry out their work on the ground practically unmolested by hostile aircraft. This undoubtedly was a factor of paramount importance in the success of our arms here. I desire therefore personally to congratulate you on your splendid work. I congratulate you, not only the flying officers, but also your mechanics, for although the officers did the work in the air, it was good work on the part of your mechanics that kept a high percentage of your machines serviceable. I wish you all bon voyage and trust that the peace now attained will mean for you all future happiness and prosperity. Thank you and good-bye.[7]

Victory

The entry into the war in April 1917 of the United States with its huge material and manpower resources, the exit of the dissolving Russian armies, and the overwhelming enemy success against Italy at Caporetto, appeared certain to have a major and probably decisive impact on the world struggle in 1918.

In the Middle East, Turkey had suffered sharp reverses in Palestine and Kut had been avenged by the capture of Baghdad in Mesopotamia. But these Allied successes were far outweighed by the absence of a hostile Russian army at Germany's back door and Allied reverses in Serbia and Rumania. Strategic military assessments concluded that the Germans would concentrate the bulk of their armed forces on the Western Front and the transfer of German divisions to France at the rate of two per week soon made it glaringly obvious that a massive onslaught in the west was in preparation. Ludendorff and Hindenburg believed that the war must be won in France before the Americans could move massive fresh combat forces across the Atlantic, which would tip the scales in favour of the Allies, leading to Germany's inevitable defeat. The prospect of an Allied offensive in France in the spring of 1918 seemed unlikely. The French wanted to wait for the coming of the Americans and for their armies to be equipped with tanks.

Ludendorff was reinforced by 35 German divisions from the Russian front. His great offensive, known as Operation "Michael", would be launched on 21 March 1918. It was a vast "gambler's throw" in which Ludendorff was prepared to stake everything and if necessary lose a million men. His strategic aim was to separate the French and British armies and destroy the British against the English Channel. The Allies knew where and when the stroke would fall and they spent the winter months strengthening their defences. Haig pressed his superiors for reinforcements but they were not forthcoming.

In the sanguinary battles of 1917 the Australian divisions in France lost heavily, suffering a total of 55,000 casualties. Trained men were scarce and the shortage resulted in the partly formed 6th Australian Division being disbanded to provide men for the divisions in France. The 4th Division was also threatened but was never broken up.

The Australian Government had pressed the British Government for all Australian divisions to be brought together as one force. The British agreed on 1 November 1917 and the Australian troops were delighted to learn that four Australian divisions were to form the "Australian Corps" and would take over a comparatively quiet area near Messines.

Signs of the coming big push multiplied in early March with German shelling of the back areas and raids by the big German Gotha bombers. The strain on the Diggers was great yet many were wishing the Germans would come so that the Allies would have the opportunity of annihilating them.

The spirit of the Australian troops as the tension rose was conveyed by the famous battle order issued by Lieutenant F. P. Bethune of Tasmania, who commanded a machine gun section. He was instructed to hold his machine gun post at all costs, so he issued the following grim orders to his Section:

Special Orders of No 1 Section, 13/3/18
1. *This position will be held and the Section will remain here until relieved.*
2. *The enemy cannot be allowed to interfere with this programme.*
3. *If the Section cannot remain here alive, it will remain here dead, but in any case it will remain here.*
4. *Should any man, through shell-shock or other causes attempt to surrender, he will remain here dead.*
5. *Should all guns be blown out, the Section will use Mills grenades and other novelties.*
6. *Finally, the position as stated, will be held.*

Bethune and his men survived, although their area was hit by German gas shells. The Lieutenant returned to Australia after the war and was a farmer there until his death in December 1942.

On 21 March Ludendorff's opening hammer blows with his huge force of 63 divisions were delivered against the British over a front of 70 miles between Vimy and Barisia in the valley of the Somme. His aim was to roll up the British forces against the sea. At 4.30 am 6,000 German guns roared into life deluging the frontline troops of the British 3rd and 5th Armies. Dense mist covered the battlefield and had not lifted when German shock troops swept forward and then cruised easily through the British defences, killing or capturing the dazed survivors. A dangerous gap was torn north of Peronne.

The British 5th was forced to retreat and at the end of the fifth day the German advance was threatening the key railway junction of Amiens. Further north the British 3rd Army, after stiff resistance, was also forced back.

In this supreme crisis Australians of the 3rd and 4th Divisions were rushed south to help avert a catastrophe. On 25 March they were rolling on motor lorries through the country north of Amiens. They passed villages where old people were hastily loading furniture on farm wagons. But when they saw the Australians they felt secure and decided to stay.

The 4th Brigade took up positions on the edge of the old Somme battlefield, relieving exhausted remnants of a British division. They held a German attack and by 27 March began to penetrate the enemy front with New Zealanders.

On 27 March the 3rd and 4th Australian Divisions were given responsibility for the British Third Army's flank. Next morning near Dernacourt, Sergeant Stan MacDougall of the 12th Brigade (4th Division) won the Victoria Cross when his brigade attacked the *German 50th Division* which was repulsed with the loss of 550 men.

An action on 4 April at Villers Bretonneux, the final ridge from which Amiens is distantly visible, cost the 3rd Division 550 casualties and next day the 4th Division lost 1,100 at Dernacourt. The 4th Division was then relieved by the 2nd Division which had just arrived from Messines. But the 1st Division which had also just arrived at Amiens, was sent north again in haste to cover Hazebrouck, an important rail junction which was threatened by a German breakthrough. The 1st barred the German advance in that sector at Strazeele on the 12th and 14th April.

Five Australian divisions had been deployed to counter the German offensive, which now faltered. The Germans had won a tactical victory, taking 70,000 prisoners, 1,100 guns and much territory. But their front line was a third longer and bulged out awkwardly with exposed flanks.

In an ambitious move on 24 April the Germans renewed the attack in the Somme area. Four enemy divisions suddenly seized Villers Bretonneux after it had been drenched with mustard gas. For the first time in the war the Germans also used tanks.

British counterattacks to retake the town during the day failed. But that night at 10 pm two Australian brigades, the 13th and 15th, the only fresh reserves in the area, were committed to the battle. The 15th attacked north of the town and the 13th across the south.

As the 13th Brigade assembled, it was seen by the enemy and fired on by machine guns from a wooded area. This fire had to be suppressed before the attack could proceed so Lieutenant C. W. Sadlier of the 51st Battalion entered the woods and courageously destroyed six machine gun posts, after which the advance swept forward. For this outstanding act of gallantry Sadlier was awarded the Victoria Cross and

Sergeant C. Stokes who went with him was awarded the Distinguished Conduct Medal.

The 15th Brigade meanwhile had swept along the northern side of Villers Bretonneux which was almost surrounded by the two brigades. Next day, Anzac Day, the confident Australians attacked the trapped Germans who were without difficulty killed, captured or driven out. The defeat of the Germans in this classic action was regarded by many military experts as one of the finest feats of arms on the Western Front. For the Germans it was a heavy defeat and contributed greatly to saving Amiens and stabilising a dangerous situation.

Meanwhile Germany was using "frightfulness" to add to the pressure of the French by bringing into action Big Bertha, a huge artillery piece which lobbed shells on Paris from a forest near Laon, a distance of 65 miles.

General Gough, the commander of the 5th British Army, had been dismissed in March and Haig offered the command to General Birdwood. Birdwood hesitated: he was prepared to forgo promotion to stay with the Australian Corps. However, when he realised that this would block the promotion of an Australian to the highest Australian command in the field, he accepted the post.

The choice of Birdwood's successor was between two great Australian generals – C. B. B. White and John Monash. Haig had never wavered in his support for Monash who impressed him deeply with his ability, efficiency and organisational brilliance. Monash considered White (in later years Chief of the General Staff in Australia) to be Australia's ablest soldier. Although clearly White's qualities were outstanding, Monash was regarded as the best divisional commander on the Western Front. Monash was appointed and White went with Birdwood as Chief of General Staff; Brigadier General (later Field Marshal Sir Thomas) Blamey, was appointed chief of the Australian Corps staff.

Birdwood cabled the High Command proposals to the Australian Government and the appointments were announced on 31 May. In addition three new Australians division commanders were appointed. Major General John Gellibrand succeeded Monash as commander of the 3rd Division; Major General T. W. Glasgow took over the 1st Division and Major General C. Rosenthal the 2nd Division.

Determined to secure a decisive result before the American divisions redressed the balance of manpower caused by the withdrawal of Russia from the war, Ludendorff struck again on 27 May. Having been thwarted in the north, he attacked at the Chemin des Dames. He again achieved a breakthrough, reaching the Marne with spearheads less than 50 miles from Paris. American troops were rushed to Chateau Thierry and Belleau Wood to help stem the tide. Their fighting effectiveness surprised German staff officers who described them as "storm troop quality". A French writer said that the Americans had begun "a vast operation of transfusion of blood" into the exhausted body of France.

After defeating the German attacks on their lines near Amiens, the Australians settled down to small-scale infiltration of the German line, taking enemy posts almost at will and bringing in prisoners. In May an Australian officer and his scouts walked over to an enemy garrison and took 21 men and an officer without having one Australian hit. This activity climaxed on a hot summer day in July when a number of German posts, together with 923 metres of the German front line, 120 prisoners and 11 machine guns were taken without German higher authorities even knowing about it.

Monash's first task as corps commander was an operation to push the Allied line forward south of the Somme and to seize the town of Hamel. Monash committed brigades from three Australian divisions to the task and they were to be supported by the new pattern Mark V British tanks which would advance with the infantry. As well the 15th Brigade was to make a feint attack beyond Ville to the north.

Ten companies of American troops were also attached to the Australians so that they could gain actual fighting experience, although at the last moment some were withdrawn because they had been committed without the direct permission of General Pershing, the American commander-in-chief.

The battle took place on 3 July. It was a brilliant success and came to the notice of military and civil leaders at the highest level. Georges Clemenceau, the 77-year-old French Prime Minister, insisted on visiting the Australians who had taken part in the battle. He received a tremendous ovation when the Diggers circled around him to hear his congratulations spoken in English.

Clemenceau told them, "We knew that you would fight a real fight, but we did not know that from the very beginning you would astonish the whole continent ..."

The tanks used were faster and more manoeuvrable than earlier models and the enthusiastic Australians, too, took instant advantage of opportunities created by the tanks.

The Australian battle commanders were full of praise for the spirit of the inexperienced American soldiers, who suffered 176 casualties. Some 1,600 German troops were taken prisoner.

In July, Foch, who had been appointed Allied Supreme Commander, was ready to seize the initiative from the Germans. He struck on 18 July on the German front between Soissons and Chateau-Thierry at a time when Ludendorff was about to mount another major offensive in Flanders. The French soldiers fought magnificently. They were well supported by the divisions of two American corps which on 24 July were combined into the 1st American Army. Foch's victory in this battle was conclusive. The Marne sector was eliminated and a week later Foch was promoted to Marshal of France. Although Ludendorff retained a gleam of optimism, some German leaders recognised that the war was lost.

Monash sent four of his Australian divisions (the 2nd, 3rd, 4th and 5th, with the 1st in reserve) into action on the Somme on 8 August 1918, the opening day of the battle of Amiens. A shocked Ludendorff was later to describe the day as "Der Schwarze Tag" (Black Day). It was an ominous turning point in the war, with the German army now in decline beyond all doubt and with the general now believing that the war must be ended. When 20 divisions, including Australian, British, American, Canadian and French troops struck on that day, enemy resistance collapsed.

More than 400 tanks spearheaded the attack with Allied combat planes harassing the German columns with machine gunfire. Along the ruptured front the enemy troops were surrendering at once as the confident Allied troops surged into their trenches. The breakdown of discipline was proof to the enemy leaders that they were losing full control over their war-weary troops. Whole divisions had failed, with many troops surrendering without resistance.

No preliminary bombardment alerted the Germans to a coming attack when the men of the 4th Army, which included the Canadian, Australian and 3rd British Corps (under General Rawlinson), surged from their trenches towards the enemy lines. Low-flying combat aircraft aided the surprise by masking the engine noise of the assembling British tanks. At 4.20 am massed Allied artillery began a creeping barrage as the Australian divisions advanced. Success crowned the Allied efforts when by 7.30 am the German front line system was broken. The 2nd and 3rd Australian Divisions then dug in while the 4th and 5th came up and by 8 am, as the fog thinned, advanced. The 4th Army captured some 13,000 German prisoners and more than 200 guns. Next day, 9th August, the 1st Australian Division joined in the action, thrusting with the 2nd Division to and over the Lihons heights. On this day, Private Robert Beatham of the 8th Battalion bombed or captured or killed the crews of four machine guns who were holding up the advance. He himself was killed and was awarded the VC posthumously.

By 15 August, the Australians had advanced up to 14 miles. The five divisions had suffered a total of 6,000 casualties.

Marshal Foch now ordered the Somme offensive to be widened to a 70-mile front between Soissons and Arras. After a brief pause the Allies struck a series of blows which sent the Germans reeling back. On 22 August the 3rd Division seized its objective north of Bray and on the 23 August the Australian 1st Division captured 2,000 enemy. The 2nd Division relieved the 1st and pressed the retreating Germans right to the Somme near the ancient town of Peronne with its moat and battlemented towers.

Mont-St-Quentin, a prominent hill not far north of Peronne, completely dominates the old town and the surrounding countryside. The Germans had turned the hill into a fortress bristling with machine guns and garrisoned by an elite Imperial Guards Division with orders to defend it to the last. Possession of Mont-St-Quentin was indispensable for the military domination of the territory in the area. Its capture by the Allies would make the German positions in Peronne untenable.

The fortress was not within the operational zone allotted to the Australian Corps. Even so Monash was keen to take it from the Germans and was very confident he could do so. He submitted proposals for the seizure to General Rawlinson. The General was surprised at Monash's audacity, but gave him permission to make the attempt. Rawlinson was amused by Monash's "cheek" when Monash claimed he could take it with three battalions. "However," Rawlinson said, "I don't think I ought to stop you."

Free to go ahead with his plan, Monash immediately gave the necessary orders. His main army strength would thrust towards the enemy from positions on the Somme river bend to the northern side of the Somme, and rush the objective. The attack was made on 31 August by the 17th and 20th battalions of the 5th Brigade. Preceded by a heavy artillery barrage they went in "yelling like a lot of bushrangers". Groups of Germans seemed bewildered and quickly surrendered. They claimed later they were taken unawares. "It all happened like lightning," a Guards regiment recorded later in its history.

The hill itself was covered with enemy troops now retreating hurriedly over the shoulders. The Australians swept up the slope to capture the "impregnable" Mont-St-Quentin. But the victors had been fighting for 12 hours and were exhausted and thinly spread. Part of the Guards division drove them from the village on the crest. However, next day the 6th Brigade, passing through the 5th, recaptured the summit while 5th Division troops crossed the moat at Peronne and took the main part of the town. The rest was seized on 2 September.

The Australian infantry had thus accomplished an astonishing feat at a cost of 3,000 casualties. Overall the fighting record of the Australians in the three days on the Somme between 31 August and 2 September had been magnificent and the most outstanding acts of gallantry had earned the award of seven Victoria Crosses, two of them to soldiers who were killed in action and a third to a corporal who died of wounds at the end of September.

The Battle of Amiens ended on 4 September and Haig now pressed on towards the Hindenburg Line. On 11 September the Australians captured the first of three lines built earlier by the British in front of the Hindenburg Line. On 18 September Rawlinson put in a major attack on the remaining lines, and by next morning a great part of the Australian front line was looking down on St Quentin canal and the Hindenburg Line beyond. The 6,800 Australian troops involved in this action had taken 4,300 prisoners.

Of Germany's allies in the east, Bulgaria had collapsed and Turkey was doomed. Foch believed victory was in sight and ordered massive simultaneous offensives by all Allied armies in France. *"Tout le monde à la bataille,"* (everyone into the battle) he declared. The first hammer blow would be launched by the British 1st, 3rd and 4th Armies (including the Australian Corps) and the 1st French against the Hindenburg Line. A major British-Belgian force would descend on Ghent and a French and American army would strike on the Meuse-Argonne salient.

The Australian Corps was given responsibility for the "main attack" through the Hindenburg Line. However, growing doubts concerning the wisdom of this task arose. The Australian troops had been pushed to the limit in operations. Battalions were so depleted that they could put only 300 men into action and only two divisions, the 3rd and 5th, were fit for combat. As well, Prime Minister Hughes told Monash that he held him personally responsible for having the Australian Corps withdrawn from operations for a rest by 15 October.

A solution to the problem was found when Monash's force was reinforced with two recently trained American divisions. "Missions" of experienced soldiers from the 1st and 4th Australian Divisions were attached to the American divisions to assist them. When they attacked at dawn on 29 September, the inexperienced Americans encountered difficulties. They were forced to advance 1,000 yards behind their barrage and although extra tanks were allotted many were destroyed by hostile fire and 21 were blown up in an old British minefield.

The last action fought by the Australian infantry in the war came on 5 October when the 6th Brigade in a brilliant action captured Montbrehain. The action cost the brigade 430 men, some the best leaders in the brigade.

All over France now, enemy resistance was crumbling. Sailors of the German navy mutinied at Kiel when called on to man warships for a grand sacrificial naval sortie. Ludendorff was dismissed. Kaiser Wilhelm renounced the throne and on 10 November fled into exile in Holland. A German Republic was declared from the steps of the Reichstag. On the next day, Armistice Day, at 11 am the guns fell silent as the "cease fire" was announced all over the Western Front.

The Flying Corps in France

The First World War was significant for the rapid development of the aeroplane in military operations. Before the outbreak, Britain had organised small air arms for the Navy (the Royal Naval Air Service) and the Army (Royal Flying Corps). Initially war in the third dimension was limited to reconnaissance activities. But soon the air crews were armed and as their aircraft became faster, stronger and more capable, new forms of air warfare emerged: air-to-air combat, air-to-ground attack and strategic air bombardment.

In Australia the opportunities for eager young men to join the miniscule Australian air service were practically non-existent. Not to be denied, many left the country to join the British air services. Among them were Robert Little of Melbourne and R. S. Dallas, a Queenslander. Both joined the Royal Naval Air Service. Little, who was killed in May 1918, was Australia's top scoring fighter ace of the war with 47 air combat victories; Dallas with 39 achieved the second highest total for an Australian. Charles Kingsford Smith, who was later world famous for his aviation achievements, served in the RFC and another great Australian aviator, H. W. (Bert) Hinkler, had a distinguished combat record in the RNAS. Many remained in the British air services and reached senior ranks.

Unlike the Canadians and New Zealanders, the far-sighted Australian military insisted that Australia should form and develop its own military aviation arm. This arm would help preserve Australian identity in air operations and more importantly would ensure that Australia would have an air force for its defence.

As a result by 1917 the Australian Flying Corps had grown to four combat squadrons. The Australian Half Flight which had been formed and sent to Mesopotamia in 1915 was later disbanded. But in December 1916 No 1 Squadron was formed at Point Cook and then sent to Egypt, arriving in April 1916.

In the same year, three more Australian squadrons were formed and were ready for combat in France by the end of 1917. They were:

> No 2 Squadron, fighter/scout, formed at Kantara, Egypt and deployed to France on 21 September, 1917.
>
> No 3 Squadron, corps reconnaissance, formed at Point Cook and deployed to France on 9 September, 1917.
>
> No 4 Squadron, fighter/scout, formed at Point Cook and deployed to France on 18 December, 1917.

Also formed in the United Kingdom during 1917 were four Australian training squadrons (Nos 5, 6, 7 and 8).

No 2 Squadron (commanded by Major Oswald Watt who had begun the war fighting in the Aviation Militaire section of the French Foreign Legion) fought the first Australian air combat in France on 2 October 1917). A patrol of four de Havilland 5s encountered German machines while returning from St Quentin. The Australians attacked but the enemy escaped: one Australian machine was forced down and its crew taken prisoner. On 20 November No 2 Squadron took part in the battle of Cambrai and lost six aircraft during daring low-flying attacks. In a letter to General Birdwood, General Trenchard, commander of the RFC, described their work: "These pilots came down low and fairly strafed the Hun. They bombed him and attacked him with machine gunfire from fifty feet [fifteen metres] flying among treetops; they apparently revelled in this work which was of great value."[8]

In March 1918, German Supreme Commander Ludendorff launched the greatest offensive on the Somme in a final bid to end the war before American troops then pouring into France were able to reinforce the Allies. Every available squadron was ordered into the air in a maximum effort to attack the huge force of 63 German divisions moving in a grey flood towards the Allied armies. Excited pilots reported the whole countryside alive with the grey-clad German soldiers.

The Australian pilots bombed and blazed away with machine guns at close range at the massed troops. On the ground the five Australian divisions in France were rushed into the battle. The strain on the pilots was great. Captain Harry Cobby of No 4 Squadron recalled how during the crisis he was unable to eat. "Champagne, brandy and an odd biscuit seemed enough," he said. It was not long before the German push ran out of steam.

On 20 March just before the Ludendorff offensive began. Cobby's squadron encountered the famous Richthofen "Circus" coming through the fog in their all-red machines. Cobby was leading a patrol of Sopwith Camels and immediately attacked. Cobby (who ended the war as the highest scoring fighter pilot in the AFC with 29 victories) recalled:

> *I managed to get my fellow in flames after a couple of bursts and turned on to a red Albatros which was on Lieutenant Pflaum's tail ... I came up under the tail of one of them, a red triplane, and fired a burst from 10 feet [3 metres] away. He heeled over and went straight down through the mist ...*[9]

The two Australian fighter squadrons Nos 2 and 4 were chosen for "circus" work – that is offensive flying by groups of squadrons. No 4 became the most successful fighter squadron in France, accounting for 199 enemy. No 2 was credited with 185. Australian casualties were 78 killed, 68 wounded and 33 taken prisoner.

Total enlistments in the AFC during the war were 460 officers and 2,234 other ranks.

As military aviation developed and expanded its activities in the war, both sides used other aircraft-not against enemy aircraft but against targets well behind the enemy front lines. The Germans used Zeppelin dirigible airships for bombing raids on the eastern counties of England. Gotha bombers carried out raids at night behind the front lines in France. The British replied in kind.

On 17 August 1918, Nos 2 and 4 Squadrons of the AFC took part in raids on the German airfield at Haubourdin near Lille. Captain A. Murray Jones led 19 machines of No 2 Squadron and Captain Cobby led 19 Camels from No 4 Squadron. As a result of the air raid, some 37 German aircraft were destroyed. Both Australian squadrons joined in an attack next day which destroyed 17 Fokker aircraft on the ground at Lomme aerodrome near Haubourdin.

By October the German war effort was in total disarray yet the German airmen fought on to the last. On 4 November, only a week before the war ended, three fine Australian pilots were killed in an air clash. One of them, Captain T. Baker of Smithfield, South Australia, was an ace with 12 air combat victories to his credit.

Naval Operations 1915-18

In 1915 the RAN light cruisers *Melbourne* and *Sydney* joined the British Navy's North American and West Indies squadrons in the Atlantic where they took part in maintaining a close watch on neutral American ports where 91 enemy vessels had taken refuge.

The two cruisers continued this Atlantic service until September 1916 when they joined the British Grand Fleet in the North Sea. Together with *Australia* which had joined the fleet in 1915, they were fully involved in the vital naval operations which continued to secure for the Allies the maritime gateways to the world.

The pre-war threat posed by accelerated German naval building to Britain's naval supremacy had been an important factor contributing to the outbreak of war. The world had waited anxiously for news of an awesome naval collision between the two giants, the outcome of which might prove decisive. They waited in vain until 31 May 1916 when the two navies clashed in the Battle of Jutland. Although the British lost a higher tonnage than the Germans, the Battle of Jutland did nothing to impair British naval supremacy and German naval thinking turned towards submarine warfare as a means of ending the war.

HMAS *Australia* would have been involved at Jutland, but to the frustration of the crew had to remain in port while the battle raged, because a collision with HMAS *New Zealand* had caused damage which could not be repaired in time. Ironically, *New Zealand* took Australia's place as flagship of the 2nd Squadron.

In May 1917 *Sydney* was involved in a duel with a Zeppelin which dropped bombs but missed and then flew off. Subsequently all three Australian cruisers were equipped with light aircraft.

On the other side of the world 74 German ships were bottled up in neutral ports just north of Australia in the Netherlands East Indies and to help curb German naval activities in the area, Australia in mid-1915 sent the cruiser *Psyche* and the sloop *Fantome* to patrol in the Bay of Bengal.

In October 1915 three RAN destroyers, *Warrego*, *Parramatta* and *Yarra*, the yacht *Komet* and cruiser *Encounter* were sent to patrol Macassar Strait in search of a reported German munitions base, but nothing was found. However, the constant patrol work by the RAN helped to frustrate German activities throughout the area including attempts by the Germans to organise anti-British uprisings in Persia (Iran), Java and Siam (Thailand).

In the same year the activities of the German commerce raiders *Wolf* and *Seeadler* in the Indian and Pacific oceans caused the deployment of British, Australian, Japanese and French warships to track them down. *Wolf* laid mines off Gabo Island which sank the British steamer *Cumberland* on 6 July 1917.

The newly built Australian cruiser *Brisbane*, which was completed at Cockatoo Island dockyard in 1916, was sent to the Indian Ocean to join the hunt. A Sopwith Baby seaplane was provided for *Brisbane*.

After destroying 14 Allied vessels *Wolf* escaped to Germany, but the *Seeadler* after successful operations in the Atlantic proceeded to the Pacific where in the Society Islands it was driven onto a reef by a sudden squall and later destroyed by fire.

By 1916 the German U-boat campaign against merchant shipping was having a disastrous effect on Britain's vital imports. In February 1917 the enemy greatly escalated the campaign by declaring they would sink at sight any vessels of any description found in the approaches to the British Isles, the west coast of France and the Mediterranean. The U-boat force was five times larger than in 1915 and Allied shipping losses by the end of April had resulted in stocks in Britain being so low they would be exhausted in six weeks. The people faced starvation and the British war effort was in jeopardy.

To meet the danger Britain undertook vigorous submarine counter-measures – convoys and anti-submarine devices.

The Mediterranean was badly infested with U-boats and in May 1917 Britain asked Australia to send the destroyers *Warrego*, *Parramatta* and *Yarra*. Australia agreed at once and offered as well to send the destroyers *Swan*, *Torrens* and *Huon* which were then based at Singapore. The Australian destroyers were refitted and used Brindisi, Italy, as a base to carry out anti-submarine operations in the Adriatic. They supported the "Otranto Barrage" which obstructed the movements of enemy submarines. Eventually the Barrage force was strengthened to 36 destroyers, together with torpedo boats, submarines, sloops, trawlers, drifters and motor launches.

By slow degrees the submarine menace was reduced until by the end of 1917 it no longer threatened imminent disaster for Britain.

When the war came to an end, an entry in HMAS *Sydney's* diary of 11 November 1918 reflected the joyous reaction of sailors who had been away from home for so long.

> *Admiral Beatty sent a signal to the Grand Fleet to splice the main brace. A tot of rum was served out to the ship's company, the first time since the ship was commissioned. Fireworks displays and all kinds of whistles – in fact anything that sound could be got out of was under way.*

In terms of casualties it had not been a costly war for the young Royal Australian Navy. The dead totalled 171 – 15 officers and 156 sailors. Of these, 6 officers and 57 sailors had been on loan from the Royal Navy.

Peace in 1918

The battles fought by heroic young Australian volunteers in faraway countries had brought a new awareness of nationhood for Australians and won recognition for Australia before the eyes of the world.

Australia in 1914 had a population of only 4,875,325 people and of these no less than 331,781 served overseas in the Australian Army, Navy and Flying Corps. They suffered grievous losses in battle. Their casualty lists totalled 212,773 of whom 60,284 were dead. It was a sanguinary outcome for a large part of an Australian generation in its prime. Hardly a family throughout the nation was left untouched.

The war gave a new word to the national lexicon – "Anzac". Anzac Day, which falls on the anniversary of the landing by the Australian and New Zealand troops on the rugged Gallipoli peninsula, was at once recognised as a most significant day in the national calendar.

The people of Australia were determined never to forget those who died and the wounded who would suffer the scars of war for the rest of their lives. Throughout the nation, in cities, country towns and public parks, they built memorials as a tribute to the fallen. Many saddened communities also planted avenues of trees in their memory.

5

THE SECOND
WORLD WAR

Commitment to War

In the early hours of 1 September 1939, German tanks (Panzers) and dive-bombing aircraft (Stukas) plunged into Polish territory and air space, scattering the pitifully weak Polish defences with their overwhelming firepower. This unprovoked aggression heralded the outbreak of the Second World War, one of the most ruinous, devastating and lethal wars in all history, resulting in the deaths of about 24 million military and 30 million civilians killed or missing.

The First World War had been confined largely to Europe and the Middle East, but the Second World War was to embrace all continents save South America and would witness the commitment of Australian army, navy and air force men to combat in widely scattered corners of the globe.

As the alarming march of international events in the 1930s had grown more menacing, Britain and France had attempted to head off the coming conflict by "appeasement" of Hitler, the German dictator. When that failed they had tried warnings and finally they issued an ultimatum demanding the immediate withdrawal of the invaders from

Poland, whose vital interests they were pledged to preserve. Hitler scornfully rejected the demands and on 3 September 1939 Britain and France declared war.

Hitler had feared a war on two fronts and was able at the last moment to eliminate one front by diplomatic manoeuvring. On 23 August the world had been stunned to learn that Hitler had entered into a non-aggression pact with his implacable enemy Soviet Russia. The pact opened the way for Hitler to attack Poland without the fear of a stab in the back on his eastern front while he fought France and Britain in the west. As an inducement Soviet Russia was promised a free hand in the Baltic states and eastern Poland. Within weeks, Latvia, Estonia and Lithuania were forced to sign pacts with Soviet Russia, granting her sea and air bases.

Hitler's "blitzkrieg" (literally, "lightning war") attack on Poland was the spark that ignited the flames of war, but the fundamental causes were not the quarrel with Poland but the determination of Germany, Italy and Japan, all of whom had fallen under the iron control of totalitarian regimes, to embark on aggressive expansion at the expense of the rest of the world.

Australia and New Zealand at once joined in the declaration of war against Germany. The Australian Government and people firmly believed that Australia must be involved because the destruction or defeat of Britain would be the destruction or defeat of the British Commonwealth and would leave Australia with "a precarious tenure on its own independence". At 9.15 pm on 3 September Australians heard on the radio the historic words spoken by the Prime Minister, Robert Menzies: "It is my melancholy duty to inform you officially that in consequence of a persistence by Germany in her invasion of Poland, Great Britain has declared war upon her and that as a result Australia is also at war."

In Australia all military districts were ordered to man coastal defences; naval mobilisation was completed swiftly with naval vessels moving to their war stations. Squadrons of the Air Force were placed on short call for combat operations. A detachment of the RAAF's No 10 Squadron was in England to take delivery of Sunderland flying boats.

Australia agreed to make the whole squadron available for service in the RAF's Coastal Command and it thus had the distinction of being the first air force squadron of any Commonwealth country to go into action in the war.

Immediately the First World War broke out Australia had offered a 20,000-strong expeditionary force to Britain. Enthusiastic recruits had besieged army barracks in the capital cities offering their services to the Empire. But there was no comparable response in 1939. The war atmosphere in Australia was low-key.

The strategic circumstances had changed. In the First World War Japan had been an ally of the British Empire and consequently of Australia. But this was no longer the case. However, the German-Soviet non-aggression pact had stunned the Japanese no less than the Allies because Japan was linked with Germany in a pact hostile to Russia – the anti-Comintern pact. Only four days before the signing of the German-Soviet non-aggression pact, Japan had suffered a humiliating military reverse at the hands of Soviet Russia at Normanhan, Outer Mongolia, losing 18,000 men. The baffled Japanese therefore regarded the German-Soviet pact as a betrayal of Japan. It aroused bitter criticism in their press. The defeat coupled with the diplomatic reverses caused the resignation of the Japanese Government. In these circumstances the Japanese declared that they would remain "independent" in the crisis. Consequently Australian fears of Japanese hostility were eased.

On 15 September the Australian Government announced that an Australian infantry division of 20,000 men would be raised to serve at home or abroad "as circumstances permit". It was later designated the 6th Division, 2nd Australian Imperial Force (2nd AIF). In November the Government announced the new division would be sent to southern Palestine for training after which it would join the British Expeditionary Force in France. The force was commanded by Lieutenant General Sir Thomas Blamey (later Field Marshal) who had served as a regular soldier at Gallipoli and was later Chief of Staff to the commander of the Australian Corps in France, Lieutenant General Sir John Monash. Monash described Blamey as having "a mind cultured above the average, widely informed, alert and prehensile". He was ably equipped to cope with the problems of a commander of an expeditionary force.

The 6th Division had three brigades (the 16th, 17th and 18th). The 16th Brigade had four battalions recruited from New South Wales, the 2/1st, 2/2nd, 2/3rd and 2/4th. The battalions of the 17th Brigade were raised in Victoria and consisted of the 2/5th, 2/6th, 2/7th and 2/8th battalions, while the 18th Brigade consisted of the 2/9th and two companies of the 2/12th recruited in Queensland, the 2/10th recruited in South Australia, the 2/11th in Western Australia and the remainder of the 2/12th in Tasmania. Artillery, mechanised reconnaissance and other arms were recruited from among the States. The division left Australia for the Middle East in January 1940.

The Australian Government also offered to the British an Australian "air expeditionary force" of six operational squadrons for overseas service. However, this plan was superseded when Britain began organising the Empire Air Training Scheme, the greatest cooperative air training plan of its kind in history. A massive rearmament effort by Germany had resulted in the build-up of predominant strength in aerial weapons and many military strategists believed that mastery of the air could well be the key to victory. To provide the air crew necessary Britain and the Dominions agreed to train a total of 50,000 each year – 22,000 from Britain, 13,000 from Canada, 11,000 from Australia and 3,300 from New Zealand. Under this scheme Royal Australian Air Force strength would increase by 11 times.

When RAN mobilisation was completed personnel strength was 10,250. The strength in warships was only slightly greater than that of 1914. It included two heavy cruisers (*Australia* and *Canberra*) four light cruisers (*Perth*, *Hobart*, *Sydney* and *Adelaide*) and five old destroyers (*Stuart*, *Waterhen*, *Vampire*, *Vendetta* and *Voyager*) as well as two sloops. Eight small vessels were requisitioned as minesweepers while the liners *Moreton Bay*, *Arawa* and *Kanimbla* were converted to armed merchant cruisers as units of the Royal Navy. Two others, *Manoora* and *Westralia*, were commissioned into the RAN.

All commissioned Australian naval ships were placed at the disposal of the Admiralty which asked for an RAN cruiser and five RAN destroyers to be made available for service beyond the Australian station. The five destroyers were sent to the Mediterranean.

Nothing could have saved Poland. Crushed between the German blitz and the Russian Bear, the Polish nation crumbled. Polish territory was partitioned between the Germans and the Soviets, and Poland ceased to exist as an independent nation. The Polish people went down to total defeat with many of their 60,000 dead having ridden horses into battle against tanks, artillery and dive bombers.

The destruction of Poland in this grossly unequal contest was followed in Europe by a "phoney" war period which ended abruptly on 9 April 1940 when the German blitzkrieg, so successful against Poland, thrust northwards to overrun Denmark and Norway.

One month later on 10 May a crucial battle began, this time involving the British and French armies, for the Germans reversed direction and invaded Belgium, Holland and Luxemburg. Having crushed all before them, they thrust into northern France, easily brushing aside the defending armies. Disaster was piled on disaster as the Allied defences crumbled. Fighting ceased in Holland on 15th May. Belgium surrendered on the 28th May and by the end of May the British Expeditionary Force and French troops isolated at Dunkirk by the lightning German advance had begun to embark for England. They only escaped because of the heroic efforts of the Royal Navy, an armada of small civilian craft and an aerial umbrella provided by the RAF.

Belatedly on 10 June the Italians declared war on the Allies and on 14 June the Germans entered Paris to parade in triumph up the Champs Elysées. On 22 June the vanquished French surrendered, accepting "merciless" terms imposed by Hitler.

In less than two months military disasters of unparalleled magnitude had overtaken the Allies. Hitler had achieved his greatest military triumph. France had been humbled and forced out of the war and Italy had declared war. "Mussolini's motives," declared the *New York Times*, "are as clear as day. He wants to share in the spoils he believes will fall to Hitler."

Only the British Commonwealth, now weakened by heavy losses, stood between Hitler and world domination. It was at this point that Winston Churchill, then Prime Minister of Britain, emerged as an inspired war leader to rally his people as they braced themselves for an inevitable onslaught on their own land. It was not long in coming. Hitler at once ordered three air fleets of the Luftwaffe to knock out the RAF in four days and pave the way for an invasion of England.

The Battle of Britain followed as the RAF fighter pilots rose to claw the Luftwaffe from the skies. They won a victory as significant as Trafalgar.

"Never in the realm of human conflict was so much owed by so many to so few," declared Winston Churchill after the Luftwaffe was defeated in the first strategic air battle in history. Some of "the few" were Australians. Of 30 Australian fighter pilots in the RAF who took part in the epic battle, 10 were killed and another eight lost in Coastal Command when they attacked German invasion barges gathered in Belgian, Dutch and French ports for the invasion of England.

No 10 Squadron of the RAAF opened its account against the German submarines when on 1 July one of its Sunderland flying boats and HMS *Gladiolus* shared in the sinking of a U-boat off the Scilly Islands.

The war at sea had been drastically transformed by the fall of France. Britain was simply not strong enough at sea to guard her home waters against the threat of invasion, maintain a major fleet in the Mediterranean and hold itself ready to send a third fleet if need be to match the Imperial Japanese Navy. However, Churchill assured Australia and New Zealand that if Japan attempted to invade their countries on a large scale Britain would sacrifice every interest except the defence of the British home islands to come to their aid.

The Mediterranean at once became an active war theatre. The British Navy was faced with the painful necessity of preventing the French Navy falling into enemy hands. On 3 July the British fired on and severely weakened the French naval force at Oran in North Africa, sinking three warships and killing 1,200 French sailors. Another force which included HMAS *Australia* attacked and damaged the battleship *Richelieu* at Dakar.

The Italian fleet heavily outnumbered its British opponents in the Mediterranean. To meet the threat, naval reinforcements were rushed to the Mediterranean including HMAS *Sydney* (Captain J. A. Collins), HMAS *Hobart* was sent to the Red Sea. *Sydney* and the destroyer *Stuart* were part of the British Mediterranean Fleet commanded by Admiral Sir Andrew Cunningham, which put to sea from Alexandria on 10 June immediately after the Italian declaration of war.

On 9 July Cunningham's fleet, which included four Australian warships (*Sydney, Stuart, Vampire* and *Voyager*), closed with the Italian fleet in the central Mediterranean. After an exchange of fire the Italian fleet withdrew towards Taranto and Cunningham followed to within 40 kilometres of the Calabrian coast. Cunningham's ships scored hits damaging the Italians and established moral ascendancy in this action known as the battle of Calabria.

Sydney after a refit was at sea again on 19 July and fought a brilliant action off Cape Spada, Crete. She was in company with a division of British destroyers on anti-submarine patrol when she encountered two Italian cruisers, the *Bartolomeo Colleoni* and the *Giovanni delle Bande Nere* and immediately raced towards them at full speed.

The Italian cruisers turned away, but *Sydney*'s accurate gunfire put the *Bartolomeo Colleoni* out of action. Collins ordered the destroyers to finish her off while he pursued the *Bande Nere* which escaped, however. Meanwhile the *Colleoni*, stationary in the water, was torpedoed by the destroyers which rescued 545 of her complement, including her commander, Captain Navarro, who however died later in a hospital ship at Alexandria. Sydney sailed into Alexandria harbour to the cheers of the Mediterranean fleet. Mussolini, the Italian dictator, was reported (in Count Ciano's diary) to have been depressed at the news because he felt the Italian sailors "did not fight very brilliantly".

The consequences of the fall of France were not lost on the ambitious Japanese who were suddenly presented with unexampled opportunities in the colonial territories of the defeated European nations, and were determined not to miss the boat. French Indochina, the Netherlands East Indies and Malaya were vulnerable, and possessed enormous resources including oil and minerals so vital to the Japanese war machine.

Nor were the consequences of the European débâcle lost on the United States, which moved to assist Britain by handing over 50 aging destroyers of the United States Navy and embarking on a huge naval building program which would outstrip the Japanese Navy.

In Australia the mood of the people had been transformed by the defeat and Britain's desperate situation. Australia's vulnerability had a profoundly disturbing effect. Men crowded the recruiting offices in unprecedented numbers and the Australian War Cabinet declared there must now be "an all-in war effort". The decision was made to send three RAAF squadrons – Nos 1, 8 and 21 – to Malaya to relieve British squadrons there for service elsewhere. Fears that the French colony of New Caledonia might fall into pro-Japanese hands prompted the Australian Government to despatch HMAS *Adelaide* to Noumea to help install Henri Surtot, a pro-Free French supporter, as governor.

During the final struggle in France a convoy of Australian troops including the 18th Infantry Brigade had been diverted to England. In April 1940 another Australian division, the 7th, was formed, A third, the 8th, was constituted after the fall of France. The 7th Division was sent to join with the 6th Division to form the 1st Australian Corps commanded by General Blamey. The RAAF also despatched one of its regular squadrons, No 3, to provide air support for the Australian army forces.

Tragedy struck on 13 August 1940 when four Australian war leaders were killed in the crash of a RAAF bomber within sight of Parliament House in Canberra. Three members of the Federal Government: the Minister for the Army (Brigadier G. A. Street); the Minister for Air (Mr J. Fairbairn); and the Vice-President of the Executive Council, Sir Henry Gullett, were killed. The Chief of the General Staff, General Sir Brudenell White, was also killed.

War in the Pacific moved closer on 23 September 1940 when Japanese army, navy and air force units occupied bases in northern French Indochina.

Four days later, Germany, Italy and Japan signed a 10-year tripartite pact. Under its terms Hitler and Mussolini committed themselves to backing Japan's efforts to bring about a "new order" in Asia, while Japan was to support Axis ambitions in Europe. The Japanese military greeted the news with great enthusiasm because it cleared the way for Japan to conquer South-East Asia.

Mussolini thought of the Mediterranean as *mare nostrum* ("our sea") and dreamed of rekindling the glories of Imperial Rome with the Mediterranean as an Italian lake. If he could seize the strategic Suez Canal from the apparently weak and effete British he could dominate the Mediterranean and begin to realise some of his grandiose plans.

So Mussolini ordered General Annibale ("Electric Whiskers") Bergonzoli and his 10th Italian Army totalling 250,000 men to advance from the Italian colony of Libya into neighbouring Egypt. The Italian push began on 12 September 1940 and by December Bergonzoli had no less than eight army divisions in position between Sidi Barrani in Egypt and Bardia, an Italian fortress just west of the frontier.

Meanwhile Mussolini's army had attacked Greece through Albania and suffered a humiliating defeat. It was the first land defeat suffered by the Axis forces in the Second World War. This was followed by a crippling blow on the Italian fleet at Taranto delivered by aircraft of the Royal Navy Fleet Air Arm. Three Italian battleships were sunk.

Waiting for Bergonzoli's army in Egypt was General Sir Archibald Wavell, the British Commander-in-Chief, Middle East. He had four divisions – the 7th Armoured, 1st Cavalry, 4th Indian and 6th Australian.

Instead of pushing ahead towards Suez, the reluctant Italians dallied at Sidi Barrani. Wavell decided to wait no longer and attacked the Italians on 9 December. The result was a spectacular and decisive victory: the British Western Desert Force destroyed four Italian divisions, taking 38,000 prisoners.

The 6th Australian Division had not been committed at Sidi Barrani. But General Iven Mackay, the division's commander was now ordered to take the fortress of Bardia. Much was at stake because it would be the first Australian land battle of the Second World War.

Australia's First Land Victory

Six battalions of the 16th and 17th Australian Brigades were to carry out the assault on Bardia, supported by all available artillery and the 7th Royal Tank Regiment. The RAF (and with it the RAAF's No 3 Squadron) was to provide air support and keep the Italian Air Force from interfering. The Mediterranean fleet with Australian warships under command was to carry out pre-assault bombardments against shore targets within the Bardia fortress.

Before dawn on 3 January 1941, the Australians moved to the start line and at 5.30 am the leading companies advanced, singing and shouting. Engineers exploded Bangalore torpedoes beneath the barbed wire defences and the infantry raced through the gaps and quickly captured Italian posts from the rear. By midday endless columns of Italian prisoners were streaming to the rear of the Australian positions.

So large were the columns of dejected prisoners that it was obvious the strength of the garrison had been greatly underestimated. It was learned later there were 45,000 Italians in Bardia.

It was not all a pushover. Some Italian pockets fought with great tenacity. One company of the 2/6th Battalion was ordered to launch a diversionary attack on Italian posts facing across the Wadi Mautered. After the fight was over only two Australian soldiers remained alive and unwounded. The 6th Division lost a total of 130 killed or died of wounds.

But in taking Bardia the Australians forced the surrender of 40,000 Italian soldiers. Bardia was not the long, drawn-out agony of Gallipoli, but in their first World War Two battle the Australians had won a great victory.

The Victories of Sidi Barrani and Bardia gave a tremendous boost to the morale of the British Commonwealth, which at that time, with the odds stacked heavily against it, was fighting desperately for survival against the Axis. The prospects seemed distinctly bleak.

The lightning British-Australian advance from Egypt had badly rattled the Italian Army. Wavell, aware of the supreme need to maintain the momentum of his highly successful advance, ordered the 6th Australian Division which had now been joined by the Australian 19th Brigade (2/4th, 2/8th and 2/11th battalions) to assault Tobruk, a strategically valuable harbour west of Bardia.

British successes in the Middle East had alarmed Hitler, who believed they might press on as far as Tripoli in the central Mediterranean. He ordered a force to be known as the Afrika Korps to be sent to Libya to put backbone into the crumbling Italian forces.

In the meantime London had directed Wavell that all possible support must be given to Greece, which was now threatened by the advance of powerful German forces through Bulgaria.

The withdrawal of substantial formations including the Australian 6th Division from his command to Greece would leave Wavell's forces in Egypt at risk. He therefore decided that after the capture of Tobruk he would advance to Benghazi, possession of which would secure the western flank of Egypt.

By 8 January 1941 the 6th Division and the 7th Armoured were on the outskirts of Tobruk. The RAF, with No 3 Squadron, RAAF, and the RN with Australian destroyers under command provided air and naval support before and during the assault on Tobruk which began on 21 January.

The Australian 2/3rd Battalion punched a hole through the wire and took five Italian posts. Other units advanced through this gap and fanned out. By the end of the day the Italian guns had almost stopped firing. An Australian officer advancing in a Bren gun carrier found 3000 Italians drawn up as if on parade ready to surrender.

Having no Australian flag available a soldier raised a Digger's slouch hat on the flagpole outside the Italian naval headquarters where an Italian admiral was waiting to surrender.

The 6th Division captured another 25,000 enemy troops, losing 49 killed or died of wounds. In total almost half the 250,000 Italian troops in North Africa when the fighting began had now been killed or captured.

It was clear after the fall of Tobruk that the Italian army and air forces were withdrawing as rapidly as possible from Cyrenaica and a race now developed with the Australian army advancing towards Barce and Benghazi and the British armoured column crossing the desert to the south. The British column arrived ahead of the Italians at Beda Fomm, some 128 kilometres south of Benghazi, capturing another 20,000 soldiers including General Bergonzoli. By 7 February elements of the

Australian 6th Division had entered Benghazi. (Giarabub, the last Italian stronghold in Cyrenaica, was captured by the Australians on 21 March.)

The plan to defend Greece from the coming German onslaught was a high-risk venture. Churchill had consulted with Australian Prime Minister (Menzies) on the use in Greece of the now veteran 6th Australian Division, and he had agreed. General Blamey regarded the enterprise as hazardous and unwise. It was another heroic gesture: Greece, the Commonwealth's one surviving ally, could not be left to face the Axis alone. As Churchill said, not to support Greece would have been fatal to the honour of the British Commonwealth.

By 3 April the 6th Division was in Greece and the 9th Division, commanded by Major General (later Lieutenant General Sir Leslie) Morshead had been given the task of garrisoning Cyrenaica. All told some 50,000 Allied troops were shipped to Greece without the loss of a man. Some Australians made the passage on the decks of HMAS *Perth*.

On 27–28 March the Italian fleet emerged from its harbours to carry out its first offensive operation of the war. The target was the shipping which was transporting Commonwealth troops to Greece. Admiral Cunningham had early warning of the Italian intention through the "Ultra" code-breaking organisation. He protected this information source by sending out a reconnaissance aircraft that was seen by the Italian fleet. The Australian warships *Perth* and *Stuart* were both actively engaged in the naval clash which took place off Cape Matapan. The outcome was a crushing victory for Cunningham whose warships sank three Italian cruisers and two destroyers. They also lost 2,400 sailors, while many more were rescued from the sea before German aircraft attacked the rescue efforts of British and Greek sailors. British losses were five aircraft.

In the last week of March, General Irwin Rommel's Afrika Korps, newly arrived from Europe, began its attack on the British forces in North Africa. The counter-offensive was under way. At Agedabia on 2 April Rommel's tanks destroyed most of the tanks of the British 2nd Armoured Division and soon his advance guard entered Benghazi. On 4 April, the 2/13 Battalion of the Australian 9th Division was the first

Australian unit to join battle with the Germans on the escarpment east of Benghazi. The Australians suffered 98 casualties and then withdrew towards Tobruk. In the confusion around Mechili, General Sir Richard O'Connor, commander of the Western Desert Force, was taken prisoner as well as part of the Australian 2/15th Battalion. Meanwhile reinforcements were rushed to Libya including the 18th Brigade of the Australian 7th Division. But Rommel was too strong and the British were pushed back out of Libyan territory, except for a garrison which remained besieged but full of fight in Tobruk.

Greece, Crete and Syria

For the conquest of southern Yugoslavia and Greece the Germans assembled an immensely strong army force of 15 divisions with powerful formations of Stukas and Messerschmitts in support.

Opposing the Germans was a force composed mainly of Australians and New Zealanders. The German attack began on 6 April and by that time only the New Zealand Division, the British 6th Armoured Brigade and two thirds of the 6th Australian Division had arrived. Most of the Greek Army was in Albania fighting the Italian army.

Salonika fell on 9 April and on 11 April the "Adolph Hitler" Division advancing in the Florina valley from Yugoslavia, attacked the Australian 19th Brigade which was spread thinly on the Olympus line. The Germans were beaten off, but they attacked again next day. After hard fighting against heavy odds, the Australians withdrew to the Aliakmon line further south. The Germans were far stronger than their opponents and because of the disastrous situation created by the Afrika Korps in North Africa where Tobruk, garrisoned largely by Australians, was now under siege, Wavell vetoed the sending of the 7th Australian Division to Greece.

By 14 April it was decided that all Greece north of the Peloponnese would be abandoned. The task of organising the withdrawal was assigned to General Blamey.

On 17 April, Yugoslavia capitulated and next day the Greek Prime

Minister, Koryzis, committed suicide. On 19 April Wavell flew to Athens to confer with Greek leaders and it was agreed that the British would leave Greece so as to avoid further devastation. The withdrawal was planned for the night of 24–25 April. Warships were to embark the troops from the beaches.

All day on 18 April the Australian 16th Brigade had been under heavy attack in the Pinios gorge north of Larissa, which was subjected to a crippling aerial bombardment that destroyed 30 British fighters and bombers. But by dawn on 19 April most units were south of Larissa, with an endless procession of trucks withdrawing towards the Brallos pass.

Fierce encounters took place on 24 April when the Germans attacked the Thermopylae line. New Zealanders and Australians of the 19th Brigade defending the line held their ground against the advancing Germans and then broke away to embark on the night of 25–26 April at Megara near Athens. On the night of the 26–27 April about 8,000 troops, including the Australian 16th and 17th Brigades, embarked from Kalamata to the south. Australian Navy warships *Perth*, *Stuart*, *Voyager*, *Waterhen*, *Vendetta* and *Vampire* took part in the evacuation.

The troops were evacuated to Egypt and Crete. Some 50,000 including the bulk of the combat units were embarked, of whom 500 were lost at sea when four transports and two destroyers were sunk by German aircraft.

The German Army marched into Athens on 26 April and next day the swastika was flying over the Acropolis.

Because of justified misgivings concerning the wisdom of ever sending an expedition to Greece, planning for an evacuation had begun even before the German attack. It was expertly planned by General Blamey and his staff. Australia had sent 17,125 soldiers to Greece of whom 320 were killed, 484 wounded and 2,030 taken prisoner.

The Airborne Invasion of Crete

Even before the victorious Germans entered Athens, they had decided to extend further their dominance of the eastern Mediterranean by seizing the strategically significant Greek island of Crete.

This German thrust would increase the threat to the oil resources of the Middle East and to the Suez Canal, already endangered by the apparently unstoppable advance of the Afrika Korps in North Africa.

The decoding of Enigma signals by British intelligence had already revealed the German intention to assault Crete and Lieutenant General Bernard Freyberg, commander of the 2nd New Zealand Division, was informed on 30 April that he was required to take command of all forces on the island and repel the expected assault.

Freyberg had just arrived from Greece as had thousands of British, New Zealand, Australian and Greek troops who were now hurriedly organised for the defence. Freyberg concentrated his defences around the port area of Suda Bay and the three airfields, Maleme, Retimo and Heraklion, all located along the northern coastal strip. The troops from Greece had been unable to bring their heavy weapons with them and in consequence would be gravely disadvantaged in the coming battle.

On 20 May the defenders of Crete heard the ominous roar of German Junkers air transports, heavily escorted by fighters, approaching the coast of Crete. As they reached their targets, the parachutists of the 7th Fleigerdivision spilled out of the air transports. To one of the defenders below they looked like "thousands of soap bubbles from a child's pipe". Many paratroopers, swaying in the wind as they floated down, were fired on and killed or wounded before they reached the ground. They landed at Maleme, Heraklion, Canea and at Retimo where the Australian 19th Brigade was waiting. Some 1,500 were dropped from transports east and west of Retimo airfield. Their slow-moving transports were easy targets and the Australians shot down seven which crashed in flames, killing all the paratroopers and crews in them. Many paratroopers who jumped clear of their transports were riddled with bullets before they reached the ground. One battalion lost 400 of its 600 men. In places it was impossible to walk a few metres without encountering clusters of German dead.

By midday on the 20th some paratroopers had been able to hold ground close to the Maleme airfield and by 21 May the New Zealanders under heavy pressure were forced to yield control of the airfield and German aircraft were landing in a steady stream. At Retimo in spite of their losses the Germans by evening had taken a vital hill overlooking the eastern end of the airfield.

It soon became apparent that Crete's defenders could not be given adequate air support and on 27 May Freyberg was told to abandon the island. A message was sent to the Australian commander at Retimo (Lieutenant Colonel Ian Campbell) to retreat, but it failed to reach him and he fought on until forced to surrender on 30 May.

The defenders at Heraklion, who included British, Australians and Greeks, killed more than a thousand German airborne troops. But on 28 May the order came to evacuate. They filed aboard cruisers and destroyers sent from Alexandria. Next day when the evacuation warships were at sea on their way to Egypt, they were set upon by 100 German dive bombers. Hundreds of the evacuees died in the air strikes, including 48 Australian anti-aircraft gunners.

The situation in other fighting areas had reached crisis point by 26 May. Freyberg informed Wavell that his position was hopeless and that night he ordered a withdrawal past Canea to a new line on Suda Bay. When the Germans followed and were nearing the new line the Australian 2/7th Battalion made a spirited charge, halting their advance. Freyberg then withdrew his force southwards over the mountain road from Suda Bay to the small village of Sfakia on the south coast. From Sfakia an evacuation began. Four cruisers including HMAS *Perth* and six destroyers including HMAS *Stuart* embarked 6000 men on the night of 29–30 May. The Australian destroyers *Napier* and *Nizam* embarked a further 1,500 on the night of 30–31 May.

Australian losses in the battle for Crete were grievous. Some 274 were killed, 507 wounded and 3,102 left behind and taken prisoner.

While the battle was lost, the resolute resistance of the garrison at Crete had inflicted heavy losses on the Germans. Some 4,000 of their most expert combat troops were killed and 200 aircraft destroyed. These losses persuaded Hitler never again to sanction such a form of attack.

In coping with the three-day battle and the evacuations, the Mediterranean fleet had been pushed to the limit of endurance. More than 2,000 sailors were killed and three cruisers and six destroyers sunk. "It was," said Admiral Cunningham, "a disastrous period in our naval history."

Syria and Lebanon

Crete was a severe reverse for Britain. To add to the now precarious military situation in the eastern Mediterranean, the Germans appeared to be poised to take over the French colony of Syria which was occupied by 45,000 Vichy French troops. Cyprus seemed also to be under threat of a German airborne invasion, though this was considered less likely in the light of the mauling taken by the German paratroopers in Crete.

Complete Axis domination of the Levant seemed likely and the British Government, urged on by General Charles de Gaulle, the Free French leader, decided on a pre-emptive invasion of Syria and Lebanon to counter it.

Already in May a steady stream of Axis aircraft were staging through Syria to support the Iraqi nationalists led by Rashid Ali. If he were to succeed and join the Axis, Allied oil supplies would be cut off. On 24 May, Commander W. H. Harrington, captain of HMAS *Yarra*, was involved in the fighting when he commanded a naval force in a combined action to disperse rebel forces on the right bank of the Shatt-el-Arab. On 31 May an armistice was signed and Britain was in control of the oil-rich country.

The Australian Army, Navy and Air Force were all committed to the Syrian campaign. Leading elements of the 7th Division's 21st Brigade crossed the boarder from Palestine at dawn on 8 June. In a difficult crossing of the Litani River the 2/16th Battalion suffered severe casualties but by 15 June the brigade occupied the coastal town of Sidon.

In a parallel advance further inland, the Australian 25th Brigade encountered determined Vichy French resistance at Merdjayoun where a counterattack forced a general withdrawal. However, by 24 June after further pressure the Vichy French withdrew.

Meanwhile on 21 June Damascus had surrendered to a Free French-Australian column after severe fighting during the advance which involved French, Australian, British and Indian troops. Some 200 Punjabis were killed in the Damascus suburb of Mezze.

On 4 July the Australians began an advance on Damour, the last major obstacle before Beirut, the principal objective of the campaign.

On 9 July Damour fell and Australian units were within five miles of Beirut. On that day the French commander accepted British armistice terms and a ceasefire became effective at midnight on 12 July.

Australian troops engaged in the Syrian campaign totalled 18,000. This compared with 9,000 British, 2,000 Indian and 5,000 Free French.

Australian casualties in the campaign totalled 1,600. Two Australians, Private James Gordon and Lieutenant A. R. Cutler (later Governor of NSW) were awarded the Victoria Cross for gallantry in action.

The RAAF No 3 Squadron which had just been re-equipped with Tomahawk fighters attacked the satellite airfield at Rayak on the first day of the Syrian campaign. The Tomahawks found no French aircraft in the air but strafed six Morane fighters on the ground. Six days later two pilots shot down two JU88 aircraft preparing to attack Allied shipping and on 28 June nine of the tomahawks attacked six Glen Martin bombers and shot them all down.

The RAN's *Perth*, *Stuart* and *Nizam* joined in spells of duty in support of the invasion, an effort the sorely tried crews found "a relaxation" after the strain of Greece and Crete. *Perth* destroyed enemy guns and an ammunition dump in a bombardment of the Damour area on 2 July.

The Siege of Tobruk

While Australians of the 6th Division fought desperate battles in Greece and Crete and the 7th Division won a notable victory in Syria, Australians of the 9th Division and the 18th Brigade of the 7th Division besieged in the Libyan port of Tobruk fought magnificently in a battle that became an epic of Australia's military heritage and won the highest praise throughout the Allied world.

The entry of Rommel's crack Afrika Korps into the Western Desert at a time when Britain was forced to withdraw troops to fight in Greece dramatically altered the war situation in North Africa. Major General Morshead, the commander of the 9th Division, had withdrawn his troops into the Tobruk perimeter by 9 April. Churchill, who dominated the strategic direction of the war, had ordered that Tobruk must be held as a bridgehead or strong point from which to hit the enemy. Wavell rushed reinforcements there, including the 18th Brigade.

Rommel's troops approached the perimeter on 10 April but were driven off by the 9th Division. Next day, however, (11 April) the Germans were astride the road from Tobruk to the east and the siege of the fortress had begun.

Rommel sent aircraft over the fortress to drop surrender leaflets which called on the Australians to fly white flags (white handkerchiefs would do!). Morshead countered by calling his brigade commanders together and telling them, "There'll be no Dunkirk here. If we have to get out, we shall fight our way out. There is to be no surrender and no retreat."[1]

Most of the Australian soldiers now manning the Tobruk defences had not yet been in action, but they were unafraid and eager for battle. Short of arms, they quickly brought into action captured Italian arms, including field guns, which they called "bush artillery".

On 13 April, enemy tanks and machine gunners appeared before the defences. They succeeded in penetrating the barbed wire and establishing a post in a section of the perimeter held by the 2/17th Battalion. This penetration called for resolute action and Lieutenant Austin Mackell at once decided they must not be allowed to stay. Taking Corporal J. H. Edmondson and five men with him he attacked vigorously, killing 12 Germans and putting the rest to flight at the point of the bayonet. Edmondson was superb, saving the lieutenant's life by bayoneting several of the enemy. Mortally wounded himself, he fought on until he could no longer stand. He was posthumously awarded Australia's first Victoria Cross of World War II.

Next day at dawn, 50 German tanks of the German 5th Light Division infiltrated the defences and made a charge towards the escarpment overlooking Tobruk harbour. While the defending artillery firing over open sights from dug-in positions engaged the tanks, the Australian infantry ignored the tanks and concentrated their attack with deadly effect on the German follow-up troops. German tank crews expected that the Australian infantry would surrender after the tank breakthrough. Instead the Australians fiercely attacked the infantry moving up behind them. By 8.30 am the battle was over with the Germans in full retreat, leaving 17 wrecked tanks, 150 dead and 250 prisoners. The garrison suffered 26 killed.

A German officer taken prisoner said: "I cannot understand you Australians. In Poland, France and Belgium once the tanks got through the soldiers took it for granted that they were beaten. But you are like demons. The tanks break through and your infantry still keeps fighting."[2]

In April, Rommel had occupied Bardia to the east of Tobruk and threatened to take Sollum. During the month his second armoured division (the 15th Panzer) joined him and he had three Italian divisions as well.

Warned by the set back encountered in mid-April Rommel now gave his undivided attention to crushing the "impudent" resistance in Tobruk. German propagandists likened the besieged Australians to "rats caught in a trap". But the Diggers quickly exploited the insult as a badge of courage by calling themselves from then on "The Rats of Tobruk".

After three weeks of aerial bombardment by the Luftwaffe which flew 677 sorties against the Tobruk harbour and anti-aircraft defences, Rommel assaulted the fortress again, this time at the high point, Ras El Medauuar, defended by the 26th Brigade. The attack began on 30 April when posts around hill 209 were shelled. After confused fighting through the night the Germans had taken seven perimeter posts and had 40 of their tanks positioned around hill 209. By 1 May they had captured 15 posts on a 4.6 kilometre front, but had suffered severe losses.

Rommel had by 3 May lost half his attacking tanks and he decided not to continue the assault. That night Morshead counter-attacked with his reserve brigade, the 18th, which came under heavy fire and captured only one perimeter post. In three days of fighting the Axis lost 950 men and the Tobruk garrison 800. In 18 days the 2/24th Battalion had captured 1,375 prisoners for the loss of 15 killed and 20 wounded.

For the first time in the war a determined German offensive had been defeated and Rommel did not again during 1941 make a serious attack on Tobruk.

After the battle Morshead received from Churchill the following signal:

> To General Morshead from Prime Minister England. The whole Empire is watching your steadfast and spirited defence of this important outpost of Egypt with gratitude and admiration.

On 15 May, Wavell mounted an offensive aimed at the relief of Tobruk, sending mobile columns of tanks and infantry from the Egyptian frontier. Halfaya Pass was captured but held only for a fortnight. Heavy fighting broke out in Tobruk when Morshead attacked in the Medauuar salient to divert the Germans from sending reinforcements away from the Tobruk area to the frontier. A month later Wavell, who had received tank reinforcements, attacked again from the Egyptian frontier but suffered disastrous tank losses. Because of this defeat, a sortie from Tobruk which was to take place at the same time as Wavell's offensive was cancelled. In August, Morshead attempted to dislodge Axis forces from the salient, but his attack (made by the 24th Brigade) failed.

By July General Blamey was pressing strongly for the relief of the Australian troops in Tobruk. He said medical evidence confirmed that the harsh conditions within the beleaguered fortress and the demands of combat since March had resulted in "a definite decline in the health and resistance of the troops in Tobruk." General Sir Claude Auchinlech who had succeeded Wavell as commander-in-chief agreed to the withdrawal of the 18th Brigade (of the 7th Division) but resisted relieving the 9th Division. Blamey had cabled Menzies who in a personal cablegram to Churchill supported Blamey. Churchill, however, asked for reconsideration, but the Australian Government insisted, and its decision to relieve the 9th Division was adhered to by John Curtin's Government, after he had become Prime Minister in October 1941. The relief was ordered and the 9th Division handed over to the British 70th Division. Only the 2/13th Battalion was still in Tobruk when the siege was raised. The battalion marched to the docks but the convoy which was to transport it from Tobruk was turned away on 25 October by German air attack.

In September 1941 the substantial build-up of modern weapons and equipment in the British Army in North Africa (now designated the 8th Army) portended a major battle. Considerable optimism as to the outcome was apparent. On the 18th November the British offensive, code-named Crusader, began with a thrust across the desert towards Tobruk. But once again the Germans soundly defeated the British armour, destroying 530 tanks. Fierce battles raged when the Tobruk garrison broke out of the perimeter to the east. The Australian 2/13th Battalion put to flight an enemy force when it charged through the enemy position with fixed bayonets.

On 10 December the siege of Tobruk ended a few days short of eight months since it began. Rommel concluded that he must abandon Tobruk because of the threat of the British thrust at El Gubi and on 7 December the Afrika Korps slipped away. He decided to stand next at Gazala but soon after retreated to Agedabia. The 2/13th battalion after a small but impressive parade left the fortress for Palestine on 16 December.

Praising the achievements of the Tobruk defenders, Auchinlech wrote:

> *Our freedom from embarrassment on the [Egyptian] frontier area for four and a half months is to be ascribed largely to the defenders of Tobruk. Behaving not as a hardly pressed garrison but as a spirited force ready at any moment to launch an attack, they contained an enemy force twice their strength. By keeping the enemy continually in a high state of tension they held back four Italian divisions and three German battalions from the frontier area from April until November.*

Between March and December 1941 the 9th Australian Division suffered the loss of 3,009 killed or wounded and 941 taken prisoner.

Lifeline from the Sea

The Rats of Tobruk had been perilously jammed into a narrow enclave between the blue Mediterranean at their backs and enemy guns to their front. Above they were menaced by the "Stuka parade". Yet throughout their ordeal they were never totally cut off. Courageous sailors of the Royal Navy and the Royal Australian Navy set up a tenuous lifeline of small warships and transports which, during the long siege, ran the gauntlet of shot and shell to bring them ammunition, food, fuel, and mail, as well as providing sea transport for relieving troops and the sick and wounded who had to be evacuated. Their story is an inspiring naval saga.

Losses in this vital Tobruk ferry run were heavy. Two RAN destroyers of the famous "scrap iron flotilla" were sunk. They were *Waterhen* and *Parramatta*. *Waterhen* went down off Salum on 28 June 1941 when attacked by dive bombers and crippled. She was the first Australian warship to be lost through enemy action in the Second World War. Fortunately no member of her crew was lost. *Parramatta*, however, suffered heavily. She was torpedoed by the submarine *U559* and rolled over and sank within a few minutes. Only 23 ratings of her total complement of 160 survived.

Other RAN ships engaged in the ferrying task were *Stuart, Vampire, Vendetta* (which alone made 39 runs into Tobruk), *Voyager, Nizam* and *Napier*. A laconic entry in the Chronicle of HMAS *Stuart*[3] recalls without heroics the hazardous experiences of the ferry task:

> *The following fits any or all of the runs. Morning of the first day, sailed from Alexandria for Tobruk with troops, ammunition and stores. Air attacks at so and so and so during the day. Arrived Tobruk in dark, unloaded and took on so many wounded, 200 troops and ammunition empties and proceeded to Mersa Matruh. Air raid at Mersa. Next day embarked ammunition and stores and sailed for Tobruk. Air attacks. Arrived Tobruk, unloaded, embarked wounded troops and empties. Tobruk continuously raided throughout stay. (During recent visits it has also been shelled at random by the enemy.)*

Air attacks on passage. Arrive Alexandria. And then 36 hours later, the same thing all over again.

As the year 1941 drew to a close Britain suffered grave naval losses in the Mediterranean. On 25 November the battleship *Barham* was torpedoed and blew up with the loss of 862 lives. On 19 December two more battleships, *Valiant* and *Queen Elizabeth*, sank at their moorings in Alexandria harbour after Italian "human torpedoes" had detonated explosives on their hulls. The Mediterranean fleet was further weakened in December when all Australian ships in the Mediterranean were withdrawn to meet the new enemy, Japan.

The RAN, too, was not spared. It suffered the greatest blow in its history when HMAS *Sydney* (the "lucky" ship) was lost off Carnarvon, Western Australia. Such are the fortunes of war that *Sydney*, which until 19 November 1941 had never lost a man in action (although attacked at least 60 times), disappeared on that day with not a single survivor from the crew of 645.

Sydney had returned to Australia in February 1941 to a warm welcome by her namesake city, including a triumphal march through the city streets. In November 1941, after escorting a troopship to Singapore, she was reported overdue. On 30 November the Government announced that she had been lost following an encounter with the disguised German commerce raider, *Kormoran*, which had attempted to pass herself off as an innocent Dutch merchantman. *Sydney* had approached *Kormoran* to within less than 1.8 kilometres. Suddenly *Kormoran* abandoned her disguise, struck her false colours and hoisted a German flag. The Germans simultaneously opened fire with everything they had and within seconds hit *Sydney*'s bridge and director tower. The apparently crippled *Sydney* fought back and the *Kormoran* eventually sank, losing 78 of her complement of 383. The *Sydney* sailed out of sight and was never seen again.

The RAAF War Effort

B ack from the Syrian campaign, No 3 Squadron, RAAF, joined the Desert Air Force in support of the 8th Army. During November 1941 No 3 was engaged in fierce air actions in which it lost nine aircraft. These reverses were avenged on 25 November when Wing Commander Peter Jeffrey, an Australian, led No 3 and the RAF's No 112 Squadron against 70 enemy aircraft over Sidi Rezegh near besieged Tobruk. In full view of wildly enthusiastic troops on the ground they destroyed 10 enemy aircraft for the loss of a single Tomahawk. No 3 claimed a further eight enemy destroyed and 12 damaged in a brisk fight a few days later.

During 1941 Australian graduates of the Empire Air Training Scheme began arriving in the Middle East and two Australian squadrons were formed. Other Australians were being posted to RAF squadrons. One of them was Clive "Killer" Caldwell of Sydney, destined to become the top scoring Australian fighter ace of the war. He had been posted to No 250 Squadron, RAF, and when flying with his squadron at El Gubi on 4 December shot down no fewer than five enemy bombers in a single engagement. After the action Caldwell reported:

> I received radio warning that a large enemy formation was approaching from the north-west. No 250 went into line astern behind me and as No 112 Squadron engaged the escorting enemy fighters we attacked the Jus [enemy bombers] from the rear quarter. At 300 yards I opened fire with all my guns at the leader of one of the rear sections of three, allowing too little deflection and hit No 2 and No 3, one of which burst into flames immediately, the other going down smoking ... I then attacked the leader of the rear section from below and behind, opening fire with all guns at very close range. The enemy aircraft turned over and dived steeply ... I opened up on another again at close range, the enemy caught fire and crashed in flames.

Caldwell had the unique distinction of being awarded the Distinguished Flying Cross and the Bar to that award simultaneously for outstanding bravery.

German submarines were wreaking havoc on Allied shipping and the RAAF's No 10 Sunderland Squadron continued to be engaged with Coastal Command RAF in combating this German menace.

On 9 August, No 452 Squadron, RAAF, flying Spitfire fighter aircraft from England with the Kenley Wing of the RAF, crossed the English Channel to take part in an offensive air operation over German-occupied France. Although new and inexperienced, the Australian pilots shot down five German Messerschmitt fighters for the loss of three Spitfires.

The Australian fighter pilots adapted so quickly to the fighter combat role that in the month of August they destroyed more German aircraft then any other squadron in Fighter Command.

It took time for the Empire Air Training Scheme to produce trained aircrews. However, in the period April-December 1941, a total of 3,000 Australian aircrew and another 1,500 ground staff arrived in England. Many were posted to nine Australian squadrons, including No 452, which were formed during the year. They were: Nos 452, 456, 457 fighter squadrons, Nos 455, 458 and 460 bomber squadrons, all formed in England, Nos 450 and 451 formed in the Middle East and No 453 formed in Singapore. In addition to those Australians who were posted to Australian squadrons, a substantial proportion of the Australian air crews were destined to serve as members of RAF squadrons.

Altogether, 17 Australian squadrons were formed and equipped with a wide variety of operational aircraft – including Hurricane, Spitfire, Buffalo, Blenheim, Baltimore, Hampden, Beaufighter, Defiant, Mosquito, Wellington, Hudson, Ventura, Halifax, Lancaster and Sunderland aircraft.

Most Australians served in the United Kingdom in RAF commands, but others operated in the Middle East, Malaya, the South-West Pacific and Burma.

The United States, Russia and Japan enter the War

The year 1941 though better than 1940 was still tough for the British Commonwealth. From a broader perspective it was perhaps the most momentous year of the war with indications of eventual victory beginning to appear.

During the year, three major powers, Russia, the United States and Japan, entered the conflict making the struggle into a war of global proportions involving the great majority of the world's population.

On 22 June 1941 Hitler had unleashed his Panzers and three million men of the Wehrmacht on an unsuspecting Soviet Russia in a campaign designated Operation Barbarossa, aimed at swiftly destroying the Soviets. Almost six months later on 7 December, Japan launched a war in the Pacific when a carrier-borne air attack caught the US Navy unaware and almost destroyed the US Pacific Fleet at Pearl Harbor, Hawaii. Simultaneously the Japanese attacked British territory in South-East Asia and the Philippine Islands. Japan's sudden but not unexpected aggression was followed by German and Italian declarations of war on the United States.

The Russian Army suffered enormous losses and fell back before the German onslaught. Stalin ordered scorched earth tactics. Britain and the United States at once offered help. The Japanese on the other hand called up a million conscripts and hastened preparations for war, not against Russia but against Britain and the United States.

It was vital to Russia's survival that Japan should not join with Germany to attack her, creating a two-front war. Richard Sorge, a brilliant Russian spy working under a journalistic cover from the German Embassy in Tokyo was able to inform the Russians, "The Soviet Far East may be considered guaranteed against Japanese attack." The Japanese militarists, he said, were certainly war-minded, but they were concentrating their combat forces for waging war on the United States, Singapore and Malaya, not Russia.[4]

Sorge's Soviet masters believed him and ordered the transfer of 18 to 20 Soviet divisions from the Far East to metropolitan Russia where they were needed to reinforce the mammoth struggle against the rampaging Germans.

The crisis in the Far East had worsened in late July when the Vichy French administration in Indochina yielded military bases in the south to the Japanese military. Japanese naval elements sailed into the excellent harbour of Camranh Bay. Combat aircraft and air transports flew into Saigon. Malaya, Singapore and the oil-rich Netherlands East Indies were now seriously threatened from French Indochina.

The United States and Britain, brushing aside any thought of appeasement, reacted strongly to the Japanese build-up, freezing Japanese assets and placing an embargo on the supply of oil and minerals to Japan. As a result the Japanese faced two choices to combat economic strangulation: yielding to US-British demands, or going to war. Angered by these economic measures the Japanese asked themselves whether they should abandon the dream of Imperial expansion, or use military force to achieve it. On 6 September at an Imperial conference it was decided to prepare for war while continuing to seek a diplomatic solution. War preparations on both sides intensified.

Australia had long felt vulnerable to a Japanese military threat. Singapore was the focus of British military power in South-East Asia and Australia relied heavily on the Singapore base as a bulwark against a hostile thrust towards Australia. Britain, forced to concentrate armed effort in Europe, was unable to send adequate forces to Singapore to combat the Japanese enemy. After a conference at Singapore in October 1940, the Australian Government had agreed to send the 22nd Brigade of the newly formed 8th Division to the island. In August 1941 a second brigade of the division, the 27th, arrived. Four RAAF combat Squadrons had joined RAF squadrons for the air defence of Malaya-Singapore.

Prime Minister Menzies believed the situation had taken an ominous turn and pressed Britain for a definite declaration calling for a halt to any further Japanese encroachment in South-East Asia.

By 3 November a plan was prepared by Admiral Isoroku Yamamoto, the Japanese Navy commander-in-chief, to carry out a surprise attack on Pearl Harbor to destroy the US Pacific Fleet in one blow. Yamamoto's plan was a massive gamble. He believed the outcome of the planned war must be decided on the first day. The attack plan was approved by the

Emperor and Imperial General Headquarters. On 26 November the Japanese Pearl Harbor task force assembled secretly at Tankan Bay in the Kuriles, and on 1 December the code signals for war were flashed out to the Japanese armed services. On 1 December, also a state of emergency, was declared in Malaya and all British, Indian and Australian forces were at battle stations. The Australian War Cabinet ordered the cancellation of Army leave and took emergency measures in the Pacific.

War Comes to the Pacific

Japan's devastating opening blows in the Second World War on 7 December 1941 were massive land, sea and air onslaughts on six widely separated points in the Pacific. They were Malaya, Pearl Harbor, Guam, Wake Island, Hong Kong and the Philippines.

The most devastating blow of all was the air strike delivered by the Japanese Navy's six aircraft carriers, *Akagi, Kaga, Hiryu, Soryu, Zuikaku* and *Shokaku*, which temporarily crippled the American Pacific Fleet at Pearl Harbor.

Death came plunging out of a clear sky at 7.55 am on a peaceful Sunday morning at Pearl Harbor when 184 Japanese carrier planes attacked, catching the Americans completely unawares and sinking four battleships tied up in "battleship row". A total of 19 American warships were sunk or disabled; 188 American military aircraft were destroyed and more than 2,400 people, 1,000 of them sailors in the sunken USS *Arizona*, lost their lives that day. Japanese losses were 29 carrier aircraft.

At the end of the first day of the Pacific War, the Japanese had achieved spectacular successes. They had disabled the US Pacific Fleet, decimated the American air forces in Hawaii and the Philippines and established bridgeheads in Malaya and Thailand.

President Roosevelt described 7 December as "a day that will live in infamy". On 8 December the US Congress declared war on Japan (with one pacifist member dissenting) and the British Cabinet unanimously supported a declaration of war on Japan after hearing a report from Churchill. In one sense the US involvement in the war was good news to Churchill, whose spontaneous comment was "so we have won after all".

Before the Japanese attacked Pearl Harbor, No 1 Squadron of the Royal Australian Air Force flew Hudson aircraft into action against a Japanese invasion force at Kota Bahru on the northeast coast of Malaya. The Japanese attack was launched two hours ahead of the Pearl Harbor attack, when they began shelling shore defences at Kota Bahru soon after midnight on 8 December.

No 1 Squadron bombed the invasion convoy, caused heavy casualties and sank the *Awagisan Maru*, a 9,700-tonne troopship, the first Japanese merchant ship to be sunk in the Pacific war. However, the success of No 1 Squadron was to be short-lived. Next day Japanese squadrons based in Thailand attacked the airfield at Kota Bahru, destroying most of the Australian Hudsons and forcing the squadron's withdrawal to Kuantan. Another Australian squadron, No 21, was attacked at Sungei Patani and seven of its Buffalo fighters were put out of action. Later in the day two Australian pilots were sent to Singora in Thailand but were attacked by 12 Zero fighters and were unable to complete their mission.

On 10 December Britain suffered one of her worst blows of the naval war when the capital ships *Prince of Wales* and *Repulse* were attacked and sunk by Japanese naval aircraft of the Japanese Navy's 22nd Air Flotilla then based at Saigon. The warships, accompanied by the Australian destroyer HMAS *Vampire* and other escorts, had sortied from Singapore into the South China Sea to seek out and destroy Japanese invasion convoys. No 453 Squadron, RAAF, was standing by at Sembawang to give fighter protection to the warships, but they were called to the scene too late. *Vampire* and HMS *Electra* rescued 796 survivors. Admiral Sir Tom Phillips and 839 officers and men lost their lives.

The loss of the two British capital ships together with the débâcle at Pearl Harbor had disastrous consequences for the Allies. The Japanese had won undisputed naval mastery of the western Pacific, exposing South-East Asia to invasion.

Meanwhile a three-pronged thrust into Malaya by Japan's 25th Army, commanded by General Tomoyuki Yamashita ("the Tiger of Malaya") was succeeding on all fronts as it pressed down the Malayan peninsula towards Singapore. By 19 December Penang Island was occupied by Yamashita whose army comprised the Imperial Guards and the 5th, 18th and 56 Divisions.

The Japanese had been spectacularly successful everywhere they attacked. The Government and people of Australia were alarmed at news of this distressing succession of military disasters to their north.

On 10 December, Guam was seized. On 22 December some 50,000 Japanese launched a major invasion of Luzon in the Philippines and were soon threatening Manila which the US General MacArthur declared an "open city", indicating that the US forces would not defend it. On 24 December, Wake Island in the central Pacific fell. On Christmas Day, Hong Kong surrendered after a 17-day siege and on the same day the Japanese landed at Kuching in British Borneo. In Malaya the Japanese were engaged in an "aerial extermination" campaign to give them almost complete mastery of the skies above the land battle.

Major General Gordon Bennett, commander of the 8th Australian Division, not yet committed to the battle, informed the Australian Government in mid-December that the military situation in Malaya was grave and urged that reinforcements be sent at once. Prime Minister Curtin warned Australians that they faced the gravest hour in their history. When advised of the meeting of Churchill, Roosevelt and their military advisers at the "Arcadia" conference in Washington, Curtin signalled them, asking them to consider the position in Malaya as of the greatest urgency. In reply Churchill assured Curtin he would do everything possible to strengthen the front from Rangoon to Darwin. He suggested that one Australian division be recalled from Palestine and sent either to India or Singapore.

At a meeting at the White House on Christmas Day it was agreed that a command known as ABDA (American, British, Dutch and Australian) would be created within the war zone. General Wavell reluctantly accepted the appointment of Supreme Commander , ABDA. Reflecting on the almost impossible task he had been saddled with, Wavell commented, "I have heard of men having to hold the baby, but this is twins."

On 3 January it was proposed that not one but two Australian divisions, the 6th and 7th, would be transferred for the purpose of reinforcing not Malaya but the Netherlands East Indies. On 5 January the Australian War Cabinet agreed.

Before the Pacific War began, the United States and Britain had agreed between them that in the event of being involved in war with both Germany and Japan the Allies would set out to beat Germany first and fight a holding war against Japan. This "beat Hitler first" strategy was confirmed in Washington, but not before a tussle between Churchill and some of the American service chiefs, notably Admiral Ernest King, who resisted the downgrading of the Pacific theatre. Curtin too opposed the strategy. He said with some passion, "We refuse to accept the dictum that the Pacific struggle must be treated as a subordinate segment of the general conflict."[5]

On 7 January the Japanese Army destroyed an Indian brigade and crippled a second in a crucial battle on the Slim river, the last natural barrier on the road to Kuala Lumpur, the Malayan capital. Five days later the Japanese 25th Division entered the city after its defenders were ordered to withdraw. Maintaining their momentum the Japanese divisions pressed southwards to Johore State, which is separated from Singapore Island only by the narrow Straits of Johore.

The Australian 8th Division was deployed in Johore and on 14 January was sent into action for the first time. Its 2/30th Battalion ambushed and slaughtered a large number of bicycle-riding Japanese soldiers at Gemas. After two days' fighting the battalion had lost 81 killed, wounded or missing compared with an estimated 1,000 enemy casualties. It withdrew in good order.

On 15 January, the partly trained 45th Indian Brigade under Bennett's command was attacked by the veteran Japanese Guards Division on the Maur river line, and were defeated. General Bennett sent two battalions of the 27th Australian Brigade to strengthen them and at Bakri, the 2/29th Battalion destroyed eight tanks while the 2/19th routed a Japanese force to their front. However, numerous Japanese forces cut the road behind them and they were forced to withdraw. For his courage and leadership during these actions Lieutenant Colonel C. G. W. Anderson, commanding officer of the 2/19th, earned the Victoria Cross. Lieutenant General Percival the

British Army commander wrote, "The award was a fitting tribute both to his own prowess and to the valour of his men."

A new threat developed on 25 January when a Japanese force landed from the sea at Endau on the east coast of Johore less than 100 miles from Singapore. Australian Buffalo and Hudson aircraft joined with the RAF to oppose the landing but were overwhelmed by a force of 50 enemy fighters.

A Japanese column on the east coast was ambushed at Jemalaung on 26 January by Australians of the 22nd Brigade. The Australians lost 89 killed or missing in this bitter fight but inflicted heavy casualties on the enemy.

Wavell had ordered Percival to prepare in secret for a withdrawal to Singapore and on 27 January, Percival concluded after the crushing defeat in Johore that he must fall back on Singapore at once. The withdrawal from Johore took four days and was successful. The Australian 22nd Brigade reinforced by Gordon Highlanders had covered the approaches to the Johore causeway and early on 31 January they were piped out of Johore by the only two surviving pipers of the Argyll and Sutherland Highlanders. The northern end of the causeway was then wrecked with demolition charges.

Victorious Japan

The Fall of Singapore

Singapore was now under siege. The triumphant Japanese, buoyed by a brilliant peninsula campaign, were poised to deliver the final blow on the proud "city of the lion".

Singapore's population had swollen to a million people by frightened refugees from the north. Churchill cabled Wavell ordering that "Singapore must be converted into a citadel and defended to the death", while Curtin warned Churchill that "evacuation of Singapore would be regarded here [in Australia] and elsewhere as an inexcusable betrayal."

Percival had 85,000 troops as against three divisions of Japanese.

Three squadrons of RAF Hurricanes arrived at the last moment to bolster the air defences. But by January, big formations of Japanese bombers were pounding Singapore's four airfields, forcing the withdrawal of all but a few fighter aircraft. Most British aircraft and Australian Hudson bombers were sent south to Sumatra. Thereafter Japanese aircraft dominated the skies and their long-range artillery maintained a constant barrage over the island from Johore. With no serviceable aircraft left the RAAF's No 21 Squadron was ordered back to Australia.

The Japanese were not long in coming. On 8 February after heavy artillery and air bombardments lasting several days, assault troops from Yamashita's 5th and 18th Divisions crossed the narrow straits in assault craft propelled by outboard motors and attacked the western side of the island defended by the Australian 22nd Brigade commanded by Brigadier H. B. Taylor. Although they inflicted heavy casualties the Australian forces were thin on the ground and were forced to pull back. The brigade received reinforcements but by 6 am next day Taylor considered the situation desperate. Next to come under attack was the Australian 27th Brigade when a third Japanese division, the Guards, also attacked in the western area, ignoring the northern area where the bulk of Percival's forces were deployed – these included the 3rd Indian Corps and the newly arrived British 18th Division. Thus the main weight of the Japanese attack fell on the Australians. Thrown off-balance by the speed of the Japanese attack and crumbling flanks, field commanders ordered premature withdrawals.

Late on 10 February Percival ordered Bennett to counterattack to regain the Krangi line. It was a hopeless mission by numerically weak forces against two Japanese divisions. Inevitably it failed, resulting in further losses and confusion. Widespread fighting continued on 11 February and on 12 February Japanese tanks advancing towards the city on the Bukit Timah road were turned back.

With the enemy enjoying control of the seas and of the skies over Singapore, Percival now withdrew his forces to a 25-mile (40-kilometre) arc around the city. A million civilians were in jeopardy and water supplies disrupted. Churchill was consulted on the "ugly" decision that had to be made. On 15 February Percival was given discretion to end resistance. Later that day he met Yamashita and at 8.30 pm fighting ceased.

The staggering defeat inflicted by the Japanese was Britain's blackest day, at the same time raising to new heights the "victory fever" which gripped the Japanese nation in the early months of the Pacific war, giving them the illusion of invincibility. It appeared nothing could stop the "rising sun". To celebrate it was decreed that every family in Japan was to receive two bottles of beer or sake.

Churchill described the loss of Singapore as "the greatest disaster and capitulation in British history". During the whole campaign the Japanese took some 130,000 prisoners and according to Japanese records their own losses were fewer than 10,000.

Australia suffered a grievous blow. Australian soldiers killed totalled 1,789 while 14,972 were taken prisoner to suffer brutal and degrading forms of captivity which, before the war ended, were to result in the deaths of one-third of their number. General Bennett was not one of the prisoners. He decided to escape and eventually reached Australia. His action caused bitter controversy and after the war an Australian Army court of inquiry found that he should have remained with his troops. A Royal Commission later reached a similar conclusion.

Some Japanese troops displayed a merciless brutality towards captured Allied forces, including women. On 12 February three days before Singapore fell, the *Vyner Brook,* a British steamship, left Singapore and two days later was bombed and sank off Banka Island south of Singapore. On board were 64 Australian army nurses of whom 22 managed to reach land in a lifeboat. Japanese soldiers appeared and after bayoneting the men in the party they ordered the 22 nurses to wade into the sea. When they were knee-deep the soldiers machine gunned them, killing all but Sister Vivian Bullwinkel who was wounded but survived the war.

Japan's strategic plan in the war was to establish "the South-East Asia Co-prosperity sphere' by seizing the colonial possessions in the region of France (Indochina), Britain, the United States and Holland. The key Malaya-Singapore area had been conquered by 15 February, 100 days ahead of the Japanese military timetable. Well before that the Japanese had embarked on the conquest of the Netherlands East Indies and the Philippines as well as the Australian administered territories of New Britain, New Ireland and New Guinea. Preceded by a declaration of war on Holland the Japanese seized the oil-rich island of Tarakan on 11 January and this was followed by Balikpapan (23 January), Kendari in the Celebes (24 January) and Ambon (31 January).

On 23 January, for the first time in history an enemy conquered Australian territory when the Japanese seized Rabaul in New Britain. The Japanese military gave priority to the capture of Rabaul not for its resources but because it was vital to their strategy of establishing air bases and naval facilities to protect from counterattack the rich resource empire which they were rapidly acquiring.

The Imperial Japanese Navy committed Admiral Chuichi Nagumo's carrier strike force which had attacked Pearl Harbor to the naval-air campaign supporting the conquest of the Netherlands East Indies. But Nagumo's first mission would be to crush the defences of Rabaul and Kavieng, and he did just that. The Japanese launched the first air attack against the flimsy defences of Rabaul on 20 January, using 109 aircraft from *Akagi* ("Red castle"), *Kaga* ("Increased Joy") *Zuikaku* ("Happy Crane") and *Shokaku* ("Soaring Crane"), all veterans of the Pearl Harbor attack. They bombed and strafed the airfields, coastal batteries and oil tankers. This overwhelming strike force was courageously opposed by the RAAF when five obsolescent Wirraway fighters of No 24 Squadron left the ground to engage them and with two others which had been sent aloft earlier were quickly shot out of the sky. That brief but heroic engagement added a page of glory to the history of Australian arms.

The RAAF commander at Rabaul, Wing Commander John Lerew, appealed for air reinforcements. The reply was, "Regret inability to supply fighters." Nevertheless he was ordered to attack the heavily escorted convoy bringing the 5,000-strong "South Seas force" which was to capture Rabaul. Lerew was then directed to evacuate all his aircrew and assist the army. Lerew's last signal from Rabaul was couched in unfamiliar Latin *Nos morituri te salutamus* – the Roman gladiator's salutation, "We who are about to die salute you."

On 21 January aircraft from *Kaga* and *Akagi* raided Kavieng while *Zuikaku* and *Shokaku* aircraft attacked airfields at Lae, Salamaua, Bulolo and Madang in New Guinea to prevent any airborne attack on Rabaul from these bases during the invasion.

The Australian garrison at Rabaul commanded by Colonel J. J. Scanlan included the Australian 2/22nd Battalion supported by two coastal guns and two anti-aircraft guns. The Japanese force was massive. In addition to the aircraft carriers they had two battleships and many cruisers and destroyers to support the 5,000-strong South Seas Force which began landing at 2 am on 23 January. Pressed by the overwhelming numbers and fire power the Australians were soon forced to withdraw. Some Australians surrendered and of these 150 were later brutally murdered at Tol and Waitavalo plantations on the southern coast of New Britain, Small craft from New Guinea later rescued 400 survivors.

Kavieng, defended by the Australian 1st Independent Company, was invaded at dawn on 23 January and the defenders were forced to withdraw after blowing up dumps and cratering the airfield runway.

Next on the Japanese invasion schedule was Ambon which was garrisoned by 2,600 members of the Netherlands Indies Army. On 17 December the Australian 2/21st Battalion known as "Gull Force" had arrived to strengthen its defence and the RAAF established its No 13 Squadron, equipped with Hudson aircraft, on the island.

The Japanese regarded Ambon as an air threat to Kendari in the Celebes and on 24 January sent more than 50 aircraft from the carriers *Hiryu* ("Flying Dragon") and *Soryu* ("Green Dragon") to attack the island. The RAAF Hudsons at Ambon were heavily engaged in air operations and after losing 17 aircraft in combat or on the ground were ordered to return to Australia. Japanese troops landed on the night of 30-31 January just after the Hudsons had left for the Northern Territory. Gull Force put up a stiff resistance but it was of no avail and by 3 February the survivors surrendered. A tough battle was fought by two companies at Laha airfield but against a concentrated attack by troops, dive bombers, fighter planes and artillery they were forced to give ground. Some 309 Australians died either in action or in mass executions by the Japanese a few days later.

Darwin Devastated

An Australian Army force known as "Sparrowforce" had joined in the defence of Timor by agreement with the Dutch authorities. It comprised the 2/40th Battalion and the 2/2nd Independent Company as well as No 2 Squadron, RAAF, equipped with Hudson aircraft, which was sent to operate from Penfui airfield near Koepang. As the Japanese danger grew, a convoy carrying American and Australian troops was despatched from Darwin to reinforce Timor. However, this convoy was attacked by Japanese aircraft before reaching Timor and General Wavell ordered its return to Darwin where it arrived on 18 February. The Australian sloops *Warrego* and *Swan* were part of the convoy escort.

On the following day Bali and Lombok were occupied by the Japanese. Java, the main prize, was now isolated.

Mainland Australia came under direct attack on the 19th February when the Japanese Navy's 1st Carrier Fleet commanded by Admiral Chuichi Nagumo, using four of the aircraft carriers which had attacked Pearl Harbor, now mounted a massive air raid on Darwin, using 188 carrier planes. Another 54 land-based aircraft from Kendari in the Celebes and Ambon joined in the attack later the same day. The Japanese were now fully into the campaign to conquer Java and saw Darwin as a potential threat to the campaign, since Darwin was the only remaining base from which fighter aircraft could be ferried to Java and it was being used as a staging area for ABDA forces reinforcing Java. The Japanese feared that Australia would become a rallying point for counter-offensives and decided that a disruptive air attack would hinder such activity and deal a sharp blow to Australian morale.

The Japanese carriers and their escorts had sortied into the Timor Sea some 352 kilometres northeast of Darwin. At dawn the carriers swung into the wind and the aircraft were launched. Darwin, taken by surprise, had one minute's warning before the Japanese bombers flying in impeccable formation appeared overhead at 4,307 metres and pattern-bombed Darwin harbour. Five American Kittyhawk fighters were on patrol over Darwin. Four were shot down. Others were destroyed attempting to take off. The Japanese admitted the loss of two aircraft.

The Darwin raid was planned and led by the brilliant air tactician Commander Mitsuo Fuchida, who had led the attack on Pearl Harbor ten weeks earlier.

The Japanese achieved their aim of temporarily wrecking Darwin's war potential, at the same time killing 243 people, most of whom were servicemen. The harbour had been crowded with shipping, a prime target for the enemy bombers: a total of 11 Australian, British and American ships were sunk. In the air and on the ground the raiders destroyed 23 aircraft. The raid caused chaos and panic, especially when the two raids were taken by many to mean that Australia's turn to be invaded by Japan had come. In what became known as the "Adelaide River Stakes", hundreds fled south on any kind of vehicle available.

Timor, the Dutch-Portuguese island, was next to be invaded. On the night of 19–20 February, after a naval bombardment of Dili in Portuguese Timor, the Japanese landed and clashed with Australians of the Independent Company (so called because it operated alone as a guerilla force) who inflicted severe casualties at the airfield. Next day Japanese troops including paratroopers landed near Koepang and after three days of confused fighting the Japanese had almost surrounded the Australian force which surrendered. The Australians lost 84 killed and were without food or water. Some 250 escaped and eventually rejoined the Independent Company.

Java Falls

The wave of Japanese conquests rolled on. Without waiting for Singapore to capitulate in February, fresh Japanese forces had swept to the south and seized Palembang, Sumatra, an oil industry centre. It was captured on the day Singapore fell. RAAF Hudsons based near Palembang bombed up and attacked the enemy convoy, scoring hits on Japanese invasion transports. However, bomb supplies gave out and the Hudsons were withdrawn to Java, where they were to fight on until on 4 March they were ordered to fly out to Australia.

Some elements of the 1st Australian Corps (6th and 7th Divisions) had arrived from the Middle East at Oosthaven, Sumatra, and were then diverted to Java where they disembarked on 18 February. On the day

Singapore fell, Curtin had cabled Churchill urging that the corps and the 9th Division should all be returned to Australia. Their return would greatly increase the security of Australia. But Rangoon in Burma was now under threat by the Japanese 15th Army. Both Churchill and Roosevelt had put pressure on Curtin to divert the Australian 7th Division to Burma "to make certain that the Burma road will be kept open and thereby China in the fight". But Curtin refused and the Corps were ordered home, except the advance element which had already disembarked in Java. They would soon be in action against Japanese invaders.

By mid-February the Japanese campaign to conquer Java was rising to a climax. A massive assault was planned: three landings were to be made on the western end of Java tasked with capturing Batavia, the capital. The convoy carrying this invasion force left Camranh Bay, French Indochina, on 19 February. A second invasion force to capture Surabaya on the eastern end of Java sailed from Balikpapan on 23 February. It included the 48th Division which had been fighting in the Philippines.

After the fall of Singapore it was Wavell's advice that further efforts to reinforce Java should not be made if they compromised the security of Burma and Australia. On 25 February, Wavell's ABDA command was dissolved and the Dutch took over. On the same day a large enemy convoy was sighted 320 kilometres north-east of Surabaya and all available warships, including HMAS *Perth*, were sent to reinforce Rear-Admiral Karel Doorman at Surabaya.

On 27 February, Doorman put to sea with his Western Striking Force of American, Dutch and British warships as well as HMAS *Perth*. His orders were to destroy the Japanese invasion convoy. The Battle of the Java Sea began at 4.16 pm when the heavy cruisers on both sides opened fire at a range of 25.6 kilometres. The Dutch destroyer *Kortenaer,* hit by a torpedo, blew up and sank. At 7.33 pm *Perth* and *Houston* opened fire and by 9.25 pm Doorman had lost two more destroyers. This was followed at 11 pm by the loss of the two Dutch cruisers, *De Ruyter* (flagship) and *Java*. Doorman went down with his flagship.

To remain in the battle would have been suicide and Captain Hector Waller of HMAS *Perth* took USS *Houston* under command and proceeded west to Tanjong Priok. With orders to try and reach Colombo the damaged *Exeter* in company with *Encounter* and USS *Pope* sortied on 28 February but were spotted by Japanese aircraft as they left Surabaya and sunk by the Japanese force.

Meanwhile, HMAS *Hobart,* in company with two British destroyers, searched on 27 February for the approaching western invading force, but sighted no enemy and in accordance with instructions proceeded through Sunda Strait. After picking up refugees in Padang, Sumatra, she continued on to Ceylon.

At 1.30 pm on 28 February, *Perth* and *Houston* reached Tanjong Priok where they refuelled and sailed again at 7 pm for Tjilatjap on the southern coast of Java. Unknown to Waller, the enemy escorting the western invasion force was in strength across their path. Three Japanese cruisers and nine destroyers converged on them, firing rapidly and launching torpedoes. About 11.05 pm Japanese torpedoes struck both *Houston* and *Perth* and some also hit the Japanese troop transports. *Perth* took four torpedoes and just after midnight on 1 March she heeled over to port and sank. *Houston,* on fire and hit by torpedoes, sank shortly afterwards.

Perth's complement totalled 681. Of these, 353, including Captain Waller, were lost. Of 324 who fell into Japanese hands, 106 died.

Captain Hector Waller was a great naval leader and his loss was a severe blow to the RAN. Admiral Sir Andrew Cunningham paid this tribute to him:

> *Hector Macdonald Laws Waller will always remain in my mind as one of the very finest types of Australian naval officer. Full of good cheer, with a great sense of humour, undefeated and always burning to get at the enemy, he kept the old ships of his flotilla – The Stuart, Vampire, Vendetta, Voyager, Waterhen – hard at it always. Greatly loved and admired by everyone, his loss on HMAS Perth in the Java Sea was a heavy deprivation for the young navy of Australia.*

The Japanese did not go unscathed. It appeared that Japanese torpedoes and gunfire were hitting their own transports, some of which were sunk and others damaged. General Hitoshi Imamura was directing landing operations when an explosion threw him into the sea. He survived to command later in Rabaul.

The final scene in the Allied military disaster of the Netherlands East Indies was now to be enacted. The British, Dutch, Australian and American soldiers in Java were doomed. There would be no reinforcements or counter-offensive to turn the tables. The Combined Chiefs of Staff had ordered that Java would be defended to the last by those combatant forces then on the island. Among them were 3,000 Australians organised into "Blackforce", which included the 2/3 Machine Gun Battalion and the 2/2nd Pioneers. The force was led by Brigadier A. S. Blackburn who as a young subaltern had won the Victoria Cross at Pozières.

The destruction of Allied naval forces in the Java Sea battle, the weakness of Allied air power and the blockade imposed by overwhelming Japanese naval dominance made the situation in Java grave. The Japanese Army was practically unopposed on the beaches and on 2 March "Blackforce" took up defensive positions 15 miles from Buitenzorg where they opened fire on Japanese attempting to cross the Tjianten river. On 5 March Blackburn was told that allied forces were falling back on Bandung. Blackburn held Buitenzorg for three days against a substantial part of the Japanese 2nd Division and suffered 100 casualties.

On 8 March the Netherlands East Indies Government accepted the inevitability of defeat and flew out of Java to Australia. The Allied Army commander, General J. Ter Poorten, then broadcast that resistance had ceased and that all Allied forces were to lay down their arms. Blackburn, influenced by the advice of his medical officers, decided against continuing resistance in the mountains and surrendered his force. Some 140 members of No 1 Squadron, RAAF, left behind in Java without aircraft, became prisoners of war.

But the suffering and loss of life did not end with surrender. The ruthless Japanese used their navy to trap and sink Allied shipping carrying the fugitives escaping from the ABDA area. On 5 March Nagumo's powerful 1st Carrier Fleet bombarded Tjilatjap where 17 ships were sunk in the harbour, although the Dutch claimed they themselves scuttled 16 of them.

Seven Australian corvettes escaped the enemy naval net to the south of Java and reached Fremantle safely on 10 March. Commander John Collins, who after the withdrawal of ABDA had stayed on to command British naval forces, boarded HMAS *Burnie* at Tjilatjap, reaching Fremantle on 8 March.

But on 4 March, the 1,060-ton sloop, HMAS *Yarra* encountered three Japanese heavy cruisers and two destroyers while escorting a small convoy to Australia. Lieutenant Commander Robert Rankin, her commander, at once signalled to his convoy to scatter and courageously took up station between the convoy and the enemy. He then ordered his gun crews to open fire with his 4-inch guns against the 8-inch guns of the cruisers *Atago*, *Takao* and *Maya*. The Japanese cruisers were untouched by the Australian gunfire but *Yarra* was quickly battered beyond recognition. Rankin ordered "abandon ship" just before an 8-inch salvo hit the bridge and killed him. *Yarra* and the entire convoy were destroyed.

Of *Yarra*'s complement of 151, a total of 138 went down with the ship or died later on rafts. The 13 survivors were picked up five days later by a Dutch submarine.

The ruthless Japanese used aircraft as well to pursue and kill refugees from Java, reaching as far as Broome in Western Australia, which was being used as an evacuation staging point. On 3 March they sent Zero fighters with long-range fuel tanks to attack flying boats and land aircraft at Broome. Some 24 Allied aircraft were destroyed and 70 people killed. These aircraft had carried refugees, including children, from Java. One Liberator, attempting to escape, took off from the airfield only to be shot down into the sea. Of the 33 people in this aircraft only one survived. As at Darwin the raid caused the impression among many townspeople that the Japanese were about invade Australia.

Meanwhile the Japanese were busily consolidating their gains north of Australia. Rabaul was developed and encircled with a protective ring of naval and air bases. In March they occupied Buka, Bougainville and the Shortland Islands in the Solomons. To the north Manus in the Admiralties was developed.

On 8 March, unhindered by the paper-thin defences, the Japanese occupied Lae, Salamau and Finschhafen in New Guinea, giving them control of the Huon peninsula and the entrance to the Bismarck Sea. However, these invaders were caught unawares two days later when 90 American carrier aircraft from *Enterprise* and *Yorktown* flew over the Owen Stanley Mountains from the direction of Port Moresby and attacked both Lae and Salamaua, sinking four transports and killing 130 men.

Defeat in Burma

In early 1942 the Allied forces in southern Burma failed to stem the advance of the Japanese towards Rangoon. However, the Japanese Army Air Force did not fare so well. It mounted a heavy air attack on 23 December but paid a heavy price, losing 27 planes to six of the defenders.

Australia was represented in the Burma campaign by many graduates of the Empire Air Training Scheme who served in RAF squadrons rushed to Burma-India to reinforce Allied forces. Australians in Blenheim bombers were sent off to bomb the docks at Bangkok in Thailand within hours of arriving. As the enemy pressed towards Rangoon the enemy air force was again badly mauled when it lost 37 aircraft in an effort to wrest air supremacy from the RAF and the American Volunteer Group.

Moulmein fell to the Japanese on 31 January and Rangoon on 8 March. Japanese army successes in Burma threatened the security of the Indian subcontinent and some strategists speculated on the possibility of a link-up in India between the armed forces of Japan and Nazi Germany.

The Japanese Carrier Fleet Attacks Ceylon

Loss of Royal Navy control of the Indian Ocean would be disastrous for Britain and Australia. The unthinkable appeared to threaten on 3 April when Nagumo's Carrier Strike Force penetrated the Indian Ocean en route to a Pearl Harbor-style air assault on Ceylon. Nagumo had five of the six carriers which had attacked Pearl Harbor: the sixth, *Kaga*, had to return to base with engine trouble.

Nagumo's aim was to drive the British Eastern Fleet out of the eastern Indian Ocean, thus protecting the Japanese defensive perimeter from Burma to Singapore. Emphasising their naval dominance at the time a second Japanese naval force, Admiral Ozawa's Second Expeditionary Fleet, sortied from Mergui, Burma, and patrolled for 320 kilometres south from Calcutta, sinking ships and causing a panic when they bombed Vizagapatam. The Japanese felt that these moves, together with the impending loss of Burma, might induce a general panic in India.

Australians were well represented in the RAF squadrons defending Ceylon and two brigades of the 6th Division were also available in Ceylon for its defence.

Intelligence reports had warned the British of Japanese intentions. The Eastern Fleet sailed on 4 April to attack Nagumo but failed to make contact. Next day Nagumo launched 85 aircraft to attack Colombo. Their approach was picked up by radar and they were engaged by Hurricane fighter squadrons in which a substantial number of Australians were serving. The Hurricanes shot down 19 Japanese aircraft for the loss of 15 Hurricanes.

Nagumo struck again on 9 April at the port of Trincomalee. Again Australian airmen were in the thick of the battle when an RAF Hurricane squadron intercepted. On this day, nine members of the RAAF serving with No 11 Blenheim Squadron were killed when the Blenheims were sent on an almost suicidal strike on the carrier fleet.

Steeling themselves to face the extreme danger the Blenheim crews made their bombing runs while every ship in the Japanese carrier force opened fire and 50 fighter aircraft attacked. Five Blenheims were shot down and the remaining four were lucky to survive. They managed to score only near misses on the Japanese ships, but destroyed a number of enemy aircraft.

On the same day a Japanese scout plane located the British carrier

HMS *Hermes* accompanied by the Australian destroyer HMAS *Vampire*. The Japanese attacked *Hermes* in waves and within 10 minutes she had been hit by 40 bombs and sunk. *Vampire* (Commander W. T. A. Moran) took 13 direct hits before breaking in two and sinking. The RN also lost the cruisers *Dorsetshire* and *Cornwall* which were sunk by Japanese dive bombers south-west of Ceylon.

The apparently invincible Nagumo now turned his carriers homewards. He had been at sea constantly since 26 November 1941 and his fleet was badly in need of overhaul. During his victorious cruise, not one of his warships had even been hit by Allied attack.

Admiral Yamamoto, his naval superior, basked in the glory of being a national hero. But in spite of Japan's spectacular achievements in the war, Yamamoto, was still ill at ease. A decisive naval battle had not yet been fought. Unless the American fleet was annihilated soon in a final showdown, American industrial might would ensure that the Americans would outbuild Japan and produce a far superior navy. Time was not on Japan's side. Military strength was beginning to build up in Australia and the Japanese Army was asking for naval support for operations in the South-West Pacific at a time when the Navy should have been concentrating its maximum strength for Yamamoto's "decisive" battle.

Yamamoto's plans for a decisive sea battle were boosted on 18 April when 16 American Mitchell bombers, launched from the deck of the aircraft carrier *Hornet*, made a totally unexpected air raid on Japanese cities, including Tokyo. The raid, led by General James Doolittle, was planned as a psychological shock to the Japanese as well as a much needed boost to the sagging morale of the Allied nations sorely tried by the cataract of disasters in the Pacific war. The raiders did little damage, but their daring exploits angered the Japanese and strengthened Yamamoto's case for a "decisive" blow against the American fleet.

After the fall of Singapore with the loss of the 8th Division and the easy Japanese conquest of the Netherlands East Indies, most Australians understandably feared a Japanese invasion. Bomb shelters were built throughout the nation (even in the extreme south) as protection against air attack. The Australian Chiefs of Staff advised the Government that Darwin could be invaded in April and that the Japanese were expected soon to advance towards Port Moresby. RAAF fighter pilots in Perth were warned to prepare for possible "one-way" bombing attacks on Japanese aircraft carriers. Pilots would be expected to fly to the target in the Indian Ocean, drop their bombs and then return if they could – depending on whether their fuel lasted. Fortunately these raids were never necessary.

The arrival in Australia of the 1st Australian Corps (less two brigades still in Ceylon) and the American 41st Division together with US Army Air Force units greatly improved morale. Already in Australia were 63,000 volunteers for the AIF who had not been out of Australia, and 280,000 militiamen. Major General Edmund Herring was sent to Darwin to take charge of Northern Territory Force. In the event of a Japanese invasion he was to take absolute control of all naval, military and air forces in the Northern Territory.

Resisting Japan

Battle of the Coral Sea

After the dissolution of the ABDA command, Churchill and Roosevelt came to agreement on the division of spheres of responsibility for the conduct of the war against Japan. Burma-India would be a British responsibility for operations while the whole of the Pacific region, including Australia and New Zealand, would be the responsibility of the United States. That meant that the strategic direction of the Pacific war, including Australia's role, would be in the hands of the American Joint Chiefs of Staff in Washington. The Pacific was divided into South-West Pacific (to be commanded by General Douglas MacArthur) and the North, Central and South Pacific (to be under the overall command of Admiral Chester Nimitz).

General MacArthur, whose forces had been fighting the Japanese in the Philippines since December 1941, was besieged on the island fortress of Corregidor in the entrance to Manila Bay. But Roosevelt ordered him to break through the Japanese cordon and proceed to Australia where he would become Supreme Commander of the South-West Pacific area.

After a hazardous escape, MacArthur arrived in Australia in March, and declared in a phrase that stuck: "I came through and I shall return."

The Australian Government on 18 April handed over operational control of all combat sections of the Australian Army, Navy and Air Force to the American general, an act which many Australians, including Gavin Long, the Australian war historian, regarded as "a notable surrender of sovereignty" on the part of the Australian Government.[6]

General Blamey was recalled to Australia from the Middle East and appointed to command Allied land forces under MacArthur. Allied air forces would be commanded by Lieutenant General G. Brett, an American, and Allied naval forces by another American, Vice-Admiral H. Leary.

The Japanese had won the "Great East Asia" empire they wanted and now they needed to consolidate their gains against a possible Allied resurgence. Convinced of their "invincibility" some Japanese naval leaders urged that Australia should now be knocked out of the war, thus depriving the Allied nations of a valuable military base from which to make a comeback. Australia should be attacked while its defences were weak.

However, the Japanese army opposed such a "reckless" undertaking. "Bitter opposition" by Australians could be expected and the 10 army divisions needed were not to be found, nor were the 1,500,000 tons of shipping required.

On the other hand, the Japanese Army was aware that General MacArthur was preparing for a counter-offensive from Australia and that retreating Allied troops, planes, ships and submarines together with Australian divisions transferred from the Middle East and American divisions coming in from the United States were building up a formidable force in the Australian area.

A compromise was reached. Strategic aims were scaled down to the capture of Port Moresby in New Guinea (from which air attacks could be made on Australia) and Tulagi in the southern Solomons. Midway Island would be captured in the expectation that it would provoke the "decisive" naval battle which Yamamoto hoped would seal the fate of the

US Navy. New Caledonia (where the Americans now had a division), Fiji and Samoa would be taken to cut the lines of maritime communications between Australia and the United States.

The Japanese moves to land a powerful army force at Port Moresby and seize Tulagi triggered the battle of the Coral Sea in which a combined American-Australian naval force inflicted the first defeat of the war against the Japanese Navy and forced the enemy to abandon (for the time being) the attempt on Port Moresby.

Two of Admiral Nagumo's carriers, *Shokaku* and *Zuikaku*, just back from the Indian Ocean raid, were sent south to take part in the attack on Port Moresby. A smaller carrier, *Shoho*, was part of the force covering the large troop convoy.

At Pearl Harbor Admiral Nimitz, aware of the Japanese intention to seize Port Moresby, sent his Task Force 17, commanded by Rear Admiral F. Fletcher, to intercept the enemy. Fletcher's force included the carriers *Lexington* and *Yorktown*, together with Rear Admiral Crace's Anzac Naval Squadron including the cruisers *Australia*, *Hobart* and *Chicago*. Crace was an Australian born Royal Navy officer commanding the Australian squadron.

On 3 May a Japanese landing force was seen disembarking at Tulagi from which a small Australian party managed to escape. Next day aircraft from *Yorktown* attacked the landing force. On 7 May American carrier planes chanced upon the *Shoho* which they sank, and next day both the American and Japanese carrier forces found each other and launched strike aircraft. *Shokaku* took heavy damage which denied her to the Japanese fleet for two months. *Zuikaku* suffered heavy aircraft losses which would keep her out of the war for a month. These losses were crucial to the Japanese fleet which would soon go into the battle of Midway without them.

The Americans lost the *Lexington* though most of her 3,000 crew were rescued. The *Yorktown* was damaged. After these encounters the opposing forces withdrew from the area. Meanwhile Fletcher had sent Crace to bar the way of the Japanese invasion convoy which aimed to sail through the Jombard passage. It failed to make it and was ordered back to Rabaul.

The Coral Sea battle was a significant Allied victory. For the first time in the Pacific War a Japanese invasion convoy was forced to turn back well short of its objective. Port Moresby was spared. The Japanese inflicted greater damage on the Americans, but they lost a strategic naval battle, Australia felt safer.

While the Japanese prepared to seize Port Moresby, No 75 Squadron, RAAF, flying Kittyhawk fighter aircraft provided by the Americans, fought a desperate battle to defend the town against Japanese air attack which aimed to destroy its air defences. No 75 Squadron had been formed on 4 March at Townsville and after minimal operational training 17 aircraft left for Moresby on 19 March.

On 4 April, led by Squadron Leader John Jackson their commander, they raided Lae, destroying or damaging 15 aircraft on the ground. Called upon for constant combat over Moresby or on raids on enemy airfields, they operated for 44 days, destroying 35 enemy aircraft and losing 12 pilots killed or missing. Jackson was killed on 28 April and on the same day with only three aircraft still serviceable the squadron was relieved by two American Aircobra squadrons of No 35 Group, USAAF. Jackson's brother Leslie succeeded him as commanding officer of No 75.

The first of three squadrons of another American fighter group, the 49th, arrived to defend Darwin in March and by the end of April had destroyed an estimated 38 Japanese planes.

Meanwhile on 5 May British forces landed on Madagascar to prevent the possibility of a Japanese invasion of this Indian Ocean island. The following day American resistance in the Philippines ended when the garrison at Corregidor surrendered. By 20 May all Burma was also in the hands of the Japanese. Some 400,000 refugees entered India in a mass exodus. In the 900 miles of fighting retreat, 13,463 British, Indian, Burmese and Gurkha soldiers lost their lives.

Attacks on Sydney and Newcastle

The setback in the Coral Sea did not deter Yamamoto in pursuit of his primary aim: a quick victory over the "remnants" of the American fleet. Convinced by his arguments, Imperial Headquarters on 5 May had issued the order for the Combined Fleet to occupy strategic points in the

Aleutian Islands and Midway Island. Yamamoto was now cleared to set sail across the Pacific for one of the greatest naval showdowns in history.

As the American and Japanese fleets moved towards each other, the Japanese Navy launched mini submarine attacks on far-off Madagascar in the Indian Ocean and against Sydney in the south Pacific. At Madagascar on the night of 30 May, a mini submarine damaged the battleship HMS *Ramillies* in Diego Saurez harbour.

On the same night, a Japanese float plane from a submarine some 56 kilometres off the entrance to Sydney harbour flew over the harbour and circled the American cruiser *Chicago* before flying off to the east. The following night the Japanese sent three mini submarines in a bid to sink warships in the harbour. One became entangled in anti-torpedo nets and its crew fired demolition charges destroying themselves and their submarine. At 11.30 pm another mini submarine fired torpedoes from near Bradley's Head. One passed under a Dutch submarine and struck the harbour bed where it exploded and sank the naval depot ship *Kuttabul*, killing 19 men. The spectacular "Battle of Sydney" now erupted with gunfire awakening the harbour and nearby suburbs. Houses were reduced to rubble in some Eastern suburbs but no civilians were injured.

While the mini submarine raid had considerable shock value, the Japanese were more successful in their attacks on merchant ships. On 3 June they sank the *Iron Chieftain* and on 4 June, the *Iron Crown*. Other ships were attacked and to avoid further losses merchant ship sailings were suspended and on 8 June a convoy system was introduced. The Japanese submarines tried shelling Sydney and Newcastle on 8 June but caused little damage and no casualties.

The Battle of Midway

By 3 June 1942, a confident Admiral Nagumo with four heavy carriers – *Akagi*, *Kaga*, *Soryu* and *Hiryu* together with battleships, cruisers, destroyers and fleet train – was nearing Midway Island in the central Pacific. The damage inflicted in the Coral Sea battle on *Shokaku* and aircraft losses to *Zuikaku* denied these two heavy carriers to the enemy fleet in the coming battle. Admiral Nimitz had only three heavy carriers,

Enterprise, Hornet and *Yorktown*, which had sailed to Pearl Harbor direct from the Coral Sea and whose damage sustained in that battle was made good in the nick of time.

Yamamoto had sent his Fifth Fleet to the Aleutian Islands far to the north in the expectation that this diversionary thrust would lure American naval units away from the central Pacific. But the American fleet was not deceived. Brilliant American intelligence work had informed Nimitz that Midway was the real Japanese objective. On the eve of battle, 3 June, his naval task force waited ready for action 300 miles northeast-by-east of the island.

At 4.30 am on 4 June, Admiral Nagumo, unaware of the presence of the American carriers, launched 108 attack and fighter planes against Midway. But Midway was ready and was not knocked out. The Japanese suffered heavy losses of aircraft. Nagumo, still unaware of the presence of the American carriers, ordered a second strike on Midway. This was probably the most damaging miscalculation of the war.

American aircraft from Midway then attacked Nagumo's carriers but this attack was a failure. At 7 am Admiral Spruance had ordered an all-out launch of carrier aircraft against the Japanese fleet. Torpedo planes from *Enterprise, Hornet* and *Yorktown* attacked but were shot out of the sky. The sacrifice of their heroic crews, however, was not in vain because their attacks drew the Japanese fighter aircraft down to a low level so that the high-flying American dive bombers which attacked next were practically unopposed. They quickly scored fatal bomb hits on *Akagi* which became an inferno and was torpedoed and sunk the next day. Within minutes *Kaga* took four direct bomb hits with fatal results. The bombs plunged through the decks of the carriers which sank in a holocaust of exploding bombs, torpedoes, ammunition and flaming fuel.

An American submarine torpedoed *Soryu* which had taken three direct hits. Dive bombers from *Enterprise* attacked *Hiryu* which was abandoned and sunk later by a Japanese destroyer. *Yorktown* was heavily damaged by aircraft from *Hiryu* and was later sunk by a Japanese submarine.

At 2.55 pm on 5 June, Admiral Yamamoto had had enough. Stunned by the loss of his four precious carriers, he ordered the retirement of the

Combined Fleet. Midway was indeed the "decisive" battle Yamamoto had sought, but the decision had gone against the Japanese. His basic mistake was that he had believed, without confirmation, that there were no American carriers near Midway.

Kokoda and Milne Bay

Midway transformed the strategic situation in the Pacific war: the Japanese Navy had suffered its first decisive defeat in 350 years. The euphoria of victory in Japan was replaced by the sting of defeat. At home a major effort was made to withhold knowledge of the Midway outcome from the public. Lantern parades and navy marches were organised in Tokyo to celebrate the "victory". The wounded were taken at night to sealed hospital wards, access to which was denied even to next of kin.

Pressure on Australia was eased when the Japanese postponed operations to seize Fiji, New Caledonia and Samoa. Conversely the American Joint Chiefs of Staff accelerated their offensive planning for the Pacific aimed at the seizure of the Japanese bastion of Rabaul. Because of the "beat Hitler first" strategy, the major part of Allied military resources were reserved for operations elsewhere in the world. Nevertheless the Joint Chiefs on 2 July issued a directive to General MacArthur and Admiral Ghormley who commanded in the South Pacific to begin a step-by-step offensive against the Japanese. Ghormley's first task was to occupy Santa Cruz and Tulagi in the southern Solomons by 1 August. MacArthur was to advance to Salamaua, Lae and northeastern New Guinea.

As a first step MacArthur ordered the assembly of a 3,200-strong "Buna Force" to establish and defend an airfield on the north coast of Papua. But the Japanese got there first. They had not given up their intention of taking Port Moresby but would now do so in an overland thrust through the Owen Stanley Mountains from Gona in Papua instead of by amphibious assault which was attempted in May and was turned back as a result of the victory in the Coral Sea.

The Japanese "South Sea Force" landed at Gona near Buna on 22 July and pushed hard along the Kokoda Trail which snaked its way across the mountains to Port Moresby. Undeterred by the pestilential climate, the Japanese advanced rapidly to take Kokoda after a spirited defence by the Australian 39th Militia Battalion.

Both sides sent reinforcements into the "green hell" of the Kokoda Trail. By 21 August the Japanese had brought in a total of 13,500 troops. On the Allied side the veteran 7th Australian Division was rushed from south Queensland. One of its brigades, the 21st, was sent to the Kokoda Trail and another, the 18th, to Milne Bay. Back in Australia MacArthur urged that the troops in Papua must "attack, attack, attack".

Although plagued with problems the tenacious Japanese pushed further ahead on 26 August and by 29 August the 21st Brigade was forced to retire from Isurava. On 1 September the brigade stopped a Japanese attack, inflicting heavy losses. But by 15 September the Japanese were only 26 miles from their objective and at night could see searchlights criss-crossing the sky over Port Moresby.

The continued retreat from Kokoda alarmed MacArthur and he decided that General Blamey must take over in Papua to "energise" the situation. On 17 September he telephoned Curtin to tell him of his concern. Curtin agreed that Blamey should go. Ironically on the day Blamey arrived at Port Moresby the emaciated Japanese received their last rice rations and three days later were ordered to fall back on Buna, a nightmare retreat that few would survive. Australian troops were to find evidence as they retraced their steps along the trail that the enemy had been reduced to eating grass, roots and wood. Some had resorted to cannibalism.

Meanwhile, as the Japanese persisted with their incredible effort on the Kokoda Trail, they also launched (on 25 August) the second phase of their plan to conquer Port Moresby – the invasion of Milne Bay, a port on the eastern end of New Guinea which had three airfields. They planned to develop an air war centre there which would provide the air cover desperately needed for the conquest of Moresby as well as for bombing northern Australia.

A shock was in store for them because Milne Bay was defended by two brigades of Australian troops – the 7th Militia Brigade and the veteran 18th Brigade of the 7th Division which had just been rushed to

Milne Bay after MacArthur had learned of the enemy's intentions. Air defence was provided by two RAAF Kittyhawk squadrons – Nos 75 and 76. The Japanese on the other hand had made a fundamental error because Milne Bay was beyond the range of adequate air cover.

On 25 August when the convoy transporting the invasion force of 1,200 Japanese was approaching, RAAF aircraft attacked. They killed 20 Japanese when they scored a direct hit on the *Nankai Maru*.

That night the invaders landed on the northern shore of Milne Bay and at dawn next day the RAAF Kittyhawks attacked, ripping open their landing barges with bombs and gunfire. The Kittyhawks were so close to the fighting which developed that when they took off from the airfield their undercarriages were barely up before their machine guns were firing. Army and Air Force were virtually fighting as one.

The Japanese attacked in force on the night of 26–27 August and after a ferocious fight the Australians withdrew. Reinforcements brought Japanese strength to 2,400 and they attacked again on 31 August, charging wildly across the open in attempts to capture No 3 airstrip. The attackers bunched and many fell before the hail of fire.

The Milne Bay military venture was a disaster for the Japanese. By 5 September they had had enough and the Rabaul command signalled to the supporting Japanese destroyers, "Try to get them out." Official Japanese figures state that 1,138 Japanese were evacuated. It was estimated 311 had been killed and 700 were missing. Australian battle casualties were 373 of whom 161 had been killed or were missing.

The battle at Milne Bay was a notable Australian victory. For the first time in the Pacific War a Japanese amphibious invasion force had been defeated on land and forced to withdraw after establishing a beachhead.

The commander of the Australian forces in New Guinea, Major General S. Rowell, reported on the battle, "The action of Nos 75 and 76 squadrons, RAAF, on the first day was probably the decisive factor."

Guadalcanal

The first American offensive of the Second World War began on 9 August when the 1st Marine Division preceded by heavy air and naval bombardments, landed on Guadalcanal and Tulagi islands in the southern Solomons.

On Guadalcanal there was no opposition on the beachhead and only token resistance further inland when the Marines occupied the airfield later named Henderson field. But at the second landing on nearby Tulagi, 1,500 Japanese troops resisted fiercely before being annihilated. American Marine losses totalled 108 killed in action.

The successful landings in the Solomons were the cause of great jubilation among Americans because for the first time in the war, American forces had wrested territory from the Japanese. They felt they were on the road to Tokyo.

For the lodgement on Guadalcanal, the American command had organised a powerful fleet including three heavy aircraft carriers and a battleship. The Australian Navy was represented by the cruisers *Australia*, *Canberra* and *Hobart*. Rear Admiral Victor Crutchley, a Royal Navy officer, commanded the Australian cruisers as well as five American cruisers.

The American purpose initially was to protect the threatened lifeline between America and Australia. There were no thoughts on either side that this was the beginning of an immense struggle crucial to the outcome of the Pacific war. The Japanese would soon regard Guadalcanal not as just another island but an island that must be held at all costs. Trying to retain it critically diminished the Japanese fleet.

When news reached Rabaul of the American landing, initial Japanese reaction was to despatch 27 bombers and 17 fighters to attack the invaders. This strike force was seen by the Australian "Coastwatcher" Lieutenant Paul Mason as the aircraft flew over south Bougainville at 9.30 am on 7 August. At 11.30 am his voice was heard at Guadalcanal with a warning. "From STO. Twenty-four bombers headed yours." Thus the Americans were able to intercept and destroy seven of the raiders. Seven Japanese cruisers and a destroyer raced southwards from the Rabaul area and at 1.45 am on 9 August they were off Savo Island where they attacked American and Australian warships guarding the invasion force. The cruisers *Canberra* and *Chicago* were silhouetted by flares as the Japanese crews opened fire. Within minutes *Canberra* was badly hit and Captain F. E. Getting, her commander, was mortally wounded. *Chicago* was hit by a torpedo but stayed afloat. Three other American cruisers, *Quincy, Vincennes* and *Astoria,* were caught in a devastating cross-fire and sunk. Having created great havoc the enemy at 2.23 am broke off the action and headed back to Rabaul, having lost 34 killed in the battle. The Savo Island naval action was the US Navy's worst sea defeat in its history.

Canberra lost 84 men killed or died of wounds and had to be sunk next day when unable to sail with the fleet. Thus the RAN, which had begun the war with six cruisers, had in the space of nine months lost three of them in combat.

Japan's Prime Minister Tojo now intervened personally in the war, demanding that top priority be given to the retaking of Guadalcanal. However, Japanese intelligence was astray: they estimated American strength at Guadalcanal at 2,000, but the actual strength was 17,000.

On the night of 18 August the Japanese sent in a mere 500 men of the Special Landing Force, together with 1,000 men of the elite Ichiki force. These men had raced from Truk in destroyers and were expected to retake Guadalcanal in three days! Instead on the night of 19 August they were virtually massacred when they attacked a strongly dug-in American marine force near the mouth of the Ilu. Ichiki next day committed *hari kari,* ritual suicide, on the beach.

Like a giant magnet Guadalcanal was attracting powerful combat forces grimly determined to annihilate each other.

The Japanese Combined Fleet commanded by Yamamoto and Admiral Fletcher's Task Force 61 clashed in the battle of the eastern Solomons on 24 August. With Fletcher's force were *Australia* and *Hobart,* which were charged with the defence of the US carriers against surface attack. The US carrier *Saratoga* destroyed a large number of Japanese aircraft in this action and sank the Japanese carrier *Ryuju,* while the Japanese seriously damaged the American carrier *Enterprise.* The Australian cruisers which had taken part in the battle were returned to MacArthur's command on 3 September.

By 18 September the Rabaul command directed that Guadalcanal must have priority over the Papuan campaign and that Horii must fall back on Buna on the north coast.

In October, after sending their 17th Division, the Japanese mounted a massive navy-army general offensive to wrest Henderson field from the Americans.

A Combined Fleet armada which included four battleships and four aircraft carriers was deployed. Losses on both sides were severe.

The situation became critical for the Americans when two Japanese battleships bombarded Henderson with 14-inch shells which turned the vital airfield into a shambles. The Japanese claimed they would unfurl the "rising sun" over Henderson by 22 October. But after some of the fiercest fighting of the war at "bloody ridge" in which the Americans inflicted a fearful slaughter on attacking Japanese troops, the enemy was forced to withdraw the remnants of its force.

By December, American strength on Guadalcanal, now known as the "island of death", had grown to 50,000, while Japanese strength had dwindled to 25,000, many of whom were starving.

When the Imperial General Staff sought Emperor Hirohito's concurrence in retreat from the island on the ground that the Japanese Navy could not transport vital supplies to the troops, he observed "our withdrawal from Guadalcanal is regrettable". At the end of January and in early February a large number of Japanese destroyers arrived and the last survivors of the Japanese garrison withdrew on 8 February. In the Guadalcanal campaign, more than 20,000 Japanese were killed or missing or died of disease. The Americans lost 1,592 killed and 4,245 wounded.

Victory in Papua

On the Kokoda Trail the Japanese who fought so desperately to reach Port Moresby were doomed when their Rabaul masters were forced to switch the main focus of their military efforts from Papua to Guadalcanal for their massive, crucial campaign.

On 28 September the 25th Brigade made a general advance towards Kokoda. When it approached Ioribaiwa it found the enemy had gone. On 2 November the brigade entered Kokoda without encountering

30. Terrible scenes ensue after the Japanese air raids on Singapore.

31. Smoke lifts over Singapore from the damaged naval base in February 1942.

32. Chaos as Japanese planes attack the American fleet in Pearl Harbor.

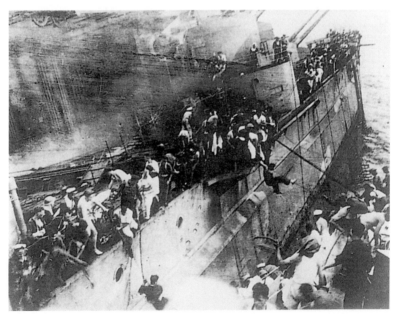

33. The crew of HMS Prince of Wales *scrambles over the side as she lists heavily before she and HMS* Repulse *both sink after an attack by Japanese aircraft.*

34. *The* Kuttabul, *sunk by a Japanese mini submarine in Sydney Harbour with the loss of 19 RAN sailors.*

35. *One of the mini submarines hauled to the surface in June 1942.*

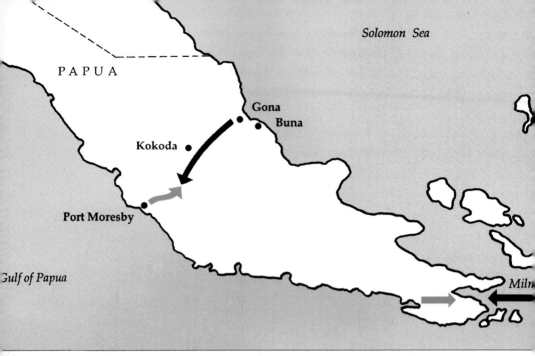

36. *The Japanese attack on New Guinea at Milne Bay, and the battle zone which developed along the Kokoda Trail.*

37. *Japanese tanks bogged down after they were brought ashore to attack Milne Bay in September 1942.*

38. A driver waits for his jeep to be dragged out of the Yalu River near Nadzab in New Guinea. Nothing was easy in this terrain, for men or vehicles.

39. On the far right of these RAF pilots resting at Darwin is Australia's top-scoring fighter ace of the Second World War, Group Captain Clive ('Killer') Caldwell.

40. The hospital ship Centaur, *which was torpedoed off the Queensland coast on 14 May 1943.*

41. In the high country, Australian troops pause briefly on the way to Finschhafen.

42. *Victoria Cross winner Lieutenant T. C. Derrick is congratulated by Lieutenant Reg Saunders, the first aboriginal to be commissioned in the Australian Army.*

43. *Ground crew load a 2,000 lb bomb into a Beaufort. The inscription reads "from Vic and his 300 thieves".*

44. Bomber crews of No 467 Squadron don flying clothing and lifejackets before a bombing raid over Western Europe.

45. Ready for an air strike at Cassino in Italy, RAAF Kittyhawks taxi onto the runway.

46. General Macarthur swore that he would return to The Philippines, and here he makes good his word, wading ashore on Leyte Island.

47. An Australian Matilda tank plunges across a river in Bougainville.

48. A Digger confers with villagers in New Britain.

49. *Flames erupt from this Liberator of No 24 Squadron when it is hit during an attack on the cruiser* Isuzu *near Sumba Island on 6 April 1945.*

50. *Diggers take shelter as Japanese shells come over in the advance from Aitape.*

51. A RAAF Liberator drops its bomb load.

52. Fires in Brunei after rocket attacks.

53. *Members of a patrol with their amphibious landing vehicle near Weston, North Borneo.*

54. *Wading ashore at Balikbapan, Australia's final landing of the war.*

55. *Lieutenant General H. C. H. Robertson receives the sword of the surrendering commander of the Japanese 18th army in New Guinea, Lieutenant General Adachi.*

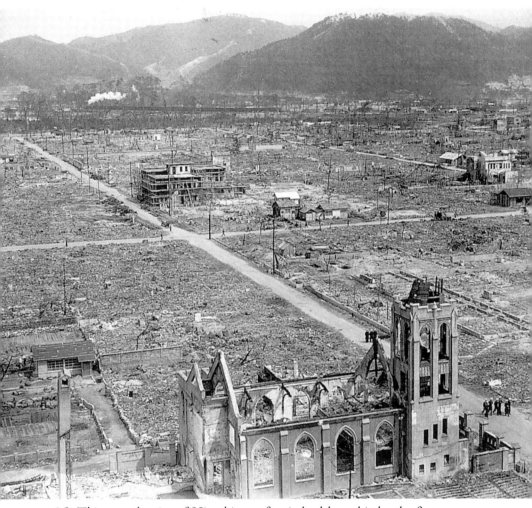

56. This was the city of Hiroshima after it had been hit by the first atomic bomb used in warfare.

57. Victory was just in time to save the lives of these Australian prisoners of war who suffered from the appalling conditions forced upon them by the Japanese in Changi Prison, Singapore. Many thousands of others perished as a result of ill-treatment even worse than this.

58. August 1945, and the RAAF takes part in a victory parade in Melbourne.

opposition and the airstrip was quickly brought into use for aerial supply.

The 16th Brigade of the 6th Division resumed the advance towards Oivi and a large-scale engagement developed a mile from that village. While the 16th Brigade maintained pressure on Oivi the 25th Brigade was sent around the southern flank to take the enemy in the rear. The enemy force was trapped and on the 11th November their main positions were abandoned as the remnants struggled to escape. Many, including General Horii, were drowned when attempting to escape across the fast-flowing Kumusi river.

The battle of the Kokoda Trail had lasted from 22 July to 16 November and ended in complete defeat for the Japanese. A total of 607 Australians had been killed and 1015 wounded. The greatest losses were suffered by the 2/14th and 2/16 Battalions of the 21st Brigade.

General MacArthur now pressed his generals to eliminate entirely all Japanese forces in Papua. The Japanese had sent 4,000 fresh troops from Rabaul and together with some 5,000 survivors from the Kokoda Trail they were dug in strongly in a fortified line between Gona and Cape Endaiadere, where they were now subjected to heavy aerial bombardment.

General Blamey planned to use the Americans of the 32nd Division to take Buna beachhead: one column was to advance along the Papuan coast towards Buna while a second column would join them from inland.

The capture of Gona and Sanananda was assigned to the Australians. By 18 November, the weary infantrymen of the Australian 25th Brigade had crossed the Kumusi River and were just south of Gona when they were fired on by the enemy. The brigade at once attacked strongly, the Diggers cheering as they charged enemy posts. But they suffered heavy losses, not only from enemy fire but from malaria and heat exhaustion. Their battleground had changed from rugged mountains to pestilential sago and mangrove swamps in which malarial mosquitoes abounded. Ants, fleas, leeches, bush mites, flies and spiders added to their discomfort. Soldiers were struck down by typhus, blackwater fever and dysentery. Losses from illness were so serious that it became a rule that no man could be evacuated unless his fever rose above 102 degrees.

The depleted 25th Brigade was reinforced on 30 November by all three battalions of the 21st Brigade whose numbers were also dwindling rapidly. As the campaign continued unabated, losses reached disastrous proportions. The 21st Brigade's strength fell to only 800 men. Nevertheless the brigade attacked again on 8 December and the next day Gona fell. The savagery of action against the fanatical resistance of the Japanese was indicated by the macabre scene after the battle, where 638 Japanese bodies lay unburied.

The United States 5th Air Force, commanded by Major General George C. Kenney, and the RAAF's No 9 (Operational) Group, commanded by Group Captain W. H. Garing, played a vital role in supporting the Papuan campaign. Kenney, a thrusting and decisive air leader, had reorganised the air elements of MacArthur's command. He formed his American squadrons into the 5th Air Force, and the Australian squadrons were placed under RAAF Command commanded by Air Vice Marshal W. D. Bostock, except for No 9 Group (commanded by Garing) which was under the control of the 5th Air Force.

No 9 Group comprised seven squadrons – No 30 with Beaufighters, No 6 with Hudsons, No 22 with Bostons, No 100 with Beauforts, Nos 75 and 76 with Kittyhawks and No 4 with Wirraways. All were fully engaged in the operations which saw the defeat of Japan in Papua.

On the Sanananda track the 16th Brigade suffered heavy casualties from enemy fire and illness which reduced their strength to 1,040 men. The 30th Brigade relieved the 16th and suffered sacrificially high losses. In one day, 6 December, the 49th Battalion lost 60 per cent of its attacking force, after which full-scale attacks against Sanananda were halted.

Meanwhile, American regiments advancing towards Buna were held up by Japanese fire from well-concealed bunkers. General Blamey was outspoken in his criticism of some of the American troops, saying his faith in them had "sunk to zero". MacArthur, angry at reports of delay at the front, put his corps Commander, Lieutenant General Robert

Eichelberger, in charge at Buna. His grim order to Eichelberger in these circumstances was, "Bob, I want you to take Buna or not come back alive."[7] Under Lieutenant General Eichelberger's direction, therefore, Buna village was taken on 14 December by the American 111/127 Battalion. But by that time it was empty of living men. The Government Station at Buna fell three weeks later.

On 8 December, Blamey ordered the 18th Brigade (Brigadier George Wootten) to add weight to the attack on the formidable Japanese defences. He was to clear the enemy from the area between Cape Endaiadere and Buna. Wootten was to take under command three American battalions and control the whole attack. On 18 December Wooten's force moved forward on a front of about 554 metres and attacked the line of Japanese bunkers with tanks and infantry. The attack was costly and more costly attacks followed. On 24 December the Japanese used concealed anti-aircraft guns to knock out tanks in quick succession.

It was not until 22 January 1943, after weeks of desperate fighting, that all organised Japanese resistance ended. In the Buna area Allied casualties had totalled 2,870 of whom 913 were Australians. Total Australian casualties in the Papuan campaign between 22 July 1942 and 22 January 1943 when the campaign ended were 2,165 killed or dead from other causes and 3,533 wounded. Of the 20,000 Japanese engaged in the campaign, some 13,000 died in battle or from wounds or disease.

Papua was one of the great victories of Australian arms. "In retrospect" wrote Gavin Long, the official Australian war historian, "it can be seen that a major achievement of the Australian Army in 1942 was to establish a tactical superiority over the Japanese troops."[8]

Since 1942 the Japanese army had maintained garrisons at Lae and Salamaua as outposts protecting the Rabaul bastion. With the fall of Papua these outposts were now under threat and the Japanese rushed reinforcements from Rabaul to strengthen them. The Japanese Army believed also that the continued Australian possession of the airfield at Wau would imperil their hold on Lae-Salamaua; they therefore ordered a 3000-strong force to take it. General Blamey, however, anticipated this Japanese move and ordered the 17th Brigade of the 6th Division to be flown into Wau from Milne Bay. The brigade began arriving on 14 January and by 24 January Japanese troops were detected approaching Wau from Mubo. By the end of January the Japanese had reached Wau airfield and had it under fire as Australian reinforcements were landing. The Australians were in action virtually from the moment they stepped from their air transports. Stiff fighting erupted in and around Wau and by the end of February the Japanese had been routed and forced to retreat to Mubo. It was the last attempt by the Japanese to add new territory to their conquests.

After the heavy raid on Darwin in February 1942 the Australian armed forces prepared vigorously to repel a Japanese invasion of the Northern Territory. But the Japanese made their moves elsewhere and fearing a counter-invasion in the Indies sent their 5th and 48th Divisions to defend Timor and Ambon.

In Timor the Australian 2/2nd Independent Company and later the 2/4 maintained a successful guerilla war, supported by supply runs by RAN warships. While engaged in one of these missions HMAS *Voyager* was lost on 23 September 1942 when she ran aground at Betano Bay on the southern coast of Timor. There she was attacked by enemy bombers. The crew of *Voyager* were then embarked on the RAN corvettes *Warrnambool* and *Kalgoorlie* and returned to Australia without the loss of a man.

After many months of raids, ambushes and generally creating havoc the men of the Independent Company had become affected by illness and fatigue. They were clearly at the limit of their endurance and the decision was made to bring them back to Australia. While en route to Timor to repatriate the 2/2nd, the RAN corvette *Armidale* was attacked by Japanese aircraft and sank within minutes with heavy loss of life. Ordinary Seaman Teddy Sheean distinguished himself at the cost of his life when, although wounded, he strapped himself to his gun and was still firing at the attacking aircraft as he disappeared beneath the waves. The 2/2nd Company was brought out two weeks later by the Dutch destroyer *Tjerk Hiddes*.

RAAF Hudsons of Nos 2 and 13 Squadrons had done much to sustain the operations of the 2/2nd and this effort was supplemented later in 1942 by No 31 Beaufighter Squadron. The gallant work of Nos 2 and 13 Squadrons in the critical period between April and August 1942 was recognised by the award to each squadron of the American Presidential Unit Citation.

Battle of the Bismarck Sea

At Rabaul, General Hitoshi Imamura, the 8th Army Commander, reacted characteristically to Japan's defeat at Wau in the New Guinea highlands by promptly despatching even greater reinforcements – the major part of the 51st Division, 6,900 men – to Lae. Another 10,000 were sent to Wewak. Japanese thinking was that while Wau remained in Allied hands, Lae would be untenable and Lae and Salamaua were the forward bases which protected Rabaul and, further north, the Philippines.

But Imamura had failed to take full account of the grave danger posed by General Kenney's air power, now strongly reinforced. He was to pay dearly for his miscalculation. On 28 February a convoy of eight transports, carrying the 51st Division troops and escorted by eight destroyers, sailed from Rabaul. En route it was to be protected by Japanese fighters and massive raids on Allied airfield were planned to dampen air reaction.

On 2 March the convoy was attacked by American heavy bombers and that night shadowed by Australian Catalinas. Weather prevented Japanese attacks on the Allied airfields and next day, 3 March, the greatest force Kenney could muster, some 90 aircraft, rendezvoused off Cape Ward Hunt and went in for the kill. Included in the attack were Beaufighters and Bostons of the RAAF.

First the Bostons carried out effective neutralising attacks on Lae airfield. The American Flying Fortresses bombing from just over 2,000 metres made their runs, later claiming five direct hits. When the Fortresses withdrew the Australian Beaufighters led the low-level attack on the convoy machine gunning the packed decks from mast-top height.

Then came the most devastating attack of all – American B25 Mitchell light bombers, using a new technique called "skip bombing".

With eight machine guns mounted in its nose each Mitchell pilot pointed his aircraft at a selected ship and poured in a devastating fire to inhibit Japanese gunners and then dropped a 500 lb (227 kg) bomb with a delayed fuse which skimmed like a flat stone across the water and tore into the hull of the enemy ship. Soon the convoy was a chaotic disaster area of burning, exploding and sinking ships. High above the lurid scene Japanese fighters were engaged in fierce dog fights with American Lightning fighters and were thus unable to attack the bombers and rescue the doomed ships. All eight Japanese transports and four of the escorting destroyers were sunk, making a total of 12 ships lost. Of the 8,740 men in the convoy it was estimated 2,890 were drowned or killed. A delighted MacArthur said the battle was the decisive aerial operation of the South-West Pacific. It was abundantly clear to the Japanese that Allied air power would make it prohibitive for their surface transports to move through areas within its range. Henceforward only submarines and barges moving at night could be used to reinforce and supply Lae and Salamaua.

After the battle, Australian squadrons continued to attack enemy bases at low level. A Boston of No 22 Squadron, piloted by Flight Lieutenant W. E. Newton, was shot down over the target at Salamaua in an attack on 15 March. Newton attempted to swim away but the Japanese at Salamaua captured and executed him. For his heroism in action he was awarded the Victoria Cross.

The Japanese military was deeply disturbed by the implication of the Bismarck Sea battle and in a head-on bid to stem the tide, Admiral Yamamoto ordered the "I" Operation which called for a maximum-effort air campaign to destroy Allied air power in New Guinea and the Solomons. To bolster the strength of air strikes planned, Yamamoto ordered navy aircraft from the four aircraft carriers of the Third Fleet at Truk to reinforce land-based strength at Rabaul, where he took over personal command.

On 7 April Japanese planes attacked Guadalcanal. On 10 April, 90 planes struck at Oro Bay near Buna. The Japanese aircraft were intercepted by a force of 50 American Lightnings and Australian Kittyhawks of No 77 Squadron which were on patrol in the area.

The attackers hit a 2,000-ton cargo ship but lost 17 aircraft in the battle.

The next target was Port Moresby where the enemy made their 106th raid of the war. Again the Japanese were outfought, losing 15 bombers and nine fighters. Yamamoto's final attack was made by more than 100 aircraft on Milne Bay. American Lightnings and 34 Kittyhawks from Nos 75 and 77 Squadrons of the RAAF rose to intercept and destroyed 14 enemy aircraft.

Four days later on 18 April, Yamamoto left Rabaul for Buin in south Bougainville on the first of a series of visits to outlying bases. But once again the Americans had decoded an important enemy signal and knew of this visit and the timetable. Lightning fighters from Guadalcanal set up an ambush and shot down his "Betty" bomber in flames as he approached his destination. He died believing his "I" Operation had succeeded but he had been deceived by pilot reports which greatly exaggerated the damage inflicted.

El Alamein

The 9th Australian Division, which in 1941 had covered itself with glory during its heroic defence of Tobruk, was afterwards assigned to the defence of Syria. When Japan declared war, it was proposed that it should return to Australia. But Curtin and MacArthur after the battle of Midway agreed the Pacific War had become less dangerous, and allowed the division to stay in the Middle East where the situation was grave. The war against Japan had already drained military resources from North Africa and on 21 June 1942 the resurgent Axis forced the surrender of Tobruk and its 35,000 defenders, much to the disappointment of the 9th Division.

The hard-pressed British 8th Army had then been forced to retreat to El Alamein in Egypt where on the 4th of July it was reinforced by the 9th Division. The Australians were in action almost at once, successfully raiding the Ruweisat ridge on 7-8 July. One of its battalions, the 2/15, fought a brilliant action named "Operation Bulimba" in which four soldiers were decorated with the Distinguished Conduct Medal. In a fierce battle on "Ruin Ridge" on 27 July, the 2/28th Battalion was surrounded. British tanks attempted to rescue the battalion but failed when 22 of their tanks were knocked out. With German tanks closing in from three sides the battalion sent a final signal, "We have to give in."

A supreme test for the 9th Division came when it played a distinguished role in the battle of El Alamein, the greatest Allied victory in North Africa, which ended in Rommel's drive to the Nile and led directly to the Axis being bundled out of the African continent.

The floor of the desert shook when 1,000 British artillery pieces roared into life on the night of 23rd October, heralding the start of the battle.

Axis defences were penetrated to a great depth. Both the Australian 26th Brigade and the New Zealand Division reached their final objectives. The 20th Australian Brigade reached their first enemy line but failed to take the final line, which was attacked by only one battalion (the 2/13th) and was more strongly defended.

Intense infantry fighting followed for a week in which General Bernard Montgomery, 8th Army commander, pursued his "crumbling" policy which was aimed at wearing down and weakening the German and Italian defences so that they would be vulnerable to a breakthrough by his armour.

On 28 October, the 9th Division struck again to the north, causing Rommel to concentrate much of his strength in that sector. For four days it became the focal point of the battle. Fierce assaults were mounted by the German 90th Light and the 21st Panzer Divisions, but the Australians held their ground.

In the early hours of 4 November an Indian brigade attached to the 51st Highland Division burst through the Axis defensive ring and British armour poured through the gap. By 5 November, Rommel's situation was hopeless and choosing to ignore a grim order from Hitler to fight on "to victory or death" he withdrew so that his shattered remnants could escape. A great Allied victory had been won and in England the church bells were rung.

The 9th Division had fought its last action in the Middle East and would soon depart for home and a new battlefield. Its casualties in the battle had been very heavy: 620 killed, 1,944 wounded and 130 taken prisoner, representing one-fifth of all Eighth Army losses. Lieutenant-General Sir Oliver Leese, the 30th Corps commander, in his report on the bravery of the Australians wrote: "They drew on their front most of the Panzer Corps, of which they destroyed a great part with their anti-tank guns. It was a magnificent piece of fighting by a great division, led by an indomitable character, Leslie Morshead."[9]

The matchless courage of two members of the 2/48th Battalion during the battle was recognised by posthumous awards of the Victoria Cross. They were to Sergeant W. H. Kibby and Private P. E. Gratwick.

From Lae to Hollandia

B y the end of 1942 the tide was turning in the Second World War. The Allies had achieved significant gains against the Axis powers worldwide and in January of 1943 Roosevelt and Churchill met at Casablanca in North Africa to take stock of the situation and chart the way ahead for victory.

At Casablanca, Allied grand strategy on the war did not change. Hitler, it was confirmed, must be beaten first. But at the same time there must be sufficient allocation of resources and manpower to the Pacific to keep the Japanese war machine in check until such time as Germany was defeated and the full weight of the Allied power could be brought to bear on Japan. The Russians highlighted the cogency of this strategy almost to the point of rupturing relations with Britain and the United States. "Don't waste effort on secondary fronts," they demanded. "Open a major 'second front' in Europe to ease the pressure on the hard-pressed Russian armed forces."

In pursuit of this aim to "Beat Hitler First", the great bulk of Allied resources had been directed against Germany with only 15 per cent allocated to the Pacific. This strategy was never seriously challenged in spite of the forceful arguments of Allied military leaders

Pacific war, notably MacArthur (backed by Australian Prime Minister Curtin) and Admiral Ernest King, the US Fleet commander, who urged an increase in the flow of resources to the Pacific.

Just before the Casablanca conference convened MacArthur had been asked to submit plans for the capture of Rabaul, and in response the general warned that Rabaul was a major Japanese bastion: an attempt to take it without adequate resources would fail. To undertake the task he needed reinforcements of five infantry divisions and about 3200 combat and transport planes.

These tenacious claims for aid for the Pacific war, however, fell on unresponsive ears. Pacific commanders would continue for some time to be "the have-nots" when it came to the allocation of resources. At Casablanca the first resources were allocated to the critical struggle against the German U-boats, followed by the "second-front" build-up in Britain, the combined bombing offensive against Germany, the campaign in the Mediterranean and aid to Russia. Then came the Pacific. As a result the desires of the Pacific commanders were largely ignored. Nevertheless they were authorised to conduct offensives against Japan which in fact would do more than just hold the line against the Japanese.

Admiral Nimitz, the US naval commander in the Pacific, was ordered to undertake a drive in the central Pacific through the Gilbert and Marshal Islands. General MacArthur (from New Guinea) and Admiral Halsey (from Guadalcanal) were to undertake mutually supporting parallel drives towards Rabaul. But since the resources needed to take Rabaul could not be shipped to the area, the orders to these commanders were scaled down to more limited objectives. They were no longer required to take Rabaul but were to prepare for its "ultimate seizure". The limited objectives assigned were:

1. The establishment of airfields on Kiriwina and Woodlark islands.
2. The seizure of the Lae-Salamaua-Finschhafen-Madang area and the seizure and occupation of western New Britain.
3. The seizure and occupation of the Solomon Islands to include the southern portion of Bougainville.

The offensives of both MacArthur and Nimitz were to converge on the Philippine Islands.

For the Allies the way to victory in the Pacific lay across the seas against island shores heavily defended by dedicated Japanese fighters. Allied combat commanders had therefore to learn new techniques in amphibious warfare and to achieve the close coordination of their army, navy and air units in maritime operations. Special amphibious craft and vehicles had to be provided and schools were established to train servicemen in their use. A combined operations school was established at Port Stephens and the 7th US Amphibious force was organised under MacArthur.

The New Guinea operations against Lae-Salamaua-Finschhafen-Madang and western New Britain would rely heavily on air support from General George Kenney's US 5th Air Force, based mainly in Papua, and the RAAF 9th Operational Group at Milne Bay and Port Moresby, with forward elements eventually to move into new air bases to be established on Kiriwina and Goodenough Islands. The greatest danger would come from Japanese air attacks mounted from Rabaul.

The RAAF had expanded enormously, from 3,489 when war began, to a total 146,000 men and women, of whom 127,246 were in Australia and the Pacific islands. Of 69 air squadrons in the South-West Pacific, 36 were American, 31 Australian, 1 British and one Dutch. The RAN had also grown, from 10,259 in 1939 to 34,498 in 1943.

In February 1943 the Australian Parliament approved legislation enabling Australian militia to be sent anywhere in the South-West Pacific which lay south of the equator. By April 1943 the Australian forces would have a strength of 470,000 and of these 286,000 would be in the 2nd AIF and available for service outside Australian territory. Of nine AIF brigades, eight were in Australia and one (the 17th) in New Guinea. Of 18 militia brigades, 14 were in Australia and four (the 4th, 29th, 7th and 15th) in New Guinea.

The veteran Australian 9th Division had played a significant role in the desert victory at El Alamein which had destroyed the power of the Axis in North Africa. Early in 1943 the division was on its way to the South-West Pacific where it faced the challenge of jungle and amphibious warfare.

The veteran 7th Division had earned the acclaim of the Australian people for its key role in the Papuan victory which saw the virtual elimination of the Japanese forces engaged, forces which until then had been spectacularly triumphant.

These two great divisions were now waiting on the Atherton Tableland in North Queensland to spearhead MacArthur's next offensive. The objective was the New Guinea port of Lae and other targets in the Huon Gulf.

From airfields in the Darwin area, squadrons of the RAAF North Western Area Command which included an American squadron of Liberator bombers were to undertake a "show of force" by carrying out offensive air operations in the Japanese occupied areas of the Netherlands East Indies. The operations were intended to pin down enemy air units in the area and to "confuse" the Japanese as to the direction of MacArthur's coming offensive.

In March 1943 three squadrons of Spitfires from the United Kingdom (Nos 452 and 457, RAAF squadrons, and No 54, RAF), were in the Northern Territory and clashed repeatedly with Japanese fighters of the 23rd Air Flotilla which frequently raided Australia's north. Wing Commander Clive Caldwell, who became Australia's leading fighter ace of the Second World War, led attacks on the Japanese raiders. RAAF Hudson bombers and Beaufighters together with Dutch Mitchells and the American Liberators carried out strikes on enemy bases.

The 3rd Australian Division, commanded by Major General S. G. Savige, a Gallipoli veteran, had also been assigned a role in the capture of Lae. Its task was to advance through the everlasting jungles and mountains between Wau and Salamaua, an enemy coastal base near Lae, and to threaten but not seize Salamaua. It was calculated that a realistic threat to the approaches to Salamaua would cause the Japanese army to react by sending troop reinforcements from Lae. Japanese Army strength was not great and Lae would be further weakened as the two veteran Australian divisions, fresh and confident, descended on Lae from the flank and rear.

Savige had taken over the command of the Australian forces in the Wau-Bulolo area, inland from Salamaua, on 23 April and as he continued the pressure towards Salamaua the enemy fought back vigorously. In May enemy troops surrounded a company of the 2/7th Battalion at Mubo but failed in eight attempts to overrun its defences.

Meanwhile the RAN and RAAF were engaged in combating Japanese submarines which were active off the Australian east coast and had succeeded in torpedoing a number of Allied merchant ships. On 14th May the Australian hospital ship *Centaur* was sunk by a Japanese submarine off Brisbane, with the loss of 268 lives, *Centaur* had been brightly lit at the time and was properly marked as a hospital ship.

The first moves in MacArthur's limited offensive in the South and South-West Pacific area came in late June 1943 when American troops were put ashore at Kiriwina and Woodlark islands. At the same time another American force (MacKechnie force) went ashore at Nassau Bay 77 kilometres from Lae. They were guided to the night landing point by lights set up by an Australian army patrol. In coordination with these operations, Marines of the South Pacific command landed at Rendova and New Georgia islands in the central Solomons. No opposition was encountered at Nassau Bay, Kiriwina or Woodlark islands but the Japanese despatched bombers which sank a transport during the landing in the Solomons, and each side lost two warships when the Japanese attempted to land reinforcements.

As the 3rd Australian Division and the Americans of MacKechnie force advanced nearer to Salamaua, the enemy as expected brought in reinforcements of four battalions. On the 14th August the Americans seized Roosevelt ridge and on the 16th the 2/6th Battalion took Komiatum Ridge. At this stage the 29th Brigade began replacing the 17th Brigade and on the 26th August the 5th Division relieved the 3rd Division.

During the advance to Salamaua the Australian troops received constant air support from squadrons of the RAAF and 5th Air Force.

During the invasion of Kiriwina and Woodlark Islands the RAN was active in the Coral Sea to guard against Japanese naval interference. In July HM ships *Australia*, *Hobart* and *Arunta* were sent to support operations in the Solomons and *Hobart* was hit by a torpedo which caused considerable damage and loss of life.

An essential preliminary to the coming battle for the Huon Gulf was an air campaign to suppress the enemy's air power and destroy its communications in the area. General Kenney had moved his American and RAAF squadrons to forward bases from which they went to work on enemy bases in New Britain (particularly the Rabaul bastion) and New Guinea. On 17 August, his 5th Air Force struck heavily at the Japanese airfields at Wewak. Liberator and Flying Fortress bombers caught the Japanese unawares on the ground, destroying 100 enemy aircraft. Five squadrons of the RAAF were engaged constantly in destroying Japanese barges which the enemy was forced to use to bring supplies from New Britain to Lae.

The reconquest of New Guinea moved a step closer on 4 September when the veterans of El Alamein stormed ashore near Lae. The assault was spearheaded by members of the 20th Brigade who blazed away with machine guns at the jungle-fringed shoreline. Seven Diggers were killed when Japanese fighters attacked their landing craft about 90 metres from the shore. Once ashore the troops advanced without opposition towards Lae. Earlier RAAF Beauforts attacking Gasmata in New Britain at a daringly low altitude were caught in a box barrage. Five were hit, two crashing in the area.

Next day (5 September) for the first time in the South-West Pacific theatre, MacArthur employed paratroopers. Watched by MacArthur from a B17 bomber, and preceded by Mitchell aircraft which strafed and dropped fragmentation bombs on the landing ground, the 503rd American Paratroop Regiment parachuted into Nadzab some 20 miles (32 kilometres) northwest of Lae and met no opposition. Australian artillerymen of the 2/4th Field Regiment and their guns were dropped in the same area to provide artillery support for the paratroopers.

On the same day, Australian Army pioneers and engineers crossed the Markham River near Nadzab and immediately set to work to prepare a disused landing ground to receive the airborne 7th Division which began arriving in Dakota transports from Port Moresby on 7 September. Tragically a bomb-laden Liberator aircraft crashed at Jackson's strip at Moresby near where the 7th Division soldiers were preparing to emplane for Nadzab killing 59 soldiers.

On 8 September with the 2/25 Battalion leading, the 7th Division began its march on Lae. Resistance increased as the division neared Lae. After a stiff fight in which 100 Japanese were killed, the division entered the ruins of Lae on the 15th September, only to be forced out again by the artillery of the 9th Division which was firing in support of its infantrymen advancing along the coast. The town fell the next day. Salamaua had already fallen on 11 September to the 5th Australian Division.

The Japanese suffered 2,000 casualties in the Lae-Nadzab operations. General Nakano of the 51st Division had been ordered to abandon Salamaua and then Lae when its fall was imminent. Some 7,800 Japanese managed to survive a long march from Lae over the mountains to the north coast where they were reorganised.

In the short, decisive battle for Lae-Nadzab, the 9th Division had lost 77 killed and 73 were missing, while the 7th Division lost 38 killed. But a stunning victory had been won. MacArthur was ecstatic.

General Kenney wanted Nadzab to provide him with airfields to increase further the pressure on Rabaul and to support the drive back to the Philippines. The ease with which Lae and Nadzab had been taken prompted him to write:

> It is hard for me to believe that anything could have been so perfect. At the last minute the Australian gunners who were to man the 25-pounders decided to jump with their guns. None of them had ever worn a parachute before but they were so anxious to go that we showed them how to pull the ripcord and let them jump … General MacArthur swore that it was the most perfect example of discipline and training he had ever seen.[10]

To exploit this success MacArthur and Blamey agreed to send the 20th Brigade to seize Finschhafen at once. The Australians landed at Scarlet Beach just north or Finschhafen on 22 September and the Japanese sent 70 fighters and bombers to attack them. The Japanese were beaten off by the American fighter umbrella. After stiff fighting the brigade linked up with troops advancing from Lae.

However, the Japanese were determined to retake Finschhafen. They sent the main body of the 20th Division to the area and on 16 October mounted a large scale counterattack at Sattelberg. Again hard fighting developed. But by 10 November enemy resistance had been crushed and Finschhafen was safe. The outstanding bravery of Sergeant T. C. Derrick of the 48th Battalion at Sattelberg was recognised by the award of a Victoria Cross.

Meanwhile the 7th Division had moved from Lae up the Markham river valley into the Upper Ramu river valley. Its main task was the guarding of the important airfield complex which would be developed around Nadzab.

Operation Jaywick

While Australian combat forces were slugging it out with the Japanese in New Guinea, a courageous party of soldiers and sailors led by Major I. Lyons of the Gordon Highlanders sailed from Australia to Singapore in the *Krait*, an inconspicuous 68-ton ketch disguised as an Indonesian fishing vessel.

Near Singapore on the night of the 26 September 1943 a six-man raiding party from the *Krait* transferred to canoes and entered Singapore harbour where they attached limpet mines to seven ships. Next day the mines exploded, destroying some 37,000 tons of Japanese shipping.

The heroes of "Jaywick", as the operation was named, returned safely to the *Krait* and after a perilous journey through Japanese-controlled seas, returned to their starting point at Exmouth Gulf, Western Australia.

"Sterilising" Rabaul

As the war progressed, the 22,000 Australians who had been captured in the early stages of the Pacific War continued to endure conditions of utmost savagery. One-third would die before the war ended from starvation, disease and the inhuman treatment of brutal Japanese guards.

In October of 1942 thousands of Australian prisoners had been sent north from Singapore to work on the infamous Burma "railway of death". They laboured incessantly under sadistic taskmasters. Rations were inadequate. Epidemics of malaria, beri-beri, cholera and dysentery caused pain, misery and death.

By November of 1943 the railway was opened. Each mile of the 400 kilometre track had cost the lives of 400 men. The prisoners had had to move 45 million cubic metres of earth and build 14.5 kilometres of bridges.

The thrusting offensives of the South and South-West Pacific commanders were rapidly nearing the proud Japanese bastion of Rabaul, where in the region of 100,000 veteran troops with ample arms and supplies waited to give battle. But suddenly MacArthur's plans for the capture of this base had to be scrapped: at the Quebec conference, attended by Churchill and Roosevelt in August, decisions went in favour of a single main effort through the central Pacific under Admiral Nimitz. Eventually it was decided that a dual advance by MacArthur and Nimitz would still proceed, but MacArthur's plans to take Rabaul were not approved. He was directed instead to "neutralise" Rabaul and gain control of the Bismarck archipelago by capturing Kavieng, the Admiralty Islands and Wewak. He was then to advance along the north New Guinea coast in a series of "step-by-step, airborne-waterborne" operations to the Vogelkop peninsula. Rabaul, the strongest Japanese base in the area, would be sterilised by naval blockade and aerial bombardment and left to "wither on the vine". Any attempt to take it by ground attack would almost certainly lead to a bloodbath, which should be avoided.

MacArthur had strongly advocated taking Rabaul which he needed as a naval base to support his drive to the Philippines. However, he was persuaded that the Admiralty Islands would provide him with excellent airfields and a fine harbour large enough to accommodate an amphibious striking force.

Meanwhile in the South Pacific, Admiral Halsey had not been idle. He bypassed the strongly held Kolombangara in the Solomons and attacked the weaker Vella Lavella whereupon the Japanese on the 6–7 October evacuated their forces from Kolombangara.

Rabaul's peril grew by the hour as Halsey and MacArthur, moving in tandem, thrust their forces closer to the enemy base. Halsey's South

Pacific forces were to land on Bougainville on 1 November, followed in December by the invasion by MacArthur's forces of Arawe on New Britain (15 December) and Cape Gloucester (26 December). As an essential preliminary for these landings, MacArthur ordered a maximum air bombardment effort to neutralise "hostile air and surface operations in the Rabaul area, starting on or about 15 October".

General Kenney's airmen were ready to go by 12 October and on that day launched their first big raid with 300 aircraft, including Beaufighters of No 30 Squadron, RAAF, one of which was shot down over the target. Some 100 Japanese planes were destroyed on the ground. Heavy explosions and huge fires from fuel dumps were observed. From Washington, the US Air Chief General Arnold cabled congratulations to MacArthur for "this Pearl Harbor in reverse".

On 20 October two squadrons of RAAF Beauforts attacked an enemy convoy off Cape St George but results could not be assessed. Gasmata was heavily attacked on 22 October by 46 RAAF Kittyhawks from Kiriwina. To add to the Japanese misery, frequent raids were continued on Rabaul at night by the RAAF Beaufort squadrons.

The Japanese commander at Rabaul, alarmed by the menace from Kenney's airmen and the steady approach by the Americans towards the Solomons, appealed strongly for air assistance. Late in October, 300 fighters from the Japanese Combined Fleet were sent from Truk, building Rabaul air strength up to 550 aircraft, of which 390 were fighters. As a result the 5th Air Force, attacking next day, lost 18 aircraft. That night three squadrons of RAAF Beauforts were sent again to bomb Tobera airfield.

Meanwhile Halsey landed the 3rd Marine Division on Bougainville (1 November) at Empress Augusta Bay which was lightly held and work began at once at Torokina to build another airfield from which aircraft could help to "take out" Rabaul.

The naval–air war now reached new heights of intensity. The Japanese responded to Halsey's invasion by immediately despatching a naval task force from Truk and on 5 November enemy naval strength in Rabaul harbour included six heavy cruisers, 10–14 destroyers, merchant ships and other vessels. Halsey struck at once on that day with carrier aircraft, severely damaging the enemy warships. Three days later three RAAF Beaufort torpedo bombers, flying through an electrical storm, carried out a hazardous night torpedo attack on a line of cruisers. One of the Beauforts was blown to pieces. Halsey struck again on 11 November with aircraft from five carriers.

In preparation for the landings in New Britain, Kenney's 5th Air Force carried out the heaviest attacks yet made in the Pacific and the RAAF bombing effort against Rabaul was more intense than ever. The enemy hardly knew how to handle the onslaught.

The noose tightened on Rabaul on 15 December when a regiment of the 1st Cavalry Division stormed ashore at Arawe and on 26 December preceded by a naval bombardment in which the RAN warships, *Australia*, *Shropshire*, *Warramunga* and *Arunta* took part. The 1st Marine Division, which had been for almost a year in Victoria, made a successful landing at Cape Gloucester.

In January the 5th Air Force concentrated on attacking New Guinea targets while the RAAF Beauforts of Nos 6, 8 and 100 Squadrons made Rabaul their main target. A force of 32 Beauforts with an escort of 33 RAAF Kittyhawks and eight Spitfires of No 79 Squadron attacked Lindenhafen in New Britain and on 21 January a still larger force of 76 RAAF aircraft struck the same target. At night the Beauforts continued their strikes on Rabaul airfields and RAAF Catalinas of 11 and 20 Squadrons harassed Kavieng at night.

In mid-February 1944, a momentous victory was won in the South-West Pacific. The Japanese Combined Fleet withdrew from Truk to escape the devastating attacks of Admiral Spruance's carrier aircraft and at the same time the enemy gave up on Rabaul. The last vigorous interception by Japanese fighter pilots over Rabaul came on 19 February. Next day all the serviceable enemy fighter planes took off for Truk and Japan's bastion of the southern seas, now without aircraft or naval combat vessels became a military tomb.

A great fortress which had stood as a barrier to MacArthur's return to the Philippines had been neutralised without the need for one Allied infantryman to fire a single rifle shot. Allied air and naval forces operating from advanced bases secured by ground forces, had been decisive.

The 100,000 Japanese army defenders, facing disease and starvation, had made ready to resist the ground assault they fully expected. But they waited in vain. Japanese officers steeped in the invincible warrior class mythology were in torment. Their frustration was reflected in their diaries, which lamented that the lack of cooperation by the Allied army was denying them honourable death in battle for the Emperor.

To complete the encirclement of Rabaul, South Pacific forces landed on Green Island on 16 February and on Emirau on 20 March.

Meanwhile MacArthur undertook a risky venture when on 29 February 1944 he sent a "reconnaissance in force" against Los Negros in the Admiralty Islands. With the invading force went HMAS *Warramunga* which provided naval gunfire support for troops landing in Hyane harbour. *Arunta* and *Shropshire* were also engaged in the operations.

To provide fighter defence and ground support for the 1st Cavalry Division, the invasion force included three squadrons of RAAF fighters (Nos 76, 77 and 79).

MacArthur's gamble paid off. The Admiralties were secured and developed as a major base to support his advance towards the Philippines.

After the departure from Truk of the Japanese Combined Fleet, an American submarine detected Japanese "heavy units" passing through Lombok Strait in the Netherlands East Indies. It was feared that an attack on Perth and Fremantle was in the making and to guard against this an Allied air attacking force was ordered to move from the Darwin area to Exmouth Gulf and Perth. Shipping was dispersed from Fremantle harbour and urgent measures taken to protect the western capital. However, the Japanese Navy made no hostile move in the Indian Ocean and normality soon returned to Perth.

In New Guinea meanwhile an American amphibious force supported by the RAN warships *Warramunga* and *Arunta* had seized Saidor on 2 January 1944 and the Australian 7th Division had captured Shaggy Ridge in the Finisterre range and forced the Japanese to withdraw to the Mindjin river. By 24 April the Huon peninsula campaign ended with the capture of Madang.

Many of the Australian divisions went home after these campaigns. In December 1943, General Blamey had directed that the Australian 6th, 7th and 9th Divisions would form I Australian Corps and move to the Atherton Tablelands in Queensland for training and rehabilitation. The Australian 3rd, 5th and 11th Divisions were allotted to II Corps for garrison duties, training and rehabilitation.

Seizing Hollandia

The breaking of the Bismarck barrier and heavy losses sustained by the Japanese forces in the South and South-West Pacific created an opportunity for MacArthur to advance rapidly along the north New Guinea coast. He wasted no time, informing the Joint Chiefs of Staff on 5 March that Japanese forces (principally General Adachi's XVIII Army) were massing in the Wewak-Madang area in anticipation of the next advance by the forces by the South-West Pacific. MacArthur therefore proposed to bypass Wewak and seize Hollandia which was weakly held. This move would "hopelessly isolate some 40,000 enemy troops". The Joint Chiefs accepted MacArthur's plan and set the target date of 15 April. This bold bypassing manoeuvre would now become the Pacific War's most momentous strategic concept, a concept that the Japanese military leaders hated most.

Following a request from General Kenney in late 1943, the RAAF had formed a mobile air task force which would move forward with MacArthur's advance along the New Guinea coast to the Vogelkop peninsula. It was designated No 10 Operational Group and was commanded by Air Commodore F. R. W. (later Air Chief Marshal Sir) Frederick Scherger, No 10 Group was assigned three squadrons of Vultee Vengeance dive bombers (Nos 21, 23 and 24) and three squadrons of Kittyhawk fighters (Nos 75, 78 and 80). The Group moved to New Guinea early in January 1944 and occupied Newton airfield (so named for Newton VC) and Nadzab and began operations in support of the Australian Army. No 10 Group was to move with the Allied advance, but No 9 Group would remain as a garrison force and was renamed Northern Command.

Unfortunately for No 10 Group, after only six weeks of operations from

Nadzab, the Vultee Vengeance squadrons were ordered to withdraw to Australia. General Kenney informed Air Vice Marshal Jones that he no longer intended to use Vengeances in operations and Jones immediately signalled Washington cancelling the delivery of Vengeances still on order. Kenney wanted the Nadzab bases for long-range Lightning fighters which would take part in the heavy air strikes in the Wewak-Hollandia area in preparation for the coming invasions of Hollandia and Aitape.

The fate of the RAAF Vultee Vengeances was a misfortune for No 10 Group but the spirits of its members rose when Kenney assigned the three Kittyhawk squadrons of the group to the Hollandia-Aitape operations.

On 22 April, covered by fast carriers of the US Pacific Fleet, MacArthur's invasion armada of 158 ships arrived off Hollandia and in the Indian Ocean a British naval force which included the RAN destroyers *Napier, Nepal, Nizam* and *Quiberon* carried out a diversionary strike against Sumatra.

When the Allies struck at Hollandia the Japanese were taken by surprise and were quickly in disarray. Opposition was minimal. Included in the invasion armada was Rear Admiral Crutchley's Task Force 74 comprising the RAN's *Australia, Shropshire, Warramunga* and *Arunta*, two US fleet units as well as three RAN landing ships *Westralia, Manoora* and *Kanimbla* carrying US assault troops. Crutchley's cruisers and destroyers had taken part in the bombardment of shore defences as a prelude to the assault landing.

The plan for the Hollandia operation included general support by RAAF Command Squadrons of North Western Area. Strikes were directed against bases which the Japanese might use to stage aircraft against the beachheads. They included bases at Babo, Manokwari, Noemfoor and in the Kai group of islands.

The plan also called for a simultaneous landing at Aitape, some 161 kilometres east of Hollandia. Elements of No 10 Group went ashore with the assault waves and with them went RAAF airfield construction teams who, in spite of sniper fire, quickly rehabilitated the Aitape airfield. By 25 April RAAF Kittyhawks were taking off from the airfield to fly patrols over the beachheads at Hollandia. But the Japanese XVIII Army at Wewak would not strike back until July.

The RAAF and the RAN beyond the South-West Pacific

By late 1942 Australia's war effort was concentrated predominantly against Japan in the South-West Pacific. But the RAN was represented further afield in the Indian Ocean and the Mediterranean, while some 14,500 members of the RAAF, mainly aircrew, were serving in Europe, the Middle East and Burma.

The crisis resulting from the sudden and spectacular entry of Japan into the war caused a large-scale transfer of aircraft and squadrons to the Asian theatre, greatly weakening air strength in the Middle East and contributing to the near success of Rommel's dangerous drive on the Nile Delta.

Nevertheless German and Italian air strength in North Africa was gradually subdued. Prominent in air operations which helped to weaken fatally Axis air power were the RAAF's two Kittyhawk fighter squadrons Nos 3 and 450. With Nos 112 and 250 RAF Squadrons, in which Australian pilots were strongly represented, they formed No 239 Wing of the Desert Air Force. Of the seven RAAF squadrons in the Mediterranean theatre, three (Nos 3, 450 and 451) were mainly Australian, two (Nos 458 and 459) were partly Australian and two (Nos 454 and 462) almost entirely non-Australian.

After the 8th Army's crushing defeat of the Axis forces at El Alamein the Desert Air Force reigned supreme in its relentless pursuit of the enemy. Nos 3 and 450 Squadrons put up a tremendous combat effort in a month of fighting during the battle, flying a total of 1442 sorties. Evidence of the havoc caused by the airmen lay everywhere in the burned out wreckage of the battlefields and airfields evacuated by the Luftwaffe.

The RAAF Kittyhawks were soon flying over Tripoli and the Gulf of Tunis destroying seaborne supplies coming from Sicily in small ships. By 13 May 1943 Tunis had fallen to the Allies, with 250,000 Axis soldiers going "into the bag".

A handful of RAAF Spitfire pilots joined with RAF pilots in an inspiring display of air fighting against the Luftwaffe over Malta. Lying in the central Mediterranean astride the enemy sea-air route to the Afrika Corps, Malta had long been a thorn in the enemy side. In a maximum air effort to crush it once and for all the enemy moved its powerful Second Air Fleet from Russia to Sicily for a final showdown. The battle now intensified and when it seemed all was lost the beleaguered defenders were greatly heartened by the sudden arrival over Malta of Spitfire fighters. The Spitfires had been flown off the decks of the aircraft carriers *Wasp* (US Navy) and *Eagle* (RN) as they neared Malta.

The air battle that now ensued was like a re-run of the Battle of Britain. German air armadas of JU88s and Messerschmitt fighters appeared all too frequently but were broken up by the spirited attacks of the Spitfires. In May 1942 the Germans gave up on Malta, conceding to the Allied airmen a significant strategic success.

With the carrier-borne Spitfires had come 10 RAAF fighter pilots who fought magnificently. Almost overnight, Queenslander Flight Lieutenant V. P. Brennan became an Australian fighter "ace" with 10 victories, and Squadron Leader A. P. Goldsmith of Sydney, who finished the war with 16.25 victories, became the second-highest scoring Australian "ace" of the Second World War.

The RAN had also become involved in the defence of Malta in June 1942 when, in the face of fierce Axis opposition, supply convoys were sent from both ends of the Mediterranean to succour the inhabitants and defenders. Four Australian "N" Class destroyers, *Nestor*, *Napier*, *Nizam* and *Norman* were sent from the Indian Ocean to provide an escort for a convoy which sailed from the eastern Mediterranean but failed to reach its Malta destination. When north of Tobruk, *Nestor* was straddled by aerial bombs and crippled. Four ratings were killed and *Nestor* had to be sunk by the British destroyer *Javelin*.

Three months later *Napier*, *Nizam* and *Norman* were back in the Indian Ocean where they were joined by *Nepal* for operations with the Royal Navy against the Vichy French in Madagascar in September 1942.

Quiberon and *Quickmatch* were part of operation "Torch" when the

British and American allies landed in North Africa on 8 November 1942, and, together with *Norman* and *Nizam* were on duty in the South Atlantic in mid-1943.

Meanwhile a courageous group of RAN reservists had volunteered in Britain for exacting and dangerous duties which resulted in their being among the most highly decorated Australian servicemen of the war. Based in England they were assigned the task of rendering mines safe. They undertook tasks in which the extreme conditions were calculated to deter the boldest spirits. Some of the mines were land mines dropped from aircraft which were difficult to get at when buried underground.

Of this group, Lieutenant Commander Leon Goldsworthy was awarded the George Cross, Distinguished Service Cross and George Medal, and Lieutenant Hugh Syme the George Cross and George Medal with Bar. Other highly decorated officers were Lieutenant Commanders John Mould and George Gosse and Lieutenants Howard Reid, Geoffrey Cliff, James Kessack and Keith Upton.

At the Casablanca conference of January 1943, the decision was taken to invade Sicily. At dawn on 10 July 150,000 British and American troops went ashore from an armada of 3,000 vessels. Eight RAN corvettes forming two minesweeping flotillas took part in the invasion. They carried out mine sweeps and anti-submarine patrols. Later they were engaged in the all-important task of escorting shipping convoys through Mediterranean waters.

At this stage of the war, the RAAF had 3,000 men and seven RAAF squadrons in the Mediterranean area. Nos 3 and 450 Squadrons, which had been part of the rapid advance of the 8th Army from El Alamein, supported the invasion of Sicily from Malta. By 17 July they had moved to Sicily where they flew close support missions for the ground troops. From Agnone airfield the two RAAF squadrons mounted 190 sorties against Axis road traffic in four days.

Sicily fell to the Allies on 17 August. A new Italian Government had been formed on 25 July. Mussolini was deposed and replaced by Marshal Pietro Badoglio. (On 28 April 1945, the Fascist dictator was captured and killed by Italian partisans.)

Resistance was slight when on 3 September 1943 Allied forces landed near Reggio on the Italian mainland, and as a huge Allied invasion convoy approached Salerno near Naples, on 8 September the surrender of Italy was announced.

By September, No 239 Wing RAF including its two Australian squadrons was based in southern Italy and by 3 October was established at Foggia, further north. A RAAF regular officer, Squadron Leader (later Air Vice Marshal) Brian Eaton, who commanded No 3 Squadron RAAF, was later appointed to command No 239 Wing which he led brilliantly in Italy. He was decorated with the DSO and Bar and the DFC.

The Australian airmen were closely involved in the advance of the 5th (US) and 8th (British) Armies from Calabria in the south to northern Italy. They carried out devastating bombing and strafing attacks on enemy troops and supplies. Included in their targets was the heavily defended Monte Cassino. After its capture they supported the entry of the Allies into Rome, which fell on 4 June 1944.

The German U-boat Campaign

At the end of 1942 the German U-boat campaign against Allied shipping was in a critical phase, threatening the Allied war effort. An invasion of Europe by the Allies could not be considered until large numbers of American servicemen could be transported across the Atlantic which was infested with some 100 U-boats. The Combined Chiefs of Staff therefore decided at Casablanca in January 1943 that the defeat of the U-boats must have first priority. Assisting the Russians was given second priority and to achieve this aim a vigorous air bombardment of the Axis must be mounted. Allied bomber aircraft were to attack Germany to achieve "the progressive destruction and dislocation of the German military, industrial and economic system and the undermining of the morale of the German people to a point where capacity for armed resistance is fatally weakened".

British air power had been growing rapidly, its personnel strength fed continually by the graduates of the great Empire Air Training Scheme. In the United Kingdom in the first quarter of 1943 were nine RAAF Squadrons: Nos 10 and 461 (Coastal Command); Nos 460, 466 and 467, heavy bombers equipped with Lancasters and Halifaxes; No 453 flying Spitfires; No 455 flying Hampdens; No 456 flying Mosquitoes and No 464 flying Venturas. No 463, another Lancaster squadron, was formed in November 1943. In May 1943 some 8,400 Australian aircrew were scattered in no less than 135 squadrons in Britain alone, while in India 330 Australians were serving in 41 different RAF squadrons.

The U-boat, the great threat to the Allies, was opposed by both the Allied navies and by Coastal Command of the RAF in which the two RAAF Sunderland squadrons Nos 10 and 461 were serving. In the desperate struggle that followed the U-boats, while sinking a huge tonnage of Allied shipping, were themselves suffering enormous losses. In May 1943 a total of 41 German submarines were destroyed and Australians sank or shared in the sinking of seven. Altogether during the war the Germans lost 817 submarines with heavy loss of life. The sailors who served in them called them "iron coffins".

In an endeavour to protect their U-boats at sea, the Germans sent long-range fighters to attack Sunderland and other anti-submarine aircraft. This resulted in casualties to Australian aircrew. At the end of the war a total of 408 members of the RAAF had been killed while serving in Coastal Command and 113 were wounded.

Operation Pointblank

Operation Pointblank was the combined US–British bombing offensive designed to devastate the heart of industrial Germany. As it got fully into stride in 1943 the Australian bomber squadrons were heavily involved, as were the many members of the RAAF serving in RAF squadrons of Bomber Command.

In May 1943 Australian bomber crews were prominent in the "Dambuster" raid which destroyed a number of dams in the industrial Ruhr. In July-August three RAAF bomber squadrons joined with the RAF in night raids on Hamburg which created huge devastation when fire storms were generated which destroyed 74 per cent of that city.

In November and December the bomber streams were targeting Berlin with four RAAF squadrons (Nos 460, 463, 466 and 467) taking part. On the night of 2–3 December the operation was a costly failure: No 460 squadron lost five of its 15 Lancasters. Bomber Command's heaviest loss of aircraft in one night occurred on the night of 30-31 March 1944 when out of 795 sent to attack Nuremburg, 95 failed to return. Again all four RAAF squadrons were in the raid, No 460 losing three aircraft. In three months Bomber Command's losses were 80 per cent of the aircraft on the strength of its active squadrons. No 460 Squadron alone lost almost 1,000 aircrewmen during the war in Europe.

The War to Come

By June 1944 Australian forces could look back on spectacular achievements by all three services in many theatres of war. There had been more Australian soldiers in Greece and Crete than those of any other nation. All three services had distinguished themselves in the Middle East and in North Africa, so that the names of Bardia, Tobruk and El Alamein are entered into the annals of Australian military history. The Navy had played an important role in the Mediterranean and in the waters of the South-West Pacific and the Indian Ocean, where the great clashes with the Japanese Navy began after Pearl Harbor. And all three services had fought over the islands of the South-West Pacific, from Papua New Guinea to Hollandia.

RAAF air crewmen, graduates of the Empire Air Training Scheme, had served in their thousands in the war over Europe, and a further crucial conflict was before them. Volume Two of this narrative draws attention to the major contribution they made in the Allied invasion of Normandy, France, at the climax of the Second World War. At this point in the story of Australians at war, all eyes turned towards the struggle in Europe.

6

THE SECOND WORLD WAR FROM D-DAY TO VICTORY

The Great Invasion

Thousands of airmen of the Royal Australia Air Force fought in the aerial bombardment campaign which, in its later stages, prepared Western Europe for Allied invasion. In Bomber Command alone, 3,486 members of the RAAF were killed.

The invasion, which came when Allied armies stormed ashore on the Normandy beaches on 6 June 1944, preceded by 25,000 airborne troops, was the climactic high point of the Second World War.

It was here at the fortified and obstructed beaches that hundreds of young Australian aircrewmen of the RAAF, flying heavy bombers, helped to destroy artillery batteries and obstacles to clear the way for the infantry, who might otherwise be in great danger on the beaches.

It was here that Australian fighter pilots in a day fighter squadron (No 453) and night fighter squadron (No 456) and more than 200 individual fighter pilots serving in Royal Air Force squadrons were sent to keep the Luftwaffe at bay as the infantry battled to seize the beaches.

Thus, although their numbers were not large, these young Australians who had learned to fly in the Empire Air Training Scheme were there to represent their country in one of the great battles of history.

A huge 80-kilometre-wide invasion fleet of 6,000 ships had ploughed through the English Channel carrying 185,000 men and 20,000 vehicles and had put them ashore. The task had only just begun. Another 2,000,000 servicemen waited to be shipped to France, to engage and defeat the Nazi forces defending "fortress Europa".

On D-Day the sky was full of Allied aircraft which flew a total of 11,000 sorties. Some Australians flew transport aircraft carrying American paratroopers to their drop zones. Others took part in air operations aimed at misleading the enemy as to the point of attack. No less than 13,000 members of the RAAF, including the men on operational squadrons, were in England at the time of the invasion.

Bomber Command dropped more than 5,000 tons of bombs in an attempt to silence shore batteries. Of the 1,136 bombers committed, 168 were from RAAF squadrons or had RAAF pilots. In 5 Group, RAF, 43 Lancasters were captained by RAAF pilots; 14 from No. 463 Squadron led by Wing Commander Rollo Kingsford-Smith; 14 from No. 467 led by Squadron L. C. Deignan and 15 from the remaining five squadrons of No 5 Group, including No 61 led by Wing Commander A. W. Doubleday. No 460 Squadron flew two missions, dropping 150 tons of bombs, and No 466 (Halifaxes) bombed a battery at Maisy which threatened both Utah and Omaha beaches, where the American Army was to land.

After the Normandy landing, Australian bombers took part in heavy and continuous air attacks on communications behind the beaches and were used also in direct support of British troops. The shock of heavy bomber attacks had a stupefying effect on German ground troops: following a close support strike, the British soldiers generally encountered only weak enemy resistance.

Heavy bomber support for the Normandy operations ended on 23 July when the strategic bombing campaign over Europe was resumed. Within two and a half months, 86,000 tons of bombs rained on the industrial areas of Germany, of which RAAF squadrons, contributed 6 per cent.

On 8 July Australian Lancasters and Halifaxes attacked Caen in daylight. Squadron Leader W. Blessing of Braidwood, NSW, was shot down and killed when marking this target from his Mosquito light bomber. Blessing, who had been decorated with the DSO and DFC, was one of the most courageous and skilful pilots in Bomber Command.

The Spitfires of No 453 Squadron led by Squadron Leader D. H. Smith were on station over the American sector of the beachhead at 8.40 am on D-Day. They saw no sign of the Luftwaffe. The German Air Force had lost the initiative on the first day and never regained it. By 25 June No 453 had moved to France and on 2 July at Liseux clashed with a mixed enemy force. The Australians claimed four enemy destroyed and five damaged.

Reflecting on the decisive defeat of the Germans in Normandy, Von Runstedt, the German army commander, said it was "all a question of air force, air force, and again air force".

On 25 April 1945, No 460 Squadron made its last raid of the war when it bombed Hitler's "Eagle's Nest" at Berchtesgaden. On 1 May Hitler committed suicide in Berlin and on 7 May the European war ended with the unconditional surrender of Germany.

The RAAF Elsewhere in Europe

In Europe in late 1944, Australian airmen were in action with fighter and bomber units of the Balkan Air Force, which supported partisans and harassed enemy communications in the Balkan countries. Others took part with No 148 (Halifax) Squadron in long and arduous flights to Poland in August 1944 to carry supplies to beleaguered Polish rebels. A number of Australians of No 178 Squadron were killed in these operations. No 451 Squadron was based in Corsica to support the Allied invasion of southern France.

In November 1944, No 3 Squadron was rearmed with the more advanced Mustang fighter and together with No 450 Squadron bombed targets in Padua, Verona and Venice. In their last sustained operations in Italy between 9 and 21 April 1945 they flew a total of 650 sorties as the

Allied armies forced the Germans to retreat north across the River Po. With German surrender in Italy the long fighting advance of the RAAF squadrons from Egypt northward came to an end. All seven Australian squadrons in the Mediterranean contributed to the final Allied victory in Italy.

In the Second World War some two-thirds of Australian aircrews served in Europe or the Mediterranean, and almost one-quarter of those who actually took part in operations lost their lives. Total RAAF losses in Europe from the commencement of operations in 1940 were 5,397 dead and 947 injured. RAAF deaths in the Mediterranean theatres totalled 1,135.

The RAAF in Burma and India

By May of 1942 Britain's bid to establish a firm line to hold the Japanese invasion of Burma had collapsed, and a desperate mass of refugees struggled north through Burma to escape the Japanese terror. Some 400,000 civilian refugees died in their bid for safety, while 13,000 British, Indian, Burmese and Gurkha soldiers lost their lives. The surviving soldiers were needed to man the frontiers of India.

Most air crew members of the RAAF posted to the India-Burma theatre served in RAF squadrons. It had been intended the RAAF squadrons would be formed for the Australian air crews but the aim was never achieved and by August 1942 some 250 Australians were scattered among RAF squadrons, with a large number concentrated in No 11 (Bomber) Squadron, which was equipped with Blenheim aircraft.

By January 1943, RAAF strength in the theatre had grown to 350 and on 19 January 1943 one of their number flying in a Beaufighter at night intercepted Japanese army bombers making a night raid on Calcutta. He was Flying Officer C. A. Crombie, who shot one of the bombers down. Return fire set his starboard engine on fire but he disregarded the danger and continued the attack, destroying a second bomber and damaging a third. His own aircraft was now well alight and his petrol tank exploded, forcing him to take to his parachute. Crombie was awarded the Distinguished Service Order for a great effort in destroying three bombers and probably a fourth.

Reinforcements of troops, airmen, ammunition supplies and equipment were rushed to India in shipping convoys and in December the British mounted an offensive in the Arakan area of Burma for the purpose of establishing airfields on Akyab island. But delays in the start of the offensive allowed the Japanese to prepare and they repulsed the British drive. By the start of the 1943 monsoon the situation was "fantastically bad" and the British Army was soon back at its starting point. General William Slim (later Field Marshal Sir William, Governor-General of Australia from 1953–60), who commanded an army corps in Burma, later wrote that the British forces had been helped by the cheering news that the Australians at Milne Bay had broken the spell of Japanese army invincibility. "If the Australians had done it in conditions very like ours, so could we," he wrote. They did, but it was to take another year.

By November 1943 a total of 795 RAAF members were serving with the RAF in Burma-India and by the following July this figure had grown to 1,091 with 590 then serving with no less than 60 RAF squadrons. The Australians were flying Hurricanes, Spitfires, Liberators, Catalinas, Mosquitos, Dakotas and a wide variety of other aircraft types. Some 200 were serving in 11 Liberator squadrons.

In January 1944 the British mounted an offensive into the Arakan and seized the port of Maungdaw. But the Japanese on 7-8 March, in a bid to regain the initiative, moved powerfully against India itself with the aim of seizing the key communications centre at Imphal. Their ultimate aim was to "liberate" India on behalf of the Indian nationalist leader Subhas Chandra Bose.

In response, General Slim rushed troops north from the Arakan front and by April the Japanese "March on Delhi" had stalled in the Imphal plain. Slim exploited air transport to airlift his forces and keep them supplied. The Japanese had only what they could carry into the operational zone.

By 22 June the Japanese offensive collapsed. Their overstretched forces abandoned a key ridge without a fight and they lost 30,000 killed and another 23,000 wounded. Many were sick and emaciated. The tide had turned in Burma. From this stage the Japanese would be on the defensive until the fall of Rangoon.

Air power played a significant role in the victory. Australians of No 84 Squadron flying Vengeance dive bombers carried out daily operations during the battle in April and May. On 17 April, Flight Lieutenant J. H. Goldfinch of the RAAF led 12 aircraft in an attack on enemy positions near Imphal, the targets being marked by mortar smoke. On 23 April the squadron bombed in support of Brigadier Orde Wingate's "Chindits" and next day Goldfinch led another 12 aircraft in a raid at Kohima. Other Australians in Nos 42, 134, 160, 215, 607 and 615 were engaged in the operations in this period.

Air supply was of great importance in the campaign. Some 126 RAAF aircrew were serving in eight squadrons of transports in No 229 Group. One of them (No 117) was commanded by an Australian, Wing Commander W. J. McLean.

To cope with the crisis when the British-Indian divisions around Kohima were surrounded, additional air transport aircraft were loaned to the Burma command from the Mediterranean command. Air operations were decisive in the defeat of the Japanese. Vice Admiral Lord Louis Mountbatten, Supreme Commander, South East Asia, in thanking the Joint Chiefs of Staff and Churchill for authorising the air transport reinforcements said: "There is no doubt that these aircraft turned the tide of battle against the Japanese and have altogether altered the outlook in northern Burma."

Under constant attack by the Allied air forces and running critically short of supplies, the Japanese retreated rapidly from India and by December 1944 the British 14th Army was across the Chindwin river, while the XV British Corps had entered the Arakan. In January 1945 the British occupied Akyab. The supporting naval forces at the occupation of Akyab included the RAN destroyers *Nepal, Napier* and *Nizam* of the 7th Destroyer Flotilla commanded by an RAN officer, Captain H. J. Buchanan. The destroyers embarked 870 troops for Akyab. When it was discovered the Japanese had pulled out of Akyab the pre-invasion naval bombardment was cancelled. Lieutenant

Commander J. M. Ramsay (who was to become Governor of Queensland after retiring from the Navy) went ashore at Akyab in a dinghy and climbed a pole on the wharf on which he secured a Union Jack. After carrying out bombardments in support of the seizure of Ramree Island the flotilla left the Burma theatre for Sydney to join the British Pacific Fleet.

In addition to a large number of RAAF air crew who supported operations in the air transport role, other RAAF members in a total of 18 RAF squadrons were in action during the crucial battles in central Burma.

Crushing air attacks were made on targets in Mandalay before its fall on 20 March. Toungoo was taken on 22 April.

Elaborate plans had been made for the attack on Rangoon but the Japanese pulled out of the city on 25 April. On 3 May, Mountbatten's land, sea and air forces took Rangoon without a fight. Wing Commander Lionel Hudson, an outstanding RAAF pilot and commanding officer of No 82 Squadron, was in Rangoon gaol before the liberation. He had crashed behind enemy lines during an offensive operation in a Mosquito on 19 December 1944. Being the most senior officer in the gaol he took charge when the Japanese left the city. He had a message painted on the gaol roof indicating that the enemy had gone. The message was seen from the air by an Allied pilot. It read:

JAPS GONE: BRITISH HERE.
An appendix in well-understood service vernacular had been added:
EXTRACT DIGIT.

The recapture of Rangoon occurred a few days before the end of the European war. Victory in Europe created an enormous surplus of air crew. In London the Air Ministry decided that all RAAF personnel in Burma-India would be progressively withdrawn from RAF squadrons and replaced from the pool of surplus RAF men now available. On arrival in Australia the former RAAF members of Burma units were either posted for service in the South-West Pacific Area or discharged, depending on the amount of operational service they had rendered.

RAAF casualties in the Burma-India theatre in the years 1941–45 totalled 242 dead and 89 injured.

The Final Campaigns

In mid-1944 American ground forces and the US 5th Air Force together with supporting forces which included the RAAF's No 10 Operational Group and RAN units had been moving rapidly along the northern coast of New Guinea and points north in preparation for MacArthur's return to the Philippines.

The RAN and RAAF from Hollandia to the Philippines

At midnight on 10 July troops of the Japanese 20th and 41st Divisions struck south of the Driniumor river mouth. The RAAF was called on for air support and from the first light next day an almost uninterrupted air bombardment by RAAF Beauforts and Beaufighters and American Aircobras began. On 14 July a naval task force under Commodore John Collins including the cruisers *Australia* and *Shropshire* joined the operations when they bombarded enemy positions along the coast. By 10 August all enemy resistance in the Aitape area ended.

After the Hollandia triumph MacArthur's American troops swiftly exploited the "amazing weakness" of the enemy by attacking Wakde Island and nearby Sarmi on the mainland on 17 May and Biak Island further west on 27 May. Two RAAF Kittyhawk squadrons were moved forward to Cyclops field at Hollandia to provide air support. Again the British Eastern Fleet, which included four RAN destroyers, sortied into the Indian Ocean and on 17 May carried out a diversionary air strike on Surabaya with 88 aircraft.

Biak had a garrison of 11,000 Japanese troops and the enemy fought back fiercely. It was not until 22 July that effective Japanese resistance ended. In the meantime a flight of RAAF Kittyhawks of No 78 Squadron had encountered a Japanese formation of 15 aircraft over Biak on 3 June and shot down nine for the loss of one Kittyhawk.

On the night of 8–9 June a Japanese naval force threatened Biak but was turned away by Rear Admiral Crutchley's combined US–Australian force. The Japanese planned to reinforce Biak and ordered the giant battleships *Yamato* and *Musashi* to escort reinforcements to the beleaguered defenders. But this plan was "suspended" when the battleships were ordered to rendezvous off the Mariana Islands where a huge American invasion force had been sighted. The American force included some 535 combat vessels and transports carrying 120,000 troops to seize the islands. The Marianas operations by the US Pacific Fleet and at the same time the invasion of Normandy made the month of June "the greatest month yet in military and naval history".

The battle of the Philippine Sea off the Marianas was a major disaster for Japan. In what was called "The great Marianas turkey shoot" American carrier pilots destroyed 480 Japanese aircraft and sank major enemy fleet units. The Americans won control of the surrounding seas and their ground combat forces seized the island. Possession of the Marianas gave the Americans air bases from which B29 "Superfortress" bombers could attack the Japanese home islands some 1,920 kilometres away.

With Japanese attention focussed grimly on the pivotal naval air struggle in the Marianas, MacArthur made two more bypassing advances in New Guinea – to Noemfoor on 2 July and Sansapor (his last) on 30 July. Noemfoor in Geelvink Bay had three airfields from which the whole Vogelkop area and Ambon could be dominated. Both landings were covered by RAN warships. Air Commodore Scherger was the air task commander for the Noemfoor operation and was directed to call forward four RAAF combat wings.

During July the Kittyhawks of No 78 Wing continued to maintain a fighter "umbrella" over Biak, Noemfoor and Hollandia.

MacArthur needed a suitable location as a base for air combat squadrons assigned to the coming operations in the Philippines. He chose Morotai in the Moluccas group, midway between New Guinea and the Philippines. It was lightly garrisoned by the enemy compared with the heavily defended Halmahera Island only a short distance away to the south.

Supported by the RAN ships *Australia*, *Shropshire*, *Arunta* and

Warramunga, an American invasion force was put ashore at Morotai on 15 September against light resistance. "No enemy air attacks were made and no calls for [naval] gunfire were received," Commodore Collins recorded. This contrasted sharply with the experience at Palau which was invaded by central Pacific forces on the same day. The strong Japanese garrison at Palau was subdued only after bitter flighting which cost some 2,000 American lives.

MacArthur's return to the Philippines was planned for November 1944, but Admiral Halsey who had been cruising off the Philippines came to the conclusion that a bolder leap was justified. He recommended that the date be advanced to October 20 and that the landing take place on Leyte in the central Philippines rather than Mindinao. The Combined Chiefs, who were in Quebec, agreed and the 100-mile long (160 km) armada left Hollandia and the Admiralties headed for Leyte Gulf where, after a spectacular naval bombardment, the men of the American 6th Army went ashore. MacArthur joined them and announced "People of the Philippines, I have returned."

The RAN was fully engaged in the Leyte campaign. Commodore Collins' Task Force 74 which included *Australia*, *Shropshire*, *Arunta* and *Warramunga*, operated as part of the 7th US Fleet. The frigate *Gascoyne* and HDML1074 were with the minesweeping and hydrographic group and *Bishopdale*, *Poyang*, *Yunnan* and *Merkur* were part of the service force. As well the destroyers, *Quiberon* and *Norman* bombarded targets on Car Nicobar in the Bay of Bengal as part of a diversionary operation by the Eastern Fleet. Three Australian LSIs (landing ship infantry) *Westralia*, *Manoora* and *Kanimbla* carried troops of the US 21st Regimental Combat Team to the Gulf.

The Australian Army had no immediate role in the Philippines but was to make a landing at Appari in northern Luzon in December. However, this landing was judged to be no longer necessary and was cancelled.

No 10 Group RAAF had been renamed the 1st Tactical Air Force and transferred from the control of the 5th Air Force to the 13th Air Force, both of which were under Kenney's orders. By October 1st TAF had under its control one attack wing (No 77), two fighter wings (Nos

81 and 78) and two Airfield Construction Wings (Nos 61 and 62), and was establishing squadrons at Morotai. In the weeks before the landing on Leyte its squadrons made daily attacks on targets in the Vogelkop and Ambon areas. These squadrons were not to move forward to the Philippines, but to Borneo, except No 3 Airfield Construction Squadron which would, in December, be sent to develop airfields on Mindoro Island in the Philippines from which Manila could be readily attacked.

Shortly after dawn the day after the landing at Leyte (21 October) *Australia* was hit by a Japanese suicide aircraft which killed 30 and wounded 64 members of the ship's company. Captain Dechaineux was mortally wounded and Commodore Collins wounded seriously. From this point on Japanese "Kamikaze" ("Divine Wind") airmen increasingly undertook one-way crashing suicide dives on Allied ships, frequently with devastating results.

Captain R. F. Nicholls of *Shropshire* who took over from Commodore Collins reported:

> *During the dawn stand-to, a low-flying aircraft approached from the land between* Australia *and* Shropshire. *It was taken under fire and retired to the westward. Observers on* Shropshire *reported that the aircraft was hit and touched the water but recovered. It then turned east again and although under heavy fire, passed up the port side of* Australia *and crashed into the foremast at 0605. There was a large explosion and an intense fire was started in the air defence position and bridges. Type 273 radar hut and lantern fell on the compass platform; both H.A. Directors and D.C.T. were put out of action and the port strut of the foremast was broken. The fire was brought under control very quickly and by 0635 the large quality of wreckage on the compass platform and A.D.P. had been cleared away. Commodore J. A. Collins suffered burns and wounds; Captain E. F. V. Dechaineux and Commander J. F. Rayment were mortally wounded ...*

Meanwhile the Japanese Navy had hatched a bold plan to destroy the American invaders. Their main fleet which included seven battleships was divided into two, with one force aiming to enter Leyte Gulf through Surigao Strait and the other through San Bernadino Strait. To lure Admiral Halsey's 3rd Fleet away from Leyte, a third Japanese force which included four carriers steamed down from Japan. Halsey raced north to meet them and sank the four carriers, one of which was *Zuikaku*, last of the six that attacked Pearl Harbor.

As the second Japanese force approached Leyte through Surigao Strait it was met in a night engagement by an American fleet which included the Australian warships *Shropshire* and *Arunta*. A tornado of Allied naval gunfire wiped out the Japanese force. Had the Japanese battleships got through they might well have sunk all the American transports and bombarded the Leyte beachhead. For a time the situation was critical when an enemy force breaking through from the north sank two escort carriers off Leyte.

In spite of the damage she had sustained at Leyte during the landing operation, *Australia* together with *Shropshire*, *Arunta*, *Warramunga*, *Gascoyne* and *Warrego* entered Lingayan Gulf on 8 January 1945 in support of yet another "leap-frogging" advance. Australia completed her bombardment task although hit five times by suiciding Kamikaze pilots who killed 44 of her crew. On her departure for Leyte Vice-Admiral Oldendorf signalled: "Your gallant conduct and that of your ship has been an inspiration to us all."

Strategy for Ground Forces

Between March and September of 1944 MacArthur's command had been receiving substantial reinforcements of American troops and by mid-1944 he commanded 18 American divisions compared with the seven he commanded a year earlier. However, six of these divisions were now tied to the defence of the bases they had captured in Bougainville, New Britain and at Aitape on the mainland of New Guinea. The General wanted to have these divisions available for the coming assault on the Philippines and it was also evident that he wanted to regain this large American dependency with American troops only.

During five years of war, Australia had built its army up to eight infantry divisions and two armoured brigades, together with a large number of RAAF combat units and RAN warships. With the agreement of the Australian Government the Australian Army divisions and brigades together with the RAAF and RAN units in the South-West Pacific had all been placed under MacArthur's operational control. But Australia's manpower resources were now at full stretch and it was proving almost impossible to maintain such a large force in the field. Curtin and MacArthur agreed therefore that by the end of 1944 Australia should maintain a reduced army of six infantry divisions and two armoured brigades for service in combat. This decision was later endorsed by the Combined Chiefs of Staff.

As early as November 1943, Prime Minister Curtin had held the view and so informed MacArthur that Australia had a special interest in the employment of her own troops to drive the Japanese from New Guinea. Thus it was clear that both Curtin and MacArthur were agreed that Australian troops would replace American troops which were providing garrisons for bypassed bases in the New Guinea-Solomons-New Britain area. Curtin told the Advisory War Council later, "We could not escape the logic of the decision that Australian troops should garrison the islands which formed her own outer screen of defence and which were mostly our own territory."

At the same time the Australian Government considered it was vital to the future of Australia and her status at the peace table that her military effort should be concentrated as far as possible in the Pacific and that Australian forces should continue to be associated with MacArthur's command in the forward movement against Japan. It was no surprise therefore when on 12 July 1944 MacArthur directed Blamey to employ Australian troops to take over responsibility for the bypassed areas by the following dates:

Northern Solomons-Green Island-Emirau Island	1 Oct 44
Australian New Guinea	1 Nov 44
New Britain	1 Nov 44

General Blamey had anticipated that Australian troops would be called on for the garrison tasks in New Guinea-Solomons, and he sought MacArthur's agreement to the commitment of six Australian brigades to hold the perimeters in these areas. This commitment would be little more than one-third of the strength of American forces engaged and MacArthur would not agree. He required 12 brigades and on 2 August 1944 directed that the minimum forces to be used in the New Guinea area would be:

Bougainville	4 brigades
Emirau, Green, Treasury and New Georgia Islands	1 brigade
New Britain	3 brigades
New Guinea mainland	4 brigades

In each of these bypassed areas the American garrisons had been holding fairly small perimeters to defend their bases from Japanese attack. The bases were large enough to prevent the Japanese shelling their airfields and supply dumps. But the Americans did not seriously consider clearing the enemy from the surrounding territory.

Blamey instructed First Army (under Lieutenant General Vernon Sturdee) to move to Lae and take command of all forces in the New Guinea territories, while II Corps (Lieutenant General Stanley Savige) would take over the northern Solomons. General Savige had the 3rd Australian Division and two independent brigades (the 11th and 23rd). The 5th Division was allotted to New Britain and the 6th Division to Aitape in New Guinea, while the 8th Brigade would continue to operate between Madang and the Sepik River.

At a conference on 11 August 1944 Blamey told his commanders that the primary role of the Australian Army in the bypassed areas would be the protection of their bases. However, his Operations Instruction of 18 October 1944 to First Army provided for offensive action to destroy enemy resistance as opportunity offered without committing major forces. He indicated, however, that at Torokina (Bougainville) the Australian forces "would not perhaps be quite so passive". An offensive operation against New Britain and the quite powerful Rabaul bastion, which bristled with armaments and well-fed troops, was out of the question. It would have to be left "to wither on the vine". The Australians would be outnumbered six to one and any attempt to take it by ground assault could lead to a blood bath for the attackers. To discourage any rekindling of the aggressive spirit by the defenders of Rabaul, the RAAF and the American AirForce would maintain a constant aerial bombardment of the base.

Few Australian troops were in action in the third quarter of 1944. The divisions of the army which had been heavily engaged in 1943–43 were mostly in Australia, resting and retraining for the final campaigns of the war in 1945. Only a small force was in contact with the enemy. The commitment of three divisions, the 6th, 3rd and 5th, and the independent brigades in the bypassed areas, meant a sharp increase in army operations.

The Solomons

On Bougainville, General Savige's II Australian Corps relieved the American Army's XIV Corps (commanded by Major General Oscar Griswold) on 12 December. Brigadier A. W. Potts commanding the 23rd Brigade had already opened his headquarters on Green Island north of Bougainville on 27 September. His task was to garrison the outlying islands in the northern Solomons. He placed his 27th Battalion on Green Island, the 8th on Emirau and the 7th on Treasury off southern Bougainville, with one company at Munda, further south.

To support the Australian army operations on Bougainville, the Royal New Zealand Air Force's No 1 Group with four fighter-bomber squadrons equipped with Corsair fighters and two Ventura bomber squadrons were also assigned to Bougainville, together with the RAAF's No 84 Army Cooperation Wing, commanded by Group Captain W. L. Hely. With the wing came No 5 Tactical Reconnaissance Squadron, RAAF, equipped with Boomerangs and Wirraway aircraft. It moved into the Piva airfield at Torokina.

On 22 December 1944, General Savige issued instructions to his corps which indicated that he would undertake a campaign to destroy Japanese forces on Bougainville. Three simultaneous offensives would be mounted. In northern Bougainville the ultimate aim was to force the enemy garrison into the narrow Bonis peninsula. In the central sector an offensive would clear the enemy from the high ground at Pearl Ridge on the Numa Numa trail. The main enemy concentrations were in the garden areas in southern Bougainville where the decisive battle of the campaign would be fought.[1]

The tasks facing the Australians in Bougainville appeared to exceed their resources. Japanese numerical strength was greater than that of II Corps. American intelligence estimated Japanese strength at 12,000 but Australian intelligence staff at Land Headquarters gave an estimate of 25,000. In fact in October 1944 Japanese strength was between 27,000 and 40,000 including naval personnel and civilian workers. As well as being outnumbered the Australians were handicapped by lack of shipping.

In the central sector along the Numa Numa trail Australians of the 7th Brigade took over responsibility from American troops on 22 November. On 18 December, supported by New Zealand Corsairs and artillery, it attacked and took Arty Hill. After this loss the Japanese sent 600 reinforcements to Pearl Ridge, the Australians' next objective. Again New Zealand Corsairs directed to the target by a RAAF Boomerang bombed the Japanese positions, and after a stiff fight costing ten Australian lives the ridge was captured.

Later the 23rd Brigade was brought in from the outlying islands and continued the advance towards Numa Numa on the east coast of Bougainville.

North from Torokina the 31st/51st Battalion of the 11th Brigade advanced rapidly towards the Bonis peninsula. At the end of January 1945 it encountered strong enemy defensive positions on Tsimba Ridge. Between 17 January and 26 February the battalion killed an estimated 148 enemy with a loss to itself of 34 soldiers. On 28 March the battalion pushed in to the north and captured Soraken peninsula.

On 8 June the 31st/51st suffered a sharp reverse when using landing craft in an attempt to outflank a strong Japanese position at Porton plantation on the Bonis Peninsula. The leading troops landed without mishap but the second landing craft grounded on coral and was caught in intense hostile fire which killed 23 Australians and wounded 106. Corsair fighter bombers were called in to bomb and strafe the enemy but the Australians were forced to evacuate while aircraft flew constantly over the area to suppress hostile fire.

On 20 June the 23rd Brigade took over in northern Bougainville with orders to contain the enemy in the Bonis Peninsula where an estimated 1,200 Japanese were deployed. The last actions in Bougainville were fought by the 8th Battalion which had been brought to Bougainville from Emirau. On 24 July the battalion attacked an enemy position, base 5, after artillery bombardment and mortar fire. A 20-year-old militiaman, Private Frank Partridge, though wounded in both arm and thigh, rushed forward under hot fire to retrieve a Bren gun from beside a fallen Australian soldier and exchanged fire with a Japanese manned bunker. He then advanced towards the bunker with a grenade in one hand and a rifle in the other. He threw the grenade into the bunker and as soon as it had burst, dived in and killed a surviving Japanese. For his courage in battle he was awarded the Victoria Cross. It was the last VC awarded to an Australian in the Second World War, and the only one awarded to a militiaman.

Meanwhile operations by the 3rd Australian Division in southern Bougainville began on 10 December 1944 when the 29th Brigade relieved the United States 182nd Regiment. By late December the 29th Brigade had crossed the Jaba River. The Northern Solomons Air Command supported the advance by ordering frequent air strikes. On 11 January 1945, Flight Lieutenant W. Vernon, RAAF, led in a strike of Corsairs against Mawaraka, which was entered by the Australians on 17 January 1945.

Against light opposition, the 25th Battalion crossed the Puriata River on 4 March and thrust the enemy from Slater's Knoll. However, in the second week of March it became evident that Japanese resistance was stiffening. Enemy artillery shelled Slater's Knoll and their infantry dug in nearby. An Australian company was surrounded and attacked persistently over a period of three days.

The Australians continued their advance towards Tokinotu and there the 25th Battalion encountered enemy pillboxes. Two Australian platoons made a bayonet charge which drove the enemy from part of its stronghold. On 22 March during further attacks, preceded by air strikes and an artillery barrage, Corporal Reginald Rattey of the 25th Battalion led his section using a Bren gun and grenades to knock out four Japanese posts. In an hour the positions had been taken. The enemy left 18 dead while five Australians were wounded, of whom two remained in action. Rattey was awarded the Victoria Cross for his actions.

A week later on 29 March, the Japanese launched a major attack with 2,700 troops and succeeded in isolating four Australian companies. After a mortar bombardment the Japanese charged with bayonets fixed. Twelve were killed. For long periods three of the forward Australian companies were out of touch. On 30 March Matilda tanks were brought up and the Japanese fled, leaving eight killed by the tanks. The Japanese attacked again on 5 April and suffered crippling losses. Between 28 March and 5 April, Australian casualties were 25 killed, but 620 Japanese bodies were counted. After this battle the Japanese withdrew and their offensive ended.

Air attacks by New Zealand Corsairs carrying 500 lb and 1,000 lb bombs, together with Mitchells and Catalinas of the US Marine Corps, continued punishing raids on the Japanese who now withdrew to the Hongorai River. Supported by artillery and Matilda tanks and air strikes, the 24th Battalion advanced further southwards and crossed the Hongorai River on 30 May. Shortly afterwards the Australians launched an offensive along the Buin Road towards the centre of Japanese power in southern Bougainville.

By July, the 3rd Division had reached the Mivo River. As the Australians pushed ahead, the enemy resisted strongly, employing a heavy artillery barrage to challenge their progress.

The Japanese planned to launch another "decisive" offensive in early September with some 9,000 troops taking part. However, news of Emperor Hirohito's surrender interrupted their plans and on 18 August a representative of the Japanese commanding general, Masatane Kanda, crossed the Mivo to negotiate the surrender. Of the 65,000 Japanese who occupied the island when the American marines invaded at Torokina on November 1943, 23,571 survived.

Japanese records show that 18,300 Japanese had died from all causes in the period of Australian ground operations in Bougainville. Australian battle casualties were 516 killed and 1,572 wounded in action.

The RAN frigate *Diamantina* and the corvettes *Kiama*, *Lithgow*, *Dubbo* and *Colac* provided naval support from time to time to the Australian forces on Bougainville. In May 1945 *Colac* was sent on a mission to Choiseul Island to search for enemy barge traffic and fought a duel with a Japanese gun which damaged her engine room. *Colac* survived the encounter and was towed to Sydney.

Australian guerillas, including Lieutenant P. Mason of the RAN Reserve, were active in Bougainville behind the enemy lines. Mason's guerilla force operated in the mountains above Kieta and killed a large number of Japanese in patrol fighting, ambushes and surprise raids. Captain C. W. Seton relieved Mason who was brought in to rest in May 1945. The guerilla leaders estimated that their native followers killed some 2,200 Japanese in eight months.

The Watch on Rabaul

Rabaul, located on the north-eastern extremity of New Britain, had been the strongest Japanese military bastion in the South-West Pacific. In 1944 it had an even greater manpower strength than Allied intelligence estimates allowed: total army–navy strength was 93,000 compared with the 38,000 estimated by Allied intelligence. These now bypassed forces were concentrated mainly in the Gazelle peninsula and anticipating the continuation of the heavy Allied air attacks they began in 1943 to build a system of underground tunnels where they stored sufficient food, ammunition and supplies to last a considerable time. The garrison waited expectantly and confidently to meet an Allied attack, believing they could inflict 100,000 casualties.

Rabaul had been sterilised militarily, and had presented no great impediment to MacArthur's advance to the Philippines. Nevertheless a watch had to be kept on such a large concentration of combat-ready enemy soldiers, and that task had been assigned to the Australian

5th Division (6th and 13th Brigades) commanded by Major General Alan Ramsay.

All thought of a major Australian offensive to seize Rabaul had to be dismissed, and the limited policy decided on was "to drive the enemy patrols back to the Gazelle peninsula and then regain control of the major portion of New Britain and contain a large force in the northern end of the island with a considerably smaller one".

On 4 November 1944 the 5th Division was landed at Jacquinot Bay – except for one battalion, the 36th, which was sent to Cape Hoskins on the north coast. Both locations were far to the east of existing Allied bases. No enemy troops had been reported in Jacquinot Bay, nevertheless the division was provided with an escort of three RAN warships: *Barcoo*, *Vendetta* and *Swan*. After covering the landing, the RAN warships sailed north and bombarded Japanese positions in Wide Bay.

In this period the rigid aerial and naval blockade of Rabaul was reinforced by air and naval units of the United States and New Zealand. RAAF Beauforts of Nos 6, 8 and 100 Squadrons struck Rabaul nine days before the 5th Division landed at Jacquinot Bay. On the day of the landing, all three squadrons bombed targets in the Wide Bay area. In December No 6 Squadron made six strikes in the Rabaul area.

Meanwhile the 36th Battalion had pushed steadily forward from Cape Hoskins to Open Bay. On the south coast, fighting developed in March 1945 when the 19th Battalion moved to secure the Waitavolo-Tol area on Wide Bay. By 10 March the Japanese were concentrated on one hill and suffering heavy casualties, mainly from artillery fire. The 12th/32nd Battalion took over from 19th and after hard fighting dispersed the surviving Japanese. In May 1945 the RNZAF's No 20 Squadron began flying offensive patrols over Rabaul from Jacquinot Bay. The pilots strafed troops and barges and bombed until 12 August when operations ceased.

The 5th Division had by May 1945 established a firm line across the neck of the Gazelle peninsula and continued its policy of containing the enemy. When the surrender of Rabaul came in August the division was very surprised to learn that the enemy they had "contained" was a force equivalent to five depleted but experienced divisions. Among those who surrendered were 19 generals and 11 admirals. The grand total of Japanese in New Britain and New Ireland in August 1944 had been 101,000.

Australian casualties in 1944–1945 in New Britain were 53 killed and 140 wounded. Another 21 died of other causes.

The Last New Guinea Campaign

Besides the troops in Bougainville and New Britain, there was a large force of Japanese that had still not been eliminated in New Guinea. These were the survivors of Lieutenant General Hatazo Adachi's XVIII Army, which included the men of the 20th, 41st and 51st Divisions who had fought against the Australians in the offensive of 1943–44. Adachi's army originally was about 100,000 strong, but by the end of 1944 it had dwindled to about 35,000.

The XVIII Army was based in the Wewak area where it had prepared to repel the invading Allies. But MacArthur had bypassed Wewak and landed instead at Aitape much further to the west. Adachi had quickly mounted an offensive against the American Army but his forces were decisively defeated in July. Now the American XI Corps at Aitape were ordered to prepare for the Philippines campaign and their base at Aitape was taken over by the 6th Australian Division, commanded by Major General Jack Stevens. Elements of the 6th Division began arriving at Aitape in October 1944.

General Blamey's instructions to the 1st Army which had operational control of the 6th Division was that in all New Guinea areas the Australian garrisons would be more active than the American garrisons had been. An operational instruction issued to the 6th Division on 16 October defined the division's role thus:

(a) to defend airfield and radar installations in the Aitape-Tadji areas;
(b) to prevent movement westward of Japanese forces in the area and seize every opportunity for the destruction of these forces;
(c) to give maximum help to AIF and Angau units in the

area in their tasks of gaining intelligence, establishing patrol bases and protecting the native population.

Air support for the Australian Army was to be given by No 71 Wing, RAAF, which included Nos 7, 8 and 100 Squadrons equipped with Beaufort bombers.

After taking over from the US 43rd Division on the Driniumor river front, General Stevens ordered extensive patrolling and then developed two simultaneous drives, one along the coastline towards Wewak, the ultimate goal, and one across the Torricelli ranges towards the garden areas to the south where the enemy was spreading rapidly in order to obtain vital food supplies.

The veteran 17th and 19th Brigades were soon in action and by January 1945 when the 19th Brigade was relieved by the 16th Brigade, it had killed 434 enemy for the loss of 36 Australians. Heavy rain which fell on 26 January caused the loss of seven soldiers of the 2/3rd Battalion who were marooned on an island in the flooded Danmap River with 27 metres of swirling flood waters on either side. They were swept away and drowned.

The 16th Brigade encountered resistance on the coast at Nambut hill in early February, but after air strikes by the RAAF with Boomerangs of No 4 Squadron and Beauforts of Nos 7 and 8 Squadrons, the infantry attacked on 18 February and finally cleared the hill.

By 19 March the 2/2nd Battalion had occupied But airfield and a week later Dagua airfield, which was still strewn with the scattered wrecks of Japanese war planes. On 19 March Blamey visited But and approved a plan for an overland advance along the coastal plain to Wewak some 33 kilometres ahead of the forward troops.

On 3 April, across the ranges, Brigadier M. J. Moten, the 17th Brigade Commander, ordered a final thrust against Maprik. Around Maprik the Japanese were dug in on dominating features and the 2/7th Battalion fought hard for ten days before the Japanese had been driven out or had been killed where they stood. The site for an airfield named Hayfield was also captured and by 14 May the first Dakota transport aircraft landed, easing the 17th Brigade's difficult supply problems.

Wewak, the Japanese XVIII Army stronghold, was attacked by troops of the 6th Australian Division on 11 May. The assault was preceded by heavy air attacks delivered by aircraft of the RAAF and by RAN bombardments carried out by the cruisers HMAS *Hobart*, HMS *Newfoundland* (on loan from the British Pacific Fleet), *Arunta*, *Warramunga* and *Swan*. Immediately the naval bombardment ended, "Farida Force" (comprising two squadrons of army commandos brought from But to Wewak by the Navy's *Swan*, *Dubbo* and *Colac*) were transferred to landing barges from which they began wading through the surf at Dove Bay at 8.34 am against "very light opposition".

In addition to the amphibious aircraft, the 19th Brigade advanced against Wewak Point at dawn on 10 May and by 8 am the objective was in their hands. The Japanese had abandoned their great base leaving rearguards to hold exits.

The 19th Brigade was heavily engaged on a hill above Wewak airfield on 14 May and took all but three enemy posts. Two of these were knocked out next day by Private E. Kenna of the 2/4th Battalion who stood in the open and fired with a Bren gun, then a rifle, then again with a Bren. The remaining post was knocked out next day by a tank, giving complete control of the Wewak coastal plane. Kenna's courage was recognised by the award of the Victoria Cross.

In June 1945 the 8th Brigade, which was operating in the Madang area, was ordered to Wewak, where it was assigned to defending the base while the other brigades pursued the Japanese who were withdrawing into the mountains to the south. As the Australians pressed inland resistance stiffened and they had to fight tough battles to capture Mt Tazaki and Mt Shiburangu. Mt Tazaki fell on 22 June after heavy attacks by three squadrons of RAAF Beaufort bombers and constant artillery barrages. The 2/8th Battalion took Mt Shiburangu on 27 June.

The RAAF was running short of bombs towards the end of the war and supplemented its supply from captured Japanese stocks. Unfortunately many proved to be duds.

Further inland, the 17th Brigade captured Kairivu on 8 August. The village was only 24 kilometres from other 6th Division forces approaching from the Wewak area.

News of the surrender of Japan came on 15 August just after 30 Beaufort bombers of Nos 7, 8 and 100 squadrons struck targets in the Kairivu area. After the strike was completed the senior controller told the airborne squadrons over the radio-telephone: "The following signal has just been received from Command Headquarters in plain language: 'Emergency. Immediate-Cancel all operations against enemy forthwith including missions now airborne.' "

Some 13,500 Japanese of the XVIII Army remained alive at the end of the war in the Wewak area. In October 1944 its strength had been between 35,000 and 40,000 and at the end of operations in August 1945, 9,000 had been killed and between 12,000 and 14,000 had died of illness. Of approximately 300,000 Japanese who were landed in New Guinea and the Solomons from January 1942, only 127,000 were alive at the surrender.

In its final campaign the 6th Australian Division lost 442 killed in action or died of wounds and 1,141 wounded. Admissions to hospital because of sickness totalled 16,203.

Critics of the Final Campaigns

Critics of the conduct of Australian campaigns in the South-West Pacific in 1944–45 have long contended that "needless and wasteful offensives" were undertaken against a "strategically impotent" enemy.

The voices of the critics grew louder as the death toll steadily rose and as the nagging feelings grew that Australian soldiers, some long-serving veterans of the Middle East campaigns now in sight of final victory, were dying needlessly in "mopping up" campaigns in bypassed areas.

The Supreme Commander, MacArthur, was himself an enthusiastic advocate of the bypassing manoeuvre, which became the Pacific war's most momentous strategic concept, a concept which the Japanese hated most but respected because it gained the most for their enemies whilst losing the fewest men.

MacArthur claimed that the bypassed Japanese were no longer capable of influencing the course of the war and should merely be contained and left to "wither on the vine". In a report to the American

Army Chief of Staff (General George Marshall) he wrote:

> *The enemy garrisons which have been bypassed in the Solomons*
> *and New Guinea represented no menace to current or future*
> *operations. Their capacity for organised offensive effort has*
> *passed. The various process of attrition will eventually account*
> *for their final disposition. The actual time of their destruction is*
> *of little or no importance and their influence as a contributing*
> *factor to the war is already negligible. The actual process of their*
> *immediate destruction by assault methods would unquestionably*
> *involve heavy loss of life without adequate compensating*
> *strategic advantages.*

However, MacArthur did not apply the same military logic when he
returned to the Philippines. General Blamey, under attack in Australia
for his "wasteful and unnecessary offensives in New Guinea and
Bougainville", pointed out that MacArthur committed his 8th Army to
the complete destruction of the Japanese who had been bypassed in the
southern Philippines, at a cost of 454 American lives. Blamey added that
he appeared not to have been criticised on the grounds that these
operations were not necessary. In later years, however, he was. Professor
Samuel Morison, the US Navy historian, said it was somewhat of a
mystery how MacArthur derived the authority to liberate one
Philippines island after another. The Joint Chiefs of Staff, he said,
permitted him to do as he pleased up to a point.

By April 1945 discontent with the "backyard" war had increased
sharply and the issue spilled over into press and parliament. On 26 April
both Blamey and Curtin were under attack in the Federal Parliament by
the Opposition Leader, Mr Menzies, who said:

> *I happen to entertain the strongest possible view that it is wrong*
> *to use the Australian forces, which, we are told, number*
> *hundreds of thousands of men – in operations in those islands*
> *which seem to me to have no relation to any first class strategic*
> *objective in this war.*

Blamey was called upon to explain and eventually both the Advisory War Council and the War Cabinet approved his general policy which was "to destroy the enemy where it could be done with light casualties, but where conditions were not favourable to the destruction of the enemy, to contain him in a restricted area by the use of a much smaller force".

The end of the war in August 1945 did not end the debate on the "backyard" campaigns nor has time extinguished it since. In commenting on the Australian soldier in the final campaigns Gavin Long paid this fine tribute:

> *Always a realist and therefore the more keenly aware of the*
> *probably doubtful value of the tasks to which he had been*
> *relegated, nevertheless the battlewise Australian soldier fought on*
> *to the end with the same devotion and skill that he had shown*
> *in the decisive battles of earlier years.*

By March 1945 the growing belief that the Australians were engaging in operations of doubtful strategic value was not confined to the Army. A similar controversial issue surfaced in the RAAF at Morotai and reached a sensational climax in April when eight distinguished young leaders asked for permission to resign their commissions.

These officers, some of whom were highly decorated fighter aces, refused to give their reasons for this action not only to Air Commodore Harry Cobby, who commanded 1st Tactical Air Force, but also to General George Kenney, commander of Far East Air Force, who was ultimately responsible for assigning air operational duties in the theatre. Kenney urged them not on any account "to throw in your badges". He said he had many air units in back areas in the theatre doing garrison duties and they were "fed up" with their role.

At this stage of the war 1st Tactical Air Force, RAAF, was under the direct operational control of the American 13th Air Force and had been directed to "continue the neutralisation and destruction of the enemy in his installations in Celebes, Ceram-Ambon and Halmahera areas". These areas had been bypassed by the advance of South-West Pacific forces to the Philippines and the large Japanese combat forces left behind in these areas had to be harassed and neutralised. This was a task primarily for air and naval forces. In pursuit of this objective 1st TAF in January 1945 alone had carried out a total of 661 sorties against Halmahera, Celebes, Morotai and the Vogelkop area of New Guinea. In a "blitz" in the period 22/25 December Cobby mustered a total of 384 RAAF Kittyhawk and 129 Beaufighter sorties against Halmahera. Australian and American aircraft were over the target area continually dropping bombs, and napalm and firing rockets and machine guns.

Many pilots believed that not only were they required to carry out secondary operations in a "backyard" war but the lives of air crew were being endangered in carrying out attacks on "worthless" targets that made no realistic contribution to winning the war.

The fundamental cause of the Air Force "mutiny" at Morotai had been the conviction of young Air Force leaders that they had been engaging in operations that were not militarily justifiable, a conviction, as we have seen, widely shared by many Australian soldiers in the Bougainville-New Guinea operations. One of the Air Force leaders, 23-year-old Group Captain Wilfred Arthur, had already, late in 1944, drawn Cobby's attention to what he believed were unjustifiable losses in men and material.

Air Commodore Cobby, the top-scoring fighter ace of the Australian Flying Corps in France in the First World War, and two senior officers were relieved of their duties in First Tactical Air Force and the Government appointed Mr J. V. Barry, KC (later Justice Sir John Barry) to carry out an inquiry. After hearing a great deal of evidence, he came to the conclusion that:

> ... *from about the beginning of January 1945 there was a widespread condition of discontent and dissatisfaction within First TAF at Morotai. The two main factors which brought about this condition were the opinions generally held about the nature of the operational activities upon which wings were engaged and the attitude of the two senior staff officers ...*

Barry's terms of reference did not require him to make a judgement on whether or not the operations in First TAF were wasteful. Nevertheless his report stated "that expenditure on the operations described by certain unit commanders far exceeded the material damage inflicted on the enemy and that, from that standpoint they were wasteful."

First Tactical Air Force was soon heavily involved in operations against Borneo and with their former leader Air Commodore Scherger (who had been injured in a road accident) now back in command the situation soon returned to normal.

The RAAF and RAN in the Final Operations

In 1944 American aircraft production had created a surplus of combat planes and General Kenney arranged for enough Liberator bombers to be provided for seven RAAF squadrons. The first three squadrons to be equipped were Nos 21, 23 and 24 Squadrons which had flown Vultee Vengeance aircraft until they were rejected. The first RAAF Liberator went into action from Manbulloo in August 1944. The Liberators carried out attacks on Netherlands East Indies targets as far afield as Borneo and Java. Later Nos 12, 25, 99 and 102 Squadrons were equipped with the long-range bomber.

RAAF Catalina squadrons, in addition to night bombing raids on the Netherlands East Indies, were employed in sowing anti-shipping mines as far north as the Philippines, Hong Kong and the China coast. At the end of the war the RAAF claimed that 23 enemy ships had been sunk by their mines and another 27 damaged.

On 25 December 1944, the German submarine U862 attacked and crippled the American ship *Robert J. Walker*, off Moruya, NSW. RAAF aircraft and US and RAN ships were despatched to the scene but the ship sank the next day after having been abandoned by the crew. The *U862* struck again the following February when it sank the motor vessel *Peter Silvester* 800 miles off Fremantle in the Indian Ocean. This was the last sinking by submarines off Australia in the Second World War. All told 19 ships were sunk by submarines off the Australian east coast during the Second World War with fatal casualties of 467.

On 15 January 1945, four pilots of No 80 Squadron RAAF went on a ferry flight to Morotai from Noemfoor, overshot their destination and were forced to land their Kittyhawk aircraft on Talaud Island, midway between Morotai and the Philippines. They were seized and interrogated by the Japanese military and then executed in a special ceremony before a parade of soldiers. After the war these terrible events were investigated and a number of Japanese were tried, found guilty and executed for the crime.

The crew and "operatives" of the *Krait* were only just back from the outstanding "Jaywick" raid on Singapore shipping when their leader Major Ian Lyons immediately planned another raid, operation "Rimau". Lyons took with him five men of the Jaywick expedition. They trained at Garden Island (now Fleet Base West) and proceeded to the Singapore area by the RN submarine *Porpoise*. After leaving the submarine on 28 September 1944 they seized a Malayan craft at Pontianak and approached Singapore. But they were detected, and all lost their lives either when resisting capture or when the Japanese executed them after capture at Singapore in July 1945. Thus the courageous venture was a total disaster in which 23 brave men died.

Tarakan

On 21 March 1945 General MacArthur had informed Prime Minister Curtin that he planned to use I Australian Corps (which included the 9th Division and was commanded by Lieutenant General Sir Leslie Morshead) to attack Borneo and seize Java. He was to be responsible for restoring Netherlands East Indies authorities to their seat of government. When this objective was achieved it was his intention to recommend to the Joint Chiefs of Staff that the mission of the South-West Pacific Area had been accomplished and that the command should be abolished.

The original planning for the operations which were designated the "Oboe" series called for a landing at Tarakan, an oil-rich island off the east coast of Borneo, followed by five more at Balikpapan, Banjermasin, Sourabaya, East Netherlands East Indies and finally British Borneo. However, on 4 April the American Joint Chiefs of Staff directed that

North Borneo was to be given a higher priority: it was to be occupied by the 9th Division immediately after they had taken Tarakan, since a landing in North Borneo would threaten Japanese communications with South-East Asia and secure oil and rubber supplies.

The Tarakan assault took place just one week before the final collapse of the Axis in Europe and at a time when the Japanese armed forces in the South-West Pacific were at the end of their tether. Victory in the war was certain, and in these circumstances it was imperative that Australian casualties should be kept to a minimum. One sure means of ensuring this objective was to call for heavy aerial bombardment of all enemy defended positions prior to assault.

Air Vice Marshal W. D. Bostock was in charge of the air preparations. For weeks prior to the assault on Tarakan, bombers of the RAAF, the 13th Air Force and the 5th Air Force ranged far and wide dropping heavy bomb loads not only on Tarakan but on enemy airfields and installations in the general area which might be used to counter the Australian attack. Two RAAF Liberator squadrons were brought up from the Darwin area to Morotai to join 1st Tactical Air Force in these operations, while No 25 Squadron based in Western Australia took part by staging its Liberators through Corrunna Downs in the western State's north-west.

The landing at Tarakan was preceded by a four-day naval bombardment and on the day of the landing Michell attack planes, Liberators and Lightning fighters of the 13th Air Force bombed and strafed the landing areas.

Naval support was provided by a large force which included the RAN's *Hobart*, *Warramunga*, *Burdekin*, *Barcoo*, *Hawkesbury* and *Lachlan*, while the LSIs *Manoora* and *Westralia* were among 56 vessels and craft in the invasion convoy which brought the assault troops to Tarakan.

On 1 May 1945, when Australian troops of the 9th Division stormed ashore they met virtually no opposition. The Japanese garrison of some 2,000 troops was heavily outnumbered by the 12,000-strong Australian invading force.

After the successful landing, the three battalions of the 26th Brigade made rapid progress and by 5 May the Australian flag was hoisted over the Tarakan airfield by the 2/24th Battalion.

The airfield was a key objective for the operation and was to be brought into use as early as possible. But heavy rain fell, the ground was waterlogged, no suitable rock was available for construction work and enemy raiders and artillery interfered with operations. As a result, and in spite of the prodigious efforts of the RAAF airfield construction squadrons engaged, unacceptable delays occurred and the airfield could not be made ready in time to receive the Kittyhawk fighters of the RAAF's No 78 Wing or the Beaufighters of No 77 (Attack) Wing. Ultimately these wings were ordered to Sanga Sanga in the southern Philippines from which they gave air cover for operations on Tarakan.

Two companies of Pioneers came under heavy Japanese fire on 7 May but forced the enemy back to an important stronghold. Here on 12 May Corporal J. B. Mackey, leading a section of Pioneers of the 2/3 Pioneer Battalion overcame a Japanese machine gun post in a hand-to-hand struggle. He charged a second post, killed the crew, and then silenced a third before he fell mortally wounded. He received a posthumous award of the Victoria Cross.

The Australians continued their advance supported by aircraft and artillery. On 22 May, after an air strike by Liberators and Lightnings which was hampered by low cloud, Lieutenant Thomas Derrick, VC, DCM, of the 2/48th Battalion led a most courageous attack on a vital feature. Two platoons were involved in some of the heaviest close-in fighting of the campaign. One Australian and 28 enemy were killed. Next morning at dawn the enemy hit back, killing two and wounding eight Australians including Derrick, who died next day. "The news of Derrick's death," wrote a battalion diarist, "had a very profound effect on the whole battalion as he had become a legend and an inspiration to the whole unit. An original member he had served with distinction through every campaign in which the battalion took part ... Tobruk, Tel el Eisa, El Alamein, Lae, Finschhafen, Sattelberg, Tarakan ..."

The Australians continued to harry the Japanese defenders of Tarakan from one position to another and on 4 June a letter was dropped to the enemy commanders suggesting a parley so that the Australians could care for the Japanese wounded. It was ignored. But on 14 June it was found that the Japanese had made substantial withdrawals and the pursuit of the retreating enemy began. Their commander had ordered his remaining forces to split up into independent groups who would fight on to the death. So the fighting went on. When the war ended the counted Japanese dead on Tarakan numbered 1,540. Another 252 surrendered before the war ended and another 300 after it.

The Australian Army on Tarakan lost 225 killed and 669 wounded. The principal objective of the operation – to provide an airfield for the support of air operations against Brunei Bay-Labuan and Balikpapan – was not achieved because insurmountable construction problems prevented the preparation of the airfield in time.

British North Borneo

A large-scale amphibious invasion convoy carrying two brigades (the 20th and 24th) of the Australian 9th Division invaded British North Borneo on 10 June.

The operation involving 30,000 men was the second phase of the Borneo campaign and aimed to eject the Japanese from Labuan, Maura Islands and Brunei.

Before the assault landing eight squadrons of Liberator bombers (six from the 13th Air Force and two from the RAAF) went in and attacked Labuan behind the beachheads to obliterate opposition. Before the Australian assault waves moved towards the beaches, naval forces also attacked, delivering an hour's intensive naval bombardment. No resistance could be observed near the beaches when the troops went ashore and by 11.29 am the 24th brigade troops were within sight of the Labuan airfield.

The 20th Brigade landings at Maura and Brooketon on the Borneo mainland were equally successful and by nightfall on 10 June the brigade had advanced nearly three kilometres towards Brunei. Three days later the Brigade entered Brunei town against slight opposition.

Brunei Bay has the best harbour on the northwest coast of Borneo and the US Chiefs of Staff had proposed that it should be used as an advanced naval base for the British Pacific Fleet. But Britain had argued against this because it was too far from the main theatre of operations.

Nevertheless the operation using Australian troops of the 9th Division supported by the US Seventh Fleet and the RAAF went ahead. The RAN was well represented in the operation by HMAS *Hobart* in addition to *Arunta, Hawkesbury, Barcoo*, and *Lachlan* together with the LSIs *Westralia, Manoora* and *Kanimbla*.

Air Vice Marshal Bostock controlled air support which was provided by the First Tactical Air Force and the 13th Air force. The 5th Air Force also loaned two groups of bombers for the pre-assault bombardment. RAAF heavy bomber Liberator squadrons based in Western Australia (Cunderdin) and the Darwin area had the task of neutralising enemy bases beyond the range of Allied aircraft based in the Philippines and at Morotai. To support the North Borneo operations, 1st TAF established on Labuan No 81 (Fighter) Wing, No 452 Spitfire Squadron, No 86 (Attack) Wing and No 83 (Army Cooperation) Wing, with a total of seven squadrons. On 18 June RAAF Spitfires and Kittyhawks at Labuan took over responsibility for close air support. Japanese air reaction to the invasion was weak, the enemy sending only an occasional nuisance raider.

On Labuan, the Japanese who survived the initial clashes withdrew into a stronghold called "The Pocket". The capture of The Pocket called for a full-scale attack with infantry, tanks and heavy artillery support. On 18 June *Shropshire* joined in with its eight-inch guns. The Japanese continued a resolute resistance and on 20 June bombers were called in to blast the position. Finally two companies of the 2/28th Battalion (veterans of the siege of Tobruk) attacked, and soon bulldozers were burying some 180 Japanese who had been killed in The Pocket.

The 24th Brigade now began operations across Brunei Bay from Labuan Island to the main Borneo island. On 17 June the 2/32nd Battalion occupied the town of Weston. Ten days later the 2/43rd and the 2/32nd moved against the town of Beaufort where some 1000 Japanese troops were positioned. During the battle for the towns Private Leslie Starcevich, a young Western Australian farmer and gold miner, overcame a series of enemy posts. His extraordinary bravery is described by a witness in his own company:

… firmly and confidently believing that he can never be hit, he walks into an enemy post preceded by a single and unbroken stream of pellets … he is quite unmoved by returning fire and stops only when the enemy has been annihilated …

Private Starcevich was decorated with the Victoria Cross, the second last awarded to an Australian in the Second World War.

Beaufort fell on 29 June, the 24th Brigade losing 7 killed and 38 wounded. The Japanese lost 93 killed.

Meanwhile the 20th Brigade, after setting up its headquarters in the Residency at Brunei, moved its battalions south towards the oilfields of British North Borneo. On 20 June, supported by Spitfires and Kittyhawks of the RAAF and the RAN's *Arunta*, the 2/13th Battalion landed in the Miri-Lutong area, securing its objectives without sighting the enemy. Next day Seria, where the Japanese had set fire to 37 oil wells, was occupied by the 2/17th Battalion. The work of extinguishing the oil fires took three months.

Having secured the coast from Papar in the north to Miri in the south, the 9th Division's objectives in North Borneo had been achieved.

In the fighting 114 Australian soldiers were killed or died of wounds, while Japanese loses were 1234 counted dead and 130 taken prisoner.

Balikpapan

On 1 July 1945 assault troops of the 7th Australian Division stormed ashore through a red haze directly against the heart of the enemy's smouldering defences at Balikpapan, where great bursts of brilliant flame were shooting skywards.

Major General Edward Milford, the Division's commander, had relied on saturation aerial bombardment and naval shelling to obliterate enemy opposition before his troops went ashore, and saw no merit in landing at a less well-defended area further along the coast from the main objective.

Not all enemy forces were obliterated, but certainly before the assault all Japanese air bases within range of Balikpapan were heavily battered. Just before the landing ten squadrons of Liberator heavy bombers from the RAAF and the 5th and 13th American Air Forces were marshalled over Balikpapan, which was then subjected to massive bombardment, followed by heavy shelling by a naval pre-invasion bombardment force which included the RAN's *Hobart, Shropshire* and *Arunta*. The landings of the 18th and 21st Brigades then followed at Klandasan near Balikpapan's built-up area. The pre-invasion attacks had been so thorough that only intermittent gun and mortar fire from the enemy was encountered by the 10,500 troops who went ashore on the first day.

The war was clearly approaching its end, with the Japanese armed forces reeling back towards Tokyo or bypassed in remote islands. Because of public controversy in Australia over "backyard" wars, political and military leaders were acutely aware of the necessity to keep Allied casualties to a minimum. The Australian government was clearly not at ease with MacArthur's plans for the Australian Army and at a meeting on 28 May the Australian War Cabinet had noted that "the operations against Borneo, the Netherlands East Indies and Malaya have assumed the nature of large-scale 'mopping up' campaigns … from the aspect of prestige it is of great importance to Australia to be associated with the drive to defeat Japan".

The Acting Prime Minister, Mr Chifley (John Curtin was gravely ill), told MacArthur in a letter that it was the desire of the Government that Australian forces should continue to be associated with his command in the forward movement against Japan but the Commander-in-Chief of the Australian Military Forces had advised that "if a reduction in our strength is to be made the 7th Division should not be employed for further operations until the overall plan is known." MacArthur replied that the 7th Division had been ordered to take part in the Borneo campaign and that the attack would go ahead unless the Australian Government withdrew the division from assignment to the South-West Pacific Area. General Blamey believed that if the 7th Division was committed to Balikpapan it would be tied down to garrison duties and unlikely to be available for forward operations.

The Balikpapan operation was Australia's biggest joint Army-Navy-Air Force operation of the war. It was MacArthur's biggest amphibious operation since the landing at Lingayen Gulf in the Philippines. It was also the last large-scale operation of the Pacific war.

MacArthur went shore with the assault waves both at Brunei and Balikpapan. According to his biographer, William Manchester[2], MacArthur did so because "the diggers still doubted the necessity for the campaign and he resolved to expose himself to heavy fire and once more show them he wasn't afraid to do what he was ordering them to do".

On 2 July the 25th Brigade came ashore and soon met heavy opposition from well dug in Japanese in the Batuchamppar area, losing 22 killed and wounded. By 21 July the Japanese had abandoned their forward positions and by August the activities of the 7th and 9th Divisions were cut back in anticipation of the end of hostilities.

At the war's end, Australian casualties in the operations in and around Balikpapan were 229 killed and 634 wounded. The Japanese lost 1,783 killed and 83 were taken prisoner. The RAAF lost five Liberators with 48 aircrew and a number of army personnel during July. Two of the Liberators were shot down while on air observation duties for the Army. One was hit by light anti-aircraft fire when flying at 61 metres over Sepinggang airfield.

RAN Warships with the British Pacific Fleet

As the ring was tightening on Japan the British Pacific Fleet, which included two battleships and four fleet carriers, entered the Pacific to take part in the main operations against Japan. The first units began arriving in Australia in December 1944 and the fleet left Sydney in February for Manus Island. On 23 March it became Task Force 57 of the American fifth Fleet and was committed to Operation ICEBERG, the seizure of Okinawa, which would provide a forward base for the bombing of Japan and a springboard for the invasion of Japan which MacArthur was planning for later in the year. Two Australian destroyers, *Quickmatch* and *Quiberon*, joined the fleet's 4th Flotilla. Later the RAN's *Napier* (Captain H. J. Buchanan, as Captain [D] 7th Flotilla), *Nepal*, *Nizam* and *Norman* also joined the fleet.

As the huge ICEBERG armada of 1400 naval and merchant ships carrying 182,000 American combat troops approached Okinawa, the

British fleet on 26 March began launching aircraft from their carriers to attack airfield targets in the Sakishima Islands to prevent their use against the ICEBERG invasion force. *Quiberon* recorded that the fleet was three times brought to five minutes' notice for air attacks but no hostile aircraft were sighted.

When the Americans assaulted the beachhead at Okinawa on 1 April, 160,000 men were ashore within an hour. They were unopposed because the Japanese, having learned a bitter lesson, kept their defenders away from the beachhead. On this day a Kamikaze crashed the base of the carrier *Indefatigable*'s island causing fatal casualties.

Japan's reaction to Okinawa was desperate. Huge waves of suicide pilots on their one-way body-crashing missions assailed the American Navy, causing considerable damage. Between 6 April and 22 June, no less than 1465 pilots on their Kikusi ("floating chrysanthemum") missions went to their deaths in a vain attempt to annihilate the American invasion fleet. The British carriers were hit several times but suffered little damage. Plans had been made for the British Fleet to proceed to North Borneo to support the Australian invasion in June but the strain caused by the Kikusi sharpened Admiral Nimitz's desire to retain it in the Ryukus Islands.

By May 1945 the Nazi regime that had tyrannised Europe for so long was no more. Hitler and Mussolini were dead. The Japanese, like the Germans, were on their knees. Whole Japanese armies were cut off from their homeland. The shattered wrecks of their once proud navy littered the bottoms of harbours, oceans and seaways.

In mid-July, the US Navy's Third Fleet with the British fleet and elements of the RAN carried out a series of heavy attacks on the Tokyo plain area while another American force struck the remnants of the Japanese Navy at Kure.

Death was raining from the skies as the "B-Sans" (B29s) from the Mariana islands scattered bombs throughout the land. In one terrible raid on Tokyo no less than 80,000 Japanese died as a result of a low-level incendiary attack by the big bombers which destroyed 41 square kilometres of the industrial areas of Tokyo. Then came the ultimate weapon, the atomic bomb, which virtually wiped out the cities of Hiroshima and Nagasaki.

The decision to use the atom bomb was a turning point. The Americans had suffered so many casualties in the bloody fighting for Iwo Jima and Okinawa that the Combined Chiefs of Staff were convinced that a conventional assault on the Japanese home islands to end the war would mean another million casualties. The use of the atomic bomb might persuade the Japanese to give up without further struggle, thus avoiding a bloodbath. After the second bomb had fallen on Nagasaki, the war was over in less than a week and the killing had ended. On 15 August the Emperor Hirohito surrendered. By radio he told his people that they must "endure the unendurable and suffer the insufferable".

The Japanese Army and Navy had given their best in courage and tenacity, but these qualities had not availed.

The RAN's *Napier* and *Nizam* were present with the British fleet in Tokyo Bay and *Shropshire*, *Hobart*, *Bataan* and *Warramunga* entered the bay from the Philippines on 21 August to take part in the surrender ceremony. On 2 September the Japanese Government surrendered to MacArthur on the quarterdeck of the US battleship *Missouri* before the assembled Allied military leaders. General Sir Thomas Blamey signed the instrument of surrender on behalf of Australia. Next day MacArthur broadcast to the world.

> Today the guns are silent. A great tragedy has ended. A great victory has been won. The skies no longer rain death – the seas bear only commerce – men everywhere walk upright in the sunlight … and in reporting this to you, the people, I speak for the thousands of silent lips, forever stilled among the jungles and the beaches and in the deep waters of the pacific which marked the way …

Sadly John Curtin, the Prime Minister who had led his country in its hour of peril, did not live to see the triumph of Australian arms. He died on 5 July 1945.

J. B. Chifley, who followed him as Prime Minister, announced the end of hostilities with these words:

Let us remember those whose lives were given that we may enjoy
this glorious moment and may look forward to a peace which
they have won for us. Let us remember those whose thoughts,
with proud sorrow, turn towards gallant loved ones who will not
come back.

The Australian government had hoped that the Australian armed services would be represented in the invasion of Japan. But there was no invasion. However, immediately after the war ended War Cabinet informed Britain that Australia wanted to take part in the occupation of Japan and offered a brigade group, a wing of RAAF Mustang fighters, two cruisers and two destroyers of the RAN. The Australian offer was accepted and would be a component in a larger British Commonwealth Occupation Force (BCOF) which was to include Indian and New Zealand armed forces as well as British and Australian Army, Navy and Air Force contributions. An Australian, Lieutenant General Sir John Northcott, was appointed Commander-in-Chief of BCOF but relinquished the command in 1946 to become Governor of New South Wales.

Overall control of the occupation of Japan was vested in General MacArthur who was appointed Supreme Commander, Allied Powers (SCAP).

As soon as the end of fighting was announced the urgent recovery of Australian prisoners of war held by the Japanese got under way. Australian repatriation teams, the first of which was parachuted into Singapore to rescue prisoners in Changi Gaol, went to work immediately to bring relief to Australian former prisoners.

Air transports, hospital ships and naval vessels were swiftly on their way to recover the Australians held by the Japanese, many of whom were starving and in urgent need of medical care. RAAF transport aircraft flew food, clothing, blood plasma, penicillin and quinine to 5500 Australians in Singapore. By the end of September most Australian prisoners of war who had been held in Singapore, Java and Sumatra were on their way home to Australia.

Australians taken prisoner by the Japanese between 1942 and 1945 were: AIF, 21,649; RAAF, 543; and RAN 324 – a total of 22,516. Those recovered were: AIF, 13,872; RAAF, 417 and RAN 237, a total of 14,526. More than a third (7990) of the prisoners did not survive. They were the victims of extreme brutality, starvation in inhuman conditions, denial of medical supplies, beatings and bashings.

No greater inhumanity to man could be imagined than the brutal activities of the Japanese army guards in Borneo whose sadistic cruelty and calculated neglect were responsible for the deaths of all but six of 2,500 British and Australian prisoners in North Borneo.

A total of 557,799 members of the three Australian armed services were sent overseas during the Second World War compared with 330,000 (from a much smaller population base) in the First World War.

Total battle deaths in all three services were 27,191 while deaths from all causes were 39,429.

By service they were:		Battle deaths in the services were:	
Army:	396,661	Army:	18,931
RAN:	37,061	RAN:	1,800
RAAF:	124,077	RAAF:	6,460
	557,799		27,191

7

MALAYA, MALTA AND THE STRATEGIC RESERVE

The Situation in Malaya

On 16 June 1948, three European rubber planters were shot to death in an execution-style killing in the Malayan town of Sungei Siput in Perak state. A party of communist Chinese terrorists were the executioners. They rode quietly into town on bicycles and after the killings rode out again into the jungle.

This atrocity was the culminating event in a widespread terror campaign of murder, arson, strikes, riots, destruction of plantations and crops, extortion and intimidation that had been going on in Malaya. Prime terrorist targets were tin mines, rubber estates, ports and factories. The terror had been instigated by the youthful (26-year-old) but remarkably ruthless Chin Peng, a communist since 1939, who by 1947 had become secretary of the Malayan Communist Party. The party's aim was to destabilise Malayan society, break down all authority and replace it with a communist-style government. A captured party document had declared: "We Malayan–Chinese Communists must conquer Malaya for China."

The Malayan uprising was far from being isolated. In the same year uprisings by communists occurred in Burma, Indonesia, India and the Philippines. A full-scale struggle was in progress in French Indochina and China itself was about to fall to the communists.

Tensions had been growing steadily between the communist and Western worlds since the end of the Second World War, to the extent that many feared another world war was inevitable.

Nation after nation in eastern Europe had yielded to the ruthless pressure of Stalin and slid behind what Winston Churchill called "the Iron Curtain".

By 1948 Poland and Czechoslovakia had become Soviet satellites and a great struggle for control of West Berlin was a flashpoint. Some 51 RAAF Dakota transport crews took part in the classic "air bridge to Berlin" airlift when the West, faced with a Russian blockade, turned to air transports to save the city from starvation. The Russians eventually were forced to abandon the blockade and Berlin returned to "normal".

In a despatch to the Australian External Affairs Minister (Dr H. V. Evatt) on 15 July 1948, the Australian Commissioner to Singapore, Claude Massey, said the Malayan uprising was not a nationalist rebellion but an insurrection of a "minority, largely an alien minority". He said there was "important evidence" that the insurrection was coordinated with other communist parties in South-East Asia with the aim of weakening Britain's position in Malaya. It was possible that the insurrection had been decided upon at Calcutta where the Burmese and Indian communist parties were "definitely known" to have received similar instructions.[1]

The British view was that the violence was communist-inspired and was part of an intensive communist drive throughout South-East Asia. The British view, and that of the Australian Commission, was supported by Dr Evatt in a cable to Mr Chifley, the Prime Minister. The Minister considered that since Britain was preoccupied with defence concerns in Europe, Australia was "to a substantial extent bound to prevent the undermining of British authority in an area whose strategic importance to Australia had been demonstrated in the Second World War". Mr Chifley, however, considered the conflict to be essentially a revolt against colonial rule.[2]

It was not surprising therefore that when Britain indicated informally that it had a need for "trained and seasoned" troops in Malaya which were difficult to provide because of heavy military commitments in Europe and the Middle East, Chifley rejected the British hint that Australian troops might be sent to Malaya to fight the terrorists.[3] "There is no question of Australia sending troops to Malaya," he said. The Australian Government did, however, supply Sten guns and ammunition as well as "walkie-talkie" radio equipment.

In 1947 alone there had been more than 300 industrial strikes in Malaya and as the level of violence and conflict grew, the Malayans demanded firm action against the rebels. The Colonial Government was on the point of taking action to meet their demands when the communists struck again at Sungei Siput, provoking anger throughout the country and prompting the declaration of a state of emergency in parts of Perak and Johore. Open military action by the terrorists had increased the rate of civilian murder to 100 a month, but the mass of the people had not risen in true revolutionary spirit to support them. On 18 June under further public pressure the emergency was extended to the whole Malayan Peninsula.

In July 1948 the Malayan Communist Party was outlawed. Police raided homes and hundreds of Communist Party and trade union officials were arrested. The communists suffered their heaviest setback late in July when British troops and police wiped out a network of hideouts near Kuala Lumpur. At least 20 were killed and 47 captured.

In the Australian Federal election of December 1949 Chifley's Labor Government was defeated by a Liberal–Country Party coalition which took office on 19 December with Robert G. Menzies as Prime Minister.

By 1950 no end to the violence seemed to be in sight and the British Government renewed its requests for support. Influential Australian newspapers carried articles and editorials encouraging Mr Menzies to increase Australian support to the British in Malaya. The Australian Communist Party newspaper *Tribune,* however, said: "Not a man, not a ship, not a gun, should leave Australia's shores for the vile war against freedom in Malaya."

Mr Spender, now Minister for External Affairs, declared in April that Malaya was of vital concern to the security of Australia.

Australia Responds

T he British Chiefs of Staff wondered whether Australia might be prepared to supply air reinforcements, the priority being first a transport squadron of Dakota aircraft for dropping supplies to Government forces operating against the terrorists. Secondly, they suggested Lincoln heavy bomber aircraft and thirdly assistance in servicing aircraft. The Australian Defence Committee advised the Government that the RAAF could meet the British needs.

At length on 31 May, Menzies announced in Parliament that Australia would send a squadron of Dakota transports to Malaya. In doing so he emphasised that events in Malaya were "part of the global pattern of imperialistic communist aggression".

Dakotas of No 38 Squadron, RAAF, arrived in Malaya by 20 June, but the Australian Government had reserved its decision on sending the Lincoln bombers because it was uneasy about public reaction to such direct involvement in combat and also had doubts about the usefulness of bombers in a campaign against guerillas. The RAF leaders in Malaya, however, wanted the bombers to saturate guerilla targets in the jungle.

In June, while Australia was weighing this question a sudden thunder of artillery and rumble of tanks heralded the outbreak of a much larger conflict in Korea.

The Korean War began in the early hours of 25 June. On 27 June the Australian cabinet met to discuss firstly the Korean War and then the Malaya situation. No decision was taken on participation in the Korean War but Cabinet made the decision "immediately" to send a squadron of Lincoln bombers to Malaya. After the Cabinet meeting Menzies declared:

> *The Korean incident cannot be looked at in isolation, nor can*
> *we in Australia regard it as remote from our own interests and*
> *safety. There are other points of possible attack on or off the coast*

> *of China. There is also at this very moment, a Communist-led campaign in Indo-China. Much nearer home there are operations of the Communist guerillas in Malaya who are making it their business to render British control of Malaya difficult and who, if they succeed, will make it impossible ... So far as Malaya is concerned we feel that Australia has some capacity to help and, in its own interests as well as those of the entire British Commonwealth, a duty to do whatever it can. I recently announced to parliament the dispatch of a squadron of RAAF transport aircraft to Singapore. I have now to announce that we are sending to Singapore pursuant to discussions with the Government of the United Kingdom, a RAAF squadron of heavy bombers ... The preservation of British authority in Malaya is vital to Australia's security ...*[4]

Two days later the Australian Government committed warships of the RAN and one day later again No 77 Mustang Squadron of the RAAF to fight in Korea under the blue-and-white colours of the United Nations. Thus within a single month Australia had committed three RAAF operational squadrons and two warships of the RAN to two wars against communist-inspired forces in Asia. As well the Australian Army was soon to be committed to action in Korea.

In July, No 1 Squadron RAAF flew its four-engined Lincoln heavy bombers to Malaya-Singapore from which it had been forced to retreat early in 1942. Together with No 38 Transport Squadron, it joined the campaign against the communist guerillas. The provision of Dakota air crews from No 86 Wing, at Richmond, NSW, was made easier because of the return to Australia of Dakota crew who had served in the Berlin airlift and were now available for service in the Malayan campaign.

The Lincoln was powered by four Rolls Royce Merlin engines. It was British designed but manufactured in Australia. Operating from the RAF base at Tengah on Singapore Island. No 1 Squadron performed faultlessly on both day and night bombing missions. It dropped 85 per cent of all bombs used in the Malayan Emergency operations. The squadron flew almost 4,000 sorties which were responsible for the killing of 23 terrorists. In one strike in the Kluang-Rengam area of southern Johore they made direct hits on the camp of the 7th Independent Platoon of the insurgent forces.

While the bombing did not kill a large number of terrorists the squadron operations had a demoralising effect. The morale of the terrorists was lowered because they were forced to move continually and often the bombing would drive them into prepared ambushes and road blocks. A large number of terrorists surrendered and on interrogation described the difficulties of life arising from the threat of air attack.

The squadron's main task was to bomb and strafe the hidden bases of the insurgents. Bombing and strafing called for great accuracy in order to avoid death and injury to civilians and damage to civilian property. Army pilots flying light aircraft sometimes guided the bombers by dropping flares to mark targets. After eight years' service in operations in the years 1950–58 the squadron was withdrawn to Australia and re-equipped with Canberra twin jet bombers.

No 38 Squadron provided a vital aerial supply service to troops in the more isolated areas of Malaya. They dropped food, ammunition and equipment by parachute in the remote and rugged jungle country to support ground troops hunting the insurgents.

In the Korean War RAAF transports were called on to provide medical air evacuation services to the British Commonwealth forces and, as this responsibility grew, more Dakota aircraft were needed. A number of machines were thus transferred from Malaya to Korea. The remaining Dakotas in Malaya joined with a New Zealand transport squadron to maintain the air transport needs of Malaya.

Malta

British defence planners, concerned with the strategic situation in the Mediterranean, proposed in 1951 that in the event of a global war Australia should commit armed forces to the Middle East region. Malaya was to have priority for Australian arms in a "cold war" situation, but the Middle East should take precedence in a "hot war".

Prime Minister Menzies appeared sympathetic towards the British view but the growing successes of the communist forces in Korea and in Indochina made him relucent to commit Australian forces to the Middle East. However, by the end of 1951 the situation was stronger both in Korea and Indochina and Australia agreed to join with Britain, France, the United States and Turkey in a Middle East defence command.

As a contribution to Middle East defences, Australia agreed to station two RAAF fighter squadrons in Malta in 1952. This would severely strain RAAF resources because the service would then have five operational squadrons deployed overseas. Of these, two were already engaged in active operations in Malaya. One fighter squadron was flying constant combat operations in Korea and two more fighter squadrons were to be based in the Mediterranean as part of the deterrent to aggression in that theatre.

The RAAF units assigned to the Middle East were the famous Nos 75 and 76 fighter squadrons. They were equipped with Vampire jets. Group Captain Brian Eaton, a highly decorated wartime leader of Desert Air Force squadrons in the Mediterranean area during the Second World War, was appointed to command. The squadrons began operating from the Royal Navy airfield at Halfar and took part with North Atlantic Treaty Organisation forces in the air defence of Malta in NATO war games. In 1953 when based temporarily in Germany, the RAAF squadrons joined with European air forces in a mock atomic war.

The Far East Strategic Reserve

By 1953–54 Australia's major area of strategic concern had swung firmly back from the Middle East to South-East Asia. This new focus was reflected in the decision to bring the RAAF squadrons in the Middle East back to Australia (they returned in 1955).

In high-level talks in October 1953 between British Commonwealth defence leaders from Britain, Australia and New Zealand, great concern was expressed at an apparent threat now coming from communist China. That communist nation was believed to be seeking to bring all

South-East Asia under communist control. First French Indochina would fall, followed by Thailand and Burma. Eventually Malaya would be under direct threat.

At the talks, which were attended by Field Marshal Sir John Harding, Britain's Chief of the Imperial General Staff, it was agreed that all three Australian armed services would, in the event of a major war, be deployed to Malaya, not to the Middle East. Clearly Australia's "Middle East first" policy in a global conflict was being discarded. Harding proposed that a Far East Strategic Reserve to be stationed in Malaya should be set up by Britain, Australia and New Zealand to act as a deterrent to Chinese aggression. It should also be available in the absence of major hostilities for counter-terrorist operations in Malaya.

The proposed Strategic Reserve was to include an army brigade to which Australia would contribute a battalion, together with supporting troops. Harding suggested that most of the forces needed for the Reserve could be provided by redeploying forces no longer needed for duty in Korea, where the Americans were planning to reduce their forces by two divisions.

However, it was not until almost two years after the fighting in Korea ended that the Far East Strategic Reserve began to take shape. Menzies announced on 1 April 1955 that Britain, New Zealand and Australia would contribute forces to the reserve.

The Australian contributions would comprise:

> Navy: Two destroyers and two frigates, an aircraft carrier on an annual visit and additional ships in an emergency.
>
> Army: One infantry battalion with supporting arms and reinforcements in Australia.
>
> Air Force: A fighter wing of two squadrons.
> A bomber squadron.
> An airfield construction squadron.

Menzies said that if the communists overran South-East Asia, Australia's existence as a free country would be at risk. The Chinese had already demonstrated their aggression in Korea, in French Indochina and in the islands off the China coast.

Reflecting the strategic policy of "forward defence" Menzies said: "If there is to be a war for our existence it should be carried on as far from our soil as possible." Menzies added that Australia could not be defended from its own soil, and required cooperation with Allies, especially the United Kingdom and the United States, two nations he referred to as Australia's "great friends" and "powerful friends".

During 1955 elements of the Australian Army, Navy and Air Force arrived in Malaya as Australia's contribution to the British Commonwealth Strategic Reserve, with the primary role of "providing a deterrent to and to be available to assist in countering further communist aggression in South-East Asia". In June 1955 Menzies revealed that the Australian forces would also be available for use in anti-terrorist operations in Malaya, but not in relation to any civil disturbances in the internal affairs of Malaya or Singapore.

The first Australian battalion committed to the Strategic Reserve was 2 RAR which had left Korea for Australia in April 1954 and after training at Canungra, Queensland, sailed for Penang in October 1955 where it joined the 28th British Commonwealth Brigade. By January 1956 the battalion had entered operations in the Kulim area of Malaya and made its first successful contact with the communist terrorists during "Operation Deuce".

The first RAN warships to serve with the Far East Strategic Reserve were *Arunta* and *Warramunga*, which began their service on 2 July 1955 when they had completed exercises with Royal Navy ships in Malayan waters. RAN ships which served in the Strategic Reserve in addition to *Arunta* and *Warramunga* included *Quiberon, Queenborough, Tobruk, Anzac, Vampire, Vendetta, Voyager, Melbourne, Quadrant* and *Quickmatch*. During their tours of duty against the communist insurgents *Anzac* and *Tobruk* were actively engaged in bombarding communist hideouts south of Jason Bay on 29 September 1956 and again on 22 January 1957. *Quickmatch* and *Queenborough* also attacked insurgent positions at Tanjong Siang. British army light aircraft were used to direct the fire of the Australian warships.

The RAAF's No 1 Squadron, long established at Tengah in Singapore, continued to fly bombing missions against the insurgents and would do so until the arrival in Malaya of No 2 Squadron, which had been equipped with Canberra jet bombers and was now assigned to the Strategic Reserve. In addition to Canberra jets, the RAAF was sending two fighter squadrons (Nos 3 and 77) now equipped with Sabre supersonic jet fighters, an improved version of the original American F86s which had won a decisive victory over the Russian-built MiG-15 jets in Korea. Australian engineers had married the F86 airframe to the Rolls Royce Avon axial flow turbojet giving added thrust to the original machine. The first commander of the RAAF's contribution to the Strategic Reserve at Butterworth was Air Commodore Keith Parsons who in the Second World War had commanded an RAF Bomber Command station at Binbrook in the United Kingdom.

With its modern aircraft the RAAF had a big responsibility for providing air power for the Strategic Reserve and for other operations. To accommodate the RAAF a new air base was needed. Butterworth, an RAF base, was chosen. Located in northern Malaya in Province Wellesley opposite Penang, it was strategically placed to dominate the Kra Isthmus and the Straits of Malacca. But the airfield at Butterworth had to be upgraded to handle modern jets and the RAAF sent its No 2 Airfield Construction Squadron to undertake Australia's biggest overseas engineering project – the new Butterworth Air Base.

RAAF airfield engineers faced major construction problems: the main runway sliced through glutinous paddy fields where the water table was close to the surface. The 300 members of the squadron were veterans of airfield construction projects in Borneo, Japan, Cocos Island and Woomera. Together with a locally recruited labour force of 600, they quickly overcame the difficulties and produced a top-rated airfield capable of handling most modern jets including the RAF's V-bomber force. Butterworth became part of a chain of interlocking air bases stretching through Malaya, Thailand, the Philippines, Taiwan, Okinawa, Korea and Japan.

The Lincoln bombers of No 1 Squadron left Singapore in July 1959 after a ceremonial flypast over Kuala Lumpur on 2 July. No 2 Squadron had flown into Butterworth on the previous day. The Canberra bombers were soon used in action against the insurgents when in September 1958 they bombed terrorist camps in northern Malaya. It was Australia's first jet bomber mission.

No 3 Squadron flew the Sabres to Butterworth in November 1958, followed by No 77 Squadron in early 1959. The Sabres were armed with the "Sidewinder" air-to-air missiles and were soon used for strikes against the insurgents.

In December 1955 shortly after 2 RAR's arrival in Malaya, Chin Peng, who had remained leader of the Malayan Communist Party throughout the insurgency, emerged from the jungle to ask for recognition of his party as a legal organisation. Tunku Abdul Rahman, Chief Minister of the Federal Executive Council of Malaya, refused. Peng returned to the jungle and eventually sought refuge in Peking.

After service in the Kulim area of Malaya, 2 RAR took part with the 28th Commonwealth Brigade in an operation at Kuala Kangsar in the State of Perak and continued that operation at Sungei Siput from October to December of 1956.

After rest and retraining at Minden Barracks the battalion served again in the operation, relieving the Royal Lincolns.

In August 1957, 2 RAR moved to Butterworth for retraining until October when it returned to Australia for a ticker tape welcome by 100,000 people in the streets of Sydney.

During its tour of duty the battalion had lost 14 soldiers, seven of whom had been killed in action against the insurgents.

On 31 August 1957 Malaya became an independent state. However, close and friendly relations continued between the British and Malaysians after "Merdeka" (independence) had been declared. Tunku Abdul Rahman, now Prime Minister, visited Australia and declared that the presence of Australian troops in Malaya was "a source of comfort to us". Australia and Malaysia he said, were together against communist terrorism and international aggression.

Old Faithful in Malaya

When 3 RAR ("Old Faithful") arrived in Malaya in August 1957 just before the Malayan people had become politically independent, the anti-terrorist campaign was dwindling. Terrorists in rising numbers were being killed, captured or were surrendering.

The battalion's operations began in northern Malaya in November 1957. Platoons of the battalion including Support Company platoons were the basis of operations. Each platoon was assigned the task of searching an area or ambushing a site. The platoon patrols lasted an average of 14 days. Sarawak Rangers were attached to battalions at platoon level and had great skills in the detection of signs of CT (Communist Terrorist) presence or passage. They proved an effective addition to each platoon.

When not on operations married members of the battalion were reunited with their wives and families in comfortable furnished bungalows together with amahs (two for officers and one for other ranks). Patrol duty in the jungle alternated with comfortable periods of domestic life with ample domestic help.

Lieutenant Claude Ducker of 3 RAR led a tracking team which achieved a significant result on 20 November 1958 when he tracked and then attacked a terrorist group.

Lieutenant Ducker recalled later, "One of our platoons found enemy tracks. We followed the footprints using an Iban tracker. Just before dark we saw signs of an enemy resting place on a rocky knoll. So I placed six men at the bottom of the knoll as a stop group and with two Ibans and two Australians I moved round the knoll. We crawled up close and attacked so as to drive the terrorists into the stop group. Three terrorists were killed. I learned later another terrorist leader who escaped our attack surrendered soon afterwards bringing with him a number of his terrorist companions." Ducker was awarded the Military Cross.

One of the terrorists killed was a District Committee Member of the Malayan Communist Party. The Malayan press claimed that he had been in charge of the ambush party which killed Sir Henry Gurney back in 1951. Gurney had been High Commissioner for the Federation of

59. Troops bound for service in Malaya board the liner Georgic.

60. *A RAAF photograph that shows precisely a supply parachute being dropped to troops on the ground by a Dakota of No 38 Squadron.*

61. A 105 mm pack howizter is hauled across a bridge by Australian artillerymen.

62. Vampires of No 78 Wing RAAF over Malta.

63. *A RAAF doctor lands in an Iroquois helicopter to tend villagers in Malaya.*

64. *A typical situation for Australians during the hard winters in Korea outside the sandbagged observation post of C Company, First Battalion RAR.*

65. *North and South Korea.*

66. *Wing Commander Lou Spence, on the right, is here receiving the decoration of the American Legion of Merit from the Commanding General of US Far East Air Force, Lieutenant General George E. Stratemeyer. Sadly, Spence was killed three weeks later while attacking a South Korean target.*

67. Pakchon, November 1950. Members of "A" company 3 RAR help a badly wounded mate.

68. *3 RAR crosses the 38th parallel during the advance into North Korea, October 1950.*

69. Australian soldiers use interpreters while interrogating captured enemy troops after the battle of Pakchon.

70. Blizzard conditions at Yonpo Airfield where No 77's Mustangs wait to strike at the Chinese army in the north.

71. *These Meteor pilots of No 77 Squadron at Kimpo are about to take off for MiG Alley. The officer speaking is Squadron Leader Dick Cresswell.*

72. *An Australian rests during construction of a gun pit.*

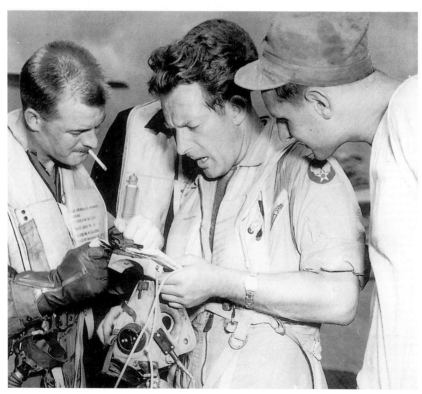

73. *Following an operation in Korea, RAAF Meteor pilots compare notes.*

PK1 K Mustang

Dakota

Meteor

74. *Australian aircraft in service in the Korean War.*

75. An American helicopter is used to evacuate Australian wounded in May 1953.

76. Australian Forces were to return to Borneo during the Indonesian confrontation period. Here, soldiers keep watch on the border between Indonesian and Malaysian territory in Borneo.

77. *Borneo, where Australians were active during the Indonesian confrontation.*

78. *A member of 3 RAR is reunited with his family at Terendak Camp, Malacca, after service in Borneo.*

Malaya at the time of his death near Kuala Lumpur, and was replaced by Lieutenant General Sir Gerald Templer, whose vigorous approach resulted in a significant improvement in the situation. When in addition Malaya was promised independence it became clear that the insurgents were likely to be defeated.

During its two years in Malaya, 3 RAR was credited with killing 14 terrorists and capturing another 32. One member of the battalion was killed in action and two died of illness. The battalion returned to Australia in October 1959 and moved to Enoggera Camp.

In July 1960 the Government of Malaya declared the Emergency over. It had lasted for 12 years and a total of 350,000 men had taken part in eliminating the insurgency. In the end the insurgents were reduced from a ruthless band of killers to a handful of starving wraiths, reduced to eating roots and berries in order to live in hiding.

In Malaya the road to victory had been long and hard. But a great victory had been won and a grand parade was held in Kuala Lumpur to mark the end of a long ordeal which had cost 12,000 lives.

The victory in Malaya was hailed as "the most significant defeat of guerilla Communists in Asia". The Australian Government could take credit for its part in helping the Malayans to survive the threat to their freedom. It had joined with Britain in a military intervention in South-East Asia which crushed a communist-led insurgency. As the Australian Official Historian (Peter Edwards) observed:

> *The intervention had been successful, helping to produce an independent, pro-western country, with healthy prospects of economic prosperity and political stability. The Cassandras, who had forecast that intervention would be unsuccessful and counterproductive, had evidently been proved wrong. The presence of Australian troops in Malaya had led, not to hostility, but to good relations with the independent and freely elected Malayan Government. No one at this time seriously suggested that similar intervention elsewhere in South-East Asia was imminent, let alone that it would prove equally successful; but the Government could have been forgiven if it drew the*

conclusion that western military intervention in South-East Asia would not necessarily prove disastrous.[5]

With the Emergency over, Australian and other British Commonwealth forces were available to take part in border operations and soon after its arrival 1 RAR, which relieved 3 RAR, was sent to the Thai-Malaya border. Platoons were assigned to three-week-long patrols in remote areas where access was by helicopter, by road or on foot.

In October 1961, 2 RAR returned to Malaya for a second tour and joined the 28th British Commonwealth Brigade at Terendak camp near Malacca. The battalion then became involved under a Malayan brigade commander in hunting down remnants of the communist bands on the Thai border. Returning to Malaya for a second tour, 3 RAR was also sent in February 1964 to the Thai border. To support the operations on the Thai border the RAAF sent a flight of four Iroquois helicopters of No 5 Squadron. They were transported to Malaya on board HMAS *Sydney*.

8

THE KOREAN WAR

The Invasion

At 4 am on Sunday 25 June 1950, the thunder of an artillery and mortar barrage shattered the silence along Korea's 38th parallel, which marked an artificial barrier between North and South Korea.

War had come to "the land of the morning calm" as the Soviet-trained and equipped army of communist North Korea, spearheaded by Russian-made T34 tanks, thrust across the parallel and headed for the South Korean capital, Seoul. Their intention was to "liberate" their blood brothers in South Korea, who had been armed and trained by the United States of America.

Thus almost exactly midway through the 20th century the world was in crisis as the long-standing tensions between the communist and the Western worlds, which had their beginning with the Russian revolution of 1917, threatened to trigger a third world war.

Korea was the unfortunate eastern country which would now become the battleground for a major test of military strength and will as the communists stepped up their drive for worldwide ascendancy by a military takeover of South Korea, which the United States had freed from Japanese control.

Because of Australia's participation in the occupation of Japan at the end of the Second World War, fate had placed elements of all three Australian armed services on duty in southern Japan not far distant from the battle zone in South Korea. As components of the British Commonwealth Occupation Force they were in Japan under the operational control of General Douglas MacArthur, the Supreme Commander Allied Powers (SCAP) and with the approval of the Australian Government they were committed to combat operations at short notice.

The Korean War had "gatecrashed" what was intended to be a farewell party at the RAAF Base at Iwakuni in southern Honshu, Japan. On the night of 24–25 June 1950, RAAF members and their wives were saying *sayonara* to Japan after four years of occupation duties. The order had come to return to Australia. Flying operations had ended on 23 June. All they had left to do was to pack up and go home.

The party festivities took place in the RAAF Sergeants' Mess and were still in progress on the morning of 25 June when the 5th United States Air Force at Itazuke (Kyushu) telephoned to say that hostilities had broken out along the 38th parallel between North and South Korea and that the 5th Air Force had been placed on standby. For operations the RAAF in Japan was directly under the control of the 5th Air Force. The commanding officer of No 77 Mustang Fighter Squadron (Wing Commander Lou Spence) at once placed his squadron on standby and ordered its members to prepare for action to counter any air attack on the Iwakuni air base. Iwakuni could be attacked and the "Double Seven" squadron had to be ready to defend it.

The North Koreans had launched a well-planned full-scale invasion of South Korea which swiftly sliced through the weak South Korean defences and within three days had seized Seoul, capital of the Republic of South Korea. The North Koreans when declaring war later that day claimed their forces were resisting an invasion by the South. As one wit put it, "If that were so, the South Koreans must have been using the seat of their pants to kick the toe of the North Korean boot."

Proof of North Korean aggression was plainly indicated in the report of two Australian military observers attached to UNCOK (the United Nations Commission in Korea). They were Major Francis Peach and

Squadron Leader Ronald Rankin. Two weeks before hostilities began they toured the front line area and, just one day before the invasion began, reported to UNCOK that the South was in no condition to carry out a large-scale attack against North Korea.

The Peach-Rankin report provided vital information upon which the United Nations could act with confidence. In unequivocal language it made it clear that the South Korean forces were organised "entirely for defence". Without tanks, air support, heavy artillery and even adequate stocks of ammunition, it was impossible for them to mount an offensive against North Korea.

On 26 June the portent of this report was explained to the United Nations Commission in Seoul which then informed the hurriedly summoned United Nations Security Council at Lake Success, New York, that the aggressive actions taken by North Korea constituted a breach of the peace. The Council passed a resolution calling for an immediate end to hostilities and the withdrawal of all North Korean forces back to the 38th parallel.

On the same day President Harry Truman, the US President, convinced that an uncontested invasion of South Korea could start a chain reaction leading to a third world war, authorised General Douglas MacArthur to use his air and naval forces to aid the hard-pressed defenders of South Korea.

Next day (27 June) the Security Council, seeking to enlist the support of other UN member states, passed another resolution, calling on all United Nations member states to furnish such assistance to the Republic of Korea as may be necessary to repel the attack and restore peace and security in the area. For the first time in history a world organisation of sovereign states would take up arms to oppose an aggressor and maintain the peace.

Australia committed armed forces to the war at once. On 29 June the RAN frigate HMAS *Shoalhaven*, which was at Kure, Japan, and the destroyer HMAS *Bataan*, which was at Hong Kong when hostilities began, were committed to action in support of the Republic of South Korea.

On the same day, while flying to Korea to make a personal

assessment, MacArthur told Roy Macartney, the Tokyo correspondent of Australian Associated Press-Reuter who was with a press party on board the aircraft, that he would "very much" like to have the Australian Mustang squadron operating in Korea. "The squadron pilots" he said, "are first class and we particularly need in Korea long-range fighters like the Mustangs." MacArthur dictated a message to Lieutenant General Horace Robertson, the Australian commander of the British Commonwealth Occupation Force, asking if Australia would commit its air element in Japan for use against the forces of North Korea operating south of the (38th) parallel. Robertson passed the request on to Australia and Macartney, after returning to Tokyo, filed a news story reporting MacArthur's request. The Australian Government was embarrassed to read Macartney's news story in the morning newspapers of 30 June. Later that day, the Prime Minister (Robert Menzies) announced that the Government agreed that the squadron would fight under the blue-and-white flag of the United Nations in Korea.

On 26 July the Australian government announced that the 3rd Battalion, Royal Australian Regiment then based at Hiro, near Kure, would also fight in Korea. A further announcement on 27 July advised that HMAS *Warramunga* would leave Sydney for Korean waters.

In Korea MacArthur saw for himself the army of the Republic of Korea in disarray, with its strength down from 98,000 to 22,000. The road from Seoul was choked with thousands of demoralised soldiers and civilians flooding southwards. It was clear that the North Koreans planned a swift conquest of all Korea before the United States and UN forces could arrive on the peninsula to save the Republic.

MacArthur warned Washington that ground troops must be committed and Truman agreed. On 1 July the first two companies of the US 24th Infantry Division arrived by air at Pusan and moved off at once to the north. For Truman the decision to intervene was "the toughest decision" of his political career. He gave MacArthur full authority to use the four divisions of the 8th Army in Korea and a naval blockade of the entire coast was ordered.

The RAAF Mustang squadron and HMAS *Shoalhaven* were cleared by General Robertson to take part in the war on 1 July. On that day

Shoalhaven was assigned the task of escorting an American ammunition ship across Tsushima Strait to the port of Pusan where both ships berthed next day. But bad weather on 1 July forced the RAAF Mustangs at Iwakuni to stay on the ground, leaving it to the RAN to perform the first operational task for Australia in the Korean war.

To the relief of the Australian pilots frustrated by the bad weather, the rain stopped next day and 16 were assigned operational tasks over Korea. The first four took off early to escort American transport aircraft which were flying wounded out of the Korean peninsula. However the four pilots made no contact with the medical evacuation aircraft and the Mustangs returned to Iwakuni.

A second Mustang mission on the first day escorted B26 light bombers of the 3rd American Bomb Group which attacked bridges across the Han River near Seoul. They were greeted by heavy anti-aircraft fire but suffered no damage.

The third Mustang mission on 2 July was to escort B29 bombers of the US Air Force which had flown up from Okinawa and then continued on deep into North Korean territory to bomb Yonpo airfield near Hamhung. Again the Australians were fired on by anti-aircraft weapons but there was no damage.

Next day (3 July) a ghastly error marred the operations of the squadron when they were sent to attack enemy forces advancing south from Seoul. In a technically brilliant operation they blew up an enemy ammunition train with rocket fire and then heavily strafed the town of Pyongtaek. Elated with an apparently successful operation they learned to their dismay when they returned to Iwakuni that Pyongtaek was still in friendly hands. Roy Macartney, now a war correspondent in Korea, was on the ground at Pyongtaek and later wrote: "I tasted to the full the bitter irony of being strafed not only by Australian planes, but by the very men with whom I had been drinking a few days before."

However, No 77 Squadron was blameless. The US Fifth Air Force had insisted that the target area was enemy held and accepted full responsibility for the disaster. Fifth Air Force operations officers were not aware that South Korean and American troops were in or near the area attacked by No 77 Squadron.

Major General Earle Partridge, who commanded the 5th Air Force, flew to Iwakuni and apologised to Wing Commander Spence, and Lieutenant General George Stratemeyer, the Far East Air Force Commander, added his expression of regret. Investigations had revealed defects in the system of target allocation in Korea.

No 77 Squadron was under strength when the Korean War began because the squadron had been winding down for its return to Australia. To build the squadron up to full operational capacity, RAAF Headquarters in Melbourne took immediate action to send reinforcements. The first reinforcement party of 40 air and ground crew left RAAF Base Richmond on 6 July. Included in this party were 12 qualified Mustang fighter pilots. They arrived in Japan on 8 July and some were in action in Korea two days later.

On 7 July the squadron lost Squadron Leader Graham Strout, who was killed in action when leading a section of four aircraft in an attack on east coast railway communications at Samchok. The other pilots in the section saw a blinding flash just after Strout had made a firing pass on the target. Next day Wing commander Spence flew to the area and found scattered white metal fragments of an aircraft on the ground. Five months later Strout's body was recovered and reburied in the United Nations Command war cemetery.

Day after day during the crisis created by the apparently unstoppable North Korean advance, the Australian Mustang pilots struck at the enemy in an "all-out" effort of close support for the ground troops. In August alone they flew 812 offensive sorties in which they pounded enemy troops, trucks, tanks, bridges and defended positions with rockets, bombs and machine gunfire. They were playing a significant role in this battle. In Washington, the State Department received many excellent reports of the work of the RAAF over Korea.

MacArthur had stripped Japan of the American occupation troops as all available units were rushed to Korea. There the United Nations forces were being compressed by the enemy within the Pusan "defence box" behind the Naktong river. The North Koreans, knowing that delay could be fatal to their aims, were relentless in their efforts to achieve victory before the US 8th Army and contingents from other nations rushed troops to save South Korea. General Walton Walker, commander of the 8th Army, declared on 17 July, "Had it not been for the Far East Air Forces there would not be an American in Korea today."

Australia and 15 other member states of the United Nations responded to the UN call for help and sent combat forces. They were: Belgium, Canada, Columbia, Ethiopia, France, Greece, Luxembourg, the Netherlands, New Zealand, the Philippines, Thailand, Turkey, South Africa, the United Kingdom and the United States. As well, Denmark, India, Italy, Norway and Sweden sent medical units. All contributing states came under General MacArthur who was appointed Commander-in-Chief of the United Nations forces in Korea.

To increase the squadron mission rate, No 77 Squadron sent ground staff to the South Korean town of Taegu within the "defence box" and there, with the sound of gunfire from the battle front nearby, they worked long hours to service, refuel and rearm the squadron Mustangs. The Australian pilots, after farewelling their wives and families at Iwakuni, would take off to attack enemy targets in Korea. After completing their first strikes they would land at Taegu and join the queue on the air base for more fuel and armament.

Off again, strike and down again at Taegu became the routine. Some pilots would carry out four strikes in one day before returning to their wives and families for the evening meal at home in Iwakuni. To keep up the heavy demand for bombs and rockets, General Robertson's VIP aircraft – a RAAF Dakota – was handed over for the task of flying in supplies from Japan. At times the shortage of rockets became so acute that the squadron armourers were pulling them straight from the General's Dakota onto the wings of the waiting Mustangs.

There was no doubt that the squadron's performance in Korea was exceptional and on 22 August 1950, General Stratemeyer, the top air commander, flew down to Iwakuni and in an informal ceremony in the squadron mess, decorated Wing Commander Spence with the American Legion of Merit.

Three weeks later on 9 September, Spence, who was also a decorated fighter pilot of the Second World War, took off from Iwakuni on a mission from which he did not return. On that day he bade goodbye to his wife and two young children who lived with him on the base and flew to Angang-Ni in South Korea where he was killed while dive-bombing enemy forces in the town. The loss of this fine leader was a heavy blow to the squadron. Eight days later Squadron Leader Richard Cresswell, who had twice before commanded the squadron in combat operations in the Second World War, arrived at Iwakuni to replace the fallen leader as commanding officer.

To reduce the strain on families at Iwakuni it was an unwritten rule that wives should not go down to the tarmac to say goodbye when their husbands were taking off on combat operations. Instead they waited in their quarters. One pilot who married a RAAF nursing sister was presented with a baby soon after the war began. He alternated between dawn patrols with his baby daughter and combat patrols over the war zone. The two tasks could cause some uncertainty: "You are apt to have finger trouble on a nappy or a rocketing mission," he remarked.

The last all-out attempt by the North Koreans to take the Naktong line and push the United Nations forces into the sea began on 31 August. The enemy crossed the Naktong at 17 points in barges, boats and underwater bridges. On the east coast they took Pohang for the second time. At a critical moment the headquarters of the 8th US Army in Korea was moved south to Pusan. However, weakened by weeks of battering from the air, the strength of the North Koreans had faded and they were unable to exploit their breakthroughs.

By 7 September the enemy offensive in the south had ground to a halt and as the North Koreans continued to hammer unavailingly against the UN defences, a dramatic change came over the nature of the war. On 16 September, MacArthur in a brilliant strategic counter-stroke (which some critics referred to as a "gambler's throw") landed the United States 10th Corps at Inchon far behind the enemy front lines and adjacent to the capital, Seoul. The move was reminiscent of the American bypassing tactics of the Pacific War which MacArthur had adopted and which had contributed heavily to the defeat of the Japanese.

The UN armada which approached Inchon totalled 260 ships including HMAS *Bataan* and *Warramunga* which formed part of the blockade and covering force. *Bataan* later bombarded enemy coastal positions and *Warramunga* fired on gun emplacements to discourage enemy attempts to escape by sea.

MacArthur's amphibious landing at Inchon had caught the North Koreans between the hammer of the 8th Army in the south and the anvil of the 10th Corps in the north. MacArthur's forces were astride the great supply route to the south and 13 North Korean divisions, desperately short of supplies, melted away. On 29 September at a ceremony in shattered Seoul, MacArthur handed back the liberated capital to the South Korean president, Dr Syngman Rhee.

Having won an historic victory, MacArthur now sought to expand the war by destroying the North Korean Army in North Korea and uniting the country under Syngman Rhee. He planned to move the 10th Corps from Seoul-Inchon to Wonsan on the east coast while the 8th Army would thrust northwards from Seoul and head for the North Korean capital, Pyongyang. On 1 October the South Korean forces began the advance across the 38th parallel and to make it legal a United Nations resolution of 7 October authorised MacArthur to proceed north of the parallel.

The Royal Australian Regiment in Korea

While the 3rd Battalion, Royal Australian Regiment, had been committed to the United Nations campaign in Korea, it took some weeks for the under-strength battalion to build up to war establishment strength of 960 men and train for the war. A recruiting campaign in Australia calling for 1,000 men to serve for three years was so successful that the army was able to choose many with good combat records in the Second World War. Experienced regular soldiers from 1 RAR and 2 RAR also joined the battalion.

The Army appointed Lieutenant Colonel C. H. Green to command the battalion. At the age of 25 Green had commanded a battalion (the 2/11th) of the 6th Division in the final New Guinea campaign. He had earlier served as a platoon commander in North Africa and Greece.

On arrival at Pusan, Korea, on 27 September the 3rd Battalion was brigaded with the British 27th Brigade which had arrived from Hong Kong. With the brigade were the Argyll and Sutherland Highlanders and the 1st Battalion, Middlesex Regiment. The Australian Government had offered to place the 3rd Battalion with the brigade which then became known as the 27th British Commonwealth Brigade. It was commanded by Brigadier B. A. Coad, a Sandhurst graduate.

After arriving in Korea to a warm welcome the 3rd Battalion was deployed in hilly country around Songju-Waegwan and there on 3 October suffered its first casualties. Captain K. Hummerston and his driver were killed when their carrier was blown up in an unmarked minefield.

Because of the collapse of enemy resistance in the Naktong River area the 3rd Battalion saw little fighting in the south but suddenly on 5 October it was ordered north to take part in a drive across the 38th parallel into North Korea. At Kaesong it joined the US 1st Cavalry Division which was to spearhead the United Nations drive on Pyongyang, the North Korean capital.

Meanwhile evidence was growing of Communist China's intention to go to war in support of the retreating North Koreans. The Indian Ambassador to Peking (K. M. Panikkar) was called in by the Chinese Government and told that should American troops invade North Korea China would enter the war. As the American 1st Cavalry and the 27th Brigade including the 3rd Battalion were pushing towards Pyongyang on 10 October, a last warning came out of China. It informed the world: "The Chinese people cannot stand idly by with regard to such a serious situation created by the invasion of Korea ... ." Within another day or so as South Korean Army spearheads reached Wonsan Chinese armies in Manchuria crossed the border and marched into North Korea. A fundamental change had come over the strategic situation.

The 1st US Cavalry Division launched its drive to Pyongyang on 9 October and two days later the Australians moved off with the 27th Brigade. On 13 October the Australians took three prisoners. Two Australians were wounded by a grenade, but they remained on duty.

Four days later on the night of 17 October when north of Sariwon,

3 RAR clashed with a large body of North Koreans whose leader called out "Russki, Russki," believing the Australians must be Russian soldiers coming to their country's aid. Major I. B. Ferguson, the second-in-command of the battalion, then drove among the North Korean soldiers in a tank, telling them through an interpreter that they were surrounded and that they had two minutes to surrender. "These two minutes were the longest in my life," Ferguson said later. "A deathly hush fell over the area and you could hear your own heart beating." But the dangerous bluff succeeded and 1982 North Korean soldiers surrendered to the Australians. It is worth noting that 3 RAR would have numbered less than 900 men, not all of whom would have been deployed in this risky action.

Pyongyang was taken by the Americans on 19 October and MacArthur flew in to congratulate the 8th Army. The magic objective of an "Iron Curtain" capital city falling to the West had been achieved. Three days later 3 RAR passed through Phongyang and fought a major action at Yongju. The battalion, riding on American tanks, was sent to the relief of American paratroopers under pressure at Sukchon. In a battle in which the Australians had four soldiers wounded, they killed 270 of the enemy. Reporting on this brilliant action Brigadier Coad wrote:

> I saw a marvellous sight. An Australian platoon lined up in a paddy field and walked through it as though they were driving snipe. The soldiers when they saw a pile of straw, kicked it and out would bolt a North Korean. Up with a rifle, down with a North Korean and the Australians thoroughly enjoyed it.

By late October, North Korean resistance appeared to be crumbling fast and the 6th Republic of Korea (ROK) Division reached Chosan and the Yalu River which formed the border between Korea and Manchuria. Victory and the end of the war in Korea seemed within MacArthur's grasp. Pyongyang had fallen and the 8th Army and 10th Corps were racing northwards to the Yalu.

But the determined Chinese were preparing a massive surprise. Largely concealed from the observation of reconnaissance aircraft, no less than nine Chinese armies of 27 divisions were advancing to meet the United Nations troops, moving as unobtrusively as possible at night and using camouflage for men, animals and equipment during the day.

The 27th British Commonwealth Brigade continued its rapid advance north of Pyongyang, crossing the Chongchon River on 25 October. At Pakchon on 25–26 October the Australians of 3 RAR were in a stiff fight known as "the battle of the broken bridge" losing eight killed in an action which saw 100 enemy killed and 350 prisoners taken. Three days later on 29 October they encountered heavy opposition, losing nine killed and 30 wounded. Next night their gallant commanding officer, Lieutenant Colonel Green, was mortally wounded when struck by a high velocity shell. He died of his wounds on 2 November.

In the face of the growing Chinese army presence now apparent in North Korea, General Walton Walker ordered the withdrawal of the forward elements of the 8th Army and the 27th Brigade and US 24th Division pulled back to the Pakchon-Sinanju-Anju area, where on 5 November a division of Chinese troops attempted to isolate and destroy the 27th Brigade. No 77 Squadron of the RAAF was on call for support in the battle area and softened up Chinese positions with rockets, napalm and machine gunfire. Major Ferguson, soon to become commanding officer of 3 RAR, described the squadron's close support as "the closest I have ever seen". This was the first occasion in the Korean fighting that Australian airmen gave direct support to Australian troops.

No 77 Squadron Moves to Pohang

Russian-built MiG-15 jet fighters were appearing in the skies over the Manchurian border at Sinuiju and the first clash in history between jet fighter planes took place on 8 November when a MiG-15 was shot down by a US "Shooting Star". To meet the mounting threat the 5th Air Force squadrons including 77 Squadron were placed on "maximum effort". Bad news came in of the shattering blow delivered by a Chinese Division against the US Cavalry Division in which 500 cavalrymen were dead or captured.

As strong evidence of Chinese intervention in Korea was confirmed MacArthur reported to the United Nations Security Council that "a new and fresh army faces us, backed up by the possibility of large alien reserves". MacArthur warned that the movement of the Chinese forces threatened "the ultimate destruction of the forces under my command".

As the United Nations divisions advanced northward their air support aircraft had to fly longer and longer missions. So in early October No 77 Squadron was relocated from Iwakuni in Japan to K3 (Pohang) on the east coast of Korea where it became an operational squadron within the 35th Fighter-Bomber Group of the 5th Air Force.

It was now late autumn and the weather grew colder with a bitter crosswind coming in from across the Sea of Japan. "Frozen Chosen" they called the place ("Chosen" was the old name for Korea), and wondered what it would be like when winter really came.

From Pohang the Australian pilots were sent to search the roads coming down from Manchuria and they found the richest targets they had seen for some time. General Partridge sent more than 600 fighters and bombers to hit bridges, cities, towns, troop concentrations and supply dumps between the front line and the Yalu river. One RAAF fight damaged 43 enemy trucks in a hectic day of patrols along the roads leading down from the border towns of Sakchu and Kangye. The trucks had been crudely camouflaged as haystacks but they were too big and square to fool the pilots.

Pohang was soon well behind the front line and General Partridge now moved his 35th Group including No 77 Squadron far to the north at Yonpo airfield near the town of Hamhung. From Yonpo, which the Japanese had developed as an air base for the Imperial Japanese Navy, the group could more efficiently support the 8th Army and 10th Corps. It was a battle to keep warm at Yonpo but the Americans generously supplied the Australian airmen with American winter-style clothing while RAAF Dakotas were used to pick up supplies of the clothing from Pusan and fly them to Pyongyang from where they were trucked to the men of 3 RAR, who were still wearing summer issue clothing.

The Chinese Offensive

General MacArthur flew to Sinanju in his Constellation VIP aircraft on 24 November to see the launch of his final "decisive effort in Korea". In a special communiqué that day he declared, "The gigantic UN pincers moved according to plan." Opposition from the enemy was slight at first but then, according to General Stratemeyer, "the whole mountainside turned out to be Chinese." A thunderbolt unleashed by the new enemy struck three divisions of the 2nd Republic of Korea Corps in the middle of the United Nations line across central Korea. The ROKs disintegrated and the Chinese than crossed the Chongchon river, ripping open the right flank of the 8th Army. The US 2nd Division which held firm around Kunu-ri bought time for the 8th Army, saving it from tactical disaster. But the 2nd Division suffered grievous losses when it was forced to make a nightmare dash through an enfiladed road south to Chasan. Firing wildly the 2nd Division troops roared down the road as the machine guns of the 40th Chinese Army raked their vehicles. The division lost one third of its strength in killed, wounded or missing.

The Chinese thrust in the centre forced the 8th Army to withdraw to prevent encirclement. The withdrawal became a retreat.

The situation was no less perilous for the 10th Corps on the east coast where the US 1st Marine Division was almost surrounded by Chinese armies in the frigid mountains around the Chosin reservoir. Annoyed by pressmen who asked him if he was retreating, Major General Oliver Smith, who commanded the division came up with a glorious piece of bluster when he replied, "Gentlemen, we are not retreating, we are just attacking in a different direction." All over North Korea the Chinese had seized the initiative. It appeared likely that the strength of the enemy forces approaching the Hamhung perimeter would force an Allied withdrawal from the area.

Airmen at Yonpo were told that the Marines had been more or less surrounded and a dangerous situation was fast developing. The wing was organising a provisional battalion of 500 men to defend the airfield if it should be attacked after a breakthrough. Every man at Yonpo including the Australians was issued with arms and required to retain them at all times. The Australians got in some target practice blazing away across the watercourse which passed outside their quarters.

On 25 and 26 November the Australian Mustang pilots flew in support of the stricken ROK Corps and the 8th Army. On 28 November all squadrons of the 35th Group flew in support of the embattled Marines at Chosin reservoir. Every plane that could be got off the snow-covered Yonpo airstrip flew to help the marines who were in trouble at Hagaru-ri where they were fighting off attack after attack by enemy forces.

Then the order came to abandon the Hamhung bridgehead. The 35th Group of squadrons including the Australians were ordered south to Pusan (K9) to relieve the impossible congestion at Yonpo. The evacuation was carried out without interruption to the "maximum effort" operations. The Mustangs took off that morning and attacked targets north of Pyongyang before flying on to their new base at Pusan.

RAAF Dakotas were sent from Iwakuni to assist in the evacuation. By 24 December all United Nations troops and their equipment had been moved out under the protective guns of UN warships and aircraft. Altogether some 105,000 troops and 90,000 Korean refugees had been moved to Pusan. By that time, the 8th Army was south of the parallel.

When the Chinese assault began in the north the 27th Brigade was moved to Kunu-ri with the 2nd US Division and then to Chasan, 38 kilometres to the south, where it controlled the main supply route.

By 5 December the United Nations had abandoned Pyongyang and after a withdrawal of 320 kilometres, 3 RAR became part of the rearguard at Uijongbu covering the approaches to Seoul. The Chinese continued to advance and on 4 January 1951 Seoul, the South Korean capital, was again in communist hands.

Except for the 2nd Division, American losses had not been heavy. They totalled 12,975. But the Inchon triumph had been cancelled out by the Chongchon debacle.

The RAN

The RAN had taken part in the United Nations advance into North Korea when HMAS *Warramunga* provided gunfire support for the 10th Corps landing at Wonsan on the east coast in October 1950 and later screened the US battleship *Missouri* when it bombarded Chongjin north of Hamhung.

By early December *Warramunga* and *Bataan* took a direct role in the operations against the Chinese offensive by joining a blockade of the Yalu Gulf which prevented the enemy from landing reinforcements in the northwest as they pursued the United Nations armies southwards.

On 4 December, the day before the fall of Pyongyang, *Warramunga* and *Bataan* were ordered to make a hazardous 45-kilometre dash at night in freezing temperatures through shoal water in the approaches to Chinnampo, the port for Phongyang. A total of 7,700 US army and navy port personnel as well as Korean troops and civilians including wounded had to be evacuated before the advancing enemy arrived. *Warramunga* grounded (but was later refloated). *Bataan* made it to Chinnampo where a flotilla of boats, barges and junks packed with refugees slipped downstream and escaped. Before leaving Chinnampo, *Bataan* took part in a spectacular demolition bombardment which saw the Chinnampo waterfront crumble into ruins.

Bataan and *Warramunga* and other UN naval units accompanied the small vessels from Chinnampo to Inchon. They then stood by to give support to the 8th Army and assisted in the evacuation of Inchon, a task which was completed on 5 January the day after Seoul was abandoned to the enemy.

In the fallout from the stunning military reversal in Korea, gloom and despondency pervaded the United Nations Command. Clearly the Chinese had won a battle that would stand in history. For the Americans it seemed almost as humiliating as the attack on Pearl Harbor nine years earlier, and they were conscious that an Asian communist army had won a battle against one of America's most famous military leaders.

In the United States President Truman declared a state of emergency.

In some quarters the possibility that Korea might have to be abandoned to the communists was by no means excluded. But this defeatist thinking was quickly extinguished when General Lawton Collins, the US Army Chief of Staff, flew to MacArthur's headquarters and then to Korea, bearing the message that there was to be no retreat.

Day after day from Pusan the Mustangs of No 77 Squadron continued to range widely over the snow-covered hills and valleys of Korea, maintaining the never-ending task of attacking Chinese troops and supplies. In the new year the squadron was assigned a hazardous mission to destroy a group of school buildings in the centre of Pyongyang, believed to be in use as a major enemy headquarters.

On 19 January 12 RAAF Mustangs comprising a bombing group of six led by Squadron Leader Richard Cresswell and a napalm group of six led by Flight Lieutenant Gordon Harvey set off in a dust haze from Pusan and flew to Pyongyang where they were greeted by anti-aircraft fire. Surprise had not been achieved because their arrival coincided with a B29 radar bombing mission on the same target. This attack alerted the anti-aircraft defences.

The six RAAF bombers attacking right on time at 13.00 hours scored four direct bomb hits and four near misses. Ten minutes later Harvey's six attacked with napalms. The Mustangs had to get right down low to have any chance of hitting the targets. The napalm group saw the bombs of the B29s exploding as they came in. Then Harvey was in deep trouble. His aircraft seemed to be on fire with smoke and flame streaming from behind. Undeterred Harvey dropped his napalms and fired rockets into the target. In an unruffled voice the other pilots heard him say, "I'm going to belly-land this aircraft." They saw him force-land in the ice and snow on an island in the middle of the Taedong river. Harvey was apparently not badly hurt and was seen to run from the aircraft and hide in a haystack.

In an attempt to rescue Harvey from imprisonment and the likelihood of torture, General Partridge placed all Allied airborne aircraft at Cresswell's disposal. Cresswell led 16 Mustangs to locate Harvey. A Navy helicopter from a US aircraft carrier was to attempt the rescue. The Mustangs could discern tracks in the snow all around

Harvey's downed aircraft but the downed pilot could not be found and the helicopter rescue had to be abandoned.

After the war ended it was learned that he had fallen into enemy hands very soon after landing and later suffered severely in captivity. In April 1951 he escaped from the notorious "Pak's Palace" prison but was recaptured six days later and punished by being placed in a two-metre hole in the ground for 45 days. Harvey survived the war and was later appointed commanding officer of No 77 Squadron when it was serving as a Sabre squadron in Malaya.

Many pilots including members of No 77 Squadron were rescued by American helicopters from enemy territory after forced landings or parachuting from disabled aircraft. When helicopter rescue attempts were being made, fighter aircraft were called to the area to cover the rescue operation and keep enemy interference at bay on the ground.

After passing through Seoul, the 27th Brigade on 5 January withdrew 160 kilometres further south through Ichon to Yoda-nae and then began a program of vigorous patrolling. Members of 3 RAR ambushed a Chinese patrol at Ichon on 16 January killing 20 enemy. An Australian patrol led by Lieutenant Angus MacDonald was surrounded and captured on 21 January. The Australians expected to be killed but were sent instead to a "correctional school" where they were instructed on the merits of communism. On 7 February the Chinese released them and MacDonald, Corporal L. Buckland and Private E. G. Light returned to the South and were flown out of Korea.

In mid-March Seoul, the battered capital of South Korea, was conquered for the fourth time in less than a year by the 8th Army now under the command of General Matthew Ridgeway. At the end of March the 27th Brigade joined in Operation "Courageous" in an advance northwards to the 38th parallel from which 3 RAR had begun its campaign five months earlier. After further advances during April, 3 RAR was relieved to the reserve at Kapyong on the Pukhan River for a well-earned rest.

On 11 April, a startled world learned that President Truman had sacked General Douglas MacArthur. Truman broke the news in Washington that the now world-famous American general, hero of the

Pacific war, then Supreme Commander of the occupation forces in Japan and finally military leader in the defence of the Western world against communist aggression in Korea, had been summarily dismissed from all posts and replaced by General Matthew Ridgeway. It was an act that needed great courage on Truman's part and was immediately followed by an intense emotional upheaval in the United States.

The issue was clear enough. MacArthur had repeatedly demanded that he should be permitted to extend the "limited" war by attacking the enemy's "privileged" sanctuary in Manchuria ... "There is no substitute for victory," he declared. In justifying the dismissal Truman said, "We are trying to prevent a world war not to start one." General Omar Bradley, chairman of the US Joint Chiefs, declared that MacArthur's policy "would have involved us in the wrong war, in the wrong place, at the wrong time, against the wrong enemy".

MacArthur had been warned repeatedly by Truman not to make political statements and by flouting presidential authority he in effect invited his dismissal for insubordination. The US Joint Chiefs of Staff had recommended his dismissal "on purely military considerations".

From Kapyong to the Hook

Hard on the dismissal of MacArthur, the Chinese Army launched a spring offensive in Korea. Their guns opened up on 22 April and the single greatest Chinese military thrust of the Korean War slammed into the United Nations armies. Some 330,000 Chinese troops went into action, fighting vigorously and regardless of losses. They had the ambitious objectives of destroying the United Nations military in Korea and delivering the South Korean capital, Seoul, as a May Day gift to Joe Stalin, the Russian communist leader.

In its critical phase the offensive would see Chinese troops and Australians of the 3rd Battalion locked together in a fierce night and day battle in which the Australians would cover themselves in glory and earn for their battalion the coveted award of the US Presidential Unit Citation. It would also see the decimation after an heroic battle of the

British Gloucester Regiment. But in the end the Chinese Army would suffer unparalleled carnage and go down to defeat.

After months of campaigning over much of Korea, the Australians on 16 April handed over their area of responsibility to elements of the 6th ROK Division and were resting at Charidai where they enjoyed pictures and a beer ration and picked wild azaleas which would garland a wreath for an Anzac Day ceremony. But their brief rest a few kilometres behind the front line was abruptly cut short. At 8.30 am on 23 April the 27th Brigade was ordered to move within an hour to defend the Kapyong valley against a threatened breakthrough by the Chinese. The night before, the 6th ROK Division had taken the full weight of the attack by the Chinese and had disintegrated, with broken formations flooding back down the Kapyong river valley and with the Chinese in hot pursuit. The brigade's task was to deploy across a seven-kilometre front using 3 RAR and the 2nd Battalion, Princess Patricia's Canadian Light Infantry, supported by the 16th New Zealand Field Regiment and a company of the US 72 Tank Battalion. Their task was to block the advance of the Chinese Army.

Kapyong was strategically important and the brigade had to defend an area six kilometres north of the town where Brigadier Brian Burke, who had just assumed command of the brigade, concentrated his force around the confluence of the Kapyong River and a smaller stream. The blocking position the battalions occupied was founded on eight clusters of men.

The Australian deployment took place with practised efficiency. Where the ground was too stony for digging the men used piled-up rocks as sangars.

As darkness approached, the flow of Koreans increased and indicated a serious collapse had taken place. Soldiers milled around in a disorderly manner and overladen vehicles clogged the road. Chinese soldiers were mingling with the retreating Koreans amid a chaos of flashing lights and random gunfire. Captain Reg Saunders, the commander of C Company 3 RAR, and the first Australian Aboriginal to be commissioned in the Australian army, found the scene reminiscent of past war experiences.

The clamour on our front became easily recognisable as that of a defeated army in retreat. I had heard it before in Greece and Crete and earlier in Korea. I must admit I felt a little dejected until I realised I was an Australian company commander and if my morale got low then I couldn't expect much from my troops. This served to buck me up and I lay down in a shallow trench and had a little sleep. The sound of small arms fire awoke me and soon after the crash of tank cannon in B Company area. I could see flashes of fire coming from the direction of battalion headquarters and I realised that the enemy were now in a good position to cut off the companies.[1]

The first assault by the Chinese came at 9.30 pm on 23 April against the American tanks, and at 12.50 am next day a major assault was launched on B Company, 3 RAR, which repulsed the attacks with heavy casualties. At daylight Chinese troops could be seen exposed in the valley between A and B Companies and were heavily counterattacked with artillery, mortar, small arms and tank fire. The Chinese were forced to pull back leaving hundreds of dead on the battlefield. In the A Company area the Chinese refused to give up the attack and rushed ahead in waves over heaps of their own dead and wounded. Robert O'Neill, the official Australian historian of the Korean War, wrote:

The Chinese seemed to have enormous numerical superiority and their attacks increased in frequency to become one continuous onrush of troops. All three Bren gunners of 1 Platoon were killed or wounded and the fighting strength of the platoon was reduced from thirty to thirteen.

A Company suffered 50 casualties but after a hard battle that raged all night was at 7 am in possession of its original area. The Chinese then had to withdraw through open country and came under fire from Australians on the heights. Major Bernard O'Dowd, A Company commander, observed later, "The situation rather resembled sitting in the middle of a wheat field at dawn potting rabbits as they dashed hither and thither."[2]

Beginning at 7 am on 24 April the Chinese turned their attention to D Company, launching attacks on its positions at half-hour intervals throughout the morning in an attempt to take the commanding high ground occupied by the company. Holding this ground was crucial to the security of the whole battalion. The New Zealand artillery brought fire to within 50 metres of the Australian positions and was vital to their defence. To maintain their fire, ammunition had to be ferried to them from as far afield as Seoul.

Lieutenant Colonel Ferguson, CO of the Australian battalion, conducted a desperate battle around his headquarters when fighting flared with Chinese infiltrators who had mingled with retreating South Korean troops. The Australian infantry in the headquarters had to fight from hastily prepared defences. The Regimental Aid Post was under fire all night but eventually made a break to a new position some three kilometres along the road south. The main headquarters body covered by US tanks had withdrawn by 6 am to the Middlesex perimeter.

D Company suffered casualties when an air strike was called on a Chinese-held position. The spotter aircraft dropped a spigot flare in error on an Australian position with the result that two US Corsair aircraft attacked with napalm in the heart of D Company defences, killing two Australians and causing fires which raced across the summit of the strategic hill 504, causing further distress. The American air attack was halted when an Australian officer ran out of cover under fire waving a marker panel.

After the napalm attack the companies were ordered to withdraw and, although hindered by Chinese fire, they were able to break clear. All elements had reached the Middlesex position by 11.30 pm.

The Canadian battalion was attacked by the Chinese on 25 April and for a time was in danger of an enemy breakthrough. However, the Chinese attack was not renewed.

Between them the Australian and Canadian infantry with the American tanks and supported by the New Zealand artillery had hurled back an all-out attack by a full Chinese division.

All three units, 3 RAR, the 2nd Battalion, PPCLI and A Company of the 72nd US Tank Battalion were awarded the high distinction of a

Presidential Citation by President Truman, "for extraordinary heroism and outstanding performance of combat duties in action against the armed enemy near Kapyong, Korea on 24 and 25 April 1951". The citation recorded that the seriousness of the breakthrough on the central front had been changed from defeat to victory by the gallant stand of these heroic and courageous soldiers [who] displayed such gallantry, determination and esprit de corps in accomplishing their mission under extreme difficulty and hazardous conditions as to set them apart and above other units participating in the campaign and by their achievements they brought distinguished credit on themselves, their homelands and all freedom loving nations.

For outstanding leadership, Lieutenant Colonel Ferguson received the immediate award of the Distinguished Service Order. Private W. H. Madden, who was taken prisoner, received after the war a posthumous award of the George Cross for outstanding courage while a prisoner. He died in November 1951 from severe illness arising from savage beatings and starvation.

The cost to the Australians in the battle of Kapyong had been high. Thirty-two members of the battalion were killed, 59 wounded and three were taken prisoner. Chinese killed in action at Kapyong totalled between 500 and 600.

By 30 April the Chinese offensive was over and they had suffered at least 70,000 casualties, while the United Nations losses were 7,000. Yet the enemy was strenuously preparing for yet another offensive.

On 28 April, immediately after the Kapyong battle, 3 RAR and two British battalions were incorporated into the 28th British Commonwealth Brigade. The 28th Brigade was then brought together with the 25th Canadian Brigade and the 29th British Brigade to form the 1st Commonwealth Division commanded by Major General (later Field Marshal Sir James) Cassels.

On 16 May the Chinese had mounted yet another major offensive with five of their armies in action. But the superior firepower of the United Nations forces and poor Chinese logistics soon had the enemy retreating in disorder, losing 10,000 taken prisoner by the UN and huge stocks of equipment and supplies. In the week from 17 to 23 May the communist losses of 90,000 were even greater than in the April offensive. It now was highly unlikely that the communists could force the UN out of Korea.

On 23 June, Jacob Malik, the Russian President of the United Nations Security Council, agreed to United States proposals to negotiate a ceasefire. Subsequently military representatives of the warring parties met first at Kaesong and later at Panmunjom to negotiate. The prospects for peace seemed favourable because both parties appeared to have given up the intention of achieving a complete victory in which they would take over the whole of Korea. When on 10 July at Kaesong negotiations actually got under way between the UN Command and the communists, high hopes were held for a successful termination of hostilities in Korea. No one believed that the peace negotiations which began that day would take more than two years before a ceasefire would be signed.

Meanwhile the first task for the newly constituted Commonwealth Division was to mount a series of patrols across the Imjin river, north of Seoul. Early in September the whole division crossed the Imjin and established a new defence line.

The Commonwealth Division and three other United Nations divisions were assigned to take part in October in a general advance to straighten the front line and drive the Chinese from the first line of high hills to the northwest of the salient.

In this operation 3 RAR was assigned the difficult task of capturing the steep-faced hill 317 which with hill 217 crowned the hill complex of Maryang San close to the Imjin River on the main Chinese defensive line. Two attempts by American units to take hill 317 had already been repelled with heavy losses.

Lieutenant Colonel (later General Sir Francis) Hassett, a Duntroon graduate, had succeeded Lieutenant Colonel Ferguson as commanding officer of 3 RAR in July.

Two companies of the battalion began the advance on Maryang San at 3 am on 3 October and took hill 199 at 8 am. They were joined by British Centurion tanks.

On 5 October B and D Companies supported by a troop of

Centurions attacked the steep eastern ridge of hill 317. Conditions were misty, which proved a mixed blessing. Navigation was difficult and artillery and mortar support was ruled out. As the Australians climbed the Chinese fired down on them and hurled grenades. But D Company penetrated the Chinese defences, killing 30 of the enemy. The company had performed magnificently, destroying a company of Chinese in deeply dug trenches.

Hassett now ordered C Company (Captain Jack Gerke) to attack the summit. The company quickly cleared the feature "Baldy" and began the final assault on the summit up a slope so steep it forced them to their hands and knees. However, the company moved so quickly that the Chinese were caught off-balance and the summit fell unopposed at 5 pm.

By 8 October, after five days of fighting, the men of 3 RAR knew they had won a notable victory against a numerically superior enemy occupying well-prepared positions of great strength. They had destroyed at least two Chinese battalions.

The battalion was highly praised by Major General Cassell, but the greatest tribute came from their proud commander, Hassett, who said of his men, "Their sheer guts is beyond belief." Hassett himself was recommended for the immediate award of the Distinguished Service Order.

Ironically only a month was to pass before the position, which had become the responsibility of another unit, was lost to the enemy and never regained while the war lasted.

The United Nations had achieved a strong defensive line in Korea by late 1951 and sought no further significant advances. The Chinese and North Koreans used a lull during ceasefire talks to build deep defensive works reminiscent of the First World War front lines. They heavily reinforced their artillery.

In 1952–53 the 8th Army's military objective was to maintain pressure on the enemy while the peace negotiations went on a Panmunjom. At the same time Allied naval and air power, while it was unable to prevent completely the flow of men and materials to the communist front line troops, exacted a heavy price from the enemy at all times.

During 1952 the United States command sought further contributions of ground forces from members of the United Nations to match the predominance of communist manpower. Australia was asked to increase her contribution, and in September 1951 Cabinet agreed to despatch a second battalion, 1 RAR, which was thereupon launched into urgent preparation for service in Korea.

Lieutenant Colonel Ian Hutchinson was appointed to command the 1st Battalion RAR which embarked by troopship for Korea, arriving on 6 April. It joined the 28th British Commonwealth Brigade on 1 June 1952. At the same time a distinguished Australian officer, Brigadier (later Lieutenant General Sir Thomas) Daly was appointed to command the 28th Brigade, taking over command on 27 June 1952. Two days later the brigade was sent into the line on the western sector of the Jameston line.

The 1st Battalion remained in Korea for a year and returned to Australia in 1953. It was replaced from Australia by the 2nd Battalion RAR on April 1953, commanded by Lieutenant Colonel C. F. Larkin. On 25 March 1953 Brigadier (later General Sir John) Wilton took over command of the 28th Brigade from Brigadier Daly.

During 19 months of static war in 1952–53, the Commonwealth Division was in the line constantly except for two months (February and March 1953). It was opposed by a Chinese Field Army of three divisions, each division having 9,500 men. The Chinese were supported by artillery regiments but their scale of firepower was much less than that of the Commonwealth Division.

Between the opposing front lines was a broad valley. At one point only 300 metres separated the opposing front line defences.

The early months of 1952 were comparatively quiet for 3 RAR, except for the night of 26–27 January. At last light two platoons captured a feature against light opposition. But the Chinese later reacted strongly and eventually the Australians were forced back with the loss of seven killed and eight wounded. Intensive patrolling was carried out by the battalion as the Australians fought vigorously to dominate forward areas.

The 8th Army gave instructions that Chinese were to be taken for interrogation purposes, but they proved almost impossible to capture: in more than a year the Australians captured only one.

On 2 July 1952, 1 RAR was tasked to capture a prisoner. In the attempt three members of the battalion were killed and 30 wounded, but no prisoner was taken. In another attempt in December 1952 a company was sent to destroy an objective code-named "Flora" and to take prisoners. One-third of the company (B Company, 1 RAR) became casualties but no prisoner was taken.

The Korean War was a hard-fought bloody struggle to the bitter end. The combined losses of 2 RAR and 3 RAR in May and June 1953 were 32 killed, 157 wounded and 9 missing. These losses occurred in patrol clashes, ambushes, bombardments and mine explosions.

As the signing of the peace agreement at Panmunjom drew ever closer, the Chinese Army made ferocious attacks in a desperate bid to gain ground before the ceasefire.

In July, 2 RAR and 3 RAR were in the front line at a notorious position known as the Hook which the Chinese had attempted many times to seize. On the night of 24–25 July, only two days before the ceasefire took effect, waves of Chinese attacked the Australians and US Marines on the Hook. In two nights some 600 artillery shells fired by the Chinese exploded in the Australian area. UN artillery fire was called in to shell the area close to the UN positions to break up repeated Chinese attacks.

Ultimately the enemy assaults failed and when dawn came some 2,000 to 3,000 enemy lay dead around the Hook. Most had been caught in the deadly artillery barrage. Casualties suffered by 2 RAR were 17 killed and 31 wounded, but the enemy dead carpeted the ground around their positions.

It was the last engagement of the war for the Australians and one of the most desperate. A 19-year-old machine gunner, Sergeant B. C. Cooper of 2 RAR, was decorated with the Military Medal for assisting to break up a Chinese attack on US Marine positions.

The RAAF in Jet Battles over MiG Alley

For the RAAF, a significant feature of the Korean War was its own use of jet fighters. After the Chinese entered the war in October 1950, numerous reports had come in of large numbers of MiG-15 aircraft being sighted in "MiG Alley" near the Manchurian border. The Mustangs of No 77 Squadron had not so far had to contend with an enemy flying high-performance jet aircraft. But with the prospect of air-to-air combat with MiG-15 jets the future of the Mustangs had to be considered. If 77 Squadron was to continue to have a leading role in the air war, it would have to be re-equipped with high-performance aircraft. The new American F86 Sabre jet fighter was the preferred replacement but the Americans were unable to make them available because of heavy demands to equip their own squadrons in Europe as well as in Korea.

So, of necessity, the RAAF settled for the British Gloster Meteor 8 jets fitted with two Derwent engines. The announcement by Prime Minister Menzies in December 1950 that the Air Force was to get Meteors caused a buzz of excitement among the pilots in Korea, although the RAAF was aware that the Meteor was not an even match for the MiG-15, which had an outstanding rate of climb and superior handling qualities at high altitudes. The MiGs were state-of-the-art in fighter technology. In building this fighter the Russians had had access to captured German swept-wing designs and had copied the jet engine from the Rolls Royce Nene.

After a lively farewell party put on by the 35th Fighter Group at Pusan, No 77 Squadron pilots flew their Mustangs back to Iwakuni and commenced conversion training in the Meteors. They had the help of four experienced RAF Meteor pilots who had been sent from England to assist.

By July 1951 the squadron was ready again for action and flew to Kimpo, near Seoul, where it was to operate with the leading American 4th Fighter Group which had been equipped with Sabres.

Overnight the Chinese, greatly assisted by the Soviets, had become a major air power. Not only could the MiGs outperform RAAF Meteors and some American jets, but they could operate in larger and larger formations.

The enemy build-up of air power had been made easy by the United Nations Command decision to respect the Manchurian border. As a result MiGs were able to take off and reach operational altitude while still in the "privileged sanctuary" of Manchuria where they were immune from attack. American air supremacy in the air over "MiG Alley" in North Korea was facing a serious challenge.

On 29 August 1951, 8 RAAF jet fighter pilots of No 77 Squadron flying Meteor jet fighters clashed with 30 Russian-built MiG-15 swept-wing jets in a hectic air battle over Chongju in North Korea.

This air combat made a first in Australian aviation history – a RAAF jet squadron in action against enemy jets.

The Australians attacked first and in the fantastic 600-mile-an-hour swirling dog fight that followed one Meteor piloted by Squadron Leader David Wilson was badly damaged and another flown by Warrant Officer Donald Guthrie went missing. American Sabres in the battle area reported seeing a Meteor smoking and spinning down. Guthrie had in fact been shot down. But he survived by taking to his parachute and three months later the enemy listed him as a prisoner-of-war. (In September 1953 when the fighting ended in Korea, he was released from prison camp.) Wilson was able to nurse his damaged Meteor back to base at Kimpo.

Sabres and Meteors were called on frequently to escort US B29 bombers which were harassing enemy communications and installations in North Korea. On 27 October the Meteors were heavily engaged fending off MiG attacks on eight B29s after they had dropped bombs at Sinanju on the Chonchon river. The B29s withdrew towards the Yellow Sea and minutes later the MiGs came barrelling through the formation and the Meteors turned to attack them. Cannon shells hit a B29 which was badly damaged and forced to make for Kimpo.

On 1 December the Australians fought their last air-to-air battle for the year over Sunchon. Above the RAAF formations of 14 Meteors were no less than 50 MiGs which swooped down in pairs to attack. A fierce battle followed with the fight ranging far across North Korea. Flying Officer Bruce Gogerly shot down a MiG-the first to fall to No 77 Squadron – but three Meteors were lost. Two pilots managed to land their aircraft in enemy territory and Sergeant (later Wing Commander) Vance Drummond, and Flying Officer Bruce Thompson were taken prisoner. Flight Sergeant E. D. Armit was posted missing believed killed.

Bravery and skill could not compensate for the inadequacy of the Meteor against the swept-wing MiG-15. So the 5th Air Force took No 77 Squadron off fighter sweeps and placed it on air defence duties. Its task was to be ready to take off at an instant's notice to intercept enemy aircraft which might attempt to attack Kimpo. But the Chinese sent only light aircraft at night on nuisance raids.

In December a dual role was assigned to the squadron: patrolling the Kimpo-Seoul area and ground attack duties. In January 1952 in their first month in the new role the squadron pilots flew 769 sorties, followed in February by 1,005. The Meteor proved a highly efficient aircraft in the ground attack role, although accurate enemy ground fire led to the loss of six pilots between January and April 1952.

The air war in 1952 was heavily focussed on the battle of the supply lines which provided support for the Chinese armies in the front line. No 77 Squadron joined in round-the-clock efforts to hamper enemy transport and to help protect American fighter bomber aircraft engaged in this air campaign. To counter the threat, the enemy ordered MiG fighters to fly further south and at lower altitudes, but the RAAF Meteors were then less disadvantaged. This resulted in RAAF Meteors destroying a number of MiGs.

In August the squadron joined in a great air assault on the northern capital Pyongyang by a total of 420 United Nations aircraft. MiG interference with this assault was slight as the marauding airmen bombed and strafed airfields, power stations, factories and anti-aircraft batteries.

During the Korean War RAAF Dakota transport aircraft made a valuable contribution to the operations not only of the RAAF and the Australian Army but to all British Commonwealth forces fighting in the Korean peninsula. Beginning with a transport communications flight within No 77 Squadron, the RAAF transport force expanded during the war to become No 30 Transport Unit and ultimately, as the workload increased, the Unit was upgraded to No 36 Squadron.

The RAAF Dakotas flew more than 100,000 passengers to Korea and carried some 6,000 tons of freight and mail.

A principal task for the RAAF Dakotas was the provision of aero-medical evacuation of wounded from Korea. The RAAF Dakotas flew 12,762 wounded to hospitals in Japan. Of these 729 later went on to Australia and 1,530 to the United Kingdom. The aero-medical evacuation service was developed by RAAF medical officers and from January 1951 to December 1953 patients were escorted from Korea to Japan by members of the RAAF Nursing Service.

The RAN Joins the Air War

Heavy fire from concealed mortars, small arms and light field guns was directed against HMAS *Murchison* (Commander A. N. Dollard) as the RAN frigate moved up the Han River on 28 September 1951.

Murchison, which had replaced HMAS *Bataan* for duty in the Korean War, vigorously returned the fire and when running the gauntlet on her return journey down the river was again engaged in a hectic battle. *Murchison* knocked out a gun on shore but herself suffered four hits.

Two days later on 30 September, *Murchison* was blasted by even heavier fire from the shore at a range so close that *Murchison*'s gunners were returning the fire over open sights. The frigate was holed by the communists in several places and three of her crew were wounded, one seriously. In response to the enemy attacks on *Murchison,* the US Navy sent aircraft from the carrier USS *Rendova* to blast the enemy shore positions.

Murchison in company with HMS *Cardigan Bay* and the ROK frigate *PF62* had been engaged in bombarding shore installations, troop concentrations, gun positions and stores dumps along the Han shoreline. *Murchison* fired 1,056 rounds of 4-inch and 1,030 rounds of Bofors ammunition in eight days. For 100 days, up to 14 small ships of the United Nations navies took part in the bombardments. *Murchison* was on the river for 44 days.

Leaders of the United Nations peace delegation at Panmunjom had called for the attacks along the Han as a "show of force" when arguments arose over the demarcation line separating the communists and the United Nations forces. The dispute ended early in November 1951 when both sides at the negotiations accepted the existing battle line as the demarcation line.

Three more RAN warships were assigned to the Korean War in the last six months of 1951. They were the aircraft carrier HMAS *Sydney* (Captain David Harries) and the destroyers HMAS *Anzac* (Commander Plunkett Cole) and HMAS *Tobruk* (Commander Richard J. Peek).

Australia sharply increased its commitment to combat operations in support of the United Nations in Korea when the RAN's aircraft carrier HMAS *Sydney* arrived in Korean waters early in October 1951. Embarked on *Sydney* was the 20th Carrier Air Group (commanded by Lieutenant Commander M. F. Fell, RN), of three naval air squadrons. They were:

- No 805 (Lieutenant Commander W. G. Bowles, RAN) equipped with Sea Fury fighters with an armament of four 20-millimetre cannon and with provision for carrying two 500 lb bombs or twelve rockets.
- No 808 (Lieutenant Commander J. L. Appleby, RN) also equipped with Sea Fury fighters.
- No 817 (Lieutenant Commander R. F. Lunberg, RN) equipped with Firefly twin seat fighters which carried radar and other devices for anti-submarine warfare.

The RAN, keen to deploy its recently acquired fleet air arm, ensured a thorough working up period for *Sydney* and gave high priority to her needs. Australia became one of three nations to deploy aircraft carriers in the war (the other two of course being the United States and Britain).

The RAN's opportunity to send the carrier to the war came when the Admiralty informed the RAN that a replacement for the carrier HMS *Glory* was needed while the latter refitted before returning to the Korean War. The Australian Government agreed but told the Admiralty that if greater emergency arose during *Sydney*'s service in Korea, the carrier might be withdrawn.

On 5 October, led by Commander Fell, Sydney's aircraft flew their first operational missions on the west coast of Korea, where the carrier had relieved the American USS *Rendova*. Two days later *Sydney* was refuelled and sailed at once to join a special force on the east coast of Korea.

On 10 October 1951, screened by British and Canadian naval units, *Sydney* was off Kojo just south of the important east coast port of Wonsan in North Korea. *Sydney* launched Sea Furies which rocketed heavy concentrations of enemy troops dug in on hills which covered the beaches. Fireflies of 817 Squadron bombed gun emplacements and the entrances to railway tunnels.

Sydney's performance was excellent. The carrier's aircraft mounted 89 sorties in one day and in "spotting" for the battleship USS *New Jersey* "did a first-class job". Three of *Sydney*'s aircraft were hit and damaged by anti-aircraft fire. The enemy had modern anti-aircraft artillery and they knew how to handle it. Small arms fire was also used to fill the air with as much lead as possible in the hope that some at least would find a target, which was not infrequently the case.

After her patrol off the east coast *Sydney* had to leave Sasebo harbour in Japan on 14 October when typhoon "Ruth" was about to strike. Precipitous seas caused *Sydney* to pitch and roll to a highly unpleasant and distressing degree. Fortunately no serious injuries resulted but one aircraft was lost overboard and another four were damaged.

Within a week the carrier was operating again off the west coast and between 18–28 October flew 474 sorties, losing 3 aircraft shot down and 28 damaged. All aircrew were recovered from enemy territory. One Firefly piloted by sub-lieutenant N. D. McMillan, with Observer P. Hancox as crew member, crashed south of Sariwon when attempting to bomb a railway tunnel. An American rescue helicopter was sent to pick them up while Sea Furies and RAAF Meteor jets provided covering fire. Several of the Meteors were hit by ground fire. The helicopter rescue under hazardous circumstances succeeded and the two Australians were flown to Kimpo.

Sydney's first fatal casualty came on 5 November. Lieutenant K. Clarkson was killed when his Sea Fury disintegrated after being hit by anti-aircraft gunfire. A month later Lieutenant R. Sinclair was lost when his Sea Fury was hit north of Chinnampo: Sinclair was fatally injured when he parachuted from his aircraft and was struck by its tail.

After *Sydney's* aircraft had flown a total of 2,366 missions for the loss of four Firefly and nine Sea Furies the carrier screened by *Tobruk* left Sasebo (Kyushu) for Australia on 27 January 1952.

Warramunga and *Bataan* returned to Korea from Australia in January 1952. *Anzac* returned in September 1952 and *Tobruk* in June 1953. The frigate *Condamine* arrived in Korea in August 1952 and *Culgoa* in April 1953. All told nine RAN warships – *Sydney, Anzac, Bataan, Tobruk, Warramunga, Culgoa, Condamine, Murchison* and *Shoalhaven* – served in Korea during the period of hostilities. Four (*Anzac, Bataan, Tobruk* and *Warramunga*) served two tours.

The RAN warships continued during 1952 and 1953 in the important tasks of blockading the enemy coasts as well as the bombardment of shore batteries and carrier screen duties. *Condamine* supported guerilla operations and frequently bombarded the west coast in defence of offshore islands. *Culgoa* fired her last shots of the war on 23 June 1953 against an enemy force invading Yongmai Do.

The War Ends

After peace talks which had dragged on for two years, the signing of an armistice brought the "limited war" in Korea to an end at 10 pm on 27 July 1953.

Although the enemy forces remained intact and undefeated in the field in Korea, the United Nations forces had won a victory that would stand in history, because the attempt of the North Koreans to "liberate" their brothers in South Korea by force of arms had been defeated.

The march of the communist powers during the "Cold War" was worldwide. Just before the Korean War began, the communist block won its greatest victory in the east when the Chinese communist armies, led by Mao Tse-tung, defeated their nationalist opponents and took control of China. Great struggles still lay ahead, but Korea, under United Nations leadership, had given hope to the free world by demonstrating a resolve to resist the spread of communism by force of arms.

Australian participation in Korea was not large in relation to Australian efforts in the previous world wars, and Australian military resources were strained to provide a modest contribution of men and weapons to the armed struggle. But the members of all three Australian services were volunteers and their courage and expertise were reflected in a contribution to successful operations that went far beyond their numbers.

A total of 18,059 Australians served in the armed forces in Korea. Of these 5,959 were RAN, 10,974 were Army and 1,126 were RAAF, Australians who lost their lives totalled 339. Of these 293 were Army, 5 RAN and 41 RAAF.

9

INDONESIA CONFRONTS MALAYSIA

"Confronting" Malaysia

In Malaya, once the emergency was over, euphoria was created by independence and by the lifting of the 12-year-old state of emergency, but this quickly evaporated when Indonesia by overt acts of military aggression and a campaign of vilification put pressure on the newly created South-East Asian state of Malaysia.

Indonesia's mercurial President Ahmed Sukarno objected wrathfully to a plan by Prime Minister Tunku Abdul Rahman to bring together Malaya, Singapore, Sabah (British North Borneo), Sarawak and the Sultanate of Brunei in a new federation to be named "Malaysia". Later Singapore withdrew from the proposed federation and a small-scale anti-Malaysian rebellion in the Sultanate of Brunei had to be put down by British forces flown in to Brunei in a RAAF Hercules transport.

However, the lurid threats emanating from Jakarta did not deter the Malayan Prime Minister who with British support went ahead with the plans for the new nation.

Australia also supported the Malaysia plan, although seeking to avoid antagonising Indonesia. But at the same time Australia saw the need to upgrade her defence capacity because of the possibility of conflict with Indonesia on the issue. However, Sir Howard Beale, the Australian Ambassador in Washington, was told that if Australian troops were "in trouble" when helping Britain to fight Indonesia in support of Malaysia, the United States would regard herself just as bound to assist Australia as she would be in a case involving ANZUS (the Australian New Zealand United States Security Treaty).[1]

It was later made clear that the US would act only in the case of "overt" attack on Australians and not in cases of subversion, guerilla war and indirect aggression. It was made clear also that US air and naval force would be used but not ground troops.

The Indonesians coined the term Konfrontasi (confrontation) for their opposition to Malaysia. A disturbing aspect of the growing tension was that Indonesia's already substantial armed forces were being boosted with Soviet arms including supersonic MiG fighters, air transports, powerful cruisers and Komar class gunboats fitted with guided missiles. Extended credit was also provided by Russia. A campaign of subversion, murder and sabotage was mounted against the "neo-colonialists" in Borneo.

Confrontation reached flashpoint on 16 September 1963, the day the new nation of Malaysia was born. While the Malaysians, ignoring the Indonesian campaign against them, celebrated the birth of their new, more viable nation, Indonesian mobs in Jakarta went on a wild rampage attacking the Malayan and British Embassies (the latter was burned down) but leaving the Australian Embassy in peace. Sukarno adopted the slogan "ganjang Malaysia" ("crush Malaysia") and cut off diplomatic relations with Kuala Lumpur. Tunku Abdul Rahman broke off diplomatic relations with both Indonesia and the Philippines when they failed to recognise the new state of Malaysia. The latter nation not only joined with Indonesia in rejecting the new Malaysia but laid claim to Sabah.

Two days later Robert Menzies told the House of Representatives that Australia would exchange notes with Malaysia, extending Australia's association with the Anglo-Malayan defence agreement to cover all Malaysia. On 25 September he made a statement intended to be taken as a major commitment to Malaysia. It included the following:

> *I, therefore after close deliberation by the Cabinet and on its behalf inform the House that we are resolved and have so informed the Government of Malaysia and the Governments of the United Kingdom and New Zealand and others concerned [i.e. presumably Indonesia and the Philippines] that if, in the circumstances that now exist and which may continue for a long time, there occurs in relation to Malaysia or any of its constituent States, armed invasion or subversive activity – supported or directed or inspired from outside Malaysia – we shall to the best of our powers and by such means as shall be agreed upon with the Government of Malaysia, add our military assistance to the efforts of Malaysia and the United Kingdom in the defence of Malaysia's territory, integrity and political independence.*[2]

Menzies pointed out that Australian army, navy and air force units had been in Malaysia for some time and had been placed there for the defence not only of Malaya, but of Sarawak, Sabah and Singapore as well.

The British had found it necessary to deploy seven battalions to contain Indonesian incursions into Sarawak and Sabah. After September Indonesia began to send regular troops on more substantial operations. On 29 December 1963 a police post in Sabah 48 kilometres from the Indonesian border was attacked. Eight Malaysians and a civilian were killed. The Indonesians were now using larger numbers in raids which were also more professionally organised and executed.

On 17 August 1964 the Indonesians began to infiltrate the Malayan peninsula itself. They despatched a flotilla of small marine craft across the Straits of Malacca from Sumatra to land some 100 infiltrators at Pontian in the State of Johore.

This action was followed on 2 September by an even bolder move when Indonesian Hercules transport aircraft flew Indonesian paratroops to Labis, a former stronghold of the communists in Johore.

Two of the Indonesian aircraft dropped their paratroopers but the third apparently crashed before reaching the drop zone. The Malaysians responded to these hostile actions by declaring a state of emergency throughout Malaysia.

In addition to these incursions the Indonesian armed forces were engaged in a substantial build-up which might indicate a major offensive. War appeared perilously close when the British promptly assured the Malaysians that in the event of further aggression on the Malayan mainland or Singapore, Britain would join a counterattack on Indonesian territory.

3 RAR is Involved

On 29 October Australian troops of 3 RAR in the Far East Strategic Reserve were involved directly in confrontation when yet another party of Indonesian infiltrators landed from the sea at the mouth of the Kesang River near the 28th Brigade camp at Terendak. The Australian Government had earlier agreed that 3 RAR could be used against Indonesian incursions in Malaya if the need arose.

The Kesang River infiltrators were quickly discovered by coast watchers, and elements of 3 RAR and supporting artillery went into action together with a force of New Zealanders and Malayan troops. A tight cordon was drawn in an area of mangrove swamps and 30 hours later most of the Indonesians had surrendered. In this first clash between Indonesian and Australian troops there were no Australian casualties. The aim of the Indonesian group had been to set up a jungle base from which to organise a program of subversion and sabotage.

Thus Australia, whilst endeavouring to be conciliatory towards the Indonesians, was being drawn into the conflict.

The Australian Defence Committee had reason to believe that Australia might now face military operations in three widely separated areas: South Vietnam, Malaysia and Papua New Guinea, and emphasised that Australia did not have enough men to become seriously engaged in combat in all three areas at once. Ministers at this point called for a study of army manpower to include "the need for compulsory military service".

Further Australian Involvement

RAAF Butterworth would be a key base if war in the air developed over South-East Asia. The RAAF Sabre fighter squadrons had long been at operational readiness. When the Indonesian infiltrators began invading Malaya more RAAF pilots and ground staff were quickly flown up from Australia to reinforce the combat squadrons at Butterworth. The Sabre fighters were placed on continuous five-minute alert. All aircraft were armed with "sidewinder" missiles and fitted with drop tanks to increase range. On 7 September 1964 elements of No 3 Squadron were ordered south to Singapore to take up alert status, which remained in force until October when the tension eased.

Because RAAF Base Darwin might be involved as a base for British bombers, a RAAF Sabre squadron was despatched from Williamtown to provide fighter defence there. Darwin's anti-aircraft defences were upgraded.

During 1964 Australian naval operations in Malaysia sharply increased to counter the threat of seaborne infiltration into Malaya. Earlier *Yarra* (Commander B. H. Loxton), and *Parramatta* (Captain R. J. Scrivenor) were involved in operations to intercept intruding fast patrol boats and submarines. The coastal minesweepers *Hawke*, *Snipe*, *Gulf* and *Curlew* patrolled off the coast of Borneo, Malaya and Singapore. Later in 1964 *Ibis* and *Teal* joined in these operations. In December 1964 *Teal* (Lieutenant K. Murray) when operating in the Singapore Straits was fired on by a vessel which then headed for Indonesian waters. *Teal* returned the fire using three Bren and two Owen guns and arrested the vessel which was then delivered to the Singapore police.

Lieutenant Murray was awarded the Distinguished Service Cross for distinguished service in the Malacca and Singapore Straits up to 24 December 1964.

A fresh crisis had developed in September 1964 when the Royal Navy sent the aircraft carrier HMS *Victorious* with two destroyer escorts through Sunda Straits to Fremantle. The Indonesians claimed the straits were in their territorial waters. *Victorious* was scheduled to return through the straits on 16 September. Tension ran high when the Indonesians indicated they would take military action to oppose this passage. Britain, however, decided to send the warships through Indonesia's Lombok Strait. Although Indonesia similarly regarded this strait as being in their territorial waters, they themselves suggested this route to the British.

Following Prime Minister Menzies' robust support of Malaysia in his September 1963 speech, the United Kingdom had hoped this would be translated into further military support from Australia. However, intelligence reports indicated that in early 1964 the border area in Borneo was under control and Australia was reluctant to send troops. Australia wanted as far as possible to avoid any deterioration of relations with Indonesia so as to maintain influence in Jakarta. In any case Australian military capacity was already almost at full stretch.

The advice of the Defence Committee was that a decision to provide troops for operations in Borneo should not be taken until there was no further possibility of deterring the Indonesians by other means. Throughout the period of conflict diplomatic relations between Australia and Indonesia continued on reasonable terms and military officers of both countries attended each other's staff colleges.

However, in April 1964 Australia did agree to send engineers to Borneo. In June the 7th Field Squadron Royal Australian Engineers and their heavy equipment arrived at Jesselton in North Borneo in the RAN aircraft carrier HMAS *Sydney*. The engineers were to build helipads, light aircraft landing fields and a 130-kilometre all-weather road from Keningau to Sepulot. As already indicated, Sydney also brought RAAF helicopters for operations in the border area of Malaya-Thailand.

There was a widespread feeling among Australians at the end of 1964 that Australia's strategic situation was deteriorating. "Confrontation", which was disturbing the security of South-East Asia, had taken a turn for the worse. While President Sukarno's denunciations of "imperialism" and "neo-colonialism" were becoming more strident, some Australians viewed konfrontasi as just a new kind of imperialism in itself.

Indonesia had vast natural resources and a huge population. The Indonesian Army had clashed in combat with Australian soldiers in Malaya, and Indonesia was Australia's closest neighbour. The Indonesian Communist Party, the PKI, was the largest communist party in Asia except for China. Signs that Indonesia was moving closer towards China as an ally coincided with the strengthening of the PKI internally. China had exploded an atomic bomb.

On 22 October 1964, Senator Shane Paltridge, the Australian defence minister, issued a revised assessment of the strategic basis of Australian defence policy to ministers saying that Indonesia posed "the only direct threat to Australia and its territories". To most Australians at this time, Indonesia was of greater concern than Vietnam. They considered that it was very important that Indonesia should be stopped from its aim of "crushing" Malaysia.

Indonesia's attacks, said Prime Minister Menzies, might create a real risk of war, and it was tremendously important that Indonesia should not become communist.

The stage was set for Australia to sharply upgrade her defence capacity and in the House of Representatives on 10 November Menzies announced very substantial manpower and equipment increases for the Navy, Army and Air Force. Of even greater significance was the announcement made at the same time of the decision not only to re-introduce compulsory military service but to require those called up for this duty to serve overseas. An editorial in the *Sydney Morning Herald* next day claimed that Australia was preparing for war with Indonesia.

The Regular Army, Menzies said, would be increased as rapidly as possible from 22,750 to an effective strength of 33,000 men and a total of 37,500. The strength of the permanent naval force was to increase by more than 3,000 in three years – from 12,569 in 1964 to 15,893 in 1967. RAAF strength would grow from 16,628 to 20,393. Both the RAN and RAAF would be engaged in an extensive new equipment program over a three-year period.

Wewak airfield in northern New Guinea, which had become a

strategically important airfield since the Indonesians took over West Irian (Dutch New Guinea), was to be redeveloped as an operational air base. RAAF airfield construction engineers would also develop Tindal, south of Darwin, as an operational air base of the RAAF. Defence expenditure would almost double.

Military advice to the government was that only the conscription of young men would make it possible for the Army to maintain an effective and efficient force in the South-West Pacific.

Imposing conscription for overseas service could be political dynamite in Australia and it was not long before a heated debate began. Labor leader, Arthur Calwell, who had been involved in the debate over conscription during the First World War, denounced the government's decision as the "lottery of death". However, the decision did not damage the government electorally in the Senate election which followed on 5 December 1964.

Young men were required to register in the calendar year in which they reached 20 years of age. Those selected were liable for two years' full-time service and three more years on the army reserve. Those called up for duty had to go overseas with the regular army unit in which they were serving.

The Army Field Force was to undergo a major reorganisation. A new division would be provided. It would be an air-portable formation suited to the South-East Asian and New Guinea terrains, where surface communications were poor.

The new division would have:

      Three task force headquarters:

      Nine infantry battalions each of 800 all ranks;

      An aviation regiment with greater numbers of fixed and rotary wing aircraft;

      An armoured cavalry regiment equipped with air-portable armoured fighting and reconnaissance vehicles;

      Other supporting arms and services.

As the end of 1964 approached, Sukarno became more menacing, claiming he would crush Malaysia "before the cock crew" in 1965.

In December, the United Nations elected Malaysia to the Security

Council. This firm recognition of the new state angered Sukarno, who withdrew Indonesia from the United Nations organisation, turned more towards China and followed policies agreeable to the PKI.

In January 1965 Subandrio, the Indonesian foreign minister, visited China; Sukarno began talking of a Jakarta-Peking-Hanoi-Phnom Penh-Pyongyang axis linking the communist nations of Asia.

In December the Indonesians trebled their combat strength in Borneo by moving brigades of regular troops from Java to Borneo opposite Sabah and Sarawak. In January the British Prime Minister Harold Wilson sent a message to the Australian government saying that he had authorised British military forces to penetrate up to 10,000 yards into Indonesian territory and that Royal Navy surveillance could be conducted between three and 12 miles off the Indonesian coast.

At the end of 1964 Britain had 18 British and three Malaysian battalions deployed in Borneo. More were needed, and Wilson advised that reinforcements were being despatched to Malaysia, but that there would still be a need for another infantry battalion and some SAS troops.

The commitment of Australian troops against the Indonesians in Borneo moved a step closer on 21 January when Tun Razak, the Malaysian Defence Minister, met Senator Paltridge, his Australian counterpart in Kuala Lumpur, and discussed the Indonesian military build-up against Malaysia. Tun Razak said he hoped Australia would agree to the use in Borneo of 3 RAR from the Strategic Reserve, as well as SAS troops and helicopters. On 27 January the Australian Foreign Affairs and Defence (FAD) Committee accepted the advice of the Australian Chiefs of Staff that 3 RAR and a squadron of 100 SAS troops be sent to Borneo. But no more helicopters were to be committed to the Malaysian area. On 3 February the Government's decision was announced. Australia, hoping to the last that a peaceful solution might be found, had certainly not rushed the decision.

Australian troops would now serve in Borneo in rotation with British and Malaysian troops. RAAF aircraft allotted to major retaliatory action against Indonesian targets were increased. RAN warships operating off Indonesia could patrol between three to 12 miles from the Indonesian coast. The conflict situation between Australia and Indonesia had clearly escalated, yet incongruously the Government decided to maintain current air projects in Indonesia and the intake of Indonesian students studying in Australia.

Australia already had a substantial commitment to the defence of Malaysia. Now there was the decision to commit combat troops to Borneo, plus a plan to send another battalion to join with American troops in combat operations in South Vietnam, and publicly to endorse the US "Rolling Thunder" air bombardment of North Vietnam. Such was the Australian Government's concern for military security in South-East Asia in early 1965.[3]

1965 – Further Commitment

Peter Edwards, the Australian official historian of the Vietnam war, suggests a link between the Australian response to the situations in South Vietnam and Malaysia. He writes:

> *The effect of the sudden Indonesian military build-up in December 1964 should not be underestimated in assessing the course of Australian policy towards Vietnam in this crucial period. As McEwen (the Acting Prime Minister) put it the two conflicts now seemed to pose "a common pattern and common threat" to Australia. The Australians were even more concerned than the Americans that a major setback to the United States in Vietnam might make the increasingly erratic and unpredictable Sukarno "uncontrollable".*[4]

The US Under-Secretary of State, George Ball, in a memorandum to President Johnson[5] claimed that Australia's concern was far greater for the fate of Malaysia than for South Vietnam. Ball argued consistently for a negotiated settlement in Vietnam. He described Indonesia as "the real prize" sought by the communists in South-East Asia.

The Australian 1st Special Air Service Squadron of 100 men was the first Australian combat force to deploy to Borneo. Commanded by Major Alf Garland it arrived at Brunei on 6 February 1965 and was employed initially on "hearts and minds" operations. These were designed to gain the confidence of the villagers of Borneo by sharing their dangers and giving them a feeling of security by day and night.

In May the squadron began four-man patrols into Indonesian territory and suffered their first casualty on 9 May when a patrol was attacked by a rogue elephant which fatally gored one of its members.

Squadron patrols set up ambushes. One ambush accounted for seven Indonesians. By the time their tour ended in August 1965 the squadron had inflicted 17 fatal casualties for the loss of one Australian.

Moving by sea and air to Borneo from the Commonwealth Brigade camp at Terendak, Malacca, 3 RAR (commanded by Lieutenant Colonel Bruce McDonald) took over from the 1/7th Gurkhas in the Bau district near Kuching, capital of Sarawak. Shortly after the battalion arrived in the first half of March 1965, two battalion members (a sergeant and a local tracker) were killed in an anti-personnel mine explosion. Two more Australians were killed in similar circumstances six weeks later.

The Australian battalion was assigned responsibility for 20 kilometres of the border astride the main approach routes from Indonesian territory to Kuching. Few roads existed in Borneo and the battalion company bases had to be resupplied by helicopter. In their early operations the battalion patrols worked on the Sarawak side of the border.

To counter the Indonesian armed forces in this undeclared war, the British military commanders conducted "Claret" operations across the Indonesian border. They ambushed Indonesian forces and attacked their supply parties as they approached the Malaysian border. Every soldier taking part was sworn to absolute secrecy and to always deny having deliberately crossed the border.

On 27 May a fighting patrol from the battalion crossed the border and killed 15 enemy troops without loss to the patrol when it triggered an ambush along a river in the Bau district. The Indonesians were using the river as a supply route and Lieutenant Patrick Beale settled with 12 of his men along the line of the river. The ambush had not long been set when Private Lawrence Jackson saw a large party of Indonesian infiltrators approaching the ambush site in two boats. Jackson alerted the platoon commander and then saw a further two boats approaching but could not attract Beale's attention. He therefore attacked them alone, killing five in the third boat and throwing grenades in the direction of the fourth boat.

On 15 June another platoon commander, Second Lieutenant Douglas Byers, set up an ambush which killed 17 Indonesian troops. Some 25 Indonesians had entered the ambush zone at 1300 hours on that day when Byers triggered the ambush. Indonesian elements which followed quickly deployed and retaliated with machine gun and rifle fire. The Australians called in artillery fire in support. In a fight which lasted 10 minutes two soldiers in Byers' platoon were wounded, neither seriously, and were flown out by helicopter.

Lieutenants Beale and Byers were later awarded the Military Cross and Private Jackson the Military Medal. Corporal Trevor Byng was awarded a Mention-in-Despataches.

A total of 30 Claret operations were carried out by 3 RAR. Four of their fighting patrols resulted in successful actions. In September 1965 3 RAR returned to Australia and in a farewell message the British commander (Brigadier W. W. Cheyne) said, "I have been highly impressed by the battalion's professionalism and their keenness to get to grips with the enemy. You have had signal success in dominating the enemy and this is borne out by your most successful contact."

To meet Konfrontasi pressure at sea the Royal Navy supported by the RAN deployed substantial naval forces in the Malaysian area. In the important May-June 1965 period, the RAN had no fewer than 11 warships operating in South-East Asian waters. Australian destroyers, frigates and minesweepers maintained constant patrols in the Malacca, Singapore and Johore Straits and off Borneo. They also joined in "war game" exercises with the Malayan Navy.

Indonesian troops crossed into Sabah on 28 June 1965. They infiltrated eastern Sebatik Island near Tawau and HMAS *Yarra* was called on to bombard the infiltrators as they withdrew. *Yarra* fired a total of 70 rounds during three runs. On 5 and 10 July the border area off Sebatik was again bombarded by *Yarra* to deter the infiltrators.

In response to the high demands of the Cold War era in South-East Asia, the RAN was expanding at an unprecedented rate. Two guided missile destroyers, HMAS *Perth* and *Hobart* were commissioned in 1965–66 and a third, HMAS *Brisbane*, was scheduled to join the Navy in 1967. These American Charles F. Adams class destroyers were armed with a guided missile fire control system capable of firing Standard Missiles from a launcher located near the stern. The RAN had another 28 vessels, including escorts, patrol boats, submarines and an escort maintenance ship, under construction in shipyards in Australia, the United States and Britain.

By 1969 the RAN would have in service a well-balanced fleet comprising an aircraft carrier equipped with modern Tracker fixed-wing anti-submarine aircraft, Skyhawk jet fighters, ground attack and Wessex anti-submarine helicopters, six destroyer escorts, three guided missile destroyers, two destroyers, four Oberon class submarines, 20 patrol boats and ships for training, logistic support and troop transport.

In this period the RAN suffered its worst peacetime disaster when the destroyer HMAS *Voyager* was lost in a collision with the aircraft carrier *Melbourne*. The collision cost the lives of 82 sailors of the 293 persons on board *Voyager*. It took place on the night of 10 February 1964, 32 kilometres south-east of Jervis Bay. Five years later on 3 June 1969 *Melbourne* was in another collision with the American destroyer USS *Frank E. Evans* in which the destroyer lost 72 of her total crew of 272. The collision occurred during an exercise in the South China Sea about 1,040 kilometres south-west of Manila. The carrier suffered no casualties in either collision but was heavily damaged in her bow section in both accidents.

Confrontation continued to demand a high rate of operational effort by the RAAF, which had more fighting units deployed overseas in 1965–66 than at any time since the Second World War. Three squadrons were deployed in the defence of Malaysia and Singapore. Another fighter squadron was based at Ubon to defend Thailand while RAAF Caribou and Iroquois helicopter squadrons were operating in

South Vietnam. Hercules transports were flying transport missions to South-East Asia and flying wounded to Australia.

The RAAF was building up to where it would be flying new fighters (the Mirage), new strike aircraft (the swing-wing F111s), new transports (updated versions of the Hercules), new maritime reconnaissance aircraft (Orions), as well as new Macchi trainers both for flying and navigation training.

Already a detachment of the new Mirage jets had been deployed to Darwin where it joined a detachment of No 30 Squadron which had been equipped with Bloodhound ground-to-air missiles for the defence of Darwin.

The growth in activity and the magnitude of the procurement program severely strained RAAF resources and to help cope with the expansion, RAAF personnel strength was increased from 17,720 in June 1965 to 19,358 in June 1966.

In direct support of Malaysia, a detachment of RAAF Sabre aircraft from No 77 Squadron flew from their base at Butterworth to Labuan airfield in north Borneo in October 1965 where it took over fighter alert duties from an RAF fighter squadron. No 77 Squadron carried out combat patrols over Borneo. The squadron was on a familiar base. When the Second World War ended, No 77 had been at Labuan flying Kittyhawk aircraft as part of the RAAF 1st Tactical Air Force. When peace came it converted to Mustang fighters and flew from Labuan to Japan as part of the British Commonwealth Occupation Force.

Neither Indonesia nor the British Commonwealth forces in Malaysia initiated air operations against each other's territories (except for the Indonesian paratroop operation in Johore). RAAF Base Darwin would have been a key target had the Indonesians decided to launch an air attack with bombers. To prepare Darwin to defend itself, a force of British Victor bombers made daily sorties against the base to test its defences. In this period the world-class military airfield at Tindal near Katherine south of Darwin was rapidly taking shape.

To test the capacity of Australia's partners in the ANZUS Treaty to reinforce Australian air defences at short notice, combat aircraft from the United States and New Zealand Air Forces flew into Australia in

October 1965 to take part in an air exercise called "Pacific Concord 1". The exercise culminated in an impressive display of bombing and air power at Evans Head in northern New South Wales, which was attended by Indonesian and Malaysian military attachés assigned to Australia. It was one of the biggest tactical air exercises ever mounted in Australia. A squadron of the latest USAF fighter jets arrived in Australia after a non-stop flight from Guam, using air-to-air refuelling facilities of the United States Air Force.

The Indonesian Coup Attempt

The course of Indonesian history changed violently on 30 September 1965 when a failed coup attempt was followed by an immense massacre of 300,000 communists and leftists in Indonesia.

The coup attempt was triggered by a lieutenant colonel of the Palace Guard. It was a plot hatched by a clique of communists and army and air force conspirators who seized six senior army generals and proclaimed a new revolutionary regime in Indonesia. The generals were tortured, mutilated and then slain.

The coup's objectives were thwarted by Major General Suharto, head of the Indonesian army's strategic command and a leading anti-communist, who led other elements of the armed services in a purge of communists. In less than six months President Sukarno had been sidelined and Suharto had virtual control of the Indonesian Government. The Communist Party (PKI) was eliminated, Sukarno eclipsed and Chinese-Indonesian relations severed. Although confrontation against Malaysia continued in Borneo, the Indonesian operations appeared to lose much of their sting.

Only 24 Construction Squadron of the Australian Army remained in Borneo after the withdrawal of 3 RAR in August 1965. By November the all-weather road the squadron was building in Sabah had entered steep mountain country and had reached the 86-kilometre peg.

Although operations had cooled down after the coup, 2 Squadron SAS was committed to operations in Borneo in February 1966. Their patrols ranged across the Indonesian border some 96 kilometres south of Kuching, but the troops were ordered to avoid contact. However, one patrol had a surprise encounter with an Indonesian party. The Australians killed five of these Indonesians without suffering any casualties themselves.

In 1963 the decision had been taken to create a fourth battalion of the Royal Australian Regiment. Original members of 4 RAR were selected from members of the three existing battalions. After inauguration at Woodside, South Australia, the battalion trained for 18 months and in October 1965 joined the British Commonwealth Brigade in Malaya. Training was then stepped up to prepare for operations in Borneo. The unit, commanded by Lieutenant Colonel David Thomson, moved into the Bau district of Sarawak. Its headquarters were located at Cambrai camp and the rifle companies occupied bases on the border at Gumbang, Stass and Bokah.

The battalion had a comparatively quiet time during its five months of operations in Sarawak, except for two significant contacts in which two members of the battalion were wounded. The unit was given maximum cooperation by the local Dyaks and its "hearts and minds" program was highly successful. The Battalion returned to Malaysia in August 1966.

On 11 August the increasingly powerless President Sukarno, much against his will, had agreed to "normalise relations" with Malaysia. After the peace agreement had been negotiated, Sukarno refused to formally farewell his Malaysian guest, the Malaysian Vice President, Tun Abdul Razak, from the doors of his palace.

A peak strength of 17,000 Commonwealth servicemen had been involved in the Borneo operations. Total casualties were 114 killed and 181 wounded. Australian losses in Malaysia in 1964–66 totalled 16 dead, of whom only four died as a result of enemy action.

Thus ended Australia's military collision with Indonesia.

The Commander-in-Chief, Far East, Air Chief Marshal John Grandy, paid tribute to the work of the Commonwealth forces under his command in the following terms:

> *Over the past three years, British, Australian and New Zealand*
> *forces of the Far East Command, have successfully taken part in*
> *an historically significant and unique military campaign aimed*
> *to bring about the peace and stability which we all now hope to*
> *see emerge in the area … Your contribution has been*
> *outstanding for its fortitude, firmness and restraint.*

The Indonesian coup of September 1965 and the ending of hostilities in the Malaysian area the following year were undoubtedly events of the greatest significance in the Cold War in South-East Asia. Alan Renouf, a former senior Australian diplomat, made the following observations on Australian policy during the crisis:

> *Australia's policy of patience, restraint and responsibility in the*
> *face of Indonesia's most serious foreign adventure was thus*
> *justified. It is a notable tribute to this policy that her friendly*
> *relations with Indonesia survived. From this phase of her*
> *Indonesian policy, Australia emerged very creditably. She had*
> *not wavered from supporting Malaysia and Singapore to the*
> *hilt, as obliged, yet at the same time had not impaired her*
> *Indonesian ties.*[5]

10

THE VIETNAM WAR

Communist Pressure in Vietnam

The communists of Asia achieved their greatest victory of the 20th century when the armies of communist China defeated the Chinese nationalist armies in the long, drawn-out Chinese civil war, and took control in 1949 of the most populous nation on earth.

A year later communism, encouraged by communist China and Soviet Russia, was on the march again in Asia as the communist North Koreans invaded South Korea. This conflict ended three years later (July 1953) without one side gaining the upper hand, even though communist China had intervened on a massive scale to support the North Koreans.

Another year later (May 1954) the cause of communism in Asia triumphed again when the communist-controlled Viet Minh inflicted a catastrophic defeat on the French at Dien Bien Phu in North Vietnam.

The fall of Dien Bien Phu convinced the French that they must bring the conflict in Indochina to an end and withdraw their military forces entirely from Vietnam.

The French had attempted to set up a strategic bastion at Dien Bien Phu in the jungle-clad interior of the north. But the Viet Minh, heavily supplied by communist China and Soviet Russia, manhandled artillery pieces through the wild northern highlands and used them to batter the airfields that served Dien Bien Phu.

With the wrecked airfields, French supplies and communications were cut off, and the defenders were in a desperate plight when 50,000 communist Viet Minh closed in for the kill. On 7 May 1954 after a 55-day siege the French remnants were overrun and forced to surrender. Only 3,000 of the French garrison of 16,000 survived the siege and subsequent brutal treatment as prisoners. It was a stunning blow to French pride.

As the grip of the Viet Minh tightened on the beleaguered French troops, world attention focussed on the grim battle where a leading nation faced surrender to revolutionaries of one of its former colonies.

On 29 March, John Foster Dulles, the US Secretary of State, called strongly for "united action" to stave off a French collapse in Vietnam. Speaking at his home on 4 April, Dulles said he saw the need for an alliance of the United States, the United Kingdom, France, Australia, New Zealand, Laos, Cambodia, Thailand and the Philippines, which should hold themselves ready to provide military assistance in Vietnam. Referring to a possible Australian contribution to that alliance, Admiral Arthur Radford, Chairman of the American Joint Chiefs of Staff, said that naval and air action was primarily, if not wholly, what he had in mind. He commended the thought that Australia should contribute an aircraft-carrier as they had in the Korean War.

Britain, however, believed air and naval intervention would not retrieve the military situation and might lead to another Korean-style war. Australia contended that intervention could not prevent the loss of Dien Bien Phu and would probably embroil the anti-communist nations of South-East Asia with communist China. It would also wreck the Geneva conference which was addressing the issue of a settlement between the French and the Viet Minh.

In the end there was no outside military intervention. "It is necessary to note," wrote Alan Renouf, "how close in 1954 the US came to armed intervention in Indochina. The US did not intervene because of Eisenhower's caution, the good sense of Ridgeway and the opposition of Britain, coupled later with that of Australia. But it was a close shave."[1]

At Dien Bien Phu the communists had won a major victory and the Geneva Accords signed on 21 July 1954 reflected that victory. France was to be stripped of her South-East Asian colonies.

Under the Geneva settlement, Vietnam was partitioned at the 17th parallel with an 8-kilometre-wide (approximately) demilitarised zone (DMZ) on either side of the parallel. To the north was the territory known as North Vietnam, governed by the communist Democratic Republic of Vietnam (DRV), while the territory below the parallel, known as South Vietnam, was governed by the Emperor Bao Dai, who in June 1954 had appointed Ngo Dinh Diem as Prime Minister. Diem was an experienced administrator who was anti-French and conducted an authoritarian regime. In October 1955 Bao Dai was deposed in a referendum and Dinh Diem became President of the Republic of Vietnam.

The ruthless communist leader Ho Chi Minh had complete control in North Vietnam and found the break in hostilities agreed to at Geneva to be to his advantage, because he needed time to convert a revolutionary movement into a stable government administration.

To Australians the Geneva decisions meant that communism had been brought much closer to their country. Australian acceptance of the Geneva Accords fell far short of endorsement. On the other hand many conceded that Ho Chi Minh's military victory could have meant that the whole of French Indochina became communist. This had been averted.

The United States did not sign the Geneva Accords, many Americans regarding the settlement as a compromise with the devil. To many observers the Accords appeared to be a means by which the battered French could withdraw with some grace after their traumatic experience in resisting the communists.

The defeat of France left South-East Asia vulnerable to the march of communism. The former French dependencies of Cambodia, Laos and a fragile South Vietnam were not expected to survive the surging communist challenge in Asia.

To provide a barrier against expected further encroachments by communist forces in South-East Asia, the United States brought together representatives of eight nations in Manila. Negotiations proceeded with remarkable speed and on 8 September, only 29 days after the decisions in Geneva, the eight nations signed a defensive treaty. The signatories were the United States, United Kingdom, France, New Zealand, Australia, Thailand, the Philippines and Pakistan.

The key provision of the treaty was that the parties agreed that military aggression against any signatory to the agreement would endanger its own peace and safety. They further agreed to act to meet the common danger (in accordance with each country's constitutional processes). South Vietnam was designated a "protocol" state guaranteed by the pact, as were Laos and Cambodia, but the latter two states later withdrew.

An organisation known as the South-East Asia Treaty Organisation (SEATO) was set up with a headquarters in Bangkok to provide administration. A combined military force similar to NATO in Europe was not to be created, but joint military exercises to which member states contributed were conducted from time to time.

In the years 1959–61 the Communist Pathet Lao faction in Laos exerted strong pressure on the Government.

At a press conference Prime Minister Menzies revealed that the position was "very dangerous". Cabinet took the view that Australia must follow the lead of the United States on the question of intervention. Military action, Menzies warned, might lead to war with China. Not to take action, on the other hand, might be the end of SEATO and result in South-East Asia falling to communism. The conflict in Laos came close to war and in the crisis the Australian Cabinet decided that "in the last resort, the overall demands of Australian security required that it provide military support for an intervention by SEATO, by the United States, and some SEATO allies, or even by the United States alone." It was a major turning point in Australian policy.[2]

Meanwhile communist pressure in South Vietnam had been growing rapidly. In late 1959 Ho Chi Minh decided to switch from the "political struggle" to the "armed struggle". He announced the formation of the National Liberation Front, which was later known as the Viet Cong

(Vietnamese communists). The Viet Cong, reinforced by 2,000 North Vietnamese troops, mounted a campaign of murder, subversion, espionage and terror. Assassinations of South Vietnamese government officials had increased from 200 in 1958 to 4000 in 1961. So bad was the situation in 1961 that the Viet Cong was able to capture Phuoc Vinh, a provincial capital only 85 kilometres north of Saigon, where they publicly "tried" and decapitated the provincial chief.

In 1959 communist armed troops in South Vietnam totalled about 2000. By 1961 communist strength had reached 17,000 and by 1964, 34,000. Together with village militia and regional forces, the communist strength totalled 106,000. In 1964 a captured Viet Cong document indicated that the Viet Cong province chief in Tay Ninh province claimed that 46 of the 48 villages in his province had been "satisfactorily organised from both a political and military standpoint". The situation there was indeed precarious.

American leaders believed that the loss of Indochina would lead to the loss of all South-East Asia to communism. In the face of relentless communist pressure, which was causing a rapid worsening of security in South Vietnam, American military assistance was sharply increased. By late 1962 American military advisers in Vietnam had grown to 11,000 and by 1963 to 16,000.

In February 1962 Lieutenant General Paul Harkins was appointed to command the Military Assistance Command, Vietnam (MACV), with headquarters in Saigon. American military aid escalated further when two American helicopter companies equipped with 32 helicopters, with pilots and maintenance staff, arrived in December 1962.

At this point the question of Australian aid to the anti-communist forces in South Vietnam came into the picture. American officials had approached Australia through the Australian Ambassador to Washington, Sir Howard Beale, asking if assistance to South Vietnam might be forthcoming in the form of equipment and Australian military advisers. The United States' view was that it was important that aid to South Vietnam should come from more than one country in the "free world" and that Australians knew more about jungle fighting than the Americans. This was followed on 31 March 1962 by a letter from

President Diem to Sir Robert Menzies (and to the heads of government of 92 other non-communist states) drawing attention to the "grave threat to peace in South Vietnam" and in addition appealing to "free world" countries to help prevent it being overwhelmed by massive subversion from communist North Vietnam backed by heavily increased support from the communist bloc.

After the South Vietnamese Government made a direct request to Australia for military aid, the Australian Government on 24 May 1962 announced that it would send 30 army instructors who were expert in counter-insurgency and jungle warfare. Referring to this decision, Athol Townley, the Defence Minister, said, "If the communists were to achieve their aims in Vietnam, this would gravely affect the security of the whole of South-East Asia and ultimately of Australia itself."

So that the Australian team of instructors operating in Vietnam would be clearly recognisable as Australians, their army uniforms were to be worn with "Australia" flashes, and an Australia flag was to fly over their headquarters in Saigon. The manifest presence of the Australians would indicate to the world that the Americans were not acting alone in their defence of the South Vietnamese against the Viet Cong.

On the equipment side, Australia provided South Vietnam with very large quantities of barbed wire, corrugated iron and generators to power perimeter lighting for use in the provision of "strategic hamlets" as a defence against Viet Cong subversion. It was an idea which had its origins in the earlier Malayan campaign against communist terrorists.

On 23 May, the day before the announcement of the commitment of 30 Australian Military advisers to South Vietnam, the Australian Government made an announcement that yet another Australian military contingent would be committed to a military role against communist forces in South-East Asia. No 79 Squadron of the RAAF, equipped with Sabre jet fighters, was to fly into Ubon, Thailand, near the border with Laos, for the defence of Thailand. This action was taken when Thailand, a member of the SEATO group of nations, became concerned about North Vietnamese troop movements near her borders.

Four of the eight SEATO nations – the United States, United Kingdom, Australia and New Zealand – responded to Thailand's call by quickly sending armed units to Thailand as a "holding force" which would take the first strain of military aggression and hold on until reinforcements arrived. Ships of the US 7th Fleet were sent to the Gulf of Thailand, but Pakistan and the Philippines, both SEATO members, took no action.

As required by the Australian Government, a request was received from Thailand to send a military force. Sabre aircraft to form No 79 Squadron were withdrawn from the two Sabre squadrons (Nos 3 and 77) then at Butterworth, Malaya, and committed to Thailand. RAAF Hercules transport aircraft flew tents, ground equipment and squadron supplies from Australia to Thailand. A camp was set up and on 1 June the squadron pilots flew their aircraft to the Ubon air base where they were quickly integrated into Thailand's air defence system. The first commander of the squadron was Wing Commander (later Air Commodore) John Hubble, veteran fighter pilot of the Second World War and the Korean war. No 79 Squadron remained at Ubon until withdrawn to Australia in 1968.

The decision to send 30 Australian advisers to Vietnam led to the formation of the Australian Army Training Team Vietnam (AATTV).

When on 3 August, at the invitation of the South Vietnam government, the training team arrived at Tan Son Nhut airport, Saigon, it became the first deployment of an Australian force in the Indochina war.

The "Team", as the AATTV became known, was a hand-picked group of career soldiers, many of whom had served in the Malayan Emergency operations. Some had served in Korea and most were infantry. The Team was a thoroughly professional army unit and was to take part in the fighting in South Vietnam for more than ten years. A large number would be decorated for their services in Vietnam, four with the highest decoration for gallantry, the Victoria Cross. Two of these VCs were awarded posthumously.

Colonel F. P. Serong, a dedicated Australian soldier, was appointed to command the AATTV. Serong was a veteran of the fighting in New Guinea during the Second World War and later commanded the Australian Jungle Warfare Training Centre at Canungra. When appointed he had just returned to Australia after two years' experience in the communist insurgency scene in Burma. General Harkins, recognising his outstanding record, asked for his appointment as a special adviser on counter-insurgency to his own staff.

Members of the Australian training team were dispersed widely throughout Vietnam from the demilitarised zone in the extreme north to the Mekong delta in the deep south, and from the Laotian and Cambodian borders to the South China Sea.

Australian jungle fighting techniques were introduced and attention was paid to details such as marksmanship, the care and maintenance of weapons and security practices when on the march or at the halt. Some Vietnamese soldiers were lacking in military skills but they were lighthearted in the face of grim news that arrived almost daily of battalions and companies being annihilated in ambushes sprung by the Viet Cong.

The Australians operated among a multiplicity of ground forces, including all the battalions of two ARVN (Army of the Republic of Vietnam) divisions as well as Ranger units and the special regiment in I Corps Tactical Zone.

In March 1963 Serong reported on the Team's achievements. He wrote, "AATTV remains in good shape and is now seeing results from its months of work. Apart from individuals trained (to the number of 20,000 in installations where we have representation) there is now in usage throughout the country a solid volume of AATTV techniques."[3]

Some members of the Team served in isolated areas such as Khe San, A Shau, A Ro and Kham Duc close to the Laos border. Captain Noel Delahunty led a Special Forces patrol of 40 soldiers tasked with setting up a camp at A Ro. Viet Cong pressure forced Delahunty's force out of the camp they established but it was recaptured when an assault force arrived in American helicopters and recovered the campsite. A Hercules transport aircraft was then used to drop a bulldozer needed for the building of an airstrip. The bulldozer fell 800 metres short of the strip site but Warrant Officer Reg Collinson, an engineer member of the Team, made his way to the bulldozer, seated himself on it and with bullets zipping about him drove it out of the jungle to the campsite. A message was then despatched which read "cutting dirt". In seven days Collinson levelled about 260 metres of runway. Unfortunately for the RAAF one of its new Caribou air transports which supplied the Special Forces camp crashed on the runway when landing and could not be salvaged.

An ARVN force suffered a severe setback at Ap Bac, Plain of Reeds, in January 1963. An American helicopter force supported the operation and lost five helicopters destroyed and another 11 damaged.

President Diem's heavy-handed repression of the Buddhists inspired disturbances in Hue where Buddhists were refused permission to display flags marking the birth of Buddha. This action sparked rioting throughout the country. A number of Buddhist "bonzes" (priests) committed suicide by drenching themselves with petrol and setting themselves alight. A photograph of a burning monk in central Saigon shocked the world. Diem's wife, Madame Nhu, further outraged world opinion by referring to the incident as a "barbecue".

On 2 November President Diem and his brother Nhu were assassinated. Political instability worsened and was accompanied by a deteriorating military situation. All over South Vietnam, Viet Cong military pressure increased. Coup after coup in addition to rebellious Buddhists and Montagnard dissidents and strikes were tearing Vietnam apart.

In 1964 the deeply troubled South Vietnamese people seemed to be on the brink of disaster. To help with the task of shoring up the defences of the South Vietnamese state, the United States began a campaign of persuasion to induce "free world" nations to have a greater direct involvement in Vietnam instead of leaving it to the United States to bear most of the burden.

At a SEATO Council meeting in Manila in April 1964 the final communiqué supported this aim by calling on members of SEATO to be prepared to fulfil their obligations under the Treaty. Those members already assisting were asked to increase their support. This communiqué did not lead to the support of all SEATO members and after the meeting the United States began looking for support from Allies outside SEATO and pointed to the need for "more flags" to be seen in South Vietnam.

In response to the SEATO call the Australian Government quickly made additional commitments to Vietnam which the White House described as "very impressive". On 29 May the Australian Cabinet agreed that the AATTV would be more than doubled in size from 30 to 83. Significantly too, Team members would now be allowed to accompany ARVN units into the field of battle and in consequence Australian casualties must be expected. Hitherto Team members had been frustrated by the ban on staying with the ARVN troops they trained when those troops were committed to combat. They welcomed the change in spite of the obviously increased risk. They would now lead Vietnamese or Montagnards in combat and when required call in artillery and air power for their support.

As well as the reinforcement of the Team, a RAAF transport flight of the newly acquired Caribou transports would be provided to assist with airlift support for the Vietnamese armed forces in the field.

As a result of the widening of the role of the AATTV the first death in action of a member of the Team was not long delayed. Warrant officer Kevin Conway, an adviser attached to a small Special Forces unit at Nam Dong, was killed in action on 6 July 1964. The Viet Cong attackers fired a barrage of mortar shells into his unit's outpost and then stormed the outer wire. Conway jumped into a mortar pit to assist the mortar operation and was killed. He was the first Australian to die in combat in the Vietnam war. The post suffered heavy losses but next morning some 55 Viet Cong dead were found, some hanging on the barbed wire.

Some Australian advisers were assigned to an organisation known as the "Combined Studies Division", a paramilitary force whose activities were directed by the American Central Intelligence Agency.

Captain Barry Petersen, a veteran of the Malayan anti-terrorist campaign, was given the task of supervising paramilitary action groups of Montagnards in the central highlands. Based on Ban Me Thout, Petersen established a special relationship with the Rhade and M'nong tribes, learning their language and eventually gaining their trust to such an extent that they bestowed upon him the honour of a tribal chieftainship.

Petersen had absolute control of the raising, training and leading of

1,000 Montagnards who wrought havoc among the Viet Cong, inflicting heavy casualties, disrupting infiltration, raiding, ambushing, patrolling and destroying their food crops.

However, Petersen's task was made difficult because the Montagnard people resented and distrusted the South Vietnamese, from whom they wanted independence. In September 1944 in a sudden flare-up, the Montagnards slaughtered a number of South Vietnamese soldiers. Petersen by skilful diplomacy was able to achieve a peaceful solution. But he now faced Vietnamese suspicion and had to leave the country.

In November 1965, Warrant Officer K. A. ("Dasher") Wheatley won the first of four Victoria Crosses awarded to members of the Team in Vietnam.

Wheatley was serving with a Civil Irregular Defence Group of Vietnamese and Montagnards engaged in an operation at Tra Bong in Quang Ngai province when it encountered a superior force of Viet Cong. Another member of the team, Warrant Officer R. J. Swanton, was badly wounded, and Wheatley attempted to carry him to safety. Having used up all his ammunition Wheatley refused to leave Swanton. He pulled pins from two hand grenades and waited for the Viet Cong to close in. The bodies of both soldiers, with gunshot wounds, were found next morning. Wheatley's VC was awarded posthumously, the first such award to an Australian since the Second World War.

Because of the primitive surface communications in the rugged jungle-clad mountains of Vietnam, airlift was a lifeline for the survival of armed forces engaged against the Viet Cong. In the early stages of the war, combat units operating any distance from coastal base were almost wholly dependent upon aerial resupply.

Thus the announcement on 8 June 1964 that the RAAF would deploy an air transport flight of Caribou aircraft to Vietnam was greatly appreciated, as a small but very useful contribution to air transport resources in Vietnam.

The Caribou was just then entering RAAF service. Manufactured by the de Havilland Company in Canada, it had an excellent payload of 6710 pounds or 31 passengers and could operate from relatively crude "dirt strips". It had a particularly good short take-off and landing performance, and its rear opening ramp-type doors allowed rapid loading and unloading.

The RAAF Caribou flight was formed on 20 July 1964 and placed under the command of an able and experienced officer, Squadron Leader Christopher Sugden, who in the Second World War had piloted Boston bombers in action in New Guinea, and Meteor 8 jets in the Korean War.

On 8 August the first Caribou of the RAAF Flight arrived at Vung Tau, a port on the south coast of Vietnam, and was assigned to the air lift system operated by the United States Air Force. Within a few months the RAAF Caribou transports with their red kangaroo insignia became a familiar sight throughout Vietnam. The flight's transport missions took it into Da Nang, Hue, A Ro, Kham Due and Khe San in the north to Nah Trang, Quang Ngai, Kontum, Dalat and Ban me Thout down to numerous airfields in the Mekong delta and to Tan Son Nhut, the major airport at Saigon.

The Caribou transport missions drew considerable ground fire from the Viet Cong when operating out of Da Nang in the northern provinces, and fighter escorts were needed because of poor security. One fighter would fly ahead and one behind the Caribou on the run into the drop zone. One Caribou took five hits from ground fire during a single mission but no passengers or crew were hit.

The Caribou were used for flare dropping operations near Tan Son Nhut where the Viet Cong were active, and frequently drew automatic fire for up to five minutes. They also carried South Vietnamese paratroopers on training jumps, but for the most part their task was air lift. Sometimes the load was cows, crated in wooden boxes and thus despatched to the ground. Sometimes the cattle broke loose in the aircraft, causing chaos.

The loadmaster did not have to be a cowboy, but certainly a knowledge of cattle handling would have been a useful skill.

"The Only Way" – Ground Troops

By December of 1964 not only was South Vietnam almost on the point of collapse, but at the same time Indonesia's confrontation with Malaysia was reaching crisis point. President Sukarno pointedly withdrew Indonesia from the United Nations organisation, spoke scathingly of "imperialism" and drew attention to his friendly links with Asia's communist nations. Indonesian troops were poured into Sumatra and Borneo.

The situation appeared grave. Some strategic analysts saw the dual threat of Indonesia and Vietnam as the two arms of a giant communist pincer movement poised to take hold of all South-East Asia.

In his book *The Vantage Point*, US President Johnson later wrote:

> *What we saw rapidly taking shape was a Djakarta-Hanoi-Peking-Pyongyang axis ... the members of this new axis were undoubtedly counting on South Vietnam's collapse and an ignominious American withdrawal. Under such circumstances, Britain, already facing financial trouble, would undoubtedly have been less eager to support Malaysia and Singapore. The entire region would then have been ripe for the plucking.*[4]

Many observers saw the Vietnam-Malaysian situations as inextricably linked. Mr McEwen, the Australian Deputy Prime Minister, in speaking of Australia's obligations in the region said that Vietnam and Malaysia were "coming to form part of a common pattern and a common threat".

Australia was being urged to provide support in both conflicts and when Malaysia asked Australia to commit combat troops, Australia agreed on 3 February 1965 to sent 3 RAR and a Special Air Service unit to Borneo to combat Indonesian infiltration. Thus, in response to strong requests, Australia was committed to war against Indonesia and at the same time was actively contemplating the commitment of an Army battalion to Vietnam.

Australia did not want Saigon to fall to the communists. A majority of American officials were advocating that a "progressive squeeze" should be applied on Hanoi and were actively considering measures for the defeat of the Viet Cong, now being rapidly reinforced from North Vietnam.

Australia's highest military advisers, the Chiefs of Staff Committee, concluded that "the only way" (to halt the downhill slide to defeat) appeared to be the United States proposal for the introduction of ground forces to South Vietnam:

> We are of the view that further bolstering of military aid to the present type will not remedy the situation in South Vietnam. Something different must be done. The proposal by the United States to introduce sizeable ground forces is such a new approach and an important one revealing a major change of policy. We feel that this is the only way of achieving a solution to the South Vietnam problem. If the military discussions with the United States reveal that a plan to isolate South Vietnam by a combined air/ground force would prove feasible it is our view that Australia should offer to contribute ground forces to the plan. Indeed the Americans would expect us, as their closest Allies in the area, to make such an offer ... The introduction of United States and allied ground forces into South Vietnam would have a profound effect throughout South-East Asia and may succeed in establishing a barrier to communism ...[5]

During December 1964 both President Johnson and the Prime Minister of South Vietnam (Tran Van Huong) asked Australia directly for further military contributions to South Vietnam. The request by Van Huong was made to the Australian Minister for Air (Peter Howson) who was in Saigon at the end of 1964. Huong made a strong direct appeal for increased Australian assistance "in every form, but particularly military".

President Johnson sent a message to Menzies on 14 December suggesting that Australia provide an additional 200 military advisers as well as minesweepers, LSTs (Landing Ship Tanks) and other vessels. Menzies responded on 17 December telling the President that Australia was anxious to do "everything in our power to be helpful" but could not release any significant number of military instructors because of the introduction of conscription. All minesweepers were committed. Referring to the question of the possible introduction of ground troops to South Vietnam he offered to send military representatives to suggested staff talks.

However, further political turmoil in Saigon including clashes between Vietnamese government and American officials delayed progress on military measures.

To underline the perils of the worsening situation the Viet Cong inflicted a savage mauling on the Roman Catholic village of Binh Gia in Phuoc Tuy province. Two regiments of Viet Cong overran the village on 28 December. The Government then sent several battalions of reinforcements in US Helicopters who were ambushed by the Viet Cong and virtually destroyed. The Viet Cong then began attacking American targets. A 300 lb bomb was detonated under the Bachelor Officers' Quarters at the Brinks in Saigon, killing two Americans and wounding 100 others. The American advisers' quarters at Pleiku were attacked on 7 February and three days later another American compound at Quin Nhon was destroyed, killing 23 Americans.

The Americans responded to this provocation by sending 45 carrier aircraft to attack North Vietnamese army barracks and port facilities at Dong Hoi (just north of the demilitarised zone).

Two weeks later, at the risk of inciting Chinese reaction, American airmen together with the South Vietnamese air force unleashed a sustained air assault on North Vietnam nicknamed "Rolling Thunder". Its objective was to cause the Government of North Vietnam "to cease its support and direction of the insurgencies in South Vietnam and Laos". The Australian Government publicly supported the American air assault.

To protect the air base at Da Nang used by American squadrons, 3500 Marines came ashore at Da Nang a few days later.

The US Secretary of Defence (McNamara) had earlier suggested that it could be helpful if Australian aircraft were to take part or stand by to protect Thailand, Laos or South Vietnam. No 79 Squadron had for some years been based in Thailand at Ubon air base close to the Laotian border where it was part of the air defence of Thailand. It would remain there until withdrawn to Australia in 1968.

American decisions on the commitment of ground forces to South Vietnam were delayed because of the political instability in Saigon but on 17 February 1965 President Johnson had declared that the United States "would persist in the defence of freedom". Shortly afterwards Australia was informed that the proposed staff talks on the commitment of Australian troops to Vietnam were to proceed as a matter of urgency and would be held in Honolulu.

Air Marshal Sir Frederick Scherger led the Australian delegation to the Honolulu staff talks. The United States military had not at this stage decided what to ask from Australia, but Scherger indicated that Australia would contribute forces to Vietnam and further, that he would recommend to his government that Australia would send a battalion and that the Australian Cabinet would agree.

As the Honolulu staff talks (30 March to 1 April) were ending, a United States National Security Council meeting in Washington was beginning. The meeting approved the introduction of two additional Marine battalions with authority to conduct counter-insurgency patrols beyond their South Vietnamese bases. Johnson had taken the fateful step of committing American ground forces to a combat role – a step which was not made public at the time. Johnson also approved "the urgent exploration" with the Korean, Australian and New Zealand Governments of the possibility of significant combat elements from their armed forces in parallel with additional Marine deployments in Vietnam.[6]

The Australian Cabinet met on 7 April and agreed to the provision of a battalion. Subsequently the Americans decided that the Australian battalion would be brigaded with the US 173rd Airborne Brigade (Separate) which would establish an enclave in the Bien Hoa-Vung Tau area.

The Australian decision was announced simultaneously by the governments of Australia and South Vietnam. Both announcements stated that the battalion was being provided "at the request of South

Vietnam". The South Vietnamese government's announcement was made in an official communiqué on 29 April and on the same day Sir Robert Menzies announced the commitment which he said had been decided in principle "weeks and weeks" before.

In his statement to Parliament, Menzies declared that the takeover of South Vietnam "would be a direct military threat to Australia and would be seen as part of a thrust by Communist China between the Indian and Pacific Oceans". The reference to the Chinese "thrust" was seen by many as an exaggeration and became something of an embarrassment to the Government.

President Johnson warmly welcomed Australia's commitment. "This action," he said, "proves again the deep ties between our countries in the cause of world peace and security." Harold Holt, who followed Menzies as Prime Minister, was to echo a similar sentiment when he said Australia would go "all the way with LBJ.". The American alliance was indeed important. For the first time in its history Australia was to fight a war in which Britain was not also taking part. Britain at the time was at full stretch in the conflict against Indonesia which was at peak intensity and in a real sense a major part of the problem of South-East Asia.

Australia chose the Regular Army's highly trained 1st Battalion RAR for the war. Vietnam was in a state of military crisis with the Viet Cong pushing hard to achieve victory before an American build-up could alter the balance. No time was lost before the battalion was rushed by air and sea to help defend the key Bien Hoa air base and hold back the Viet Cong threatening Saigon, the capital. "It was a frantic time preparing at such short notice," Corporal Lex McAulay recalled. "We even got those wraparound First World War leggings – you know puttees! Puttees for jungle warfare!"

Nevertheless, no better trained nor better equipped professional military force had ever left Australia. Its commander was Lieutenant Colonel I. R. W. (Lew) Brumfield, who had served in 3 RAR in the Korean War.

The battalion, together with a cavalry troop, signal troop and the 1st Australian Logistic Support Company, began moving to Vietnam within

25 days of the government decision. The advance party travelled by chartered civil airliners and RAAF Hercules transport, while the main body together with heavy equipment, supplies and vehicles sailed to Vung Tau in the former aircraft carrier HMAS *Sydney* which was now a fast troop transport. *Sydney*, escorted by the destroyer HMAS *Duchess*, left Port Jackson without fanfare in the dead of night at 1 am, 27 May 1965.

The battalion settled in at Bien Hoa in rather spartan conditions compared to the lavish circumstances of the "sky soldiers" of the 173rd Airborne. The battalion's first task in Vietnam was to protect the Bien Hoa air base, which had been mortared by the Viet Cong some months earlier with extensive loss and damage to American bombing aircraft and installations.

Initially, at the request of the Australian Government the battalion had been limited to "local security operations" within 35 kilometres of the airfield, but this restriction was soon lifted and in August the battalion was cleared to operate in provinces contiguous to Bien Hoa.

On 26 June on returning from an operation 1 RAR lost its first soldiers. Their mission had been to secure a base area for an incoming American brigade and on arrival back at Bien Hoa a hand grenade exploded accidentally as a soldier jumped down from a truck. Three Australians and one American soldier were killed and another 11 Australians were injured.

On 28 June the battalion joined in a major airborne sweep with American and Vietnamese troops into War Zone D north of Bien Hoa. More than 10,000 troops were taking part. The task of the Australians was to secure a fire support base that would extend the range of artillery support.

Some of the Australians found themselves in a waist-deep morass when they hit the ground from the helicopters. But they secured the fire support base. The Viet Cong had melted away, allowing their stronghold to be penetrated with ease. However, they returned as soon as their opponents left the area.

A rapid American build-up of military strength was under way in Vietnam in 1965. By May US strength was 82,000. By June it was 125,000 and at the end of the year 200,000.

General Westmoreland wanted to see more Australians in his command. He recognised them as thorough professionals: "Small in numbers and well trained, particularly in anti-guerilla warfare, the Australian Army was much like the post-Versailles German Army in which even men in the ranks might have been leaders in a less capable force."[7]

In July President Johnson asked for an increased Australian contribution. Although Australian military leaders warned of the uncertainties of the military situation in Malaysia, they agreed that the Australian force in Vietnam should be built up to a battalion group. On 17 August the Government agreed and by September a 105 mm Howitzer battery, additional armoured personnel carriers, engineers, light aircraft and logistic support were added, bringing Australian strength at Bien Hoa to 1,300.

In October 1965 1 RAR took part with the 173rd Brigade in a search and destroy operation in the Iron Triangle area near Ben Cat in which 106 Viet Cong were killed. In preparation for the helicopter assault, B52 bombers blasted the area but did not help greatly. The helicopters moving the troops in received ground fire as soon as they appeared and an American armoured personnel carrier was blown up by a mine, wounding nine Australians. Other Australians were killed and wounded by sniper fire and booby traps. Australians casualties were two killed and 37 wounded.

Vo Dat in Binh Tuy province was one of the richest rice-growing areas in Vietnam and from 21 November to 16 December 1 RAR was assigned to operation "New Life", aimed at preventing the rice harvest falling into enemy hands. During the operation 1 RAR was ordered to seize Duc Hanh, a fortified hamlet surrounded by a moat. In a highly successful attack by the Australians the hamlet was taken with 8 Viet Cong killed and 86 prisoners. The Australians suffered no casualties and 134 tons of rice was removed or destroyed.

An old neck injury forced Colonel Brumfield to return to Australia and command was taken over by Lieutenant Colonel Alex Preece, then the commander of the AATTV.

In January 1966 after rest and recreation at Bien Hoa over

Christmas, and entertainment provided by Bob Hope, it was back to war with the 1st Battalion leading a mission to destroy the Viet Cong stronghold in the Ho Bo woods area four kilometres east of the Iron Triangle.

The Diggers had a B52 heavy bomber strike and an artillery barrage laid on before they assaulted their target area in helicopters, which came under immediate fire. The battalion suffered casualties from both snipers and booby traps as they advanced. A vicious fight developed. Second Lieutenant James Bourke's platoon led D Company in the assault and came under Viet Cong fire from both flanks. Bourke reported later:

> Delaney got hit and went down. Then Smith, poor bugger. He took two bullets through the eye. One came out of his forehead and the other came out of the back of his head. I could see brains exposed, but he was still moving a little so I knew he wasn't dead yet. I yelled out to the rest of the boys to give me some cover and went forward to try and bring Delaney and Smith back. But when I got to Delaney some bastard got me from a slit in the washout. There was a tunnel behind it and firing slits all along. I dropped Delaney, and he was all right because he was below the level of the slits. My face was a bit of a mess though. The bullet had gone in through the cheek, broken my jaw and taken out a handful of teeth. I remembered noticing how blue the sky was and hearing birds singing, while I looked at my blood dripping on the sand. – I'm dying, I thought. Then I decided I'm not and told myself to find cover.[8]

Delaney survived his wounds and incredibly so did Smith. Australian casualties were eight killed, including an engineer and 29 wounded in action.

In the Ho Bo woods, operation battalion losses were heavy but results were outstanding. The Diggers killed 27 Viet Cong when they overran successive camouflaged bunkers. Viet Cong were seen emerging from, and disappearing into, trapdoor entrances. As the operation proceeded the Australians uncovered an amazing multi-level labyrinth of underground tunnels containing a headquarters complex, dispensaries and a hospital. An astonished Digger declared that there was enough space underground to house "a flaming division".

The village above where the fortunes of war had placed the battalion was the living quarters and recreation area for the huge command post below. The Diggers had captured the Saigon-Cholon-Gia Dinh Special Sector Committee and the political headquarters of Military Region 4 as well. Altogether 128 enemy were killed. The Battalion captured 59 weapons, including 30 automatic weapons, 20,000 rounds of ammunition, 100 Chinese grenades, clothing and medical supplies.

But the most notable achievement of the operation was the capture of 100,000 pages of enemy documents, one of which was the most important intelligence find of the war – a detailed order of battle for Military Region 4, naming members of the entire Viet Cong organisation.

Battalion members and attached engineers braved the hazards of the airless passage to search the tunnels thoroughly. One engineer lost his life when caught in a trapdoor. This tunnel system was put out of action but the enemy soon had it operating again and it was used to shelter Viet Cong troops who attacked Saigon in the "Tet" offensive of early 1968.

After the Ho Bo woods success 1 RAR had a quiet time for more than two weeks at Bien Hoa. During February the battalion was transferred from the operational control of the 173rd Brigade to the 1st Infantry Brigade (US) for an operation to protect engineers building a road near Ben Cat. During this operation Australian patrols handed in intelligence reports indicating that a major enemy attack was likely, and the 1st Brigade, acting on this information, brought in reinforcements of an infantry battalion, tanks and artillery.

At 2 am on the night of 24 February the shadowy figures of the Viet Cong suddenly emerged from tunnels to charge what they thought was an easy target, but encountered instead withering sheets of automatic fire together with devastating blasts of canister shot from tanks and dozens of Claymore mines that cut swathes of destruction.

Dawn revealed a ghastly scene of carnage. Many of the enemy had blundered into the Australian positions and next morning 50 Viet Cong bodies were collected along the perimeter.

Later in the day Australian engineers assisted in burying some 180 bodies in the crater left by a B52 bomb burst. The Americans lost 11 killed and the Australians only one man wounded. He was Lance Corporal Walter Brunalli, who had led an isolated patrol which fought with determination and bravery.

On 8 March 1966 Harold Holt announced that the Australian commitment to Vietnam was to be increased to a self-contained task force of two battalions and from 30 March to 9 April 1 RAR joined the US 1st Infantry Division which was to support the arrival of the task force in Vietnam.

Towards the end of April the battalion withdrew to Bien Hoa. During an Anzac Day parade and church service members met the new Prime Minister, who was visiting Australian forces in Vietnam. In a farewell address, General Westmoreland told members of 1 RAR: "I have never seen a finer group of men. I have never fought with a finer group of soldiers."

It was a fine tribute. In 1966 the Vietnam conflict had not yet become unpopular, and the battalion, joined by returned veterans of the Training Team, were welcomed home by an enthusiastic crowd, 20 deep, when they marched through Sydney. Those who came to cheer the veteran soldiers were startled when a woman covered with red paint emerged from the crowd and in a bizarre gesture pressed herself against Lieutenant Colonel Preece, who was leading the march, thus transferring paint onto his uniform.

The Task Force

The commitment of the 1st Australian Task force to Vietnam in mid-1966 came at a time of growing belief that the slide to defeat of the South Vietnamese forces had been halted. The Task Force commitment trebled the strength of the Australian armed forces in

Vietnam from 1,500 to 4,500. In making this substantial commitment, Holt warned Australians that "a long period of fighting is the prospect we have to face". His words were prophetic, for Australian military operations in Vietnam were to last for 10 years.

The strength of United States forces in Vietnam had by 1966 almost doubled from 200,000 to 385,000 and South Vietnamese forces rose from 691,000 to 735,000. In addition, the forces of the Republic of Korea increased to 45,000, which included the Korean 9th and Capital Divisions.

Reflecting a more favourable outlook for the Allies in 1966, General Westmoreland in his "Report on the Vietnam War" said: "By the end of 1966 sufficient forces had been deployed together with their logistic support so that the total allied military establishment was in a position for the first time to go over to the offensive on a broad and sustained basis."[9]

Australian forces in Vietnam as a whole now came under a new organisation, Australian Forces Vietnam (AFV) commanded by Major General K. Mackay, with Air Commodore J. Dowling of the RAAF as Deputy Commander, Brigadier O. D. Jackson was appointed commander of the Task Force which had been assigned two battalions of the Royal Australian Regiment: 5 RAR, which had been formed on 1 March 1965 at Holsworthy and was commanded by Lieutenant Colonel J. A. Warr; and 6 RAR, which had been formed on 6 June 1965 at Enoggera, Queensland, and was commanded by Lieutenant Colonel C. M. Townsend.

Among members of the Task Force's 5 Battalion who stepped ashore, bayonets fixed, at the port of Vung Tau on 1 May were the first national service conscripts to serve in Vietnam. They had been ferried ashore in landing craft from HMAS *Sydney*. Both battalions of the Task Force included a proportion of national servicemen who, in 1965, had begun to flow into the Army. Before embarking for Vietnam the young "nashos" had been fully trained and fully integrated into the regular battalions. They had all completed the demanding course at the Jungle Training Centre at Canungra and other training areas before embarking for Vietnam.

As well as a Task Force, Australia also committed two RAAF operational squadrons to Vietnam. No 9 Squadron, equipped with eight Iroquois helicopters, was commanded by the RAAF's most experienced helicopter pilot, Wing Commander Ray Scott. It was based at Vung Tau airfield and would be under the operational control of the Task force commander. In addition, the RAAF Caribou transport flight was upgraded and named No 35 Squadron. It was commanded by Wing Commander Charles Melchert and was placed under the operational control of the United States 7th Air Force. The RAAF appointed a Task Force Air Commander who would also be the RAAF Officer Commanding at Vung Tau where all RAAF units were based. He was Group Captain Peter Raw, who had served with distinction in the Second World War as a young bomber pilot.

Strategic airlift played a significant role in the Vietnam War and two squadrons of RAAF Hercules supported by Qantas and domestic charter flights supplied Australia's needs.

Hercules transports had the vital task of flying home the wounded. The combination of flying and medical skills in aero-medical evacuation from Vietnam was one of the finest Australian service achievements of the Vietnam War.

Phuoc Tuy province south-east of Saigon was chosen as the location and area of operations for the Australian Task force, whose objective was to break the hold of Viet Cong in the province and help reassert the government control.

The Task Force was moved into Nui Dat, which was some 32 kilometres inland and lay along Route 2, which bisected the province.

Nui Dat was a jungle-covered knoll rising some 60 metres above the surrounding mainly flat terrain. It was chosen because it was away from population centres yet was centrally placed within the province. A logistics base for the Task Force was established alongside a stretch of beach on the eastern side of Vung Tau peninsula.

Phuoc Tuy province had been infiltrated by the Viet Cong who had organised the D445 Provincial Mobile Battalion. Enemy main force troops in the province totalled some 6000 men comprising the 5th Division which included two regiments (274 and 275) each with some 2,000 men.

On 24 May 5 RAR began moving into Nui Dat. Captain Robert O'Neill, an officer in B Company, described the airlift from Vung Tau to Nui Dat in American helicopters:

> *The morning of May 24 was dull and misty. Reveille was very early as the companies began taking off in helicopters shortly after dawn in approximately half company groups. My lift took off at 0936 hours, punctual to a few seconds. The helicopters seemed to be amazingly close together in the air. From a distance they looked like a line of cherry stones hanging and bobbing on strings – the country looked quiet and sleepy, clad in small wraps of white mist which clung around the tall trees.*[10]

Before the day was over the Task Force was to lose its first soldier in action. In a fire fight which developed with the Viet Cong, Private Errol Noack was hit by a burst of machine gunfire. He was with a party sent to fetch water. Noack was flown out of Nui Dat in a medical evacuation helicopter (known as a "Dust Off") but died before reaching hospital at Vung Tau. He was the first Australian national serviceman and the first member of the Task Force killed in action in Vietnam.

Victory at Long Tan

The 1st Australian Task Force won a stunning victory in Vietnam on 18 August in a ferocious battle in which 245 enemy soldiers were killed.

In this encounter in a Long Tan rubber plantation near the new base at Nui Dat in Phuoc Tuy province, the heavily outnumbered Australians vanquished Viet Cong formations comprising the D445 Battalion and elements of the 5th Viet Cong Division.

Young Australian national servicemen of D Company of the 6th Battalion, who had been called into the army only in the previous year, shared in the triumph which cost 18 Australian lives and earned the company the award of the United States Presidential Unit Citation for "extraordinary heroism in operations against an opposing armed force".

It was Australia's greatest victory in its 10 years participation in the war and one of the classic actions of Australian military history.

The newly arrived Task Force had set up a strongly defended base at Nui Dat in the heart of the important enemy province Phuoc Tuy. This challenge angered the VC and they reacted violently with the intention of inflicting a sharp defeat on the "arrogant" Australians and hopefully swaying Australian domestic opinion against the war by inflicting sacrificial losses on their armed forces in Vietnam.

The Viet Cong battle plan was straightforward enough. It was master-minded by a senior officer of the 5th Viet Cong Division, Colonel Nguyen Than Hong, who directed that the VC attacking force was to approach the Australians at Nui Dat undetected and then fire mortars and recoilless rifle shells into their base. It was calculated that this action would lure the Australians out of their strong defensive positions to look for the mortar bases and to search the area from which they were fired. The VC would be waiting to trap them from prepared ambush positions among the rubber trees and whatever Australian "mercenaries" were sent would be quickly wiped out.

So 275 Regiment moved steadily towards its appointment with destiny. From radio intercepts and visual sightings, the Task Force became aware of the presence of strong enemy forces within 5 kilometres east of its base. Company-sized Australian patrols were sent out to intercept the enemy, but the patrols found nothing.

Then on the night of 16–17 August the Task Force was struck by a barrage of mortar bombs and recoilless rifle shells which wounded 24 Australians. The Task Force replied to this attack with a countering artillery barrage.

The Diggers had to be ready in case the mortar attack was followed up by ground attack. They grabbed their weapons and stood to in their weapon pits, peering into the murk. But no enemy approached. At dawn, B Company of 6 RAR was sent to search for the enemy mortar positions and found five mortar sites and weapon pits for 35 men.

Next day D Company of the 6th Battalion took over the search from B Company which was soon back in "the Dat" where singer Col Joye

79. *The guided missile destroyer HMAS* Perth, *which was to become a veteran of the Vietnam War.*

80. The RAAF sends the Caribou transport flight into Vietnam in August 1964.

81. Colonel F. P. Serong (far left), Australian's most experienced jungle warfare expert, watches a training exercise with Vietnamese officers at Dong Da.

82. Watched by Montagnards, a Caribou transport plane lands at a primitive airstrip to bring support to the Australian training team.

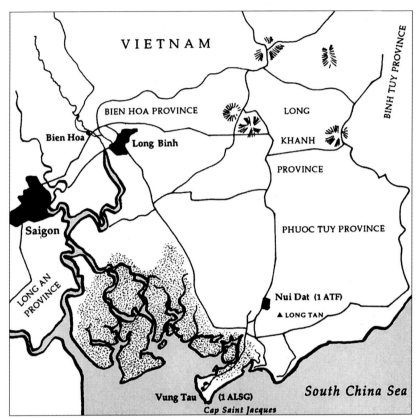

83. The area of South Vietnam in which the Australians were active. (Black shading indicates towns and grey the river delta.)

84. *Montagnards gather around a Caribou at Plei Mrong. The airmen are distributing toys and clothing, gifts from the RAAF in Australia.*

85. *Men of 1 RAR on a search and destroy operation move through paddy fields as their American transport helicopters depart.*

HMAS Sydney

HMAS Vendetta

HMAS Brisbane

HMAS Hobart

HMAS Perth

86. *Australian ships of the Vietnam War.*

87. Australians move across a road as Vietnamese rural life goes on as usual.

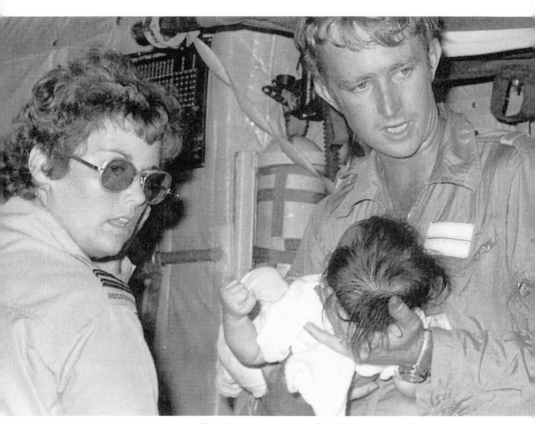

88. In all, 288 Vietnamese children orphaned in the war were flown to Australia.

89. Delta Company of 6 RAR boards an American Chinook helicopter.

90. *A helicopter brings supplies to Australian troops during an operation.*

91. *Choppers saved the lives of wounded men in Vietnam by their ability to fly them to medical help immediately.*

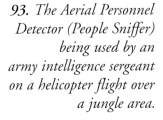

92. Ten hours after the Battle of Long Tan, a wounded Australian is found and tended by his comrades. Long Tan was a spectacular victory for the Australians in Vietnam.

93. The Aerial Personnel Detector (People Sniffer) being used by an army intelligence sergeant on a helicopter flight over a jungle area.

94. *An Australian member of the training team instructing Montagnards at the special forces camp at Pleiku in 1969.*

95. Australian Centurion tanks and a helicopter act in concert during an operation in Vietnam.

96. The region in which Australians were deployed during the Gulf War.

97. A RAN Seahawk helicopter hovers over HMAS *Adelaide during operations in the Gulf.*

98. Sunset in the Gulf with an RAN 50-calibre machine gun outlined against the sea.

99. Seven Australian women made history during the Gulf crisis by undertaking combat-related roles in war.

100. HMAS *Westralia, the biggest ship in the Australian Navy.*

101. Australians continued the United Nations presence in war-torn Somalia.

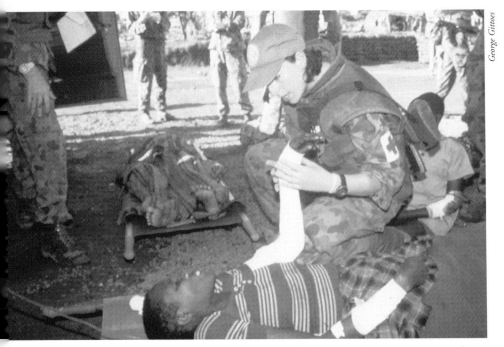

George Gittoes

102. Captain Carol Vaughan Evans of the Australian Army attends victims of the Rwanda genocide at Kibeho in 1995.

and his party of entertainers had arrived by helicopter to stage a rock concert.

Led by Major Harry Smith, D Company left base at 11 am on 18 August. In the afternoon, with Second Lieutenant David Sabben's platoon in front, they moved at a fast pace towards the Long Tan rubber plantation. The route took them through low scrub, swamp and paddy fields in hot and stifling conditions. The young soldiers each carried 60 rounds of ammunition and three days' rations. They test-fired their weapons and through the humid air they could hear the faint beat of rock music coming from "the Dat", reminding them of their disappointment at missing out on Col Joye and Little Pattie.

Meanwhile leaflets were fluttering down into Long Tan village from a RAAF helicopter engaged in psychological warfare. Gathered in the village was part of the force about to attack the Australians. The leaflets urged them instead to desert the VC, but no doubt few were in the mood at that particular time to give up the struggle.

At 3.15 pm the company entered the Long Tan rubber trees on a frontage of some 400 metres. Lieutenant Sharp's 11 platoon had just crossed a clearing when a squad of six to eight Viet Cong appeared. The platoon opened fire, killing one. The battle of Long Tan had begun.

At 4.08 pm, as the company continued its advance along the edge of the plantation, the Viet Cong attacked in force, pouring a withering fire from at least a company. Major Smith recalled, "Everything just went mad. Eleven platoon is being surrounded and overrun. The whole company is under fire from mortars, rifles and machine guns." At the same time torrential rain was falling, and Lieutenant Sharp called for artillery support. A New Zealand battery of 105 mm artillery pieces responded immediately.

Major Smith then ordered Sharp to withdraw his platoon, but it was pinned down by an incredible volume of hostile fire, and menaced by repeated assaults by enemy infantry bursting through the foliage. Sharp, a national serviceman who had been commissioned, was killed shortly afterwards, and Sergeant Bob Buick took over and maintained control, shouting to be heard above the noise of battle.

Major Sharp wanted air support. He called for an air strike with napalm directly in front of 11 platoon to cover its withdrawal. When the American strike planes arrived overhead the whole company was in danger of being surrounded. Canisters of coloured smoke were set off to pinpoint the target. But the torrential rain and the canopy of trees hid the smoke and spared the enemy from air attack. The four F4 Phantoms which could be heard flying over the battleground were forced to divert to a secondary target, Nui Dat East.

Not only were the soldiers denied direct air support but they were running perilously short of ammunition. At 5 pm Major Smith called for helicopters to drop ammunition to keep his weapons firing. The beleaguered soldiers were grimly aware that the monsoonal downpours might work against the resupply choppers as well. But they were not to be denied. Two RAAF helicopters risked the appalling conditions and the danger of ground fire from a low altitude to fly in fresh supplies of ammunition. They were flown by two gutsy crews captained by Flight Lieutenants Cliffe Dohle and Frank Riley. The choppers were at Nui Dat to transport the concert party back to Vung Tau and were promptly diverted to the vital ammunition resupply task.

Cascading rain forced the two Iroquois "slicks" to fly at tree-top level, thus exposing them to the danger of ground fire from hundreds of Viet Cong troops. Tracer rounds passed through both doors of one of the choppers and the crew could see a machine gun firing straight at them.

The soldiers of D Company set up smoke signals to guide the RAAF to their position. The RAAF crews found the company and quickly dropped the boxes of ammunition wrapped in blankets (the blankets were for the wounded), to the waiting troops. The boxes fell right on target and over the radio the chopper crews heard an exultant Digger voice, "You bloody beauty, that was smack on."

Ian McNeill the Australian official historian wrote later, "The RAAF was roundly praised for their skilful and daring feat. It marked the beginning of a new period in inter-service cooperation and understanding".[11]

With the powerful support of the four batteries of Australian, American and New Zealand artillery which thundered incessantly, and aggressive fire from D Company soldiers, the enemy were stopped in their tracks. A D Company soldier describing the carnage said:

> *A solid line of them – it looked like hundreds – would suddenly*
> *rush us. The artillery would burst right in the middle of them*
> *and there would be bodies all over the place. The survivors*
> *would dive for cover beside these bodies, wait for the next*
> *attacking line, get up and leap over the dead to resume the rush.*
> *They were inching forward all the time over their piles of dead.*[12]

To support D Company in its hour of peril, B Company of 6 RAR was ordered to return post-haste to the battle area while A Company also raced out in armoured personnel carriers (APCs) of 3 Troop, 1st APC Squadron, commanded by Captain Adrian Roberts. On their timely arrival in the plantation rested the fate of D Company. With the carriers went Lieutenant Colonel Townshend, who took charge of the relief force.

Wasting no time, the carriers passed through the Nui Dat wire and made the difficult crossing of the Suoi Da Ban creek now in flood from the heavy rain. Within a kilometre of the battle area, the relief force encountered an enemy force numbering well over 100. Soldiers of 2 Platoon dismounted and advanced on foot, blazing away at the Viet Cong. The APCs joined in the battle and the outgunned Viet Cong fled.

At 6.55 pm when the relief force approached D Company, the light was fast fading, but the Viet Cong could be seen massing for a final assault. Soon afterwards, however, the firing stopped as well as the rain and the enemy troops began rising from the ground and receding into the rubber trees.

The Viet Cong had suffered horrendous casualties and hundreds of wounded were in desperate need. The extent of the Viet Cong catastrophe was not fully appreciated until next day when the Australians moved back into the battle area and counted 245 bodies in the plantation and the surrounding jungle. Many more enemy dead had been hauled away. Captured documents and the questioning of prisoners indicated that the Viet Cong force comprised 275 Regiment (reinforced by North Vietnamese troops) and D445 battalion. Thus D Company of 108 men, supported by artillery, had faced some 2,500 men.

Australian battle casualties were 18 killed (17 from D Company and 1 from 1 APC Squadron) and 24 wounded. With the fighting over except for artillery fire, helicopters were urgently needed to fly the wounded to hospital. The first helicopter, an American Army "dust off" machine, was called in around midnight followed by six RAAF Iroquois. A helicopter pad had been prepared and artillery fire was temporarily suspended while the choppers were guided to the pad by a dim glow from the APCs which had been formed into a hollow square.

An Australian infantry company had survived against heavy odds and the Task force had won a victory that would live in Australian military history. Congratulations poured into Nui Dat, acclaiming the Australian victory. Prime Minister Holt sent a message and another came from General Westmoreland which read:

> *For General Mackay from General Westmoreland. Your troops have won a spectacular victory over the enemy near Baria. Aggressiveness, quick reaction, good use of fire power and old fashioned Australian courage have produced outstanding results.*

Major Smith drew attention to the vital supporting role of the artillery. Enemy casualties in the immediate D Company area had been caused by small arms fire (50 per cent) and artillery fire (50 per cent) he said.

Major Smith visited No 9 Squadron, RAAF at Vung Tau to thank personally the helicopter crews who had faced the dual hazards of the elements and enemy fire to deliver the crucial supply of ammunition when D Company had no hope of resupply by other means.

Professor Robert O'Neill, then a captain with 5 RAR, highlighted the cardinal error of the Viet Cong in launching their operation within range of the artillery at Nui Dat. "The intensity and accuracy of the defensive (artillery) fire which the gunners laid around the beleaguered company was of critical importance to the outcome," he wrote.[13]

Artillery support was absolutely vital because the adverse weather and approaching darkness ruled out air strikes in support.

The Australian victory at Long Tan was headline news at home and in the United States. "It ranks with some of the great stands in military history," a newspaper editorial declared. As well as the unit being awarded the Presidential Unit Citation, fifteen Commonwealth decorations were awarded to individual soldiers.

Predictably, however, having built up feverish hopes in their minds for a great triumph against the Australian "mercenaries", the mendacious Viet Cong spokesmen were not about to let a few facts kill their version of the outcome. They broadcast through Hanoi and Beijing radios the news of "a major Viet Cong victory at Long Tan in which 700 Australians had been killed and two squadrons of tanks destroyed." As if to confirm news of the victory the Viet Cong D445 regiment was honoured with an "heroic unit citation". More than 20 years later the Viet Cong were still holding to their fairytale view of the battle of Long Tan.

After the mauling they suffered at Long Tan, the Viet Cong lay low for a time to lick their wounds. The standing of the Australians rose high and Australian military dominance led to an extension of Task Force control over Phuoc Tuy province.

Search and Destroy

In October 1966 the RAAF lost its first helicopter in the Vietnam War when supporting 5 RAR in operations against a Viet Cong base in Nui Thi Vai, a mountain in western Phuoc Tuy province from which the VC threatened the flow of Allied forces along the important Route 15 from Vung Tau to Bien Hoa and Saigon. The Viet Cong were caught by surprise in their caves and tunnels. Ten were killed and the rest scattered.

However, a RAAF helicopter supporting the operation overshot the 5th Battalion position, crashed into the jungle and caught fire. The helicopter was carrying army engineers and explosives. Some of the crew and army passengers were seriously injured. Sergeant Gordon Buttriss, a helicopter crewman who was not badly hurt in the crash, completely disregarded his own safety and immediately took steps to clear all crew and passengers from the aircraft. Just as every one was safely behind rocks away from the helicopter, ammunition began to explode and the fire became intense, threatening to set off the explosives. For his courageous actions, Buttriss was awarded the George Medal.

In November, both 5 RAR and 6 RAR together with the Special Air Service squadron launched a search and destroy operation against Long Son Island. The troops flew into Long Son in American helicopters while the SAS squadron surrounded the island in small boats. RAAF helicopters kept the troops supplied with food, ammunition and water and flew out a total of 376 Viet Cong suspects. Shortly after the operation 13 Viet Cong arrived at Vung Tau in sampans to surrender.

In an attempt to deny the Viet Cong access to rice production in the central rice bowl of Phuoc Tuy Province, the Task Force erected a barbed-wire barrier and laid a minefield from the Horseshoe near Dat Do to the coast. The project became a serious embarrassment because the South Vietnamese Government forces failed to patrol it adequately and the Viet Cong stripped the field of many of its mines and used them as booby traps. General Westmoreland, commenting later on this project, said:

> One ingenious project the Australians attempted had an
> unhappy ending. In an effort to secure a portion of Phuoc Tuy
> province, the Australians laid some 20,000 anti-personnel
> mines, but South Vietnamese militia that were charged with
> protecting the field failed to keep out VC infiltrators. The VC
> removed roughly half the mines and used them for their own
> purposes throughout the province.

The situation was bad and the minefield had to be cleared. The Australians devised an ingenious mine-detonating device towed by a tank, and the device detonated the mines which exploded harmlessly behind the vehicle.

In the Federal election of 26 November 1966, Prime Minister Holt's coalition government was returned to office with a substantial majority of 39 in the Lower House. Vietnam policy was at the forefront of election issues, and clearly a majority of Australians supported involvement.

A month later, Holt announced a substantial build-up in the Australian military contribution to Vietnam, bringing the total of Australian forces committed to 6,300. The RAN would now also be directly involved in combat operations when the Guided Missile destroyer HMAS *Hobart* was committed to operations off Vietnam under the operational control of the US 7th Fleet. Australia thus became the first nation other than the United States to commit all three of its armed services to Vietnam.

As well, the RAAF's No 2 Canberra jet bomber squadron with 400 personnel would move from Butterworth, Malaysia, to Phang Rang near Cam Ramh Bay in the 2 Corps Zone of South Vietnam. A RAN Clearance Diving team and 498 additional Army personnel were also committed.

The Australian combat build-up in Vietnam continued in July 1967 when Australia announced additional helicopter support including eight RAN helicopter pilots and supporting staff, who would join the US army 135th Assault Helicopter Company at "Blackhorse" near Xuan Loc in 3 Corps Zone. The Australian Army Navy and Air Force would now all be operating helicopters in the Vietnam War.

In mid-1967, Clark Clifford, a US White House adviser visited Allied capitals (including Canberra) with General Maxwell Taylor, urging governments to increase their military efforts in Vietnam. "In the main," he later wrote, "our pleas fell on deaf ears."

Clifford, who later became Defence Secretary in succession to McNamara, said that Holt "presented a long list of reasons why Australia was already close to its maximum effort".

Nevertheless, on 17 October Holt announced a decision to send a third Australian battalion with helicopter support to Vietnam. He also added a squadron of Centurion tanks with 250 personnel, and eight more helicopters for the RAAF's No 9 Squadron. The total Australian commitment would now be 8,000 men.

On 14 February, 5 RAR lost three officers killed in a landmine explosion. Three days later 6 RAR lost 7 killed and 26 wounded. On 21 February two horrific landmine explosions killed seven and wounded 22 members of 5 RAR. The battalion was engaged in a sweep of the Long Hai hills to destroy enemy bases and caches when a mine detonated under an APC, killing most of the leading section of a platoon. RAAF helicopters were called in to evacuate the wounded from heavily mined country at the foot of the Long Hai hills. So great had the congestion become in the military hospital at Vung Tau that a special RAAF C130E Hercules of No 37 Squadron was flown up from Richmond to evacuate 48 litter and three walking wounded to Australia so that pressure on the hospital facilities could be eased.

The RAAF had a distinguished history of involvement in aero medical evacuation. Except for a few patients in the early stages the RAAF handled all Australian sick and wounded from Vietnam, not only soldiers, but members of the RAN and some civilians as well as RAAF casualties. The Royal New Zealand Air Force and New Zealand Army also took advantage of the RAAF service as far as Richmond, NSW from where the casualties were taken over by New Zealand authorities.

When they became available, the improved C130E model Hercules were used in a regular service every two weeks between Vietnam and Australia, solely for aero-medical evacuation. In addition special flights were undertaken to relieve the critical bed state at 1st Australian Field Hospital, Vung Tau.

The 3,164 patients evacuated through the RAAF system from Vietnam to Australia were from the following:

Australia Regular Army	2,777
Royal Australian Navy	24
Royal Australian Air Force	158
NZ Army	194
RNZAF	3
Civilian	8
TOTAL	3,164

On 6 August 1967, A Company of 7 RAR (commanded by Lieutenant Colonel E. H. Smith) lost six Australians killed in action and 17 wounded when they clashed at Suoi Chau Pha with a battalion-sized force of the Viet Cong 274 Regiment. Five RAAF helicopters, disregarding enemy fire, evacuated the casualties to hospital.

RAAF Jet Bombers in Action

The Canberra jet bombers of No 2 Squadron RAAF arrived at Phan Rang, Vietnam, on 19 April 1967, to add weight to the Allied bombing effort in Vietnam. As with all other combat commitments in Vietnam they came under United States operational control. This control was exercised by the United States 7th Air Force commanded by General William Momyer who was at Phan Rang to welcome the Canberra squadron when its aircraft touched down.

The squadron became a tactical unit of the US 35th Tactical Fighter Wing and part of a comprehensive air support system in South Vietnam. The Canberras were required to launch eight aircraft every 24 hours, seven days a week, and to attack targets anywhere within the four corps areas into which Vietnam was divided for military operations.

The Canberras wasted no time getting into action. On 23 April they carried out eight strikes, dropping 42 bombs of 500 lb, each on 11 targets ranging from 2 Corps to 4 Corps in the Mekong Delta. Within three years they had struck over 9,000 targets and dropped over 50,000 bombs. They had an exceptional record for accuracy.

Within four days of arriving at Phan Rang the Squadron flew missions in support of the Australian Task Force to the south. Bombing from just over 3000 m the Canberras hit Viet Cong tunnels and bunkers 16 kilometres northwest of Nui Dat, after which troops of 7 RAR assaulted the area in a helicopter-borne operation.

When the Viet Cong launched the "Tet" offensive in early 1968, a deluge of bombs cascaded almost endlessly on Viet Cong targets throughout South Vietnam. No 2 Squadron Canberras contributed to bombing operations in support of Allied forces from Khe Sanh in the extreme north to Saigon and the Mekong delta in the south.

The enemy besieged a US Marine force and South Vietnamese Rangers at Khe Sanh, apparently to repeat the achievement of seizing Dien Bien Phu from the French as they had 14 years earlier. But Westmoreland had an armada of 2,000 planes and he unleashed an awesome aerial campaign in which No 2 Squadron joined. On 3 and 4 February 1968, flying at 8,600 metres and guided by radar, the squadron blasted the besiegers at Khe Sanh. No 2 Squadron attacked them again during the successful Allied breakout in April.

During the siege, Khe Sanh was entirely supplied by aircraft. All enemy attempts to overrun the defenders were defeated. "The key to our success at Khe Sanh was firepower, principally aerial firepower," General Westmoreland declared.

Within the perimeter of Phan Rang air base, living conditions were reasonably comfortable for the RAAF, but beyond the perimeter wire was Viet Cong country. Occasionally parties of guerillas broke through the wire to attack the air base installations. Over a period of three and a half years no less than 784 mortar rounds and rockets exploded in the base. RAAF Airfield Defence Guards contributed to the security of the base and were involved in clashes with guerilla raiders. RAAF Corporal Noel Power led a patrol which ambushed enemy sappers and was awarded a Military Medal for his part in the action.

Members of No 2 Squadron often had the unreal experience of watching open-air film shows when just off the screen a real battle scene was unfolding beyond the perimeter wire.

Year of the Monkey

General Vo Nguyen Giap, the Viet Cong's top war strategist, masterminded one of the most extraordinary military campaigns of the 20th century when he launched the "Tet" offensive which erupted suddenly throughout South Vietnam in early 1968.

Giap used the traditional holiday period of the Buddhists' sacred "Tet" celebrations as a smokescreen behind which he mounted his massive offensive against no less than 100 cities and towns throughout South Vietnam. Saigon itself became a battlefield. The world was staggered by the sheer audacity of the Viet Cong guerillas who, disguised as South Vietnamese soldiers, stormed the United States Embassy and occupied it. US troops landed on the roof of the building by helicopters and took six hours to flush them out again room by room.

As though they had a death wish, the Viet Cong guerillas swarmed from tunnels and jungle hideouts into the cities against Westmoreland's very large army of well-equipped and confident troops, who mowed them down in their thousands, including those besieging Khe Sanh near the Demilitarised Zone in the far north.

It was the Tet "Year of the Monkey" and the Viet Cong attempted to mask their intentions by announcing beforehand that they would observe a seven-day truce for "Tet" from 27 January to 3 February. But they had no intention of keeping their word. However, the Allies were not taken by surprise. Warned by intelligence reports, Westmoreland ordered General Frederick Weyand, 11 Corps Field Commander, to strengthen US forces in the area around Saigon.

The massive build-up of American armed forces together with "free world" contributions and the strengthening of the ARVN (Army of the Republic of Vietnam) had, by the end of 1967, arrested the Allied downhill military trend and the enemy now had a pressing need to reverse his deteriorating fortunes. Westmoreland was confident all enemy thrusts would be crushed. "I hope they try something because we are looking for a fight," he declared. "Frankly those of us who had been in Vietnam for a long period found it hard to believe that the enemy would expose his forces to almost certain decimation by engaging us frontally at a great distance from his base areas and border sanctuaries. However, in 1968 this is exactly what he did and in doing it he lost the cream of his army."

On the night of 29 January the stage had been set and General Weyand sent a flash signal to commanders ordering them to place all forces on maximum alert. That same night the enemy struck.

Weyand had ordered a tight defensive screen to be thrown around Saigon and two-thirds of the Australian Task Force (including 2 RAR) was already conducting operations around the vital Bien Hoa-Long Binh complex near Saigon. In "Operational Coburg", as the operation was named, the Australian infantry inflicted heavy casualties on the attacking enemy, killing 181 by body count. Bien Hoa was never put out of action. During Coburg, helicopters of No 9 Squadron were based forward to Fire Support Base "Andersen" in daylight hours, returning each night to Vung Tau. General Weyand sent a signal commending the Australian Task Force for its "exceptional performance in defeating the enemy 'Tet' attacks against the critically important Bien Hoa/Long Binh complex".

Meanwhile on 1 February, A Company of 3 RAR (commanded by Lieutenant Colonel Jim Shelton), which had just arrived at Nui Dat from Australia, was ordered to defend the provincial capital, Baria, where D445 battalion had launched attacks on five targets. Altogether some 600 enemy troops were operating in the area. They were attempting to persuade the citizens to join in a "popular uprising".

A Company moving from Nui Dat in armoured personnel carriers rammed their way to the sector headquarters in Baria and began a gutsy series of fire fights and rescues of American civilian workers. One of the Australian platoons killed 15 Viet Cong holed up in one of the houses. By 2 February more than 40 enemy had been killed and the Viet Cong had ceased to be an effective force in the town.

Viet Cong action had cut the road between Vung Tau and the Task Force at Nui Dat, so RAAF Caribou transports were called on to fly supplies and equipment from Vung Tau airfield to Nui Dat. In three successive days the Caribou airlifted a total of 220,412 kilograms of freight.

In mid-February 3 RAR was sent north to protect Fire Support Base Andersen which was astride the enemy communications and thus a thorn in his side. The Viet Cong launched three full-scale assaults to eliminate the base. At one stage they pushed through the wire but were halted by machine gunfire from the APCs and American gunners.

By March 1968 the Tet offensive had ended as a military disaster for the Viet Cong. Yet it had had a deep political impact in the United States where opposition to the war was stiffening.

President Johnson on 31 March announced that he was restricting the bombing of North Vietnam and made a renewed offer to the North Vietnamese for negotiations. He then made the surprise announcement that he would not seek another term as President of the United States. He gave as a reason for withdrawal from the presidential race his belief that it would heal the "partisan divisions" that were racking the nation.

General Westmoreland was replaced as US commander in Vietnam (this was a decision taken before the Tet offensive began) and appointed Chief of Staff of the US Army. His replacement was his deputy, General Creighton W. Abrams. Clark Clifford was to replace Robert McNamara as Secretary of Defence.

The North Vietnamese response was swift. They agreed to negotiate in Paris in May and at the same time General Giap rushed plans for a new offensive to coincide with the opening of the projected peace talks.

However, before Giap could launch his new offensive, the Americans, South Vietnamese and Allied forces struck on 8 April, beating the enemy to the punch. Westmoreland employed 79 battalions in 111 Corps zone in an offensive known as Toan Thang ("Complete Victory"). When the operation ended on 31 May the total of enemy killed had reached 7,600. Altogether the enemy had lost 120,000 men during the first six months of 1968. Toan Thang went a long way to disrupt Giap's plans for another Tet-style attack on Saigon.

Giap's army struck again on 7 May, launching 119 attacks against cities, towns and military targets. Six days later on 13 May the Paris peace talks were under way.

In Vietnam, parties of Viet Cong infiltrated Saigon and during street fighting in the city, three Australian and one British pressmen were killed when they drove a jeep into a Viet Cong trap in Cholon, a Saigon suburb. The fighting seemed to have no clear military objective but was apparently designed to create the impression in Paris that Saigon, "under siege", was in a chaotic state.

Enemy military plans for the offensive had fallen into Allied hands and this enabled Westmoreland to dispose his forces advantageously to meet the attacks.

The Australian Task Force was ordered to occupy, ambush and

block positions straddling the enemy infiltration routes to and from Saigon. The Task Force assigned 1 RAR commanded by Lieutenant Colonel (General Sir Phillip) Bennett and 3 RAR to set up Fire Support Base "Coral" and then establish the blocking positions and send out patrols. Units assigned to Coral included both New Zealand and Australian artillery units which were to support the infantry operations. Later 52-ton Centurion tanks of the Australian 1st Armoured Regiment were committed.

Delays and confusion during the occupation of Coral on 12 May had caused a loss of vital time so that the Australian troops there had barely enough time to dig weapon pits. There was no time for barbed wire or Claymore mines. A North Vietnamese battalion had observed the activity at Coral and decided to attack that night. An American briefing officer told the Australians they would not have to search out the enemy. "Charlie", he said, "will come looking for you."

Charlie was not long in coming. About 2,500 metres distant from Coral a North Vietnamese party suddenly appeared where D Company, 1 RAR, commanded by Major Tony Hammett, was preparing an ambush site. The Australians killed one of the North Vietnamese and Hammett, expecting trouble, ordered his men to "dig, dig, dig". He also ordered a 50 per cent stand-to.

Hammett's company was suddenly hit at about midnight when the enemy opened fire with rocket-propelled grenades (RPGs) killing two Australians by tree bursts and wounding nine.

About an hour later a picket reported the presence of some 400 enemy only 50 metres from Coral's defences. "They were all gibbering excitedly," the picket reported and their attack came in a barrage of rocket, mortar and small arms fire which swept through the vulnerable fire support base. Then a rush by NVA of the 275th Battalion overran the 1 RAR mortar platoon positions. Lieutenant Anthony Jensen, the mortar platoon commander, called for artillery fire and the Australian gunners fired three Splintex rounds (each containing thousands of small darts) which cut a swathe through the enemy attackers. American "Spooky" aircraft (DC3s equipped with mini guns) and helicopter gunships joined in the battle. When it was over the mortar platoon had lost five killed and eight wounded. Total Australian losses were nine dead while 52 North Vietnamese had been killed.

When the North Vietnamese returned to the attack against Coral three days later they were repulsed by three companies of 1 RAR. They lost 34 killed while 1 RAR lost five killed and 19 wounded.

Shortly after the Coral encounters the Task force set up a new fire support base named "Balmoral" to the north of Coral. A column of the heavily armed Australian Centurion tanks and elements of the 3rd Battalion arrived at Balmoral only a few hours before the base was attacked (at 3.45 am on 26 May) by two battalions of North Vietnamese regular troops.

Next day 3 RAR accompanied by four Centurion tanks attacked an extensive bunker system manned by an aggressive enemy. Led by Major Hammett the Australians had a highly successful day, destroying bunkers and killing enemy occupants. "The tanks were superb. My men were patting them and fussing over them back at Coral," said Hammett. On 28 May the North Vietnamese again attacked Balmoral and suffered a sharp reverse losing 47 killed.

In early June the Task Force returned to Nui Dat. The enemy had suffered crippling losses. Sickness, air strikes and lack of progress at Paris caused many individuals and groups to surrender.

An experienced Viet Cong battalion commander who surrendered near Saigon said he could no longer lead men to certain death in "illogical, futile attacks against inconsequential objectives, attacks which North Vietnam was ordering in order to provide a fulcrum for her diplomats in Paris"

The RAN in Combat Operations

HMAS *Hobart*, one of the RAN's new guided missile destroyers, was the first of four RAN warships to be committed to naval operations in Vietnam. By agreement of the US and Australian governments they were to be under the operational control of the US 7th Fleet. The other three were *Brisbane*, *Perth* and *Vendetta*.

After joining the US 7th Fleet at Subic Bay in the Philippines, *Hobart* (Captain G. R Griffiths) carried out her first operation on 31 March 1967. She provided naval gunfire support for a patrol of US Marines entangled with the Viet Cong in Quang Ngai province south of Da Nang. Shortly afterwards *Hobart's* gunfire killed 15 Viet Cong attacking an ARVN post, north of Cap Mia.

Gunfire from *Hobart* and other RAN destroyers at times meant the difference between victory and defeat in infantry operations ashore.

The US Navy's Sea Dragon operations involved the bombardment of military targets in North Vietnam and the suppression of coastal traffic supplying the Viet Cong. *Hobart* was assigned to the Sea Dragon Task Force and on 16 April was under fire after shelling barges in a river mouth north of Cap Falaise in the Gulf of Tonkin. *Hobart* then joined the screen for the aircraft carrier *Kittyhawk* whose aircraft were carrying out strikes on North Vietnamese targets.

Hobart was repeatedly straddled by coastal defence batteries when attacking a ferry complex, south of Dong Hoi.

HMAS *Perth* (Captain P. H. Doyle) took over from *Hobart* on 14 September and on 18 October was hit by a North Vietnamese shell when engaging enemy artillery. Four sailors were wounded, two of them seriously.

Perth was relieved by *Hobart* (Captain K. W. Shands) in April 1968 and on 17 June when off Cap Lay at night was mistakenly attacked by a US swept-wing fighter which fired a missile. It struck *Hobart* amidships, killing Ordinary Seaman R. J. Butterworth and wounded two others. *Hobart* had identified the aircraft as "friendly", nevertheless it attacked again, killing Chief Electrician R. H. Hunt and wounding several sailors. The attacking aircraft appeared to be about to make a third attack when *Hobart* opened fire on it.

Captain Shands then proceeded to Subic Bay for repairs and was back on the gunline by 26 July. On 22 August *Hobart* was off Cap St Jacques and opened fire on a Viet Cong base camp on Long Son Island in support of operations by the Australian Task Force.

In total *Hobart* carried out three deployments in Vietnam, firing 42,475 rounds. *Perth* served three times firing 30,711 rounds; *Brisbane* twice firing 15,651 rounds, and *Vendetta* once firing 13,709.

RAN Helicopter Flight

The Vietnam War created an insatiable need for helicopters and a contingent of RAN helicopter crews and technical sailors was committed to the war in 1967. It was designated the RAN Helicopter Flight Vietnam (RANHFV) and made history by being the first RAN helicopter force to go into action in support of ground forces, including the Australian Task Force.

The Flight, of some 50 RAN personnel, included eight pilots, four observers, four aircrewmen and supporting technical sailors. In Vietnam it was integrated with the United States Army's 135th Assault Helicopter Company.

The integrated US-Australian Navy unit began operations in November 1967 and in the following month moved to Camp Blackhorse near Xuan Loc in Long Khan province. In that month the RAN pilots flew 860 hours in support of American, Australian and Vietnamese troops. On 8 January 1968 eight company aircraft were hit by ground fire during the insertion and extraction of troops.

In the marked increase in operations during the Tet offensive of 1968, Blackhorse came under threat of enemy rocket and mortar attacks. RAN crew survived attacks while on the ground during the planning of a mission.

On 22 February 1968, Lieutenant Commander P. J. Vickers was fatally wounded by enemy fire when descending on a pick-up zone to lift ARVN troops. Two more members of the Flight, Lieutenant A. Casadio and Petty Officer O. Phillips were killed on 21 August when their gunship was hit by a rocket-propelled grenade, causing it to crash through trees and explode near Blackhorse.

A replacement RAN Flight led by Lieutenant Commander G. R. Rohrsheim arrived in Vietnam in September 1968 and in November moved with the 135th Company to Bearcat, northeast of Saigon. At Bearcat the Australians came under mortar and rocket fire. In six days, 99 rounds landed in or near the company area.

A total of 35 RAN pilots served in the RANHFV and flew a grand total of 33,734 hours. Four RAN contingents were sent from Australia, the fourth serving at Dong Tam in Dinh Tuong province where helicopter operations continued until June 1971. The unit was then withdrawn from Vietnam, arriving back in Australia on 16 June 1971. Five members of the unit had been lost in action over a period of 15 months between February 1968 and May 1969.

To meet the serious threat of underwater attacks on shipping, small teams of RAN frogmen were sent to Vietnam. The first Contingent, Clearance Diving Team 3 (CDT3) arrived in Vietnam in February 1967 and was attached to the Vung Tau harbour defence unit.

Commanded by Lieutenant M. Shotter, the unit carried out inspections of anchor blades, rudders and propellers while hull searches were conducted on request. The divers were called on to assist in the disposal of dangerous ordnance and to inspect objects thought to be floating mines. For their service in Vietnam, the First Contingent was awarded the US Navy Meritorious Unit Commendation.

Between February 1967 and May 1971 a total of eight RAN clearance diving team contingents served in Vietnam and were employed in a wide range of vital maritime tasks requiring a high degree of expertise and courage.

The Final Years

The Tet offensive of 1968, for all the catastrophic losses inflicted on the Viet Cong, appeared to be a turning point leading ultimately to the ending of the Vietnam war.

By May 1968 a basic change had occurred in American strategic policy on Vietnam. Major emphasis was henceforth to be placed on training and equipping the South Vietnamese force so that they could assume the dominant role in the conflict and progressively relieve the US forces of their combat role.

In November 1968 President Johnson ordered the end of aerial bombing and naval shelling of North Vietnam. His successor, Richard Nixon, came to power with the promise of reducing American commitment. He promised the end of the war and the negotiation of an acceptable peace.

Within weeks, Nixon announced that US troop withdrawals from South Vietnam were "high on the agenda". His strategy was disengagement by American forces and the "Vietnamisation" of the war. Fighting the war would again be the responsibility of the South Vietnamese, whose forces would be doubled and provided with ships, planes, helicopters and more than a million rifles. They were to be well supported so that they could hold their own against the Viet Cong.

While moving to withdraw the US from the fighting, Nixon enunciated the "Guam" doctrine which laid down that American allies and partners would have to accept the primary responsibility for their own defence. Allied armies such as the ARVN must do their own fighting.

Commanded by Lieutenant Colonel P. L. Greville, 4 RAR on 1 June 1968 became the seventh battalion of the Royal Australian Regiment to serve in Vietnam. The battalion took over the operational responsibilities of 2 RAR (Lieutenant Colonel N. R. Charlesworth) which returned to Brisbane on HMAS *Sydney* on 13 June. In the same year 9 RAR (Lieutenant Colonel A. L. Morrison) arrived at the Task Force base from Woodville in South Australia to take over the responsibilities of 3 RAR at Nui Dat. Before returning to Australia 9 RAR carried out eleven major operations in Phuoc Tuy, Long Khan, Bien Hoa and Binh Tuy provinces.

In early 1969, 5 RAR (Lieutenant Colonel C. N. Khan) returned to Vietnam for a second tour of duty, assuming the responsibilities of 1 RAR. The arrival of 8 RAR (Lieutenant Colonel K. J. O'Neill) in November of the same year brought to nine the number of battalions of the RAR to serve in the war.

On 8 May 1969, 6 RAR (Lieutenant Colonel D. M. Butler) arrived to begin its second tour of duty. Of the total of nine RAR battalions, seven (1, 2, 3, 4, 5, 6 and 7) served two tours in Vietnam and two (8 and 9) served one. For three years Australia had three battalions serving together in the Task Force while a fourth battalion was serving at the same time in Malaysia.

During the 4th Battalion's tour of duty in Vietnam, New Zealand infantry assigned to the Task Force were placed under its command. The

4th Battalion's first large-scale operation was a successful entry with 3 RAR into the Long-Binh-Bien Hoa complex area with the task of dominating enemy rocket activities. It was again in the area during the Tet period of 1969. But Viet Cong activity was much more subdued compared with the major campaign of 1968.

Bushrangers

A Major task and one of the most important for RAAF helicopters in Phuoc Tuy province was the air lift of the Australian Army's Special Air Service reconnaissance patrols into and out of the jungle. When enemy troops threatened an extraction (a "hot" extraction) the United States Army provided gunships (heavily armed helicopters) to cover the extraction with their weapons. Sometimes gunships could not be provided for the task and on 21 August 1966 a RAAF helicopter went down without gunship support to pick a patrol up from the vicinity of a company-sized enemy force. When the helicopter landed the SAS patrol then ran from cover to the helicopter under fire. The SAS troops and RAAF door gunners both opened fire on the Viet Cong who attacked with small arms fire. The SAS patrol made it to the helicopter and spasmodic hostile fire continued until the helicopter had reached about 310 metres.

The work of the SAS patrols was highly regarded. General Westmoreland described their activities as contributing significantly to the successful operations of the Australian Task Force. He said:

> *This highly trained reconnaissance group provided continuous surveillance throughout the area of operations, detected the enemy and permitted the infantry battalions to concentrate rapidly on forces moving through the zone of established base areas.*

A close partnership developed between the SAS and No 9 Squadron. The SAS commanding officer in a letter to Wing Commander Scott wrote: "My blokes think your blokes are doing a tremendous job for them. The joy of seeing the aircraft coming to pick them up really has to be experienced to be fully appreciated." Another senior army officer was of the opinion that "the rapport that developed between 9 Squadron and the SAS Squadron was extraordinarily close. Probably almost unique".

The services of RAAF helicopters were in great demand and to meet Task force requirements, long hours of flying by RAAF helicopter pilots were taken for granted. One pilot had only one half day off in a month. In March 1967 No 9 Squadron flew 181 hours longer than the authorised time and at the end of 1967, with only six helicopters available, the squadron had amassed a total of 50,674 sorties.

The Australian Government had announced in October 1967 that Australian personnel in Vietnam would increase to 8,000 and that eight additional helicopter crews, including RAN and New Zealand Air Force crews, would be assigned for duty with No 9 Squadron to help cope with the increased demand. The squadron also received new and more efficient helicopters (the Iroquois "Hotel" model) with aircraft strength increased to 19 machines. Sixteen of these were Hotel models and three were the older "Bravo" models.

Until 1968 all major airborne insertions of Task Force troops had been carried out by United States Army helicopters because the RAAF did not have sufficient machines for major movements.

However, on 29 July, 1968, with more helicopters available, the RAAF undertook the airlift of the entire 3rd Battalion into Fire Support Base "Coolah" and landing zone "Wattle" 16 kilometres north of Nui Dat. It was the biggest assault troop lift to be undertaken by the RAAF to that time.

Before the landings, an artillery barrage and air strikes prepared the way and just before the landing US helicopter gunships "brassed-up" the area. Then 10 RAAF helicopters carrying A and B companies of 3 RAR flew in. Another air mobile force of RAAF helicopters then landed C and D companies at Wattle. At the end of the day the RAAF had air transported 711 troops as well resupplying other units throughout Phuoc Tuy province. It was the busiest day of the war for the RAAF helicopters to that time. By Christmas 1968, No 9 Squadron had flown 100,000 sorties in support of the Task Force. It had carried more than 150,000 passengers and had evacuated 2,000 casualties from the field of battle.

Although by 1968 No 9 Squadron had doubled the number of helicopters on squadron strength, the RAAF crews became convinced as a result of their experience in action that the squadron needed the more heavily armed gunship version of the helicopter. A gunship was capable of providing greater gunfire support for the ground forces and could lay down heavy suppressive fire during dust-off operations which all too often faced fierce enemy resistance.

When a gunship or light fire team was needed it was obliged to call upon the US Army, and not infrequently this support was not available.

With official sanction, the RAAF acquired gunship kits from the United States Army, and the Squadron converted a number of their Hotel model Iroquois helicopters to the gunship role. The greater lift capacity of the Hotel model allowed for the carriage of two seven-tube rocket pods, two 7.62 mm mini guns capable of firing 4,800 rounds a minute and two sets of twin-mounted side-firing M60 machine guns with a total ammunition load of 4,000 rounds.

No 9 Squadron adopted the familiar Australian term "Bushranger" for their gunships and flew the first Bushranger mission on 11 April 1969. On 11 May in an action in a rubber plantation the Bushrangers reported that a sweep of "friendlies" resulted in a body count of 14. Seven were attributed to the squadron and another seven to an American Cobra helicopter.

The Australian soldiers fighting in the jungle fully appreciated the efforts of the RAAF helicopter crews supporting them in their battles and being always on hand when soldiers were wounded to land near them and quickly fly them to hospital. Sometimes the soldiers would send messages of thanks and on other occasions expressed their gratitude in a typical Digger way – rolling out the barrel. Shortly after the RAAF had brought out a number of wounded on 19 July 1969, No 9 Squadron received $30 from C Company of 9 RAR to buy ale for the crews of the helicopters "who helped them out of a nasty situation". After losing one killed and eight wounded at the hands of the Viet Cong force surrounding them, the Diggers of 9 RAR, out of ammunition, were relieved to see the Viet Cong dispersed by the timely arrival of Bushrangers and RAAF dust-off helicopters.

Canberras and Caribou Transports

By the middle of 1970, No 2 Canberra jet bomber squadron was still operating from Phan Rang base and had achieved bombing results which were not only the highest in the 35th Tactical Fighter Wing of the USAF's 7th Air Force, but the highest in any aviation unit in South-East Asia. The toll exacted on the Viet Cong by the RAAF Canberras included destruction or damage to thousands of bunkers, military structures, tunnel complexes, trench lines and sampans.

Initially the Canberras flew on night bombing missions but gradually they were moved on to daylight missions. Wing Commander Anthony Powell, a RAAF Forward Air Controller serving in Vietnam with the USAF, demonstrated that the Canberras were suitable for tactical daylight bombing and as a result Canberra missions under the control of Forward Air Controllers began.

A very successful FAC controlled strike at Dak To during a critical battle was described as "magnificent". No 2 was soon firmly established as a valuable unit of the tactical air forces in Vietnam.

By 1969 about 70 per cent of the squadron's missions were being flown in the Mekong delta area where their characteristics could be best applied. The delta region gave superior results because of its flatness and the fact that the altitude of targets, which were almost always just a metre or two above sea level, could be fed into the bombsight with precision.

The squadron maintenance flight achieved a close to perfect score in serviceability of 96 per cent. Maintenance crews in achieving this result worked 24 hours a day on a two-shift basis. A minor problem encountered was damage caused by shrapnel which came from the Canberra's own exploding bombs. As a result the squadron was directed to increase its minimum bombing altitude from 310 metres to 370 metres. Even so shrapnel hits remained a source of danger to the Canberras.

An event which ever since has been shrouded in mystery occurred on

3 November 1970 when a Canberra jet bomber vanished during a night bombing mission over South Vietnam.

The young crew members, Flying Officer Michael Herbert, 24, the pilot, and Pilot Officer Robert Carver, 24, the navigator, were carrying out a "Combat Sky Spot" bombing mission in support of the South Vietnamese Army near Da Nang. The radar bombing operator passed target information to the aircraft which then reported it was turning on a heading of 120 degrees. After that was silence. All bombing missions were suspended and the command swung into a widespread search for the missing Australians. But no clue as to their whereabouts or the cause of their loss has been discovered.

In early 1971 the South Vietnamese Army, growing in strength and confidence, was assigned the major task of thrusting into Laos in a massive attempt to disrupt the flow of arms and supplies along the "Ho Chi Minh" trail through Laos and into Cambodia and South Vietnam.

The operation was named "Lam Son 729/Dewey Canyon" and the South Vietnamese ground forces were given direct and indirect support by American and South Vietnamese air power. From 5 February to 15 March, No 2 Squadron was involved in an intense bombing campaign in support, but only within the borders of South Vietnam. There strikes were carried out in the northwestern corner of Military Region I, where they flew a significant proportion (25 per cent) of the total sorties. Squadron Leader Brian O'Shea, a Canberra pilot, said "the night sky in the area seemed to be brightly lit like a Christmas tree as Canberras, Phantoms, F100s, C130 gunships, A7s and A6s and other aircraft joined in the air offensive".

As the Lam Son air operations reached their peak, the squadron lost a second Canberra. Piloted by Wing Commander John Downing, commanding officer of the squadron, the Canberra was shot down by a surface-to-air missile. Downing and his navigator, Flight Lieutenant Allen Pinches, took to their parachutes and survived. They spent a tough night in mountainous country before being picked up next day by an American dust-off helicopter. The Canberra crew were the first members of the RAAF to be brought down in this way.

Although the South Vietnamese troops inflicted heavy casualties on the North Vietnamese, the flow of supplies along the Ho Chi Minh trail was only temporarily slowed. An armada of US helicopters were used to airlift the South Vietnamese troops into Laos and 107 were lost with another 600 damaged.

On 30 March 1971, McMahon, the Australian Prime Minister, announced that No 2 Squadron and three Caribou aircraft of No 35 Squadron and their crews were to be withdrawn from Vietnam.

The Canberras carried out their last combat missions on 31 May. The final bombs were loaded on to the wing of Canberra A84-244 and on the last bomb the armourers painted the words:

76,389th AND LAST BOMB
COMPLIMENTS TO "CHARLIE"
FROM NO 2 SQUADRON
RAAF UC DAI LOI.

The Canberras flew out of "Happy Valley" (Phan Rang) for the last time at dawn on 4 June 1971. A few hours later the squadron was once more on Australian soil after an absence abroad of nearly 13 years. The squadron had left Darwin for Butterworth, Malaya, on 29 June 1958 and until the homecoming from Phan Rang had never returned. For its service with the US 7th Air Force, the squadron was awarded the United States Air Force outstanding unit award.

"Wallaby Airlines" as No 35 Squadron, RAAF, was widely known throughout Vietnam, had carried a total of more than 500,000 passengers and 78 million pounds of freight by mid-1970. They achieved these results although they frequently operated from remote, primitive strips where overruns were short and rough, where navigational aids were few and there was constant danger from hostile fire from the ground. Many were hit and a number destroyed by enemy fire. No crew member was killed, but many were wounded in action. On a typical day a crew would land on up to 10 airstrips ranging from major bases to temporary dirt strips.

Priority for transport requirements was given to the Australian Task Force as much as possible, and the squadron began a daily courier service between Saigon and Vung Tau. When Luscombe airfield at the Task Force base at Nui Dat was opened for operations the daily Wallaby courier schedule included this field.

On 19 January 1969 the crew of a RAAF Caribou had a lucky escape when subjected to mortar fire while taxiing at Katum, a Special Forces outpost close to the Cambodian border. The Caribou, piloted by Flight Lieutenant Tommy Thompson, was hit in more than 100 places by shrapnel. Thompson was wounded in the right leg and his co-pilot, Flying Officer Rod McGregor, was cut by flying glass. Thompson decided to turn the aircraft around and take off again as fast as possible. The cargo was unstrapped and discharged and the damaged aircraft was quickly back in the air.

Another Caribou was mortared at That Son, a South Vietnamese army training base, on 29 March 1970. This time there was no escape. The aircraft received a direct hit and was destroyed by fire.

The Team Goes Home

An astonishingly high number of military decorations were awarded to members of an elite Australian military unit whose unique contribution in the Vietnam War added a new chapter to Australia's proud military heritage.

They were the members of the Australian Army Training Team, Vietnam (known as the Team).

Professional regular soldiers all, they were the first Australians to serve in combat in Vietnam and remained in that country from August 1962 through difficult and dangerous years until withdrawn at the direction of the Government in December 1972. While the Team was concentrated mainly in the critical northern provinces, individual members were located widely throughout South Vietnam from the Mekong delta in the south to the Demilitarised Zone in the extreme north.

Originally the team was only 30 members strong, but it reached an ultimate peak of 222. Of the 990 members who saw active service in Vietnam, 33 were killed and 122 wounded.

Including four Victoria Crosses, members of the unit were awarded a total of 113 British decorations, as well as 245 United States and 376 Republic of Vietnam awards, together with the US Army Meritorious Unit Commendation and the Republic of Vietnam Cross of Gallantry with Palm, unit citation.

The proud first commander of the Team, Brigadier F. Serong observed, "In its ten years of continuous combat it stands as the most highly decorated unit in the annals of British warfare."

We have read that the first to be awarded the Victoria Cross, posthumously, was Warrant Officer K. Wheatley. The second member of the Team to be awarded the Victoria Cross (posthumously) was Major Peter Badcoe.

Badcoe was a man who did not appear to know the meaning of fear. His repeated acts of fearlessness while in action north of Da Nang in Thua Thien province earned him the Victoria Cross in early 1967. His citation records his outstanding acts of bravery on 23 February, 7 March and in his final battle on 7 April 1967 when he was cut down and killed by a burst of machine gunfire.

Two more members of the Team were to be decorated with the Victoria Cross for acts of exceptional bravery when attached to mobile strike forces ("Mike Forces") of Vietnamese and Montagnard tribesmen operating in the 11 Corps area, near the junction of the borders of Laos, Cambodia and South Vietnam.

They were Warrant Officer 2 Ray Simpson, who was decorated for his outstanding courage on 1 and 11 May 1969 in Kontum province near the Laotian border. In the same area Warrant Officer 2 Keith Payne earned the Victoria Cross two weeks later. Both Australians were leading their companies against regiments of the North Vietnamese Army.

Simpson was a veteran of the Second World War, the Korean War and Malayan operations. He also completed three tours of duty as a volunteer with the Team. During the withdrawal of his company he took a lone covering stand to protect soldiers bringing out the wounded.

Payne had saved the lives of many indigenous soldiers and a number of his American counterparts serving with him. The citation for his award stated that his "repeated acts of exceptional personal bravery and unselfish conduct in this operation were an inspiration to all

Vietnamese, United States and Australian soldiers who served with him".

In the first half of 1970 Australians of the Team were fighting a lonely war in small groups in the remote border areas of Vietnam where the North Vietnamese army was infiltrating southwards and seizing Special Forces outposts. In early April the North Vietnamese laid siege to Dak Seang in Kontum province and soon the Montagnard defenders were in a desperate plight. Another force of Montagnard mercenaries commanded by Australian Major Patrick Beale and with Australians Captain Peter Shilston and Warrant Officer P. N. Sanderson as company commanders, was airlifted by helicopter from Pheiku to the threatened area. However, they could not land at Dak Seang and their helicopters encountered heavy ground fire at an alternative site. But they fought their way to Dak Seang.

Beale had been told to "get in there and relieve Dak Seang". After a close quarters battle that raged for 11 days and cost Beale's small force 100 killed and wounded, the siege was raised.

Shortly after the bloody epic at Dak Seang members of the Team were progressively withdrawn from the northern outposts, and by August 1970 the Australian Army's long association with the Special Forces came to an end.

Under the Vietnamisation policy the ARVN forces were to be doubled. To help cope with the expansion the Australian training team was also doubled (including the addition of 65 corporals) and its main effort was concentrated in Phuoc Tuy province. Australians were assigned to Mobile Advisory Training Teams (MATTS) and served with the Regional and Popular (Territorial) forces.

In August 1971 the end of Australia's combat role in Vietnam was announced. However, a residual force known as the Australian Army Assistance Group (AAAG) commanded by Brigadier Ian Geddes was to remain. This force continued its training operation until ordered home after the election of a new (Labor) government on 2 December 1972.

The Australian Combat Role Ends

The peace talks in Paris and American withdrawal plans from Vietnam did not halt the war in embattled South Vietnam, although the tempo of operations had slowed markedly after the heavy Viet Cong losses of 1968. In mid-1969 North Vietnamese troops made an aggressive move against Binh Ba, a town of some 3,000 people only five kilometres north of Nui Dat. Its purpose was to demonstrate that the North Vietnamese army was capable of moving freely into villages and hamlets in Phuoc Tuy province.

On 6 June the Viet Cong in the town fired an RPG at an Australian tank passing through. By 10.30 am the Australian ready reaction force from Nui Dat comprising D Company of 5 RAR, together with Centurion tanks and armoured personnel carriers commanded by Major Murray Blake, approached from the south and was greeted by a hail of RPGs from a row of houses in the town.

After receiving clearance from the District Chief, Blake ordered an attack into the centre of the town. For eight hours Australians and North Vietnamese fought it out. Another Australian infantry company was brought up from Nui Dat and the RAAF sent a Bushranger helicopter gunship team to work the town over. More than 100 enemy were killed for the loss of one Australian killed and 10 wounded.

Next day the Viet Cong Chau Duc company occupied part of the notoriously anti-Australian village of Hoa Long immediately south of Nui Dat. Major Claude Ducker led C Company 5 RAR with tank support and personnel carriers in an attack which quickly routed the Viet Cong without losing a man.

The Chau Duc company of the Viet Cong and Hoa Long village suffered another heavy blow on the night of 11–12 August 1970 when 19 of its members who had entered the village were killed and 10 captured in a successful ambush three kilometres south-west of Hoa Long. The ambush was set up at night by members of 8 RAR and was the battalion's most successful ambush of the war. Two groups of heavily laden figures totalling about 50 Viet Cong were detected coming from Hoa Long and were caught in a devastating crossfire and a bank of Claymore mines.

In July 1969 6 RAR/NZ carried out a highly successful operation in the Courtenay rubber plantation, killing 90 enemy and capturing 10 for the loss of 3 Australians. By constant ambushing during operation "Mundingburra" the battalion helped to break the links between the enemy in his jungle hideouts and his military and civilian contacts in the hamlets, and inflicted severe reverses on the enemy along Route 44.

In December of 1969, 6 RAR was assigned the difficult and dangerous task of clearing the enemy from their lairs in the rocky Mao Tao mountains in the northeastern corner of the province. This area had long been a logistics base and the Viet Cong province headquarters. The battalion had many enemy contacts and discovered a massive bunker complex and large caches of food. The battalion set up a fire support base on top of Mao Tao.

During 6 RAR's tour in Vietnam (its second) the helicopters of RAAF No 9 Squadron flew 14,700 hours in support of the Australian Task Force and of these 3,700 were in direct support of 6 RAR throughout Phuoc Tuy province. Canberra jet bombers of No 2 Squadron also supported the battalion as did No 35 Squadron Caribou aircraft, which at some stage of the 12-month tour carried every member of the battalion. Particularly admired were the dust off activities of the helicopters, whose pilots frequently ignored hostile fire to winch out wounded Diggers and fly them within about 30 minutes to the 1st Australian Field Hospital at Vung Tau.

An Infantry officer of 6 RAR who was wounded in action and later awarded the Military Cross was unstinting in his praise. "The RAAF choppers performed magnificently," he said. "They got me out of sticky situations a number of times."

A close bond developed between the soldiers and the helicopter crews because of the dangers they shared. A young New Zealand officer serving in 6 RAR/NZ, Lieutenant Stanley Kidd of Papakura, New Zealand, planned to present a "Ho Chi Minh" rubber sandal originally owned by a Viet Cong soldier to the squadron. On its sole, Lieutenant Kidd had written: "To those magnificent men in their flying machines, 9 Squadron, RAAF." Sadly, fate stepped in. Just before he was to return home at the expiration of his tour of duty, he was killed. Nevertheless, the sandal and a bottle of whisky did reach the RAAF mess, and all the members toasted his memory.

The performance of the RAAF helicopter operations was officially recognised by the award of the Gloucester Cup for 1969–70, the third successive year. Maintenance standards were exceptionally high, with the squadron meeting a daily requirement of 13 aircraft out of a unit strength of 16.

A reduction of the Australian military commitment to the Vietnam conflict was foreshadowed by Mr Gorton, the Prime Minister, on December 1969 and confirmed on 22 April 1970 when he announced that Australia would withdraw 8 RAR from Vietnam without replacing it. It had been scheduled to complete its tour of combat duty in November 1970.

Just prior to this announcement the United States had also foreshadowed a further withdrawal of 180,000 Americans from Vietnam, and had made it clear that the total withdrawal of all American combat forces was intended.

Ironically, with the end of western intervention now in sight the announcements of the coming withdrawals appeared to generate greater opposition to the war. In Australia thousands joined in street demonstrations calling for the withdrawal of foreign troops and for an end to conscription in Australia.

The organisers of the street demonstrations were delighted with the public response.

In Vietnam the Diggers fought on, but while most were unmoved, many were appalled by the excesses of a minority of demonstrators whose actions debased the courage and sacrifice of the dead and the maimed. As military historian Ian McNeill put it:

> *What angered the men in the Team (AATTV) was that they could not understand how they could be at war while people in Australia were allowed to parade behind enemy flags, wear enemy badges, shout enemy slogans and collect money for the enemy's support.*

From the beginning of involvement in Vietnam, efforts were made by the Australian servicemen to assist local communities and ease the distress of civilians caught up in the path of military conflict. As Australian forces built up in Vietnam, so funds and resources were channelled into the provision of schools, medical and dental aid, markets and water supplies and other civil construction, together with immediate assistance in the form of food and clothing. All units took part in programs and in the later stages of the war the Army 1st Australian Civil Affairs unit was established at Nui Dat, employing the full-time effort of 300 men. The RAAF employed voluntary services and official funds to provide MEDCAPS (medical civil aid programs) and help in agricultural production, social welfare, water supply and even light industry.

In April, May and June of 1970, 7 RAR (Lieutenant Colonel R. A. Grey) in Vietnam for its second tour, killed 39 enemy in an operation designed to destroy elements of D445 battalion. Together with 2 RAR (Lieutenant Colonel J. M. Church) also on its second tour, 7 RAR took part in operation "Cung Chung" aimed at denying enemy access to villages along highway 15. However, the enemy were becoming more elusive, and when contacted moved rapidly away to new areas.

The last two battalions assigned to Vietnam were 3 RAR (Lieutenant Colonel F. P. Scott) and 4 RAR (Lieutenant Colonel J. C. Hughes). Both arrived in 1971 for their second tours. The Task Force assigned the battalions to Operation "Overlord" to counter moves by the North Vietnamese Army and D445. Intelligence information indicated that the enemy were concentrating northeast of Nui Dat for attacks on hamlets in the area. The Task Force employed 3 RAR and tanks of the Armoured Regiment to drive the enemy towards a blocking force comprising 4 RAR and the US 8th Cavalry. A major clash occurred with the enemy who, however, managed to escape the trap and reach safe havens in the border area.

The enemy, firing from the ground, had destroyed a large number of American helicopters (107 destroyed, 600 damaged) in the Lam Son 791 operations in Laos. Encouraged by this success, the North Vietnamese issued orders to their troops to attack helicopters at every opportunity.

As a result six RAAF Iroquois had been hit during March by enemy ground fire. One was shot down and burst into flames in the notorious Long Hai hills area, killing an army corporal on the ground and a medical orderly in the aircraft. Survivors were winched out by Wing Commander Peter Coy, CO of No 9 Squadron, who was forced into a dangerous hover near jagged rocks in adverse wind conditions.

During operation Overlord in June, No 9 Squadron flew a total of 183 sorties in one day, and during a resupply mission close to enemy positions, a RAAF helicopter was seen taking ground fire. It then crashed and burned, killing Flight Lieutenant Everitt Lance and a crewman, Corporal David Dubber.

The Task Force fought a final major action on 21 September when 4 RAR clashed with the 33rd North Vietnamese regiment which had attacked a Regional Forces base north of Nui Dat. Fierce encounters followed with the Task Force calling up a formidable array of helicopter gunships and strike aircraft to blast the enemy. After more fierce fighting the enemy withdrew to the north. Five Australians had been killed and 30 wounded.

The final war mission for the RAAF was a people sniffer assignment on 19 November, when a lone chopper was despatched, but no signs of the enemy registered on the sniffer.

Of the two Australian Battalions still in Vietnam in 1971, 3 RAR was the first to return home. RAAF helicopters airlifted 500 members of the battalion on to the deck of HMAS *Sydney* on 6 October and on 16 October operational control of Nui Dat was passed to the Vietnamese Province Chief.

On 9 December, *Sydney* had returned to Vung Tau and 4 RAR sailed for Australia, as did No 9 Squadron, RAAF, President Nguyen van Thieu, the South Vietnamese leader, came aboard to thank the Australian servicemen for their contribution over the years in the conflict, and bid them farewell.

Army logistics support elements and the remaining Caribou aircraft of No 35 Squadron followed early in 1972.

Only the Australian Army Assistance Group remained to help the Vietnamese and this group stayed until December 1972 when it was ordered home, arriving in Australia by RAAF Hercules on 20 December.

Four weeks later on 23 January 1973 a ceasefire agreement was signed in Paris and on 29 March the last planeload of American troops left Tan Son Nhut.

Thus ended Australia's combat role in Vietnam. It had begun with the arrival in Saigon (now known as Ho Chi Minh City) in August 1962 of 30 Australian army advisers and ended 10 years later, making it Australia's longest war. It was not quite the end of the war for RAAF Hercules aircraft, which as the enemy closed on Saigon were sent on mercy missions to bring war orphans from Tan Son Nhut to Bangkok to begin a new and hopefully better life. Other Hercules, wearing the livery of the United Nations, flew into Vietnam bringing food and medical supplies to refugees.

In 10 years a total of 50,190 members of the Australian Army, Navy and Air Force served in the Vietnam conflict. The services sent the following contributions:

Army	42,437
RAN	3,310
RAAF	4,443
Total	50,190

More Australians served in the Vietnam War than in any other war save the two world wars.

Australian fatal casualties were:

Army	478
RAN	8
RAAF	14
Total	500

The professionalism and valour of the Australian Army, Navy and Air Forces engaged in combat in Vietnam over 10 years impressed the world. The nine RAR battalions engaged fought brilliantly and never lost a battle. The training Team made an outstanding contribution to Australian military history.

Sadly the peace agreement signed in January 1973 in Paris did not last. Hostilities between North and South Vietnam were soon resumed and culminated on 30 April 1975 in the unconditional surrender of the Republic of Vietnam. This was followed by the saga of the "boat people" when hundreds of thousands of Vietnamese astonished the world by risking death to escape the new regime in flimsy, overcrowded boats. Upwards of 600,000 got away to a new life in democratic countries.

The outcome in 1975 was certainly not what was expected in countries which sent forces to help save South Vietnam from communist takeover. Air Chief Marshal Sir Frederick Scherger, chairman of the Australian Chiefs of Staff at the time 1 RAR was committed to the war commented later: "It never was conceivable to us that America could lose – no way; but lose she did."[14] He was not alone. President Johnson, according to Alan Renouf, could not conceive that what he called "a mob of night-raiders in black pyjamas" could defeat the greatest power in the world.[15] They did, and it was the United States' first defeat in war.

It is perhaps too early to evaluate historically the intervention of free world countries in Vietnam. But the fall of Saigon should be placed in a wider context. The impact of the struggle on South-East Asia, and indeed in much of the world, was enormous. The effort and sacrifice of the free world countries helped to buy time for larger and more populous and significant areas of South-East Asia to achieve stability in the turbulent post-Second World War years. They helped them to survive Cold War pressures until the communist monolith in eastern Europe collapsed and the danger passed.

11

THE GULF WAR

Australia's 11th war erupted suddenly in August 1990 in a turbulent area of the world – the oil-rich Arabian Gulf.

Hostilities began on 2 August when the Gulf state of Iraq invaded, crushed and claimed to have annexed its neighbouring state of Kuwait. Small in area, Kuwait had been made enormously wealthy by the exploitation of its oil resources, but militarily it was no match for Iraq.

No civilised country could have executed a more blatant act of naked aggression. The United Nations Organisation, dedicated to the prevention and resolution of military conflicts, was quickly involved in steps to free the victims of the Iraqi invasion.

At a meeting on 2 August, the United Nations Security Council had no difficulty in deciding on strong action. It demanded that the Iraqis immediately and unconditionally withdraw their armed forces from Kuwait. Countries throughout the world froze Kuwaiti assets.

President Saddam Hussein, the Iraqi dictator, had a brutal and lawless record. At the time of the attack on Kuwait, Iraq had one of the largest armies in the world, which had been built up and battle-tested in a long, indecisive war (from 1980 to 1988) against an equally strong Iran. His army was supported by a modern air force of more than 1,000 aircraft and a small missile-equipped navy. Hussein had in the past resorted to the use of chemical warfare weapons, and it was known that he was more than just dabbling in the development of nuclear weapons.

Hussein had calculated that his lightning conquest of Kuwait would take the world by surprise and dissuade any country that entertained thoughts of intervention.

He was wrong. He was confronted at once with a remarkable display of solidarity in the international community, which quickly translated verbal condemnation into positive action against him.

On 3 August the United States and Britain announced that they would send naval vessels to the Gulf, and the following day it was clear that Iraq would not have Soviet support, for the Soviet Union joined with the United States in calling for a world ban on the sale of arms to Iraq.

On 6 August Iraq had not responded to the demand to withdraw from Kuwait, and the United Nations Security Council tightened the screws by passing Resolution 661. The resolution declared that the United Nations were determined to bring the invasion and occupation of Kuwait to an end, and involved wide-ranging sanctions against Iraq and Kuwait.

By 10 August it had become clear that a Multi-National Naval Force (MNNF) would be formed for service in Gulf waters and that Australia would commit naval units to the force. Australia's initial contribution to Gulf operations would, therefore, be predominantly naval.

Following a telephone conversation between President George Bush and Prime Minister Robert Hawke, the Australian government announced that two RAN frigates (HMAS *Darwin* and HMAS *Adelaide*) and the replenishment tanker HMAS *Success* would be committed in support of measures to enforce sanctions banning trade of all goods to and from Iraq except for medicine and, in humanitarian circumstances, foodstuffs.

The Prime Minister, in announcing the commitment of the three RAN warships and their 600 sailors said, "We join with the rest of the world in saying that we will not tolerate, will not stand idly by, while any member of the international community purports to break the rules of civilised conduct in this way."

At 10 am on Monday 13 August, after intense preparations, *Darwin*

(Captain Russ Shalders) and *Adelaide* (Captain William Dovers) sailed from Sydney amid emotional scenes to join the Multi-National Naval Force, first stopping at Jervis Bay to embark Seahawk and Squirrel helicopters.

Success (Captain Graham Sloper), which had been en route to Melbourne, returned to Sydney at once and sailed for the Gulf two days later after embarking a Squirrel helicopter.

Success had no adequate self-defence weapons against air attack except for three obsolescent 40 mm Bofors. This provided an opportunity for the Army: approval was given for a detachment of the Army's 16th Air Defence Regiment to sail on board *Success*. They brought with them their RBS70 anti-aircraft weapon system to provide additional protection for *Success*. Thus the first Australian soldiers assigned to duty in the Gulf would be fighting from the deck of an Australian warship. The RBS70 weapons and eight soldiers to operate them joined *Success* at Fleet Base West (HMAS *Stirling*).

The RAAF too was immediately involved. It provided essential air transport to the Task Group ferrying equipment and naval personnel from Richmond to the West. Hercules transports were also flown to Diego Garcia in the Indian Ocean carrying additional stores and equipment for the Task Force.

The RAAF also provided F111C, F/A-18 Hornets, Macchis and Orions which carried out many mock attacks on the RAN ships as they sailed to Western Australia and then on to Diego Garcia. The aim of these "work-up" training exercises was to enhance the readiness of the RAN warships for combat, especially against hostile aircraft. Protective measures against chemical and biological attack were practised.

The Task Group had to be prepared to meet the worst-case scenario of an all-out war in the Middle East. The emphasis in the work-up operations was on anti-air warfare and damage control. Captain Shalders said that for the Task Group the operational exercises with the RAAF made for a period of "unbelievable intensity". He said:

In my experience it was the most demanding and professionally stimulating period of naval activity I'm ever likely to be

involved in. The RAAF provided the loyal opposition at a level
of intensity I'd not thought possible. With the exception of an
18-hour period in the middle of the Bight, the Task Group was
hounded relentlessly.[1]

On 21 August, Hawke sought parliamentary support for the government decision on the Gulf War and moved a motion condemning Iraq. He told the House of Representatives, "We are not sending ships to the Gulf region to serve our allies. We are going to protect the international rule of law which will be vital to our security, however our alliances may develop in the future."[2]

The House adopted his motion with only one member dissenting.

Less than a month after being committed, the Task Group crossed the boundary of the area of operations to begin "Damask" the RAN designation for the Task Group's Gulf Operation. On 9-10 September a meeting took place between the commanders of the Multi-National Naval Force (15 nations had agreed to send naval contributions to the force). At the meeting the RAN Task Group was allocated the key "Alpha" area of the Gulf of Oman through which shipping passed on its way to the United Arab Emirates and the Straits of Hormuz. Commodore Chalmers knew that Alpha was the most likely area to become the scene of action in enforcing the United Nations sanctions, and for that reason had claimed it for his Task Group.

Initially the RAN had authority only to identify, contact, interrogate and warn vessels. However, the Australian government decided to expand the powers of the Task Group and on 10 September Commodore Chalmers was informed that his force would now be permitted to halt, board and verify suspicious vessels and to use warning gunfire to divert and if necessary seize ships breaching United Nations sanctions. The RAN Task Group could also enter the Straits of Hormuz. Chalmers was very pleased. He considered the rules now established to be "terrific – very robust".

Darwin intercepted its first merchant ship on 3 September. After detecting the vessel on radar, *Darwin* left the Group to quiz the ship about its cargo, nationality and destination. It was a Maltese tanker in ballast sailing from Pakistan to the Suez Canal. By 12 September the two Australian warships had intercepted 80 cargo ships but all were allowed to proceed. Within a range of 160 kilometres they were tracking up to 200 contacts.

On 14 September, an incident occurred which meant that Petty Officer Gary Eadie of HMAS *Darwin* opened fire with a 50-calibre machine gun across the bows of an Iranian tanker, *Al Fao*. *Al Fao* had entered the Gulf of Oman and was heading towards Iranian territorial waters when it was challenged. Captain Shalders ordered the firing of shots after *Al Fao* had repeatedly failed to obey orders to stop. Further warning shots had to be ordered before *Al Fao* eventually stopped. Boarding parties from *Darwin* (led by Lieutenant Commander Norman Banks) and the USS *Brewton* then joined in the First Multi-National boarding operation. At first the master of *Al Fao* refused to drop a ladder. Then he did so, and the RAN team boarded the ship. In the oppressively hot conditions and dressed in uniform, lifejacket, body armour and carrying radios, weapons and water bottles, the boarding party found the work exhausting. After it had confirmed that the 40,000-tonne tanker was in ballast the ship was permitted to proceed into the Arabian Gulf.

On 22 January 1992, President Bush praised Australia's contribution to the Gulf War and pointed out that the RAN and US Navy were the first two navies of the Multi-National Naval Force to jointly board a tanker to enforce United Nations resolutions. During an address to Federal Parliament that day, President Bush said:

> *In the Persian Gulf, we stood together against Saddam Hussein's aggression. Indeed, the first two Coalition partners in a joint boarding exercise to enforce the UN resolutions were Australians from HMAS* Darwin *and Americans from USS* Brewton. *During the war, the joint defence facilities here in Australia played an invaluable role in detecting launches of Iraqi Scud missiles. And today, two of the three navies represented in operations enforcing the embargo against Iraq are of Australia and the US.*

When, on 1 October, the Iraqi ship *Al Wasitti* refused to stop, it was necessary for *Adelaide* as well as British and American warships to fire adjacent to the ship. It stopped when a force of British marines went aboard from a helicopter.

On the same day warships from three nations including *Darwin* sent boarding parties to land on the 3,500-tonne *Tadmur* which was attempting to sail from Aden to the Straits of Hormuz without being inspected. The uncooperative Iraqi crew made the boarding difficult.

Another uncooperative Iraqi ship was the 140,000-tonne tanker *Amuriyah*. The master of *Amuriyah* ignored all challenges. Sirens were sounded at close quarters to attract the master's attention and *Darwin*'s helicopter buzzed the tanker and hovered near the bridge with a written warning displayed. Aggressive manoeuvring was tried and two US fighter aircraft from the American aircraft carrier *Independence* buzzed the tanker. Then *Darwin* fired .50 calibre rounds down to 100 metres ahead and a US warship fired five-inch rounds. But the *Amuriyah* sailed serenely on ignoring the "pirates". When Coalition boarders, including Lieutenant Commander Banks (leading a RAN team), landed by helicopter on the foredeck, the master used water cannon to frustrate them. He had to be handcuffed while the ship was searched.

The maritime blockade by the coalition naval forces was highly successful and the Iraqis were forced to suspend most of their maritime activities. Yet President Saddam Hussein, although his country was now cut off from vital supplies by sea, gave no indication that he would agree to the demands of the United Nations by withdrawing his army from Kuwait.

The Iraqi economy was heavily dependent on external trade, and by the end of November that trade was winding down to a standstill. The Iraqis were forced to tie up their shipping in ports and assign the crews to other duties. Sanctions were working. The Iraqis were not getting any oil out to pay their bills and very little food and materials were entering the country by sea. In achieving this remarkable result the UN navies had carried out the following tasks:

26,343 recorded challenges

996 boarding and

51 diversions.

The Ultimatum

For the Iraqis, greater trouble lay ahead. Hussein was playing for time and stubbornly refused to budge on the issue of withdrawal from Kuwait. Enormously powerful land, sea and air forces had been built up in the region aided by a massive strategic airlift and the United nations was ready, if necessary, to use them. They were not prepared to wait.

So on 29 November 1990 the United Nations Security Council set a deadline. On that day Council passed resolution 678 which gave authority to member states "to use all necessary means" against Iraq unless that nation withdrew from Kuwait on or before 15 January 1991. Force would be used to expel Iraqi forces from Kuwait if it did not begin to pull out by that date.

On 4 December, Prime Minister Hawke informed the Australian parliament that Australia was prepared to make available its Naval Task Group in support of the UN resolution, should it become necessary.

Australia was committed to a combat role should a clash of arms occur. As tensions rose, the RAN Task Group was authorised to pass through the straits of Hormuz into the Arabian Gulf where it would come under US Navy operational control, but continue under Australian command. It was obvious that maritime surveillance in the Gulf of Oman had sharply declined in importance and if Australia was to continue to play a useful role it needed to operate in the Arabian Gulf.

Before the ultimatum to Iraq expired, the question of the relief of the RAN ships on duty in the Gulf area had to be resolved. They had been committed for a three-month term and the decision was taken to relieve (on 3 December) *Adelaide* and *Darwin* with the guided missile destroyer *Brisbane* (Captain Christopher Ritchie) and the newer guided missile frigate *Sydney* (Commander Lee Cordner). *Success* would be relieved by the 40,870-tonne *Westralia* (Captain John Moore), the RAN's largest warship.

The Department of Defence considered a number of options for the commitment of RAAF RF111, Orion, Hornet and Hercules aircraft to operations, but no deployments were approved. However, with naval operations under way in the Gulf of Oman, RAAF Hercules transports became an essential link in the logistics chain that brought mail and supplies to the RAN Task Group.

Brisbane and *Sydney* sailed for the Gulf from Sydney on 12 November. Before departure the Navy had undertaken a rapid and complex installation on *Brisbane* of two "stand alone" Phalanx close-in weapons systems which had involved the removal of boats and davits and was accomplished in seven weeks. A number of additional enhancements to increase the capabilities of both warships had also been undertaken.

On 3 December Commodore Don Chalmers handed over command of the RAN Task Group to Commodore Christopher Oxenbould and on 16 December the 2nd RAN Task Group entered the Arabian Gulf.

Commodore Oxenbould held the view from the intelligence briefings he had received that there would be a shooting war in the Gulf.

> *Saddam Hussein was not going to withdraw. Furthermore I thought a war would be the best outcome. The alternative to such a massive force backing down in front of Saddam Hussein could only lead to further international instability. Such conclusions added significant impetus to our preparation for hostilities.*[3]

The RAN Task Group on entering the Gulf became part of the largest fleet of warships since the Second World War. At the height of the conflict the Allied naval forces in the Gulf comprised four aircraft carriers, two battleships, 10 cruisers, more than 50 destroyers and frigates and more than 100 logistic, amphibious and small craft. Its principal role was to establish sea and air control of the Arabian Gulf while providing strike support for the Allied effort ashore. Against this awesome Allied force the Iraqis had more than one thousand aircraft and a missile-equipped navy.

On 23 December, *Sydney* sailed from Bahrain for patrol duties in the Gulf, where tension mounted as the ultimatum deadline came closer with no apparent solution to the deadlock. Only one other anti-air warfare naval unit (US *Worden*) was at sea in the northern Gulf at that time. A pre-emptive strike by the Iraqi air force appeared possible.

However, that task of enforcing maritime sanctions still had to be continued, and Sydney was suddenly sent on a high-speed passage (30 knots for nearly 30 hours) down the coast of Oman to join US and British Naval units on Christmas morning. The task was to intercept the so called "Peace Ship" *Ibn Khaldoon* sponsored by pro-Iraqi Libya in an attempt to discredit the United Nations coalition against Iraq.

The ship was loaded with food and medicines and it had been made known that its intention was to break the UN sanctions barrier. In order to maximise the propaganda value of their passage, more than 241 men, women, children and journalists had been embarked as passengers. *Sydney* was wanted partly so that the interception task would be given an international flavour.

Sydney intercepted the *Ibn Khaldoon* at 5.45 am on Boxing Day off Al Masirah Island, but the *Ibn Khaldoon* failed to stop after repeated demands by Commander Lee Cordner to do so. US marines were then placed on board by helicopter. Within 30 minutes they had seized control in a particularly effective operation. Struggles occurred with passengers who tried to seize weapons carried by the boarding party, shots were fired into the air, and stun grenades were used in order to gain control. It was confirmed that *Ibn Khaldoon* was carrying prohibited goods and it was held in custody.

In the New Year, tension continued to rise. There could be no relaxation of vigilance because of the possibility of pre-emptive Iraqi air strikes using anti-shipping missiles. Floating contact mines were detected and Silkworm missile shore batteries added to the hazards. All male personnel in the Task Group were directed to be cleanshaven to make the fitting of chemical protection masks more effective. Tablets were taken for protection against chemical nerve agents and all personnel were inoculated against plague.

Intense efforts were made in the first half of January 1991 to prevent the outbreak of hostilities. In Geneva, James Baker, the US Secretary of State, met the Iraqi Foreign Minister, Tariq Aziz, but nothing came of that meeting. Two days before the ultimatum expired the Secretary

General of the United Nations, Javier Perez de Cuellar, flew to Baghdad in an attempt to persuade Saddam Hussein to withdraw from Kuwait, but he could make no progress. A defiant Saddam Hussein told his army the day before the deadline expired that they must be prepared for "the mother of all battles" and warned the world that should the Americans attack, they "would swim in their own blood".

The American Navy's Midway Battle Group was retitled "Battle Force Zulu" on 11 January 1991. Rear Admiral D. March, who commanded Battle Force Zulu, wanted the Australian naval units to become part of his carrier group, and on 12 January *Brisbane* and *Sydney* assumed their assigned sectors around *Midway* as part of that carrier's anti-air warfare protective screen. Next day tactical control of all three RAN units was formally passed to Rear Admiral March and they were then fully integrated into Force Zulu.

On 11 January Iraqi Air Force jet aircraft had made feints towards the Coalition naval forces in the Gulf. The jets came from Iraq and flew within weapons release range before turning away. More feints were made in the following days.

Just before hostilities began, *Sydney* was detached from the anti-aircraft screen to escort *Success* in a replenishment assignment in the northern area of the Gulf. The assignment was particularly tense with hostilities expected at any moment and a growing further threat from a large number of drifting mines which the Iraqis had released.

In the circumstances, with the threat of war only hours away, the morale of the men and women in the RAN Task Group was very high.

Numerically the Coalition forces now assembled in the Gulf were far stronger than the Iraqi forces. Coalition contingents totalled 700,000, of whom 500,000 were Americans. American naval strength in the area was 75,000. RAN strength was 884. Iraqi forces were estimated to total 480,000.

Desert Storm

The United Nations deadline for Iraq to leave Kuwait expired at midnight on 15 January with nothing occurring to indicate that the Iraqis were going to comply with United Nations demands. Under the dynamic leadership of America's General H. ("Stormin") Norman Schwarzkopf, the Coalition forces launched combat operations to free Kuwait by force of arms in an operation designated "Desert Storm".

The initial assault against Iraq was an all-out air offensive in which missiles and manned navy and airforce combat planes were employed intensively. The first Coalition aircraft took off from Dharan air base in Saudi Arabia early in the morning of 17 January.

In the Northern Gulf at 2.30 am on 17 January US battleships and destroyers launched the first Tomahawk missile strikes which were quickly followed by the launching of carrier based strike planes from *Midway* and *Ranger*. Amazingly members of the RAN were able to watch as missiles were fired from an American battleship and then see (on CNN television) these same missiles exploding hundreds of miles away on targets in Baghdad.

The pre-battle tensions of the Australian sailors were released when they watched the awesome display of military power and knew that what they hoped for had become a reality – the Coalition had struck first.

The air strategy was designed to cripple Iraq's military without laying waste to the country. Within six hours the Pentagon was able to claim the Coalition controlled the skies over Iraq.

In announcing that hostilities had begun, President Bush said, "We will not fail. Sanctions were tried for well over five months and we and our Allies concluded that sanctions alone would not force Saddam from Kuwait."

For the first few days of hostilities, the Iraqi air force did not retaliate against the Coalition fleet in the Gulf. But on 24 January, two Iraqi Mirage maritime strike planes, escorted by three MiG 23 fighters, were detected flying down the Kuwaiti coast. The two Mirages were quickly downed by missiles fired by Saudi Arabian F-15s, and the

MiGs turned away soon afterwards. Two days later (26 January) large numbers of Iraqi air force planes were reported quitting the war and seeking sanctuary in neutral Iran. Whether the pilots had mutinied was not known.

Iraqi naval vessels also attempted to seek sanctuary. Many were attacked in the Gulf by American carrier aircraft and British Lynx helicopters. In the Iraqi Navy 138 naval vessels of all types were either destroyed or put out of action.

On 25 January *Success* departed the war for Australia and on 5 February was replaced in the RAN Task Group by *Westralia*. Two frigates (one Danish, the other Norwegian) escorted *Westralia* into the Gulf.

Westralia created Australian naval history: She carried into the war seven women (two of them officers) who were members of her crew. It was the first time that women members of the RAN went to war in combat roles in a RAN warship. One of them (Able Seaman Natalie Collis) found the experience was "like something that only happens in books or on television. It especially hit home when Commander Moore addressed the ship's company explaining that people were dying around us, and this situation certainly was real".

"The Mother of all Battles"

General Schwarzkopf, after receiving the go-ahead from the White House, launched the ground offensive against Iraq at 4 am on 24 February. The war was over 100 hours later on 28 February when all military operations ceased. As the guns fell silent President Bush declared, "Kuwait is liberated; Iraq's army is defeated; our military objectives are met ... this is a victory for all mankind and the rule of law."

Coalition losses had been amazingly light – 131 killed in action and another 100 in accidents. The US Defence Department estimated enemy killed at around 100,000 but warned that the estimate could be out by 50 per cent either way.

Resistance had been slight with enemy troops "jumping up like squirrels" to surrender, while others retreated in disarray. Too late on 26 February Saddam Hussein ordered his troops to withdraw from Kuwait.

Many had already abandoned their posts and a very large number were trapped and decimated in a disorderly retreat on the road north to Iraq. "The mother of all battles" had become "the father of a hiding".

For the ground war the Coalition naval forces in the Gulf switched their attack to close support of Coalition army forces. One drove north and quickly captured Kuwait City, another west into Iraq to engage Iraq's Republican Guard and a third group thrust towards the Euphrates River at Nasiriya.

When the ground offensive began *Sydney* (after 47 days at sea) and *Westralia* were in port at Dubai where the opening phase of the ground war could be watched on television. Next day *Sydney* was at sea again relieving *Brisbane* in the anti-air warfare protective screen. *Brisbane* had had a particularly active day, controlling six fighter combat air patrols and four tanker aircraft.

While no Australian units served in the land campaign, a number of individual Australians of all three services attached to British and American units were involved. For a courageous battlefield rescue of two wounded soldiers, RAN helicopter exchange officer with the RAF, Lieutenant Commander Peter Nelson, was awarded the Air Force Cross.

When the fighting began, commercial air services in the Gulf were suspended and RAAF Hercules transports flew missions into Muscat and Dubai to deliver cargo and mail for the RAN.

Before hostilities began on 17 January, two RAAF Hercules were positioned at Singapore and a Boeing 707 at Nicosia, Cyprus, to be available if needed for the evacuation of Australian civilians from the area of conflict.

During the intense hostilities phase of the Gulf War, 40 members of the Australian Task Group Medical Support Element (TGMSE), both men and women, were serving in the United States hospital ship USNS *Comfort*. Originally two medical teams from Australia served on *Comfort* but in January 1991 when it seemed likely there would be more Australian casualties, the two medical teams were replaced by four teams under the command of Surgeon Captain Michael Flynn. Described as one of the world's largest trauma centres, the 69,000-tonne *Comfort* has 12 major operating theatres and 1,000 beds.

On 17 February *Comfort* was off Bahrain with an amphibious task force which sailed north through oil slicks and black fog from oil fires set off by the Iraqis.

Although the full use of their medical skills was not called upon, Captain Flynn, said, "The unit fulfilled its primary task of enabling access to advanced medical treatment facilities for the RAN Gulf Task Force."

The involvement of RAN fleet units with Iraq did not end with the ceasefire in February 1991. One Australian frigate was needed for sanctions enforcement duty. *Westralia* remained in the Gulf until *Darwin* returned in mid-1991 to resume ship monitoring duties. *Sydney*, *Darwin* and *Canberra* were involved in this duty until Australia discontinued the operation after *Sydney* completed the final deployment in 1993. However, on 30 April 1999, the Australian commitment was re-established when the frigate HMAS *Melbourne* was sent to the Gulf on ship-monitoring duties.

Mine Clearance

The more than 1,000 sea mines in the Arabian Gulf posed a considerable threat, and Australia committed an RAN Clearance Diving Team (CDT3) to assist in the task of removing them. The team of 23 sailors led by Lieutenant Commander John Griffith arrived in the operational area on 30 January and initially were involved in preparations for an amphibious assault on Kuwaiti beaches, which was cancelled.

With fighting over, the team cleared mines from four ports, dealt with 60 sea mines and surveyed 32 shipping wrecks. After 3½ months the team returned to Australia having earned a high international reputation for its skill and professionalism.

The members of the RAN Task Group received tremendous welcomes when they returned to Australia. Vice Admiral Stanley Arthur, the US Navy Central Commander, described the RAN's service in the Gulf as magnificent. "The US Navy," he said "will be proud to sail in harm's way with the RAN, anytime anywhere."

The Australian nation was deeply grateful that all the young men and women of the RAN who risked their lives in this conflict came home safely, mission accomplished.

The Army and the Gulf War

The Middle East has been a breeding ground of terrorism, and although terrorist acts were not thought likely in Australia during the conflict with Iraq, the Australian Regular Army was made responsible for "resolving in support of civil authorities, high risk terrorist incidents". The Australian Special Air Service (SAS) was required to be on call and when in January 1991 war with Iraq appeared inevitable the counter-terrorist elements of the SAS were placed on full alert both in Australia and overseas. No terrorist incident occurred during the war, but such an event could not be discounted.

The defeat of Iraq triggered a revolt by Iraq's dissident Kurdish minority who had endured barbarous treatment by the oppressive regime of Saddam Hussein.

The Kurds had mistakenly thought that the United Nations having gone to war with Hussein would force Iraq into giving them independence. Instead the United Nations remained silent while the Iraqis brutally crushed the revolt with tanks, artillery and heavy weapons. Two million Kurds fled towards the borders and soon thousands were dying.

Calls for help were made and on 16 May 1991 Australia sent a 75-strong Army contingent of four medical teams, and dental, preventative medicine and field engineer teams.

Water and bacteriological testing was conducted in 33 locations as well as pest control, fumigation programs and health surveys. The engineer team established nine water points. The Australian team withdrew in June and the humanitarian tasks were continued by civilians under UN auspices.

After the ceasefire the Australian Army also sent three Australian army engineers to join a team of United Nations experts to investigate nuclear, chemical and biological warfare capabilities in Iraq. Also on the team were a RAAF officer and a RAN expert on nuclear, biological and chemical medicine.

Tension arose between the UN inspections teams and Iraqi authorities. In September 1991 two of the Australian army officers were held at gunpoint in a Baghdad car park after they had removed documents and videotapes purporting to give details of Iraqi nuclear capacity. The two officers said they had evidence the Iraqis had continued to develop nuclear capacity after the Gulf fighting ended. Later, Iraqi nuclear installations were blown up.

12

KEEPING THE PEACE

The mission in Australians to the armed forces is primarily the defence of the nation. Increasingly, however, since the Second World War, they have been making significant and growing contributions to world peace by serving not only in combat operations but as peacekeepers and observers of military activity in disturbed areas of the world.

More than 180 countries now belong to the United Nations, whose stated objective is "to maintain international peace and security".

In the early years after the United Nations Organisation was formed it sent missions to troubled areas of the world as a means of securing its peaceful objectives. The peacekeepers took part in supervising ceasefire agreements, providing buffers between belligerents and undertaking humanitarian tasks. These activities are designed to help preserve peace after the combatants have put aside war as a means of achieving their objectives.

Because of the "Cold War" that soon developed after the Second World War, this activity was circumscribed by many vetoes in the Security Council. UN peacekeeping efforts were almost paralysed by Communist-bloc non-cooperation.

This situation changed dramatically with the end of the Cold War and currently some 45,000 United Nations peacekeepers are directly involved in duties around the world.

The world still has many turbulent places where the hold on peace is tenuous. The ultimate disaster of nuclear holocaust appears much less likely, but serious conflicts continue to arise, and millions all over the world are hoping that the great task of promoting and preserving peace, undertaken by the United Nations, will succeed. Few countries have done more to promote those aims than Australia

Peacekeeping has worked well in Cambodia where an Australian General (Lieutenant General John Sanderson) was military commander. But it has been far from successful in the former Yugoslavia.

Australia has no plans to maintain standby forces specifically for peacekeeping and has no units specifically available for the peacekeeping role. However, the Australian Defence Department has established a Peacekeeping Centre at RAAF Base, Williamtown, to coordinate and further develop existing experience. Training encompasses the development of doctrine, negotiation and conflict resolution skills, and peacekeeping techniques.

Australia's peacekeeping role had small beginnings. It started when Australia was called upon by the United Nations to provide four military observers to join the United Nations Commission for Indonesia (1947–51) during the conflict between the Indonesian revolutionaries, led by Dr Ahmed Sukarno, and the Netherlands East Indies authorities.

From this modest beginning, Australia's commitment by early 1993 had grown to 2,000 servicemen and women deployed overseas in support of international peacekeeping operations. They were serving in seven United Nations missions to countries which had been ravaged by war.

As well as in Indonesia, Australian peacekeepers have served for more than 40 years in United Nations, American and British sponsored peacekeeping operations in Korea, India-Pakistan, Iran-Iraq, Afghanistan, Israel, Lebanon, Palestine, Namibia, the Gulf of Oman and the Red Sea, Sinai, Cambodia, Somalia, Western Sahara and Zimbabwe and Rwanda.

Peacekeeping operations can be dangerous and many lives have been lost. Six Australians have been killed. One was Major Susan Felsche, the first Australian woman peacekeeper to die. An Australian Army doctor, she was part of the Australian contingent to the UN Mission for the referendum in Western Sahara; she was killed in an aircraft crash in that area. Another Australian, Captain Peter McCarthy, was killed when a land mine exploded in Lebanon in 1988. It was in Lebanon on 23 October 1983 that horrific explosions killed 241 US Marines and 58 French paratroopers on peacekeeping duties in Beirut. Terrorists detonated explosives in trucks after they had been driven into the peacekeepers' headquarters.

A long-lasting commitment by Australia to peace between India and Pakistan began in 1950 when an Australian general, Major General R. H. Nimmo, was appointed Chief Military Observer to the UN Military Observer group in India-Pakistan after the ceasefire in the India-Pakistan war.

Major General Nimmo remained in the post until his death in 1966. Australia added a contingent of six military observers who joined the UN observer group. The Australian contingent remained until withdrawn late in 1985. For the period 1975–79 an RAAF Caribou transport and a detachment of 12 RAAF men provided air transport for the unit.

Korea

In 1950, when war was imminent in the Korean peninsula between the communist northern regime and the South Koreans, two Australian military observers, Major Francis Peach and Squadron Leader Robert Rankin, were sent by the United Nations Commission on Korea (UNCOK) to inspect the military situation along the 38th parallel, which was the artificial dividing line between the two Korean regimes. They carried out their task at a time of high tension and only days were left before the North Koreans unleashed their invasion of South Korea on 25 June 1950 with overwhelming force, sweeping all before them. Professor Robert O'Neill, the official Australian historian of the Korean War, claimed that the work of these two officers was "one of the most consequential reconnaissances ever conducted by officers of the Australian armed services".

It was a critically important reconnaissance because the Peach-Rankin report gave the United Nations Security Council immediate and neutral confirmation that the North Koreans and not the South Koreans (contrary to the claims of the North) were the aggressors.

The report cleared the way for legally sanctioned intervention by member states of the United Nations, and Australia. Fifteen other member states sent military contributions. The war that followed UN intervention was the first major test of military strength between the West and the Communist world, with the United States providing the predominant part of UN military strength.

Had there been no United Nations intervention in Korea, the North Koreans would have been victorious, giving further worldwide impetus to the communist bid for domination.

Israel and the Middle East

In April 1948 the United Nations Truce Supervisory Operation (UNTSO) was established to supervise armistices and truces following the war between the Arabs and Israelis. In 1956 four Australian officers were posted for duty with UNTSO as military observers. This number had increased to 13 in 1982 after the Israeli invasion of Lebanon. During the Australian operations in Malaya and during Confrontation and the Vietnam war, Australian army reservists were used to help man the contingent.

The Iran–Iraq War

When the bitter struggle from 1980 to 1988 between Iran and Iraq ended in a truce, 15 Australian army officers joined with officers of other United Nations forces in supervising the ceasefire. The Australians served only on the Iranian side of the truce line because the

Iraqis refused to allow them in their area. These officers endured harsh conditions, living in underground bunkers and eating local rations of bread, soup and rice. They were exposed to dangers from mines, chemical weapons, artillery fire and disease.

Afghanistan

Mines sown in Afghanistan during the Russian occupation were estimated at up to 30 million and caused a difficult and dangerous problem for the inhabitants after the Russian withdrawal.

In 1989 a team of Australian Army field engineers joined United Nations mine clearance teams which trained Pakistan-based Afghan refugees in mine ordnance recognition and clearance techniques. The knowledge gained by the Afghan refugees was to be utilised on their return to their homeland.

When the last Australian team was withdrawn in 1993, 95 Australian experts had served with a program that had trained 14,498 Afghans.

Zimbabwe

In a peacekeeping operation organised by the British Commonwealth, 1,548 troops from five Commonwealth countries monitored a ceasefire in Rhodesia (now Zimbabwe). The Australian Army contribution totalled 152. They arrived in Rhodesia in December 1979. The Commonwealth force monitored the ceasefire leading up to a general election in which independence was achieved for the Republic of Zimbabwe.

Egypt-Israel Treaty of Peace

Australia's expertise in directing peacekeeping operations was confirmed in 1994 when a senior Australian Army officer, Major

General David Ferguson, was appointed to command the Multinational Force and Observers, Sinai. "The force working under me will continue to undertake their mission in accordance with the requirements of maintaining peace between Israel and Egypt," General Ferguson said.

In mid-1994 a contingent of 28 Australians was serving with the force, whose personnel totalled 2,400. The force was organised by Israel and Egypt to monitor the Camp David Accords of 1978 under which Israel withdrew from Egyptian territory it had occupied since the 1967 Arab-Israeli war.

Australia contributed to the Force at the outset of the mission in 1982 by providing a joint RAN/Army/RAAF detachment of eight Iroquois helicopters and 89 personnel.

In 1986 Australia withdrew from the force in order to reduce peacekeeping commitments. But in 1993 Australia rejoined the mission by committing a 26-strong contingent.

Namibia

A ustralia despatched a large army contingent to Namibia in 1989 in support of the United Nations Transition Assistance Group. Namibia was the last colony in southern Africa to become independent, and the purpose of the Assistance Group was to supervise elections, the withdrawal of South African forces and Namibia's transition to independence.

At its peak, the Australian contingent totalled 309 including the 17th Construction Squadron and the 17th Construction Workshops. The contingent was responsible for construction engineering support and for mine clearance.

The Western Sahara

T he Sahawri people of Western Sahara (formerly Spanish Morocco) took up arms in 1975 when the Spanish Government ceded the territory to Morocco and Mauretania. Spain did not want its former territory to have self-determination. But Polisario, the Popular front in Western Sahara, began fighting both Morocco and Mauretania to achieve independence. Mauretania renounced its claim but Morocco continued to fight.

A ceasefire was declared on 6 September 1991 and a United Nations mission in Western Sahara was established. Its task was to supervise a referendum which would decide whether the Sahawri people wanted independence or incorporation into Morocco. Australia provided the UN Mission with a 45-strong army communications unit. This allowed the force commander to coordinate the activities of the Mission. The Australians were required to deploy to 13 locations throughout the country, the tour of duty for members of the contingent being six months.

Due to serious disputes the referendum was postponed several times and the Mission has been limited to monitoring the cease-fire between the parties.

Cambodia

The Australian armed forces played a major role in one of the most ambitious and complex United Nations peacemaking operations the world has seen and, given the difficulties and dangers faced, arguably the most successful.

Cambodia, once one of the states of French Indochina, had endured in recent years an exhausting four-sided civil war, the nightmare of the "killing fields" as well as chronic political turbulence and corruption.

The achievements of the United Nations Transitional Authority in Cambodia (UNTAC) which included a 488-strong Force Communications Unit from Australia whose military direction was in the hands of a distinguished Australian, Lieutenant General John Sanderson, has won world-wide praise.

Senator Gareth Evans, Minister for Foreign Affairs, who strongly supported the Cambodian initiative, summarised the achievement.[1]

During the eighteen months of the operation (1992–93) repatriation of nearly 370,000 displaced persons from the Thai border was completed successfully. All political prisoners were released and political parties were established and were able to operate and campaign widely and with a degree of security. The UN organised elections were held without serious incident and with massive popular participation, leading to the establishment of a provisional government linking all parties who won seats. There were unquestionably flaws in the UNTAC operation, but the success of the elections has given Cambodia its first real chance in over 20 years to escape from civil war and political repression and to build a stable and prosperous country.

The United Nations commitment to the Cambodian mission followed the signing in Paris in October 1991 of a treaty to restore peace, and the formation in February 1992 of oversight of the disarming of 250,000 men, the resettlement of refugees and the holding of free elections.

Australian defence personnel, both men and women, were given the task of establishing the Force Communications Unit. The unit was based on the 2nd Signals Regiment, but was reinforced by many other units including 20 personnel each from the RAN and RAAF. From 5 May to July 1993 Australia also contributed 115 troops, six Blackhawk helicopters, and an infantry platoon protective party from the 2/4 Battalion, RAR. The Blackhawks had an important role in the coordination of the elections and carried out a number of casualty evacuation tasks.

Somalia

Some 937 Australian troops took part in the largest Australian overseas operation since the Vietnam War when the Australian Government responded to yet another request from the United Nations for the commitment of troops to a peace enforcement task in support of humanitarian objectives.

Operation "Solace", as the Australian operation was called, was undertaken to assist with the distribution of humanitarian aid and the restoration of order in Somalia where thousands faced death from starvation.

An Australian Army battalion group was committed. They were mainly members of 1 Battalion, Royal Australian Regiment, supported by armoured personnel carriers, artillery, field engineers, signals, and a company-sized battalion support group.

The troops were to serve for 18 weeks in Somalia. Five Hercules transports of the RAAF flew in an advance party and the main body arrived in two groups, one on 15 and the other on 18 January 1993.

The RAN's HMAS *Tobruk* and HMAS *Jervis Bay* were assigned to transport troops, armoured personnel carriers, heavy equipment and vehicles from Townsville to Mogadishu. *Tobruk* remained in Somalian waters as a command ship providing communications and logistic support to the ground forces.

Somalians faced mass starvation due to the breakdown of law and order, and the task of the battalion group was to assist in ensuring that desperately needed aid reached the starving Somalians in the 17,000 square kilometre Baidoa Humanitarian Relief Sector in south-west Somalia.

A bitter civil war had broken out in Somalia following the overthrow of President Siad Barre in January 1991 and the collapse of the Somali state. With the country divided by warring factions, lawlessness was rife.

The Australian troops dramatically improved the quality of life for the people in the Baidoa region. They helped to deliver 8,311 tonnes of humanitarian aid and protected ten convoys a week. They won widespread international praise for fostering and protecting humanitarian relief efforts, restoring law and order and re-establishing functional legal, social and economic systems.

Large quantities of weapons including 544 rifles and 145 machine guns were seized.

Repairs were made to much of the local infrastructure including schools, the police station and the orphanage.

On 2 April Lance Corporal Shannon McAliney, a member of the Royal Australian Infantry, was accidentally shot dead on patrol during battalion operations.

The RAAF was tasked to airlift the Operation Solace troops back to Australia. Using two B707s and three Hercules aircraft the RAAF shuttled the troops from Baidoa to Mogadishu where they were picked up by the B707 airlift. Seven loads of 120 troops with full field kit and weapons were then flown from Mogadishu to Townsville. The operation was completed by 23 May 1993.

Australian forces remained in Somalia in 1994 to coordinate all UN movements by land, sea and air, while others held key positions in the UN Force headquarters.

Rwanda Genocide

The worst example of genocide in African history, costing the lives of close to one million men, women and children, began its horrific course in the state of Rwanda in April 1994.

It led to the decision by the Australian Government to send a medical support force and substantial financial aid to help ease the suffering in that country.

The genocide was triggered on 6 April 1994 when the President of Rwanda was killed in the crash of a transport aircraft shot down near his capital, Kigali.

Next day, the majority Hutu people of Rwanda set out to eliminate the entire Tutsi minority people who they held responsible for the killing and branding them "the enemies of the state".

There were no sanctuaries in Rwanda and for months this small African state was covered with corpses and mutilated bodies in their hundreds were floating down the rivers.

In response to this unbelievable human disaster, Australia agreed to send a medical team, to support the United Nations peacekeepers who had been sent to Rwanda from African member states of the United Nations, including Ethiopia, Zambia and Tunisia.

The initial Australian Defence Force contingent was deployed for six months and in February 1995 a second rotation was committed for a further six months.

The Australian force was based on three companies:

A medical company as the core of the operation
A logistic company to supply the physical needs of the force, and
A rifle company to provide security in an extremely tense
military situation.

Most of the 309 members of the first contingent were Australian Army personnel, but the force also included 18 RAAF (including six women) and six RAN members.

The Australian advance party flew to Rwanda in a USAF Galaxy transport aircraft from Townsville in August 1994 and occupied the Central Hospital in Kigali.

After the medical needs of the United Nations peacekeepers were attended to there was excess capacity available for the care of fugitives from the genocide and from displaced persons. The Australians treated hundreds of local civilians for gunshot wounds, machete wounds, injuries from exploding land mines as well as tropical diseases and motor accident injuries.

A second Australian contingent arrived in February 1995 and in April, 50 members of the contingent with an Australian infantry platoon for protection, were sent to Kibeho where they were forced to endure seeing tragic events which were to test their mental, professional and physical fitness.

On 20 April the Rwanda Patriotic Army ordered two of its battalions to surround some 120,000 displaced people at Kibeho where the Australians were witness to episodes of unmitigated horror and suffering as 3,000 to 5,000 people were killed by the Rwandan troops.

The Australian contingent at Kibeho continued their humanitarian medical efforts after the killing was over and the camp had been reduced to little more than 1,500 survivors.

In May 1995 the decision was taken to withdraw the Australian contingent. In a tribute to the 650 Australians all told who served in the force, Major-General Peter Arnison, Land Commander, Australia said: "Your presence, courage, steadfastness, discipline, skills and compassion saved many hundreds of lives which would have been lost had you not been there."

The bitter legacy of the Rwanda genocide has led to severe criticism of the United Nations organisation.

President Clinton, the US President, made a television broadcast in which he deplored UN failure to act to stop the slaughter.

ROLL OF HONOUR

**Australians who have received
the Victoria Cross, the highest award
for gallantry.**

Captain Neville Howse
Vredefort, Orange Free State
24 July 1900

Trooper John Bisdee
near Warm Bad, Transvaal
1 September 1900

Lieutenant Guy Wylly
near Warm Bad, Transvaal
1 September 1900

Lieutenant Frederick Bell
Brakpan, Transvaal
16 May 1901

Sergeant James Rogers
near Thaba 'Nchu', Orange Free State
15 June 1901

Lieutenant Leslie Maygar
Geelhouttboom, Natal
23 November 1901

Lance Corporal Albert Jacka
Gallipoli
19-20 May 1915

Lance Corporal Leonard Keysor
Lone Pine, Gallipoli
7-8 August 1915

Lieutenant William Symons
Lone Pine, Gallipoli
8-9 August 1915

Corporal Alexander Burton
Lone Pine, Gallipoli
9 August 1915

Corporal William Dunstan
Lone Pine, Gallipoli
9 August 1915

Private John Hamilton
Lone Pine, Gallipoli
9 August 1915

Lieutenant Frederick Tubb
Lone Pine, Gallipoli
9 August 1915

Captain Alfred Shout
Lone Pine, Gallipoli
9 August 1915

Second Lieutenant Hugo Throssell
Gallipoli
29-30 August 1915

Lieutenant Wilbur Dartnell
East Africa
3 September 1915

Private William Jackson
France
25-26 June 1916

Private John Leak
Pozières, France
23 July 1916

Lieutenant Arthur Blackburn
Pozières, France
23 July 1916

Private Thomas Cooke
Pozières, France
24-25 July 1916

Sergeant Claud Castleton
Pozières, France
28 July 1916

Private Martin O'Meara
Pozières, France
9-12 August 1916

Captain Henry Murray
near Gueudecourt, France
4-5 February 1917

Lieutenant Frank McNamara
Palestine
20 March 1917

Captain Percy Cherry
Lagnicourt, France
26 March 1917

Private Jorgan Jensen
Noreuil, France
2 April 1917

Captain James Newland
France
7-9 and 15 April 1917

Private Thomas Kenny
Hermies, France
9 April 1917

Sergeant John Whittle
France
8-15 April 1917

Lieutenant Charles Pope
Louverval, France
15 April 1917

Corporal George Howell
near Bullecourt, France
6 May 1917

Lieutenant Rupert Moon
near Bullecourt, France
12 May 1917

Captain Robert Grieve
Messines, Belgium
7 June 1917

Private John Carroll
St Ives, France
7-10 June 1917

Private Reginald Inwood
Polygon Wood, Belgium
20-21 September 1917

Second Lieutenant Frederick Birks
Belgium
20 September 1917

Sergeant John Dwyer
Zonnebecke, Belgium
26 September 1917

Private Patrick Bugden
Polygon Wood, Belgium
26-28 September 1917

Sergeant Lewis McGee
east of Ypres, Belgium
4 October 1917

Lance Corporal Walter Peeler
Broodseinde, Belgium
4 October 1917

Captain Clarence Jeffries
Passchendaele, Belgium
12 October 1917

Sergeant Stanley McDougall
Dernacourt, France
28 March 1918

Lieutenant Percy Storkey
Bois de Hangard, France
7 April 1918

Lieutenant Clifford Sadlier
Villers-Bretonneux, France
24-25 April 1918

Sergeant William Ruthven
Ville-sur-Ancre, France
19 May 1918

Corporal Phillip Davey
Merris, France
28 June 1918

Lance Corporal Thomas Axford,
Hamel Wood, France
4 July 1918

Private Henry Dalziell
Hamel Wood, France
4 July 1918

Corporal Walter Brown
Villers-Bretonneux, France
6 July 1918

Lieutenant Albert Borella
Villers-Bretonneux, France
17-18 July 1918

Lieutenant Alfred Gaby
Villers-Bretonneux, France
8 August 1918

Private Robert Beatham
east of Amiens, France
9 August 1918

Sergeant Percy Statton
near Proyart, France
12 August 1918

Lieutenant W. D. Joynt
Peronne, France
23 August 1918

Lieutenant Lawrence McCarthy
France
23 August 1918

Lance Corporal Bernard Gordon
east of Bray, France
26-27 August 1918

Private George Cartwright
near Peronne, France
31 August 1918

Private William Currey
Peronne, France
1 September 1918

Sergeant Albert Lowerson
Mont St Quentin, France
1 September 1918

Private Robert Mactier
France
1 September 1918

Lieutenant Edgar Towner
Mont St Quentin, France
1 September 1918

Corporal Alexander Buckley
Peronne, France
1-2 September 1918

Corporal Arthur Hall
Peronne, France
1-2 September 1918

Corporal Lawrence Weathers
near Peronne, France
2 September 1918

Sergeant Gerald Sexton (Maurice Buckley)
near Le Verguier, France
18 September 1918

Private James Woods
near Le Verguier, France
18 September 1918

Major Blair Wark
France
28 September to 1 October 1918

Private John Ryan
France
30 September 1918

Lieutenant Joseph Maxwell
north of St Quentin, France
3 October 1918

Lieutenant George Ingram
Montbrehain, France
5 October 1918

Corporal Arthur Sullivan
North Russia
10 August 1919

Sergeant Samuel Pearse
North Russia
29 August 1919

Corporal John Edmondson
Tobruk, Libya
13 April 1941

Lieutenant Arthur Roden Cutler
Syria
19 June to 6 July 1941

Wing Commander Hughie Edwards
over Germany
4 July 1941

Private James Gordon
near Jezzine, Syria
10 July 1941

Lieutenant Colonel Charles Anderson
Malaya
18-22 January 1942

Private Arthur Gurney
Tel El Eisa, Egypt
22 July 1942

Private Bruce Kingsbury
Papua
29 August 1942

Corporal John French
Milne Bay, New Guinea
4 September 1942

Sergeant William Kibby
El Alamein, Western Dessert
23-31 October 1942

Private Percival Gratwick
Miteiriya Ridge, Western Desert
25-26 October 1942

Flight Sergeant Rawdon Middleton
Italy
28-29 November 1942

Flight Lieutenant William Newton
New Guinea
16 March 1943

Private Richard Kelliher
New Guinea
13 September 1943

Sergeant Thomas Derrick
New Guinea
24 November 1943

Corporal Reginald Rattey
Bougainville
22 March 1945

Lieutenant Albert Chowne
New Guinea
25 March 1945

Corporal John Mackey
Tarakan Island
12 May 1945

Private Edward Kenna
New Guinea
15 May 1945

Private Leslie Starcevich
Borneo
29 June 1945

Private Frank Partridge
Bougainville
24 July 1945

Warrant Officer 2nd Class, K. A.
Wheatley
Vietnam
13 November 1965

Major Peter Badcoe
Vietnam
23 February to 7 April 1967

Warrant Officer 2nd Class, Ray
Simpson
Vietnam
6-11 May 1969

Warrant Officer 2nd Class, Keith
Payne
Vietnam
24 May 1969

INDEX

NOTES

AUSTRALIANS IN THE BOER WAR
1 A J Hill, *Chauvel of the Light Horse*, p.19, Melbourne University Press, Melbourne 1978.
2 A G Hales, *Campaign Pictures of the War in South Africa*, p.l72, Cassell, London, 1900.
3 R L Wallace, *The Australians in the Boer War*,

Australian War Memorial.
4 Arthur Conan Doyle, *The War in South Africa*, pp.481–2, George Bell, London, 1900.

THE FIRST WORLD WAR
1 A B Facey, *A Fortunate Life*, p.256, Penguin Books, Ringwood, Victoria. Facey was

severely wounded at Gallipoli and two of his brothers, Roy (of the 11th Battalion) and Joseph (10th Light Horse) were both killed on the Peninsula.
2 C E W. Bean, *The AIF in France*, 1916, p.444, Angus and Robertson, Sydney, 1934.
3 Quoted in Bean, *ibid*,

pp.658–60.
4 Bean, Vol V, *The AIF in France*, p.349.
5 H B Gullett, *Sinai and Palestine*, p.397, Angus and Robertson, Sydney, 1933.
6 Frank Dalby Davison, *The Wells of Beersheba*, p.85, Angus and Robertson, Sydney 1934.
7 F M Cutlack, *The*

Australian Flying Corps, p.171, Angus and Robertson, 1934.
8 Quoted in Cutlack, *op cit*, p.188.
9 A. H. Cobby, *High Adventure*, p.76, Robertson and Mullins, Melbourne 1942.

THE SECOND WORLD WAR
1 Chester Wilmot, *Tobruk*, p.87, Angus and Robertson, Sydney.
2 *Ibid*, p.107.
3 Held in Naval Historical Section, Navy Office
4 Richard Sorge's spying activities came to an abrupt end in October 1941 when he was arrested by the Japanese. He was hanged for spying in 1944.
5 Melbourne Herald, 27 December 1941.
6 Long, *The Six Years War*, p.181, Australian War Memorial.
7 R L Eichelberger, *Jungle Road to Tokyo*, p.21, Viking Press, New York, 1950.
8 Gavin Long, *The Six Years War*, p.259.
9 Nigel Hamilton, *Monty*, pp.832–4, Hamlyn Paperbacks, Feltham, 1981.
10 George C Kenney, *General Kenny Reports*, p.292, Duell, Sloan and Pearce, New York, 1949.

THE SECOND WORLD WAR FROM D-DAY TO VICTORY
11 II Corps report
2 *American Caesar*, Arrow Books, London, 1979, p.373.

MALAYA, MALTA AND THE STRATEGIC RESERVE
1 Peter Edwards, *Crisis and Commitments*, Allen & Unwin in association with the Australian War Memorial, p.33
2 Edwards, *ibid*, p.43
3 Edwards, *ibid*, passim.
4 Current Notes on International Affairs, Vol 21, No 6, June 1950,pp.420–1
5 Peter Edwards, *op. cit.*, p.192

THE KOREAN WAR
1 Norman Bartlett, *With the Australians in Korea*, Australian War Memorial, 1954, p.94.
2 Robert O'Neill, *Australia in the Korean War*, 1950–53, Australian War Memorial, Australian Government Printing Service, Canberra, 1987, p.142

INDONESIA CONFRONTS MALAYSIA
1 Peter Edwards, *Crisis and Commitments, op. cit.*, p.263

2 CPD, House of Representatives, 25 September 1963, p. 1339
3 Peter Edwards, *op. cit*, p. 350
4 The Pentagon Papers, Bantam Books, New York, 1971
5 Alan Renouf, *The Frightened Country*, Macmillan, 1979, p.438

THE VIETNAM WAR
1 Renouf, *The Frightened Country*, op. cit, p.123
2 Peter Edwards, *Crisis and Commitment*, op. cit, p.227
3 Quoted in Ian McNeill's *To Long Tan*, Allen and Unwin, in association with the Australian War Memorial, p.44
4 Lyndon B Johnson, *The Vantage Point*, Holt, Rinehart and Winston, New York, 1971, p.136
5 M Sexton, *War for the Asking*, Penguin Books. 1981, pp.63–66. Italics are the authors.
6 National (US) Security Action Memorandum No 324 of 6 April 1965, published in *The Pentagon Papers*, Vol II, Gravel Edition, Beacon Press, Boston, 1971–72, p.703.
7 William C. Westmoreland, *A Soldier Reports*, Doubleday, New York, 1976, p.258
8 John Rowe, *Vietnam, the Australian Experience*, Time-Life Books,

Australia, in association with John Ferguson, Sydney.
9 Report on Operations in South Vietnam, January 1964–June 1968, General W C Westmoreland, US Government Printing Office, Washington DC, USA
10 Robert J O'Neill, *Vietnam Task*, Cassell, Melbourne, 1968, p.35
11 Ian McNeill, *op.cit*, p.322
12 *Ibid*, p.328
13 *Ibid*, p.84
14 Harry Rayner, *Scherger*, Australian War Memorial, p.154
15 Alan Renouf, *The Frightened Country*, op. cit., p.245

THE GULF WAR
1 Journal of the Australian Naval Institution, May 1991
2 CPD, House of Representatives, 21 August 1990, p.1194
3 Presentation on 6 November 1991 to the Australian War Memorial 50th anniversary celebrations.

KEEPING THE PEACE
1 Gareth Evans, *Cooperating for Peace*, Allen & Unwin, p.107–8

ACKNOWLEDGEMENTS

Grateful thanks go to the following who provided material for this book:

Australian Defence Force – picture numbers 3, 22, 23, 35, 40, 43, 51, 60 (RAAF), 63 (RAAF), 72, 73, 74, 80, 81, 83 (RAAF), 89, 91, 92, 95, 96 ((RAAF), 98 (RAN), 99-101 (RAN), 102. Australian War Memorial

(catalogue numbers are given after picture number where relevant): 2. A2744; 4. EN131; 6. V6392; 7. A3869; 8. H11559; 9. J2522; 10. J450; 12. E105; 13. E4947; 14. E715; 15., 16. 109; 17. E4851; 18. E4328; 19. 1347; 21. 184/3; 24. 5409; 25. 8860; 26. P784/213/061; 27. 10997; 28. ME39B; 32. VIIP224;

33. VIIP232; 37. 26632; 39. 14497; 41. 16722; 42. 83166; 44. 26268; 45. V4/Sec4/P174; 46., 47. 18392; 48. 17956; 49. 18413; 50. 128814; 52. 28816; 53. 18680; 54. 10436; 55. 131583; 56. 19296; 57. 19199; 58. V1687; 61. CUN/674/MC; 64. HOB3881; 66. 148927; 67. 146958; 68. 501286;

70. 146985; 76. 147312; 77. LES/66/174/MC; 79. DUN/1199/MC; 82. DVN/64/436/MC; 85. VN/66/1031/(1)(4); 86. SHA/66/7/VN; 88. CUN/66/161/VN; 90. EKN/67/141/VN; 93. FOR/66/664/VN; 94. CUN/71/403/VN; Jeff Isaacs 75, 87.